HOLMAN *QuickSource*™

BIBLE ATLAS

WITH CHARTS AND BIBLICAL RECONSTRUCTIONS

**INTRODUCTION AND
GEOGRAPHY OF THE BIBLE LANDS
BY PAUL H. WRIGHT**

Holman QuickSource Bible Atlas
© 2005 by Holman Bible Publishers
Nashville, Tennnessee
All rights reserved

Maps © 2000 by Holman Bible Publishers
Nashville, Tennessee
All rights reserved

ISBN 978-0-8054-9445-7

Dewey Decimal Classification: 220.9
Subject Heading: BIBLE—ATLASES

The Holman Editorial Staff gratefully acknowledges the contribution of
Dr. James McLemore and the staff of *Biblical Illustrator*
(G. B. Howell, current editor) for consultation on *Holman QuickSource
Bible Atlas with Charts and Biblical Reconstructions*. Many of the visual resources
contained herein are from the archives of the *Biblical Illustrator*. For additional
information about the *Biblical Illustrator* go to the following Web address:
www.lifeway.com and then do a search on **Biblical Illustrator**.

The Agricultural Year © Thomas V. Brisco.
Used by permission.

Unless otherwise noted, Scripture passages
are taken from the Holman Christian Standard Bible® (HCSB),
copyright © 2001 by Holman Bible Publishers. All rights reserved.
Unless otherwise noted Old Testament Scripture passages are taken from
the New International Version (NIV), copyright ©1973, 1978, 1984
by the International Bible Society.

Printed in China

8 9 10 11 12 13 14   15 14 13 12 11 10

CONTENTS

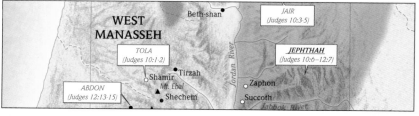

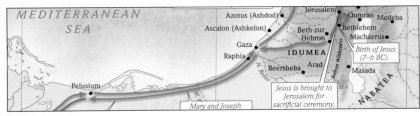

KEY:
Maps
Charts
Reconstructions

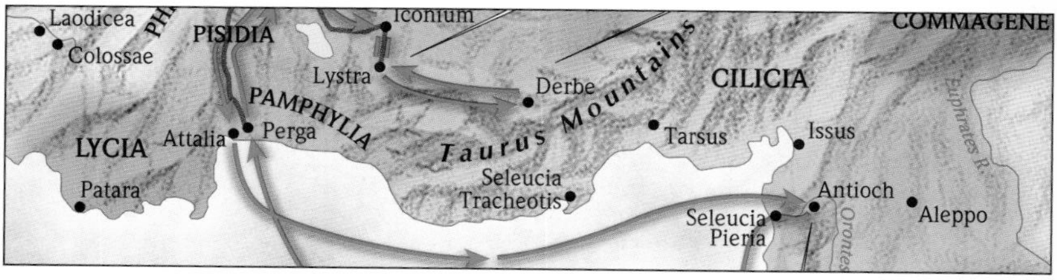

TIME LINE

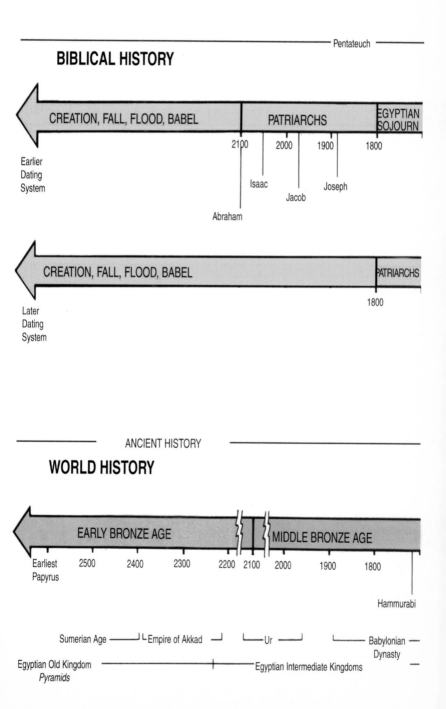

Pentateuch

BIBLICAL HISTORY

CREATION, FALL, FLOOD, BABEL | PATRIARCHS | EGYPTIAN SOJOURN

2100   2000   1900   1800

Earlier
Dating
System

Isaac

Jacob

Joseph

Abraham

CREATION, FALL, FLOOD, BABEL | PATRIARCHS

1800

Later
Dating
System

ANCIENT HISTORY

WORLD HISTORY

EARLY BRONZE AGE   MIDDLE BRONZE AGE

Earliest   2500   2400   2300   2200 2100 2000   1900   1800
Papyrus

Hammurabi

Sumerian Age ——┘└ Empire of Akkad ──┘   └── Ur ──┘   └── Babylonian ──
                                                              Dynasty
Egyptian Old Kingdom ────────────────┼──────── Egyptian Intermediate Kingdoms
Pyramids

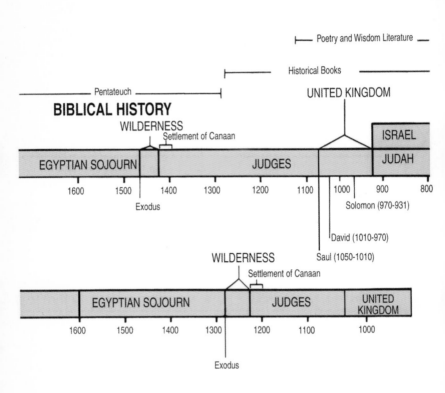

Poetry and Wisdom Literature

Historical Books

Pentateuch

BIBLICAL HISTORY

WILDERNESS

Settlement of Canaan

UNITED KINGDOM

ISRAEL

EGYPTIAN SOJOURN | JUDAH | JUDGES

1600 1500 1400 1300 1200 1100 1000 900 800

Exodus

Solomon (970-931)

David (1010-970)

Saul (1050-1010)

WILDERNESS

Settlement of Canaan

EGYPTIAN SOJOURN | JUDGES | UNITED KINGDOM

1600 1500 1400 1300 1200 1100 1000

Exodus

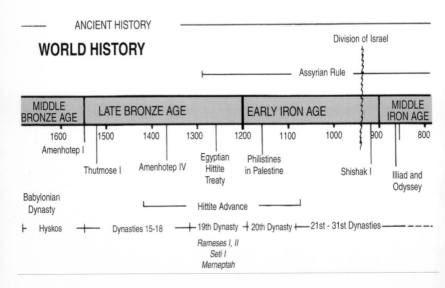

ANCIENT HISTORY

WORLD HISTORY

Division of Israel

Assyrian Rule

MIDDLE BRONZE AGE | LATE BRONZE AGE | EARLY IRON AGE | MIDDLE IRON AGE

1600 1500 1400 1300 1200 1100 1000 900 800

Amenhotep I

Thutmose I

Amenhotep IV

Egyptian Hittite Treaty

Philistines in Palestine

Shishak I

Illiad and Odyssey

Babylonian Dynasty

Hyskos — Dynasties 15-18 — 19th Dynasty + 20th Dynasty — 21st - 31st Dynasties

Hittite Advance

Rameses I, II
Seti I
Merneptah

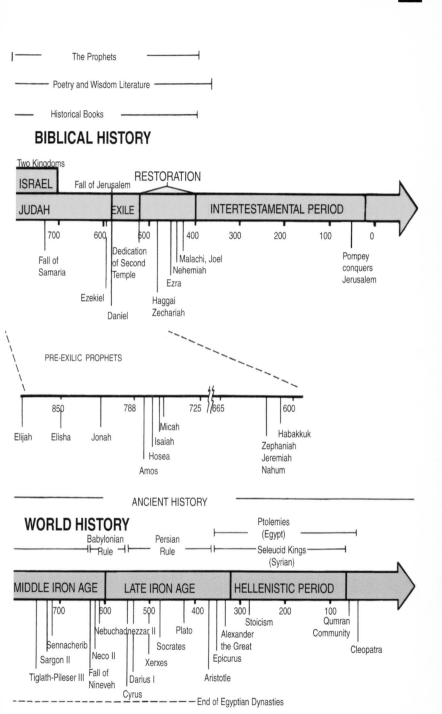

|———— The Prophets ————|

——— Poetry and Wisdom Literature ———|

——— Historical Books ———|

BIBLICAL HISTORY

Two Kingdoms

ISRAEL Fall of Jerusalem RESTORATION

JUDAH EXILE INTERTESTAMENTAL PERIOD

700 600 500 400 300 200 100 0

Fall of Samaria

Dedication of Second Temple

Malachi, Joel
Nehemiah
Ezra

Pompey conquers Jerusalem

Ezekiel

Haggai
Zechariah

Daniel

PRE-EXILIC PROPHETS

850 788 725 665 600

Elijah Elisha Jonah

Micah
Isaiah
Hosea

Amos

Habakkuk
Zephaniah
Jeremiah
Nahum

ANCIENT HISTORY

WORLD HISTORY

Babylonian Rule Persian Rule

Ptolemies (Egypt)

Seleucid Kings (Syrian)

MIDDLE IRON AGE LATE IRON AGE HELLENISTIC PERIOD

700 600 500 400 300 200 100

Sennacherib
Sargon II
Tiglath-Pileser III

Nebuchadnezzar II
Neco II
Fall of Nineveh
Cyrus

Plato
Socrates
Xerxes
Darius I

Stoicism
Alexander the Great
Epicurus
Aristotle

Qumran Community

Cleopatra

End of Egyptian Dynasties

CHURCH HISTORY

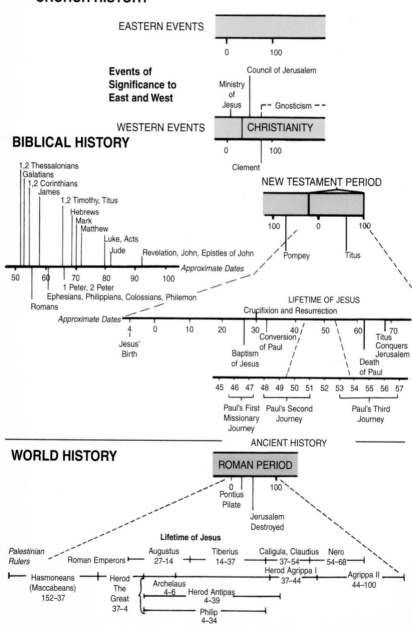

EASTERN EVENTS

0   100

Events of
Significance to
East and West

Council of Jerusalem

Ministry
of
Jesus

┌-- Gnosticism -- ┐

WESTERN EVENTS   CHRISTIANITY

BIBLICAL HISTORY

0   100

Clement

1,2 Thessalonians
Galatians
1,2 Corinthians
James
1,2 Timothy, Titus
Hebrews
Mark
Matthew
Luke, Acts
Jude
Revelation, John, Epistles of John

NEW TESTAMENT PERIOD

100   0   100

Pompey   Titus

Approximate Dates

50   60   70   80   90   100

1 Peter, 2 Peter
Ephesians, Philippians, Colossians, Philemon
Romans

LIFETIME OF JESUS

Crucifixion and Resurrection

Approximate Dates

4   0   10   20   30   40   50   60   70

Jesus'
Birth

Conversion
of Paul

Baptism
of Jesus

Titus
Conquers
Jerusalem

Death
of Paul

45 46 47 48 49 50 51 52 53 54 55 56 57

Paul's First
Missionary
Journey

Paul's Second
Journey

Paul's Third
Journey

ANCIENT HISTORY

WORLD HISTORY

ROMAN PERIOD

0   100

Pontius
Pilate

Jerusalem
Destroyed

Lifetime of Jesus

Palestinian
Rulers

Roman Emperors

Augustus
27-14

Tiberius
14-37

Caligula, Claudius
37-54

Nero
54-68

Herod Agrippa I
37-44

Agrippa II
44-100

Hasmoneans
(Maccabeans)
152-37

Herod
The
Great
37-4

Archelaus
4-6

Herod Antipas
4-39

Philip
4-34

CHURCH HISTORY

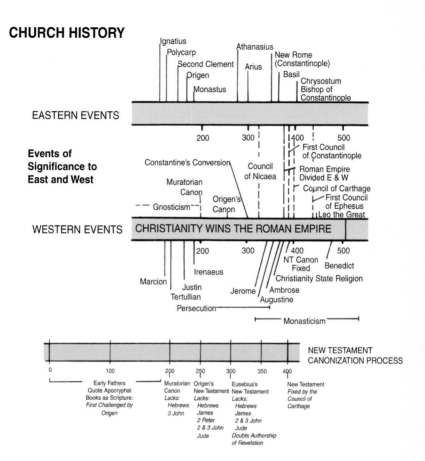

EASTERN EVENTS

Ignatius
Polycarp
Second Clement
Origen
Monastus
Athanasius
Arius
New Rome (Constantinople)
Basil
Chrysostum Bishop of Constantinople

200   300   400   500

Events of Significance to East and West

Constantine's Conversion
Muratorian Canon
Gnosticism
Origen's Canon
Council of Nicaea

First Council of Constantinople
Roman Empire Divided E & W
Council of Carthage
First Council of Ephesus
Leo the Great

WESTERN EVENTS   CHRISTIANITY WINS THE ROMAN EMPIRE

200   300   400   500

Marcion
Justin
Tertullian
Irenaeus
Persecution
Jerome
Augustine
NT Canon Fixed
Ambrose
Christianity State Religion
Benedict

Monasticism

NEW TESTAMENT CANONIZATION PROCESS

0   100   200   250   300   350   400

Early Fathers Quote Apocryphal Books as Scripture: *First Challenged by Origen*	Muratorian Canon *Lacks:* *Hebrews* *3 John*	Origen's New Testament *Lacks:* *Hebrews* *James* *2 Peter* *2 & 3 John* *Jude*

Eusebius's New Testament *Lacks:* *Hebrews* *James* *2 & 3 John* *Jude* *Doubts Authorship of Revelation*

New Testament *Fixed by the Council of Carthage*

ANCIENT HISTORY ——————————————— MEDIEVAL HISTORY ———

WORLD HISTORY

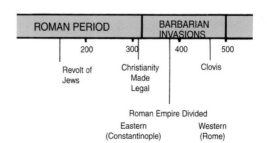

ROMAN PERIOD   BARBARIAN INVASIONS

200   300   400   500

Revolt of Jews
Christianity Made Legal
Clovis

Roman Empire Divided
Eastern (Constantinople)   Western (Rome)

CHURCH HISTORY

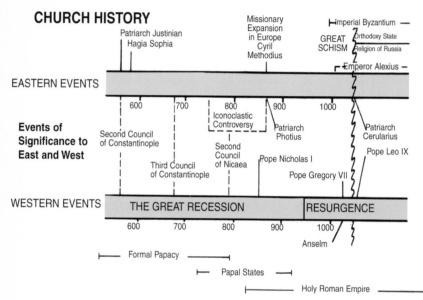

Patriarch Justinian
Hagia Sophia

Missionary
Expansion
in Europe
Cyril
Methodius

⊢Imperial Byzantium ——

GREAT
SCHISM

Orthodoxy State

Religion of Russia

Emperor Alexius —

EASTERN EVENTS

600   700   800   900   1000

**Events of
Significance to
East and West**

Second Council
of Constantinople

Iconoclastic
Controversy

Second
Council
of Nicaea

Patriarch
Photius

Pope Nicholas I

Third Council
of Constantinople

Patriarch
Cerularius

Pope Leo IX

Pope Gregory VII

WESTERN EVENTS

THE GREAT RECESSION   RESURGENCE

600   700   800   900   1000

Anselm

⊢— Formal Papacy ——⊣

⊢— Papal States —⊣

⊢— Holy Roman Empire ———

Doctrines Addressed by the Early Church Councils

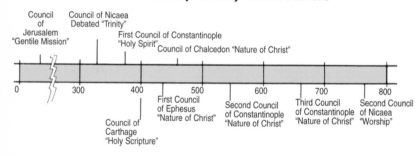

Council
of
Jerusalem
"Gentile Mission"

Council of Nicaea
Debated "Trinity"

First Council of Constantinople
"Holy Spirit"

Council of Chalcedon "Nature of Christ"

0   300   400   500   600   700   800

First Council
of Ephesus
"Nature of Christ"

Second Council
of Constantinople
"Nature of Christ"

Third Council
of Constantinople
"Nature of Christ"

Second Council
of Nicaea
"Worship"

Council of
Carthage
"Holy Scripture"

⊢————— MEDIEVAL HISTORY —————⊣

WORLD HISTORY

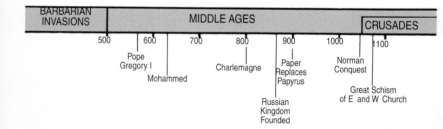

BARBARIAN
INVASIONS

MIDDLE AGES

CRUSADES

500   600   700   800   900   1000   1100

Pope
Gregory I

Mohammed

Charlemagne

Paper
Replaces
Papyrus

Russian
Kingdom
Founded

Norman
Conquest

Great Schism
of E and W Church

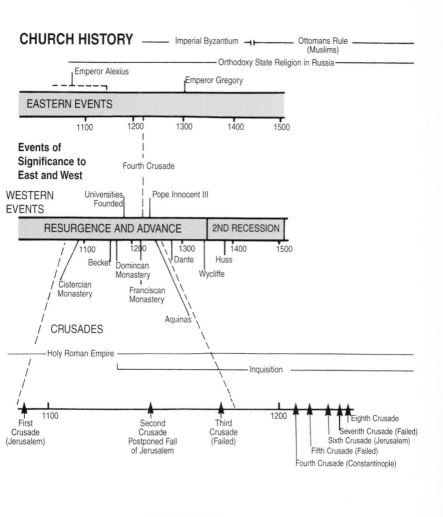

CHURCH HISTORY —— Imperial Byzantium —┤├—— Ottomans Rule ——
(Muslims)

—————————————— Orthodoxy State Religion in Russia ——————

┌ Emperor Alexius
├ ─ ─ ─ ─ ─ ┐   ┌ Emperor Gregory

EASTERN EVENTS

1100   1200   1300   1400   1500

**Events of
Significance to
East and West**

Fourth Crusade

WESTERN   Universities,   Pope Innocent III
EVENTS   Founded

RESURGENCE AND ADVANCE   2ND RECESSION

1100   1200   1300   1400   1500
Becket Domincan   Dante   Huss
        Monastery   Wycliffe
Cistercian
Monastery   Franciscan
            Monastery
                     Aquinas

CRUSADES

—— Holy Roman Empire ——————————————————————

                  ┌──────────── Inquisition ────────────

First   1100   Second   Third   1200
Crusade   Crusade   Crusade
(Jerusalem)   Postponed Fall   (Failed)   Eighth Crusade
                             of Jerusalem   Seventh Crusade (Failed)
                                                                    Sixth Crusade (Jerusalem)
                                                        Fifth Crusade (Failed)
                                                  Fourth Crusade (Constantinople)

——————————— MEDIEVAL HISTORY ————————┤

WORLD HISTORY

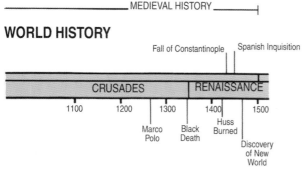

Fall of Constantinople   Spanish Inquisition

CRUSADES   RENAISSANCE

1100   1200   1300   1400   1500
              Marco   Black   Huss
              Polo   Death   Burned
                              Discovery
                              of New
                              World

CHURCH HISTORY

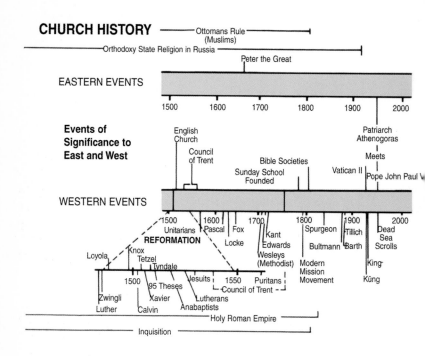

Ottomans Rule
(Muslims)

Orthodoxy State Religion in Russia

Peter the Great

EASTERN EVENTS

1500   1600   1700   1800   1900   2000

Events of Significance to East and West

English Church

Council of Trent

Bible Societies

Sunday School Founded

Patriarch Athenogoras Meets

Vatican II

Pope John Paul

WESTERN EVENTS

1500   1600   1700   1800   1900   2000

Unitarians   Pascal   Fox   Kant   Spurgeon   Tillich   Dead Sea Scrolls

REFORMATION

Locke   Edwards   Bultmann   Barth

Loyola   Knox   Tetzel   Tyndale   Wesleys (Methodist)   King

1500   Jesuits   1550   Puritans   Küng

Zwingli   Xavier   Council of Trent   Modern Mission Movement

Luther   Calvin   95 Theses   Lutherans   Anabaptists

Holy Roman Empire

Inquisition

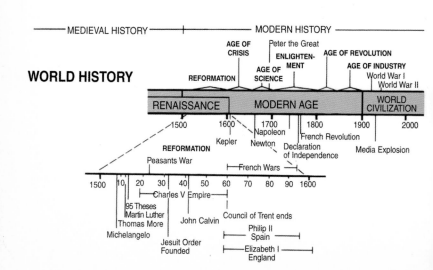

MEDIEVAL HISTORY ——— MODERN HISTORY ———

WORLD HISTORY

AGE OF CRISIS   Peter the Great

ENLIGHTEN-MENT   AGE OF REVOLUTION

REFORMATION   AGE OF SCIENCE   AGE OF INDUSTRY

World War I
World War II

RENAISSANCE   **MODERN AGE**   **WORLD CIVILIZATION**

1500   1600   1700   1800   1900   2000

Kepler   Napoleon   French Revolution

Newton   Declaration of Independence   Media Explosion

REFORMATION

Peasants War   French Wars

1500   10   20   30   40   50   60   70   80   90   1600

Charles V Empire

95 Theses   Council of Trent ends

Martin Luther

Thomas More   John Calvin   Philip II Spain

Michelangelo

Jesuit Order Founded   Elizabeth I England

FOREWORD

The Holman QuickSource Bible Atlas has two divisions.

GEOGRAPHY OF THE BIBLE LANDS

The first division focuses on the narrow strip of land that is broadly called Palestine, Israel, or the Holy Land. This is the land God promised to Abraham and that came fully under Israel's control during the time of David. This part of the atlas looks at the major regions of Palestine, giving attention to the geographical and climatological features of each region. This section of the *QuickSource Bible Atlas* was written by Paul H. Wright, director of Jerusalem University College Institute of Holy Land Studies. Dr. Wright is a graduate of Trinity Evangelical Divinity School (M.A.), Institute of Holy Land Studies (M.A.), and Hebrew Union College (Ph.D.).

MAPS OF BIBLE LANDS

The second division of the *QuickSource Bible Atlas* begins with Noah, follows the Bible's story line from Genesis to Revelation, and contains information on the expansion of Christianity to the third century. This division is arranged in sections according to the major divisions of biblical history. Each section includes maps, charts, and biblical reconstructions that illuminate that epoch of history. The *QuickSource Bible Atlas* ends with charts that summarize the development of the biblical canon and explains weights and measures of the Bible.

GEOGRAPHY OF THE BIBLE LANDS: INTRODUCTION

"Long ago God spoke to the fathers by the prophets at different times and in different ways. In these last days, He has spoken to us by His Son" (Heb. 1:1-2). The writer of the book of Hebrews reminds us how God revealed Himself to people in the past.

As creator of the universe, God stands outside of time and space. He nevertheless chose to enter a real flesh-and-blood world in order to create, and then redeem, mankind. For hundreds of years God communicated His words and will to an eager, yet usually recalcitrant, people who made their homes in the lands hugging the southeastern shore of the Mediterranean Sea. Then, in what the Apostle Paul called "the completion of time" (Gal. 4:4), God Himself bent down to enter the human race, choosing to dirty His hands and feet in a small, noisy, and very needy corner of the Roman Empire called Galilee (cp. Phil. 2:5-8).

Unlike sacred books of the world's other great religions, the Bible is full of stories of real people living in real places. God's decision to communicate eternal truths through fallible human beings, to wrap His message around mankind's experiences with rock and soil and water, is both mind-boggling and humbling. It also suggests that a full understanding of God's revelation cannot be gained without an appreciation of the physical context in which that revelation was given.

▶ THE ANCIENT NEAR EAST

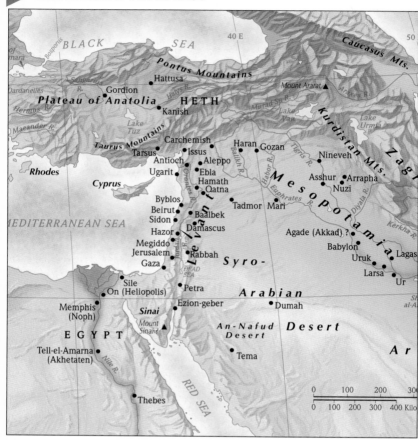

The writers of the Bible knew well the land in which God chose to reveal Himself, for it was their home. They were intimately familiar with the rugged terrain of Judah, with cold winter rain and scorching desert heat, and they had experienced the relief offered by a small spring of water or the shelter of a crevasse in a mighty rock. They knew what it meant for the hills surrounding their city or village to be filled with enemy troops or to lie down at night secure after a bountiful harvest. Time and again the Bible's historians, prophets, and poets used such information to enliven the divine message they had to tell. Geographical information fills the biblical text, and the biblical authors assumed that their readers knew even more. The land of the Bible has rightly been termed the "playing board of biblical history" (James M. Monson, *Regions on the Run*, Rockford, IL: Biblical Backgrounds, 1998, p. 3). It is difficult at best to understand fully the instructions (the Bible) without the board (the land) on which the events of the Bible were played out.

The rugged terrain characteristic of the wilderness of Judah.

Many people journey to the lands of the Bible with the hope of walking where Jesus walked. In spite of the established pilgrimage spots in the Holy Land, however, it is just not possible to say with certainty that Jesus stood on spot X when he healed such-and-such a person or delivered such-and-such a teaching. On the other hand, the location of many biblical cities, hills, valleys, and the like are known, and by carefully studying the geographical settings of the Bible, the serious reader can enter more deeply into its world. It becomes possible to follow Joshua's army into the hill country of Canaan after laying waste to Jericho. One can climb to the crest of the hill on which David's Jerusalem stood and still experience the energy of the Songs of Ascent (Pss. 121–134). Jesus must have often gazed over the Sea of Galilee in the early mornings from the hills above Capernaum (cp. Mark 1:35); doing so today helps the serious Bible reader appreciate Jesus' call to ministry—and one's own place in the kingdom of God.

A calm Sea of Galilee at dusk with snow-capped Mount Hermon in the distance.

There is yet another reason understanding the geography of Bible lands is important for understanding the Bible. God created the features of the lands of the Bible in the way that He did—and then chose to bring His people there (Gen. 12:1-3; 13:14-17; 15:12-18)—for a reason. In fact, the lands of the Bible are uniquely suited to teach lessons about the nature and character of God as well as the ways that His people should respond to Him.

The various natural features of the lands of the Bible combine to form a setting in which personal or national security was always in doubt. With limited rainfall, an overabundance of rocks but scarcity of good soil, and a position situated alongside a major international highway on which the armies of the world marched, the lands of the Bible were well acquainted with lifestyles that demanded their inhabitants depend on God to survive. In today's maddening times, the lands of the Bible offer lessons of peace and security that should be heard and heeded.

2 ▸ THE ARCHAEOLOGICAL PERIODS OF THE NEAR EAST

TERM	APPROXIMATE DATES
Paleolithic (Old Stone Age)	?–18,000 BC
Epipaleolithic (formerly Mesolithic—Middle Stone Age)	18000–8300 BC
Neolithic (New Stone Age)	8300–4500 BC
Chalcolithic (Copper Stone Age)	4500–3300 BC
Early Bronze Age	3300–2000 BC
Middle Bronze Age	2000–1550 BC
Late Bronze Age	1550–1200 BC
Iron Age	1200–586 BC
Babylonian and Persian Periods	586–332 BC
Hellenistic Period	332–63 BC
Roman Period	63 BC–AD 324
Byzantine Period	AD 324–638

PALESTINE

Most of the events described in the Bible took place within the borders of the modern state of Israel plus the West Bank and areas currently under the Palestinian Authority. For many Bible readers this entire region should be called *Israel*, while others prefer the term *Palestine*. Theological or political considerations usually play a decisive role in what this land is called today, just as they have throughout history. Indeed, theological and political positions often claim support from names found on a map. The names Canaan, Israel, and Palestine (or Palestina) have all been used at various times in history to designate the land that lies between the Mediterranean Sea and the Jordan River. When speaking geographically, however, Bible atlases and encyclopedias commonly refer to this land as Palestine rather than Israel, without intending to make a religious or political statement. For this reason, the term *Palestine* is used in this volume as well.

3 ▶ MODERN POLITICAL DIVISIONS OF ANCIENT PALESTINE

Some biblical events took place in lands that lie outside of the modern state of Israel. These lands include Egypt; Mesopotamia (modern Iraq); Persia (modern Iran); Edom Moab and Ammon (all in modern Jordan); Phoenicia (modern Lebanon); Aram (modern Syria); regions such as Galatia, Phrygia, Lydia, and Mysia (all in modern Turkey); Macedonia and Achaia (both in modern Greece); Cyprus;

4 ▶ MODERN STATES AND THE ANCIENT NEAR EAST

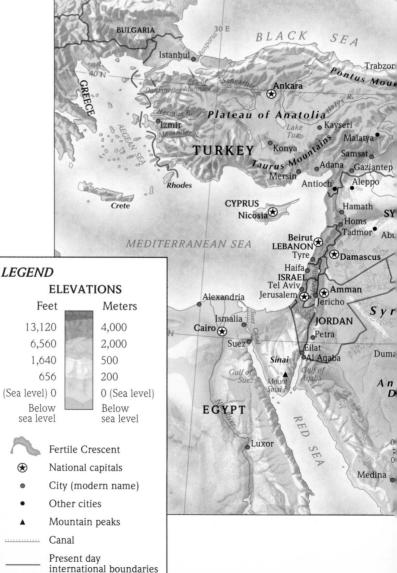

Crete; and Italy. Other lands in North Africa (Libya and Cyrene), or located in the Arabian peninsula or in northeastern Africa (Cush and Sheba), are also mentioned in the Bible. Each of these is properly a "land of the Bible," as well, and should be of interest to serious Bible readers.

Names for the Bible Lands

CANAAN

The origin of the word *Canaan* remains uncertain. Some relate it to the Akkadian word for a costly blue-purple dye (*kinahhu*)—or the cloth dyed that color—that was derived from murex shells found along the Phoenician coast. Others find its origins in the Akkadian word designating a class or type of merchants (*kina 'nu*) dealing in this type of dyed cloth. Support for this latter suggestion is found in passages such as Isaiah 23:8 and Zephaniah 1:11.

ISRAEL

Genesis 32:28 connects the name *Israel* with a Hebrew verb meaning "to struggle or strive": "Your name will no longer be Jacob, but Israel, because you have struggled with God and with men and have overcome." It is unclear, however, whether the author of Genesis 32 is providing the actual etymology of the word or simply punning on the name *Israel*.

PALESTINE

Palestine is derived from the word *Philistine*. It was first used by the Greek historian Herodotus in the fifth century BC to refer to the geographical area of the southeastern Mediterranean coast. Some English editions of the KJV uses *Palestina* as an alternate name for Philistia in Exodus 15:14 and Isaiah 14:29,31.

HOLY LAND

The term *holy land*, so familiar to Christians as a synonym of Israel, is in fact a very rare biblical term. Its only true occurrence is Zechariah 2:12, part of a vivid prophecy of the restoration of Israel: "The LORD will inherit Judah as his portion in the holy land, and will again choose Jerusalem." The HCSB, NIV, NASB, and RSV also mention the "holy land" in Psalm 78:54: "Thus he brought them (i.e., Israel) to the border of his holy land, to the hill country his right hand had taken." The NKJV, reading the Hebrew text more literally, however, translates this phrase as "His holy border" instead.

At just over 8,000 square miles, Palestine is about the size of New Jersey, but its variations in topography and climate more closely resemble those of California.

Climate

The climate of Palestine is largely a product of the land's narrow dimensions between desert and sea. The vast Arabian Desert to the east of the rift valley encroaches to within less than 100 miles of the Mediterranean, pinching Palestine between an extremely hot, dry desert climate and the more temperate climate of the sea. Moreover, in the Sinai Peninsula to the south, the eastern extremity of the Sahara meets the Arabian Desert, and both touch the Mediterranean coast. Because Palestine is narrowly wedged between the desert and the sea, any minor change in global weather patterns will have significant or even drastic effects on its annual climate.

Palestine's climate is also affected by topography. Because of sharp variations in topography, the local climate within Palestine can differ widely in a space of just a few miles. The main ridge forming the backbone of the hill country—the watershed ridge—runs north-northeast to south-southwest, at right angles to the prevailing rains off the Mediterranean. Most of the rain that falls in Palestine falls on the western side of the watershed ridge, leaving the eastern slopes and the rift valley under a dry rain shadow. Rain also falls in a narrow north-south band in the higher hills that rise east of the rift but quickly tapers off further east under the harsh effects of the Arabian Desert.

That is, higher elevations in the northwestern part of the country receive ample amounts of rainfall, while lower elevations to the southeast receive scant rainfall. Mount Carmel, which juts into the Mediterranean Sea in the northern part of the country, receives over 32 inches of rainfall per year. By contrast, the Dead Sea, only 80 miles to the southeast but below sea level, receives less than 2 inches of rainfall per year. Jerusalem receives about 25 inches of rain per year, about the same as London, but unlike London, all the rain of Jerusalem falls over the course of five or six months.

5 CROSS SECTIONAL VIEWS OF LONGITUDINAL ZONES

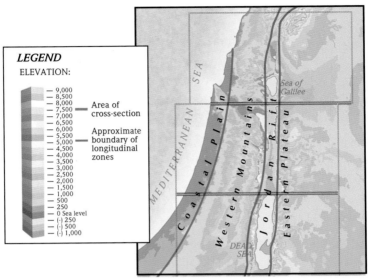

LEGEND

ELEVATION:

— 9,000
— 8,500
— 8,000
— 7,500
— 7,000
— 6,500
— 6,000
— 5,500
— 5,000
— 4,500
— 4,000
— 3,500
— 3,000
— 2,500
— 2,000
— 1,500
— 1,000
— 500
— 250
— 0 Sea level
— (-) 250
— (-) 500
— (-) 1,000

Area of cross-section

Approximate boundary of longitudinal zones

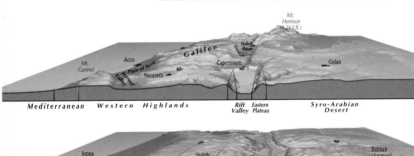

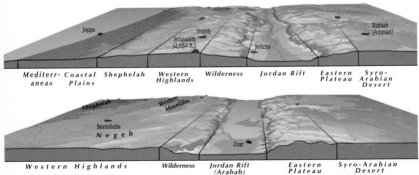

It is possible to speak in general of three "rules of rainfall" for Palestine:
1. North is wet; south is dry.
2. West is wet; east is dry.
3. High is wet; low is dry.

There are two primary seasons in Palestine, a rainy season (usually mid-October through mid-April) and a dry season (usually mid-May through September). Short transitional seasons mark the change between the two. Palestine's agricultural year is determined by these seasons, as were the times of ancient Israel's major festivals (see below).

6▶ THE AGRICULTURAL YEAR

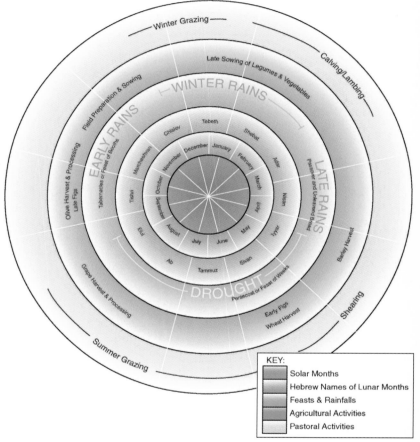

The rainy season begins with the early rains of late October and November. These rains clear the air of dust and loosen the soil for planting grain (Deut. 11:14; Ps. 84:5-7; Jer. 5:24; Joel 2:23; cp. Ps. 65:10). If the rains are late, farmers anticipate famine (cp. Prov. 25:14; Amos 4:7). The early rains are followed by heavy winter rains that fall in December, January, and February (Ezra 10:9-13). During the winter months, storms typically roll into Palestine from the northwest, dumping heavy waves of rain for three or four days. Between storms, the land experiences clear, sunny skies and moderate temperatures. The storms lessen in March and early April, as the latter rains give the heads of grain their final growth (cp. Zech. 10:1; Mark 4:28).

Snow falls every year on Mount Hermon but only some winters in other parts of Palestine. Snow typically falls at night (temperatures rarely dip below freezing during the daytime) and in the higher elevations of the hill country (above 1,700 feet); it is wet and heavy, and usually melts the next day (cp. Job 24:19). Snow was rare enough in ancient Israel to receive special notice by the biblical writers (e.g., 1 Chron. 11:22; Job 6:15-16; 38:22-23).

7 ▶ CLIMATE PATTERNS OF ANCIENT PALESTINE

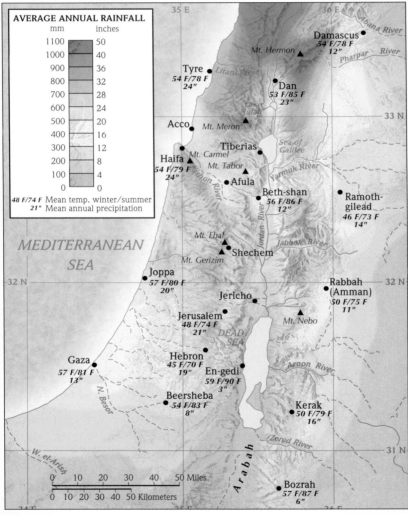

The average August daytime temperature in Jerusalem, a city located 2,600 feet above sea level, is 86° Fahrenheit; at night, the temperature averages 64°. The highest temperature ever recorded in Palestine was 129° Fahrenheit on June 21, 1945, near Beth Shan in the upper Jordan Valley. On May 24, 1999, Jericho set a record temperature of 124° Fahrenheit. Both Beth Shan and Jericho lie below sea level in the Rift Valley.

Natural Routes

What Palestine lacks in natural resources, it makes up for in location. Palestine's geopolitical importance lies in its role as a passageway between three great land masses, Africa, Europe, and Asia, as well as between the Mediterranean Sea and the Red Sea (Indian Ocean). Because the land is bisected by major trade routes, political powers who controlled Palestine during the biblical period become major economic players in the ancient Near East, just as they do in the modern Middle East today. Routes that carry trade, however, also carry armies, and throughout history Palestine has been overrun numerous times as foreign powers have sought to secure the region for themselves. The international routes that cross Palestine also make the land a meeting place of cultures where new ways of life and faith challenge those that have already taken root in its soil.

8 ▶ INTERNATIONAL ROUTES

LEGEND
- City
— International Coastal Highway
— King's Highway
— Sea routes
— Other routes

| 0 | 100 | 200 | 300 Miles |
| 0 | 100 | 200 | 300 Kilometers |

> *"There is no land which is at once so much a sanctuary and an observatory as Palestine; no land which, till its office was fulfilled, was so swept by the great forces of history, and was yet so capable of preserving one tribe in national continuity and growth; one tribe learning and suffering and rising superior to the successive problems these forces presented to her, till upon the opportunity afforded by the last of them she launched her results upon the world"* (George Adam Smith, *The Historical Geography of the Holy Land*, Hodder & Stoughton, 1931, p. 91).

It is possible to reconstruct many of the important routes of ancient Palestine by comparing the location of the land's gravitation points (e.g., population centers, gateway cities, seaports, and the like) with topographical features that act either as channels for traffic or barriers to travel. For instance, in the rugged Cenomanian hill country, most traffic stayed on the tops of ridges, with the primary routes into and out of the hills following the continuous ridges that separate wadi systems (e.g., "the road going up to Beth Horon"—Josh. 10:10 NIV). Routes tended to follow the easiest—but not necessarily the shortest—distance between two points, avoiding where possible rugged mountainous regions, swampy and sandy areas, and deserts. Most of the natural routes of antiquity can still be followed, even though, thanks to modern road-building machinery, many highways in Israel today violate the land's natural topography.

It is also possible to reconstruct ancient routes in Palestine by looking at the movement of persons through the land in the biblical story. For instance, we read that Abraham entered Canaan from the north, stopped at Shechem and Bethel, then continued south toward the Negev (Gen. 12:4-9). [See **THE MIGRATION OF ABRAHAM**, p. 74.] In doing so he followed a well-worn natural route through the middle of the hill country, a route that in part makes use of the watershed ridge forming the spine of the hill country of Judah. The portion of this "Patriarchal Highway" that goes through the hill country of Ephraim was described in detail by the writer of Judges (Judg. 21:19).

Many local routes crisscrossed Palestine. The Bible provides the names of some of these. Typically a road was named after its destination (e.g., "the road to Shur"—Gen. 16:7; "the road toward Bashan"—Num. 21:33; "the way to the wasteland of Gibeon"—2 Sam. 2:24, etc. [NIV]). "The king's highway" (Num. 20:17) is the only clear biblical exception to this rule (but cp. Isa. 35:8). [Several important routes are shown on **INTERNATIONAL ROUTES**, p. 16.]

Two major international routes ran the length of Palestine in antiquity, one west of the rift valley and the other to the east (p.16).

The western route is often called the International Coastal Highway or *Via Maris* ("the Way of the Sea"). The biblical name "the road through the Philistine country" (Exod. 13:17) refers to the southern portion of this route as it hugs the Mediterranean coast in the vicinity of Gaza. Historically, the International Coastal Highway was the principal highway carrying international traffic between Egypt and Mesopotamia. North of Damascus, this route followed the arc of the Fertile Crescent, but once in Palestine it worked its way through the hills and valleys of Galilee to the coast. Strategic cities in Palestine along this route in the biblical period (from north to south) were Hazor, Megiddo, Aphek, Gezer, and Gaza.

The eastern international route ran due south out of Damascus through the highlands of northern Transjordan to Rabbath-ammon (modern Amman, Jordan). From here one branch connected the capital cities of the Old Testament nations of Ammon, Moab, and Edom (Rabbath-ammon, Kir-hareseth, and Bozrah, respectively) before continuing south to the Red Sea and the great inland spice route of Arabia. The Bible calls this route "the king's highway" (Num. 20:17; 21:22). An eastern branch, the "desert road of Moab" (Deut. 2:8), skirted Moab and Edom along the edge of the desert. Less a route of armies, the international highway in Transjordan carried the wealth of the Arabian Peninsula (e.g., gold, frankincense, and myrrh) to the empires of the ancient Near Eastern and Mediterranean worlds.

Palestine's importance on the larger world scene lies in its position as a land bridge. In the bigger picture, however, the biblical writers used Palestine's natural highways as a tangible illustration of the "ways" in which God's people should walk (for example, see Jer. 6:16; Deut. 5:33; Isa. 26:7).

Roman Roads

In the late first and early second centuries AD, the Romans built an extensive road system in Palestine, part of a larger road system tying together their far-flung empire. For the most part these roads followed the old natural routes of the biblical period but with sophisticated technological improvements (e.g., grading, curbing, paving, etc). Some of the mileposts marking these roads remain, allowing intrepid hikers to follow their course today. Jesus often walked between Jericho and Jerusalem (Matt. 20:29; cp. Luke 10:30); in His travels He no doubt followed the natural route, which was upgraded to the status of a Roman road about a hundred years later.

Eventually larger powers—the Assyrians (2 Kings 15:29), Babylonians, Persians, Greeks, Seleucids, Ptolemies, and Romans—seized the Huleh Basin to secure their position in the area. By New Testament times, the Huleh sat in the middle of Jewish and Gentile populations. In offering the wealth and opportunities of the world, this region became a true testing ground of faith.

THE LAND OF PALESTINE

The land of Palestine can be divided a number of ways. For the purpose of the *QuickSource Bible Atlas*, we will look at four broad regions: the southern regions (Judah/Judea), the central regions (Israel/Samaria), the northern regions (Galilee), and the eastern regions (Transjordan).

A view from the front of the so-called "treasury" building of the narrow entryway into the Nabatean city of Petra.

9 ▶ THE NATURAL REGIONS OF PALESTINE

LEGEND
- City
- ○ City (uncertain location)
- ▲ Mountain peak

MEDITERRANEAN SEA

Sidon

Damas

Tyre

Mt. Hermon

Pharpar

Rosh HaNiqra
(Ladder of Tyre)

Litani River

Dan

UPPER GALILEE

Hazor

Huleh Basin

Acco

Mt. Meron ▲

Capernaum

LOWER GALILEE

Sea of Galilee

BASHAN

Mt. Carmel

Sepphoris

Cana

Dor

Megiddo

Nazareth
▲ Mt. Tabor

Caesarea

Mt. Gilboa

Beth-shan

Ramoth

SAMARIA

Tirzah

Jordan River

Joppa

Aphek

Mizpah ▲
Shechem
▲ Mt. Gerizim

Shiloh

GILEAD PLATEAU

Bethel

Jericho

Jerusalem

Rabbah (Amm

Gezer

Heshbon

Ashdod

Ekron

Shephelah

Western Mountains

Medeba

MISHOR

Ashkelon

Gath

Gaza

Hebron

Wilderness of Judah

En-gedi

DEAD SEA

Dibon

Arnon River

Beersheba

Arad

JUDAH

MOAB

Kir-hareseth

Jordan Rift

Negeb

Eastern Plateau

Wilderness of Zin

Tamar

EDOM

Arabah

W. el-Arish

Bozrah

Kadesh-barnea

Petra

Plain of Asher

Plain of Acco

Jezreel Valley

N. Harod

Plain of Dor

Plain of Sharon

N. Yarkon

N. Besor

Plain of Philistia

Coastal Plain

Kishon River

0   10   20   30   40   50 Miles

0 10 20 30 40 50 Kilometers

THE SOUTHERN REGIONS
(Judah/Judaea)

The southern portion of Palestine, generally corresponding to the land of the southern kingdom of Judah, is composed of six distinct geographical regions: the hill country of Judah, the Shephelah, the Philistine coastal plain, the biblical Negev, the wilderness of Judah and the land of Benjamin.

10 ▶ PHILISTINE PLAIN, SHEPHELAH, JUDAH, AND THE DEAD SEA

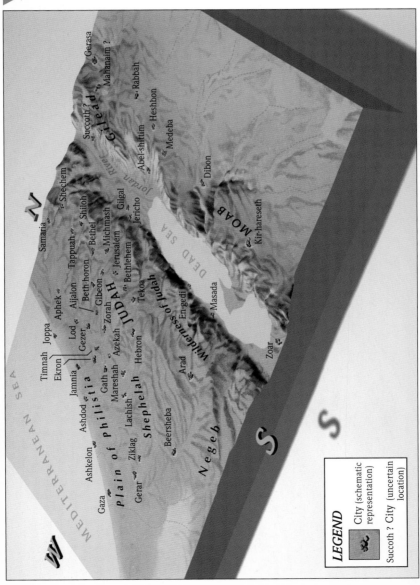

LEGEND

City (schematic representation)

Succoth ? City (uncertain location)

The Hill Country of Judah

The hill country of Judah formed the heartland of the Old Testament kingdom of Judah, as well as the New Testament province, Judea. In area the hill country covers approximately 480 square miles (40 miles x 12 miles), the size of an average county in the United States. The high point of the hill country, at Halhul (cp. Josh. 15:58) just north of Hebron, is 3,347 feet in elevation.

Joshua 10:40, summarizing Joshua's conquests in the southern part of Canaan, recognizes the natural geographical regions of the land of Judah: "So Joshua subdued the whole region, including the hill country, the Negev, the western foothills and the mountain slopes, together with all their kings." In this translation (NIV), "western foothills" translates the Hebrew term shephelah, *while "mountain slopes" refers to the wilderness slopes to the east. Similar verses are Deuteronomy 1:7 and Jeremiah 17:26.*

11 ▶ JOSHUA'S CENTRAL AND SOUTHERN CAMPAIGNS

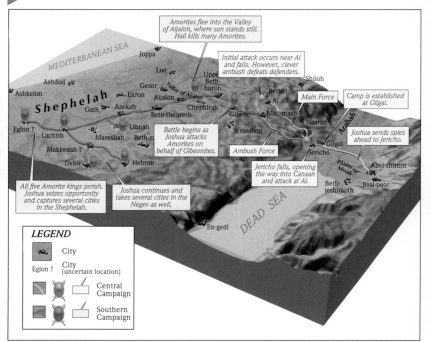

Amorites flee into the Valley of Aijalon, where sun stands still. Hail kills many Amorites.

Initial attack occurs near Ai and fails. However, clever ambush defeats defenders.

Camp is established at Gilgal.

Joshua sends spies ahead to Jericho.

Battle begins as Joshua attacks Amorites on behalf of Gibeonites.

Jericho falls, opening the way into Canaan and attack at Ai.

All five Amorite kings perish. Joshua seizes opportunity and captures several cities in the Shephelah.

Joshua continues and takes several cities in the Negev as well.

MEDITERRANEAN SEA · Joppa · Lod · Upper Beth-horon · Shiloh · Ashdod · Gezer · Valley of Aijalon · Bethel · Main Force · Ashkelon · Ekron · Aijalon · Ai · Shephelah · Gath · Azekah · Chephirah · Gibeon · Michmash · Beth-shemesh · Naaran · Arabah · Eglon ? · Libnah · Jerusalem · Lachish · Mareshah · Beth-zur · Gilgal · Ambush Force · Makkedah ? · Jericho · Plains of Moab · Abel-shittim · Debir · Hebron · Beth-jeshimoth · Baal-peor · En-gedi · DEAD SEA

LEGEND

🐎	City
Eglon ?	City (uncertain location)
⚔	Central Campaign
⚔	Southern Campaign

The wadi through the limestone cliffs of the Qumran area in Israel.

The watershed ridge, running north-northeast by south-southwest, forms the backbone of the hill country of Judah. From it wadis flow westward to the Mediterranean Sea and eastward to the Jordan Valley and Dead Sea. As these wadis cut through the hard Cenomanian limestone, they form deep, V-shaped valleys with steep, rugged sides. Because the limestone is bedded, it breaks on the wadi slopes into natural terraces that have been improved with considerable effort through the centuries into numerous small but fertile plots of agricultural land. Adequate winter rainfall, plentiful springs, and rich terra rosa soil have allowed farmers and villagers in the hill country of Judah to produce ample crops to sustain life. Since antiquity the traditional crops of the hill country have been grapes, figs, olives, pomegranates, and almonds (cp. Deut. 8:8). Grapes, figs, and olives, in addition to bread, were the staples of life.

Pomegranate blossoms taken at Sabaste, Israel.

Young grapes growing near Tel Lakhish (Isa. 5:1-7).

From earliest times, the traditional crops of the Judean hill country have had symbolic value. Grapes symbolized a full life of serenity and peace (1 Kings 4:24; Ps. 128:3) and, in particular, people living under the blessing of God (Ps. 80:8-11,14-15; John 15:1-7). Figs, identified with the tree of knowledge (cp. Gen. 3:7), were also a symbol of prosperity and peace (Isa. 36:16; Hab. 3:17). Biblical writers used olive trees to speak of beauty, fertility, and endurance (Gen. 8:11; Ps. 128:3). Pomegranates symbolized beauty, love, and fertility (Song 4:3,13), and the almond, blooming in mid-January as the harbinger of spring, hearkened to the hastening of events (Num. 17:8; Eccles. 12:5; Jer. 1:11-12).

The major cities of the hill country of Judah—Hebron, Bethlehem, and Jerusalem—are located just off the central watershed ridge. They are linked together by the main route through the hill country, the central ridge route or Patriarchal Highway, which follows the line of this ridge. Of the hill country cities, Hebron has always held pride of place in terms of geographical and agricultural advantage, and it was there that David, born in Bethlehem and destined to find glory in Jerusalem, first reigned as king over Israel (2 Sam. 5:1-5).

Countryside between Jerusalem and Bethlehem.
Olive trees can be seen in a small orchard.

The rugged wadis that drop out of the hill country tend to isolate the cities and villages of the watershed ridge from the International Coastal Highway to the west and the rift valley and King's Highway to the east (see **INTERNATIONAL ROUTES**, p. 33). A few natural routes following the continuous ridges that divide these wadi systems link Hebron, Bethlehem, and Jerusalem to the world beyond. Down one of these ridges that connects Bethlehem with the Elah Valley in the Shephelah (the "Husan Ridge Route"), a young David brought food to his brothers fighting the Philistines (1 Sam. 17:12-19). It was probably along this same route that Philip met an Ethiopian eunuch traveling from Jerusalem to Gaza (Acts 8:26-40).

Because of its rugged isolation and natural defenses, Judah has always been relatively closed to foreign cultural influences. The large powers of antiquity (Egypt, Assyria, Babylon, Greece, and Rome) were occasionally drawn into the hill country to fight against the Canaanites, Israelites, or Jews living in Jerusalem but seldom went out of their way to settle there. As a result, the local inhabitants of Judah tended to value stable and conservative lifestyles. It was here that Jeremiah preached the "old-time religion" of Moses, that Isaiah spoke of a coming Messiah to deliver His people (Isa. 40:9-11), and that Judaism took its formative steps in the centuries leading up to the New Testament. More than any other region in Palestine, the hill country of Judah represents the land in which God chose to dwell among His people.

During the biblical period the hill country of Judah was the "irreducible minimum" of God's promised land, the cradle of Israelite and Jewish life. On its protected ridges and slopes, God's people were given opportunity to take root and prosper. Their success was mixed and depended on their willingness to obey Him (Deut. 11:11-12; 28:1-68; Ps. 80:1-19).

The Shephelah

The Shephelah (lit. "lowland," translated "western foothills" by the NIV) is the area of low, rolling Eocene hills between the hill country of Judah and the coastal plain (Deut. 1:7; Josh. 9:1; 10:40; 15:33-36; 1 Kings 10:27; 2 Chron. 26:10; Jer. 17:26). This region covers approximately 250 square miles (25 miles x 10 miles), and its hills vary in elevation from 300 to 1,200 feet.

A hard mineral crust called nari, three to five feet thick, covers the hills of the Shephelah, rendering them practically useless for agriculture. Only small trees and shrubs grow on these hills naturally. The broad valleys of the Shephelah, however, are quite fertile and particularly well suited for grain (wheat and barley), but vineyards and orchard crops also do well there. These valleys are the extension of the major wadi systems flowing west out of the hill country of Judah and are fed by ample runoff rainfall from the hills.

Five valleys of the Shephelah have figured prominently in the political history of Palestine. From north to south, they are the Aijalon, the Sorek, the Elah, the Guvrin, and the Lachish.

Several verses in the Bible mention the agricultural possibilities of the Shephelah. First Chronicles 27:28 mentions the sycamore tree, which produces an inferior type of fig, and the olive tree.

The Lachish Valley is named after Lachish, the second most important city in Judah during the late monarchy. The capture of Lachish by the Assyrian king Sennacherib in 701 BC (2 Kings 18:14,17; 19:8) and again by the Babylonian king Nebuchadnezzar in 587 BC (Jer. 34:7) signaled the fall of the entire Shephelah to foreign powers.

The definitive line of a wall at Lachish running from the south, northeast up to the high place.

Politically, the Shephelah has always functioned as both a bridge and a buffer between the hill country and the coastal plain. The east-west orientation of the five valleys of the Shephelah provides easy access for the people of the coast to move into the hill country (e.g., the Philistines or international powers such as Egypt, Assyria, Babylon, Greece, and Rome). On the other hand, if the inhabitants of the hill country are to have any thoughts of expanding their influence in Palestine, they must first secure the agricultural lands and highways of the Shephelah. For this reason the valleys of the Shephelah historically have functioned like saloon doors of the Old West, swinging either in or out depending on the strength and ability of those pushing from either side. At times, however, a king in Jerusalem would attempt to close the doors altogether, building fortifications in the Shephelah as a front guard for his heartland in the hill country (2 Chron. 11:5-12).

As Judah's buffer zone toward the coast, the Shephelah witnessed assault after assault on Jerusalem. This was the region that Judah could scarcely afford to lose yet over time could scarcely control.

The Philistine Coastal Plain

▲ Joppa.

Palestine's coastal plain stretches from north of Mount Carmel to the Sinai Peninsula. The portion of this plain that lies between the Yarqon River, a stream flowing through Joppa (the modern city of Tel Aviv), and the Nahal Besor just south of Gaza is commonly known as the Philistine coastal plain. This was the heartland of the Philistines during much of the time of the Old Testament.

The Philistine coastal plain extends approximately 50 miles along the Mediterranean coast, varying in width from 10 miles in the north to 25 miles in the south. The plain rises gradually eastward to the hills of the Shephelah. Sand dunes dominate the coastline, but inland the sand mixes with alluvial and loess soils (from the Shephelah and Negev, respectively) to form a decent agricultural base. Historically, the major agricultural crops grown on the coastal plain have been grain, but citrus orchards are common in the area today.

The shoreline of the Mediterranean coast is stiff and uninviting except for a small natural harbor at Joppa (modern Tel Aviv), Judah's desired seaport. For this reason, most traffic on the plain during the biblical period was land-based, moving north and south along two branches of the International Coastal Highway. One branch, tracking just behind the coastal dunes, linked Gaza, Ashkelon, Ashdod, and Joppa before turning inland to Aphek (1 Sam. 4:1; New Testament Antipatris—Acts

12 MEDITERRANEAN COASTLINE

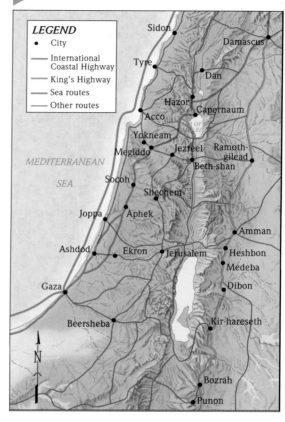

LEGEND
- City
— International Coastal Highway
— King's Highway
— Sea routes
— Other routes

Sidon
Damascus
Tyre
Dan
Hazor
Acco
Capernaum
Yokneam
Megiddo
Jezreel
Ramoth-gilead
MEDITERRANEAN
Beth-shan
SEA
Socoh
Shechem
Joppa
Aphek
Amman
Ashdod
Ekron
Jerusalem
Heshbon
Medeba
Gaza
Dibon
Beersheba
Kir-hareseth
N
Bozrah
Punon

23:31), located at the head of the Yarqon River. An inland branch followed the western edge of the Shephelah, connecting Gerar, Gath, and Ekron to Aphek.

The openness of the Philistine coastal plain makes this a true international region. This was the homeland of the Philistines, and from their five cities (Gaza, Ashkelon, Ashdod, Ekron, and Gath—1 Sam. 6:17-18) the Philistines attempted to push into the hill country at the same time that Israel was trying to expand its influence toward the coast.

Eventually large powers from the outside—Assyria and Babylon from the east, Greece and Rome from the

Panoramic view of the ancient tel of Gath.

west—swept down the coastal plain with their eye on the wealth of Egypt, running over the local inhabitants in the process. The Philistines disappeared from history, although their name lives on in the term *Palestine*. The Israelites and Judeans, able to find refuge in the rugged hill country to the east, survived as the spiritual ancestors of both Jews and Christians today.

The Philistine coastal plain was the highway of southern Palestine. Judah wanted to take advantage of the opportunities that living on this highway offered but, more often than not, was run over by mighty empires of the day in the process.

The Biblical Negev

▲ Excavated storerooms at the site of ancient Beer-sheba in the Negev.

The biblical Negev (lit. "dry land" or "south") is a geological depression reaching inland from the southern Philistine coastal plain to a point 12 miles west of the southern end of the Dead Sea. The western basin of the Negev overlaps the southern end of the coastal plain, and the city of Gerar rightly belongs to both regions. The Negev was the natural southern border of the United Kingdom of Israel (1 Kings 4:25) and the southern kingdom of Judah (2 Kings 23:8).

Topographically the biblical Negev is composed of three broad, shallow basins joined end to end and oriented west to east. These Negev basins receive, on average, 8 to 12 inches of rain per year. When plowed, their powdery, windblown loess soil can retain sufficient water to grow grain. More often than not, however, the rainfall is inadequate for agriculture, and so historically the Negev has been more a land of the shepherd than a land of the farmer. As with the coastal plain, the water table under the Negev basins is high, allowing the residents to dig wells without much difficulty (Gen. 21:25-34; 26:17-33). The arid Negev was a suitable home for the bedouin lifestyle of Abraham, Isaac, and Jacob (Gen.13:1-7; 25: 27; 26:12-17).

South of the biblical Negev is a "great and terrible wilderness" (Deut 1:19, HCSB) in which ancient Israel was never really at home. Solomon was able to pierce this wilderness all the way to Ezion-geber (near modern Eilat), where he sailed his ships on the Red Sea (1 Kings 9:26), but 80 years later Jehoshaphat failed in an attempt to do the same (1 Kings 22:48-49; 2 Chron. 20:35-37). Archaeological excavations have found numerous small settlements throughout the Negev Highlands, perhaps evidence of attempts by strong Judean kings such as Uzziah to settle the region (2 Kings 26:10); they were successful only when Edom could be contained in the southern hills opposite the rift valley (cp. 1 Kings 22:47). By New Testament times this entire region had been taken over by the Nabateans, traders from the eastern mountains, who controlled the traffic in spices from Arabia to Gaza and the Mediterranean Sea.

The biblical Negev was Judah's doorway to the south. For ancient Israel, its value lay not in natural resources but in its strategic position fronting Egypt, Edom, and the great trade routes of the desert.

The Wilderness of Judah

 The wilderness of Judea as viewed toward the Dead Sea from atop the Herodium.

Tucked between the hill country of Judah and the rift valley, the wilderness of Judah is the largest area of exposed Senonian chalk west of the Jordan River. In a distance of 10 to 12 miles, the ground drops over 4,600 feet from the watershed ridge to the surface of the Dead Sea, which, at more than 1,300 feet below sea level, is the lowest spot on the face of the earth. The view east from the watershed ridge is dramatic and has been likened to a sailor standing on the narrow deck of a huge ship with the angry billows—here a jumbled mass of brown-white chalk hills, rounded and bare—churning below.

Two Hebrew terms designate the wilderness of Judah. The more common, *midbar*, refers to the higher areas of the wilderness, where shepherds are able to graze sheep and goats during the winter months (1 Sam. 17:28; Jer. 9:10). The more remote areas, south and east, are called Jeshimon, "waste" or "desert" places, where even the shepherd would not go. It was to the Jeshimon that David retreated when fleeing from Saul (1 Sam. 23:19; 26:1-3).

In the biblical period the only spots of permanent settlement in the wilderness were at the edge of the rift valley where a few springs provide water (e.g., Jericho, Engedi) and in a small valley above the cliffs west of the northern end of the Dead Sea (the Buqei'a), where runoff rainfall can collect from the hills. Two small towns in the hill country at the edge of the wilderness, Anathoth and Tekoa, were the homes of Jeremiah and Amos respectively. These prophets spoke vividly of the wilderness or wilderness-like conditions in their prophetic messages (e.g., Jer. 2:6; 3:2-3,21; 6:1-5; 9:1-2; 17:5-6; Amos 2:10; 4:7-12). One difficult natural route leads from Bethlehem to Engedi through Tekoa; another drops from Jerusalem to Jericho, skirting Anathoth on the way. The rest of the wilderness is essentially devoid of water supplies and human habitation.

One of few natural waterfalls in Israel is located at Engedi on the west side of the Dead Sea.

While many Americans may associate the term *wilderness* with dense woods, the wilderness of Judah is exactly the opposite. The Judean wilderness brings the harsh conditions of the desert to the doorstep of Jerusalem. The biblical writers often used the hard life of the wilderness to illustrate God's judgment and the need for His people to depend on Him.

The Dead Sea, 50 miles long by 11 miles wide, is the lowest spot on earth (approximately 1,350 feet below sea level), and by far the world's saltiest body of water.

The minerals of the Dead Sea include sodium, magnesium, calcium chloride, bromide, sulfur, potassium, potash, and bitumen; these account for 33–38 percent of the content of the Dead Sea by weight, compared to a 15-percent mineral content in the Great Salt Lake and 3–3.5 percent in the oceans. Surprisingly, 11 kinds of bacteria live in the Dead Sea, and some fish congregate around the mouth of the Jordan River. The name "Dead Sea" is really a misnomer, for since antiquity the mineral content in the water has been known to provide healing for a variety of diseases. The Dead Sea's high salt content makes it virtually impossible for a person to sink in its waters.

The Land of Benjamin

Joshua allotted the tribe of Benjamin a narrow strip of land wedged between the hill country of Judah to the south and Ephraim to the north (Josh. 18:11-28). Benjamin's territory climbs from the Jordan River up the harsh hills of the wilderness and over the central watershed ridge to the city of Kiriath-jearim, overlooking the western slopes of the hill country. The land of Benjamin is thus a cross section of the hill country of Palestine, with the eastern half the land of the shepherd and the western half the land of the farmer.

Benjamin's allotment included four important cities critical for anyone seeking to control the hill country. The first, the oasis city of Jericho (the City of Palms—Deut. 34:3; Judg. 3:13), is the gateway into central and southern Palestine from the east (Josh. 2:1; 1 Kings 16:34). The second, Bethel, faces the powerful tribes of Ephraim and Manasseh to the north (Gen. 28:19; 1 Kings 12:29; 2 Kings 2:2-3). The third, Gibeon, lying just west of the watershed ridge, is Benjamin's gateway to the Aijalon Valley, Gezer and the west (Josh. 9:1–10:15). The fourth, facing south, is Jerusalem, allotted to Benjamin but conquered by David as his own royal city (2 Sam. 5:6-10). Each of these was an important Canaanite city in the days of Joshua.

As the watershed ridge passes through the land of Benjamin, it broadens into a smallish plateau about 25 square miles in size. This "central Benjamin plateau" is actually a broad saddle in the hill country, slightly lower in elevation than the hill country to the north and south. Four cities that play a prominent role in the biblical story lie on the plateau: Gibeah (the hometown of king Saul— 1 Sam. 10:26; 15:34); Ramah (the hometown of Samuel—1 Sam. 2:11; 8:4; 15:34); Mizpah (the adminis-

Round Neolithic defense tower at Old Testament Jericho.

trative capital of the hill country after the destruction of Jerusalem by the Babylonians—2 Kings 25:23-25); and Gibeon. Gibeah, Ramah, and Mizpah are located on the Patriarchal Highway, south to north, with Gibeon to the west. Bethel lies on a smaller and higher plateau three miles north of Mizpah, while Jerusalem is the same distance south of Gibeah. The many biblical events that took place in and around these cities testify to the critical importance of the land of Benjamin.

The central Benjamin plateau is well watered, and its terra rosa soil and relatively flat topography combine to form a highly desirable agricultural area. The nahals Aijalon and Sorek drain the plateau to the west and south, while the Wadi Qilt cuts dramatically through the chalk wilderness east-ward from the plateau. Several powerful springs in the Wadi Qilt combine to provide a steady flow of water to the plains around Jericho.

▲ View from atop the tel of New Testament Jericho showing the lush greenery of the oasis.

Herod the Great built a large and elaborate summer palace on the banks of the Qilt where the wadi spills out onto the plains of Jericho. His palace contained sumptuous reception and banqueting halls, a Roman bath complex, a sunken garden, a swimming pool, and an arched bridge spanning the wadi. Recent archaeological excavations on the site have also uncovered what is thought to have been a synagogue dating to the first century BC, the oldest known in Palestine to date. New Testament Jericho grew up around Herod's palace and the adjacent lands of his influential friends. Here Zacchaeus collected taxes for Rome. Jesus' encounter with Zacchaeus showed his followers and critics alike what true repentance really was (Luke 19:1-10).

The central Benjamin plateau is the heartland not only of Benjamin but also of the entire hill country and the scene of much of the biblical story. A look at the sweep of biblical history shows that the people of the land of Benjamin lived in a true testing ground of faith. It is therefore with great significance that the apostle Paul identified himself as a Benjaminite (Rom. 11:1).

Jerusalem

The biblical writers held Jerusalem in high esteem. Verses such as Psalm 48:1-2 ("His holy mountain, rising splendidly"), Psalm 122:1 ("Let us go to"), and Isaiah 2:2-3 ("[it] will be raised above the hills," HCSB) are rooted in soaring theological expectations about God's chosen city. At the same time, they are also grounded in the physical reality of the land. Jerusalem is a city of hills and valleys, and most steps taken on its streets either go up or down. Today Jerusalem is a beautiful city, with surprising vistas and new horizons as the sun and clouds play upon its huddled mass of gray to golden walls, domes, and towers; the same, from all accounts, was also true in antiquity (cp. Song 6:4).

> The Talmud, Judaism's monumental codification of the oral law, speaks of Jerusalem in lofty terms: "Whoever has not seen Jerusalem in its splendor has never seen a lovely city" (Succah 51b); and "Of the ten measures of beauty that came down to the world, Jerusalem took nine" (Kidushin 49b).

Historically, the Kidron and Hinnom Valleys have marked the limits of settlement in Jerusalem, although, over the course of the last 150 years, the city has spilled over the surrounding hills and valleys on every side. The Kidron Valley, on the east, separates the old walled city from the Mount of Olives. The Hinnom Valley (the "Valley of the Sons of Hinnom") curls around the western and southern sides of the city, with the watershed ridge and Patriarchal Highway beyond. The Hinnom formed the border between the tribal inheritances of Judah (to the south and west) and Benjamin (to the north and east) (Josh. 18:16). North of the city the ground rises gradually, without natural defense, and this has been the preferred direction of attack since antiquity.

It was in the southern portion of the "Valley of the Sons of Hinnom" (Hb. *ge bene-hinnom*) that kings Ahaz and Manassah of Judah apparently sacrificed their sons by fire to the pagan god Molech (2 Kings 21:6; 2 Chron. 28:3; cp. 2 Kings 23:10). Some scholars think that the ancient Israelites also dumped refuse from the city into the Hinnom Valley to be burned (today's Dung Gate, the lowest part of the walled city and natural exit of surface drainage, opens toward the same area). Over time the Hebrew name of this valley, *ge bene-hinnom*, was shortened to *gehenna*. By intertestamental times, *gehenna* was used to refer to a place of fiery judgment reserved for the wicked (2 Esdras 7:36; cp. Matt. 5:22).

13 ▶ JERUSALEM IN THE TIME OF DAVID AND SOLOMON

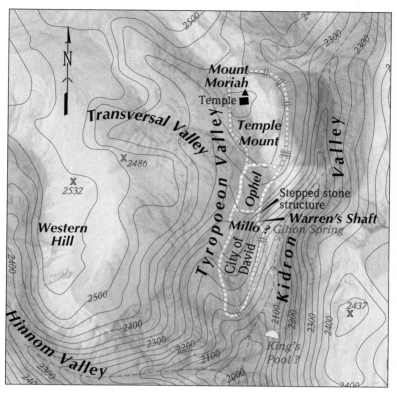

A smaller valley—today usually called the Central Valley, although it was known to Josephus as the Tyropoeon Valley or "Valley of the Cheesemakers"—divides the hill lying between the Kidron and Hinnom into two parts, a smaller, eastern hill and a larger, higher western hill. Settlement in Jerusalem began on the southern end of this eastern hill, above the Gihon Spring. A second, less powerful spring, En-rogel, lies further down the Kidron Valley (1 Kings 1:9, 43-45).

David's city, about 12 acres in size, encompassed only the southern end of the eastern hill (2 Sam. 5:6-10; 1 Chron. 21:18-30) (see Map 5). His son, Solomon, built the temple on the higher extension of this hill to the north (1 Kings 6:1-38; cp. 1 Chron. 22:1). Over the course of the next 200 years, houses were built on the western hill as the city's population slowly grew. Hezekiah enclosed the western hill by a massive wall in the late eighth century BC in response to the Assyrian threat against his kingdom (2 Chron. 32:5). The Bible calls this area of the city the *Mishneh* ("Second" or "New Quarter," 2 Kings 22:14; Zeph. 1:10).

The elevation of the hill on which David's Jerusalem and Solomon's temple were built is lower than that of the surrounding hills (i.e., the Mount of Olives, the western hill, and the hills to the north and south). This fact was not lost on the psalmist, who clearly knew the topography of Jerusalem when he wrote of the city under siege, "I raise my eyes toward the mountains. Where will my help come from? My help comes from the LORD, the Maker of heaven and earth" (Ps. 121:1-2). But mountains around the city can also shelter and protect: "the mountains surround her. And the LORD surrounds His people, both now and forever" (Ps. 125:2).

▲ The Mount of Olives viewed from the Temple Mount.

After the destruction of Jerusalem by Babylon, the city was restricted to the eastern hill, only to grow gradually during the centuries between the Testaments to again include the western hill and northern extension of the Tyropoeon Valley. The most significant change to Jerusalem by New Testament times, however, was the 35-acre artificial platform built over the Temple Mount and graced by a magnificently rebuilt temple. This massive engineering feat was accomplished under the sponsorship of Herod the Great, although he probably incorporated earlier Hasmonean elements into his project. The extent and function of the so-called "Third Wall" north of the New Testament city remains a matter of debate; many scholars attribute at least parts of it to Herod Agrippa I (AD 41–44), who apparently began to incorporate the northern hills (the "Bezetha") into the walled city. The Romans destroyed the entire city in AD 70.

The hills and valleys of Jerusalem determined the shape and character of the city over time as well as its natural limit of settlement. The city's topography was well-known by the biblical writers, who incorporated images of its terrain in their divine message.

14 JERUSALEM IN THE NEW TESTAMENT PERIOD

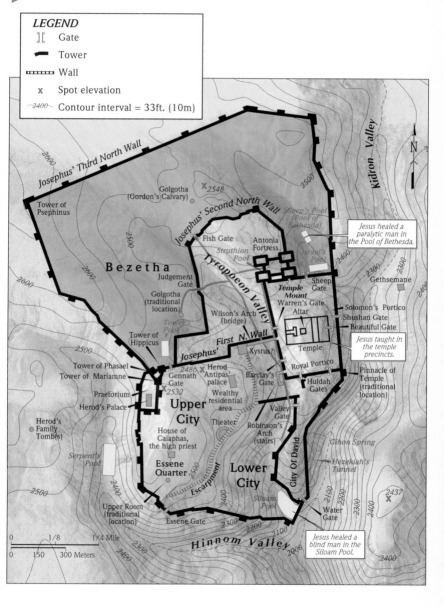

LEGEND

- ⨟ Gate
- ▬ Tower
- ▭ Wall
- x Spot elevation
- ~2400~ Contour interval = 33ft. (10m)

Kidron Valley

Josephus' Third North Wall

Tower of Psephinus

Golgotha (Gordon's Calvary) x2548

Josephus' Second North Wall

Sheep's Pool (Pool of Bethesda)

Jesus healed a paralytic man in the Pool of Bethesda.

Fish Gate

Antonia Fortress

Struthion Pool

Israel's Pool

Bezetha

Judgement Gate

Golgotha (traditional location)

Tyropoeon Valley

Sheep Gate

Temple Mount

Warren's Gate

Altar

Gethsemane

Solomon's Portico

Shushan Gate

Beautiful Gate

Tower's Pool

Wilson's Arch (bridge)

Tower of Hippicus

First N. Wall

Josephus'

Xystus?

Royal Portico

Temple

Jesus taught in the temple precincts.

Tower of Phasael

Tower of Mariamne

Gennath Gate x2486

Herod Antipas' palace x2532

Barclay's Gate

Huldah Gates

Pinnacle of Temple (traditional location)

Praetorium

Wealthy residential area

Herod's Palace

Upper City

Theater

Valley Gate

Herod's Family Tomb(s)

House of Caiaphas, the high priest

Robinson's Arch (stairs)

Gihon Spring

Serpent's Pool

Essene Quarter

Lower City

City Of David

Hezekiah's Tunnel

Escarpment

Siloam Pool

2437 x

Upper Room (traditional location)

Essene Gate

Water Gate

Jesus healed a blind man in the Siloam Pool.

Hinnom Valley

0   1/8   1/4 Mile

0   1/50   300 Meters

THE CENTRAL REGIONS
(Israel/Samaria)

The central portion of Palestine generally corresponds to the heartland of the northern kingdom of Israel and the territory of New Testament Samaria. It is composed of five distinct geographical regions: the Hill Country of Ephraim, the Hill Country of Manasseh (Samaria), the Sharon Plain, Mount Carmel, and the Jordan Valley.

15 ▶ **PLAIN OF DOR, PLAIN OF SHARON, SAMARIA, JORDAN VALLEY, AND GILEAD**

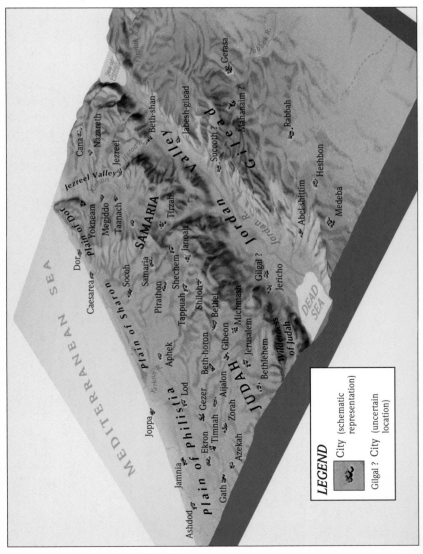

LEGEND

City (schematic representation)

Gilgal ? City (uncertain location)

The Hill Country of Ephraim

The hill country of Ephraim is a rugged area of hard Cenomanian limestone lying north of the tribal inheritance of Benjamin. The region is 15 miles south to north, from Bethel to the Wadi Kanah (Josh. 16:8; 17:9-10), and stretches 27 miles east-west, from the Jordan Valley to the Plain of Sharon. The hill country of Ephraim thus corresponds to the heartland of the tribal territory of Ephraim (Josh. 16:1-10). The high point of the hill country of Ephraim is the hill of Baal-hazor (2 Sam. 13:23), 3,333 feet in elevation, located five miles northeast of Bethel.

The hills of Ephraim are well watered, receiving up to 30 inches of rain annually in regions west of the watershed ridge. This, plus the numerous small springs that dot the wadis, provides ample water resources for agriculture. Like the hill country of Judah, the hills of Ephraim are terraced, and their rich terra rosa soil provides excellent crops of grapes, figs, olives, pomegranates, and almonds.

The main center of the hill country of Ephraim during the biblical period was Shiloh, tucked among the hills in the upper reaches of the Nahal Shiloh just west of the watershed ridge. Small but broad valleys in the vicinity of Shiloh provide a nice agricultural base, and its relative seclusion made this a natural center for the ark of the covenant while Israel settled the land (Josh. 18:1; 21:1-3; Judg. 21:12, 19-23; 1 Sam. 1:3; 4:1-4). Shiloh was a large walled city during the middle Bronze II Age (18th through 16th centuries BC) but only a small village during the time of the judges. Because of its rugged terrain, the hill country of Ephraim is largely closed to outside traffic and cultural influences. This is a land of farms and small villages, well suited to the agricultural life of ancient Israel.

The Hill Country of Manasseh

The hill country of Manasseh is a large hilly region situated between the hill country of Ephraim and the Jezreel Valley, approximately 32 miles east-west and 22 miles north-south in size. This region generally corresponds to the heartland of the portion of the tribal territory that was allotted to Manasseh west of the Jordan River (Josh. 17:7-10) and to the New Testament region of Samaria.

Geologically, there are three subregions within the hill country of Manasseh, each about the size and shape of the Judean Shephelah and each oriented north-northeast by south-southwest. Today these regions are often called Eastern Samaria, Central Samaria, and Western Samaria.

The two highest hills in all of Manasseh, Mount Ebal (3,084 feet) and Mount Gerazim (2,891 feet) (Deut. 11:29-30; Josh. 8:30-35) dominate the southern end of Central Samaria, while the northern end terminates in Mount Gilboa (1,600 feet) (1 Sam. 31:1-8). Central Samaria is separated from Eastern Samaria by a narrow chalk depression forming a direct natural link between Shechem and Beth-shan (1 Sam. 31:12). Central Samaria receives approximately 20–25 inches of rainfall per year.

Mount Ebal lies near the ancient city of Shechem.

The broad valleys, relatively gentle hills, good soil, and adequate rainfall of Manasseh give shape to a land where shepherds and farmers, grain fields and orchards thrive. This mixed economy provides a stable economic base for the region, allowing its inhabitants to live and prosper off the land.

The city of Shechem (modern Nablus), located at the head of Nahal Shechem between Mounts Ebal and Gerazim, is the natural center of Manasseh. Historically Shechem was also the natural "capital" of the entire hill country, the point from which kingdoms and would-be kingdoms radiated throughout central Palestine (cp. Gen. 33:18–34:31; Judg. 9:1-57; 1 Kings 12:1,25; cp. Josh. 8:30-35). Unlike Jerusalem, Shechem's geographical position is open and inviting. Valleys carrying natural routes extend from Shechem in four directions—toward the east, south toward Bethel and Jerusalem, northwest through Nahal Shechem to the coast, and northeast to Beth-shean with a side route down the Wadi Faria to the Jordan Valley. While these valleys provide Shechem with a strong agricultural base, they also open the region to easy invasion.

Jeroboam, the first king of the northern kingdom of Israel, established his capital at Shechem (1 Kings 12:25).

Mount Gilboa.

Later in his reign, and perhaps as a defensive measure to protect his kingdom against pressures from the south and west, Jeroboam moved his capital to Tirzah, a city nestled in the chalk pass connecting Shechem with Beth-shean at the head of the Wadi Faria (1 Kings 14:17; 15:21,33; 16:15). From this relatively isolated position, Jeroboam was able to consolidate his kingdom's holdings in Gilead to the east (Transjordan). A generation later, Omri, the father of Ahab, moved the capital again, this time to Samaria (1 Kings 16:23-24,29), a prominent hill in Nahal Shechem with easy access to the coast, where it remained until the destruction of the northern kingdom (2 Kings 17:1-6). From Samaria the Israelite kings were able to expand their influence to Phoenicia and the coast (cp. 1 Kings 16:31).

Following common practice in the ancient Near Eastern world, biblical writers often used *Samaria*, the name of the capital city of Israel, to refer to the entire northern kingdom (cp. 1 Kings 13:32; 2 Kings 17:24; Jer. 23:13; Hos.10:7). *Samaria* also became the official name of the Assyrian province in central Palestine after the fall of Israel to Sargon II in 722 BC The name was maintained for the region throughout the time of the New Testament (e.g., John 4:4) and is commonly used by Israelis for the region today.

The city of Samaria was a thriving Hellenistic city in the third and

Long colonnaded street built by the emperor Severus at NT Sebaste which was the OT city of Samaria.

second centuries BC before it was destroyed by John Hyrcanus, the Hasmonean Jewish king and nationalist, in 106 BC. Herod the Great rebuilt the city and renamed it Sebaste, the Greek form of "Augustus," in honor of his emperor in Rome. Here Herod settled foreign mercenaries who had helped him put down resistance from Jewish nationalists at the beginning of his reign. On the high point of the site, over the ruins of Ahab's palace, Herod built a magnificent white limestone temple that he dedicated to Caesar Augustus.

The hill country of Manasseh—New Testament Samaria—is a blessed land with easy access to the world beyond. Ancient Israel grew rich and complacent here. With barbed words the Prophets Amos and Hosea laid bare the self-centered people of this land, who serve as a warning for people who live in similar conditions today.

The Plain of Sharon

The portion of the coastal plain between Mount Carmel and the Yarkon River is known as the Plain of Sharon (1 Chron. 5:16). The northern boundary of the Sharon is actually Nahal Tanninim (the Crocodile River), a small stream flowing westward from the Mount Carmel range to the Mediterranean Sea. The Plain of Sharon is approximately 10 miles wide and 30 miles long and rises only slightly to the western foothills of Manasseh.

Like the Philistine coastal plain to the south, the Plain of Sharon is primarily composed of sand mixed with alluvial soils that have washed down from the eastern hills. Along the coast, three parallel ridges of solidified sand (*kurkar*) block the flow of water from the hills forming swamps that impede agriculture. When drained, as today, the Sharon is an agricultural breadbasket, particularly well suited for citrus.

Because of its sandy swamps, the Plain of Sharon of antiquity was home to an exuberant fertility of scrub and oak forests, undergrowth and wildflowers (cp. Song 2:1). Like the heights of Mount Carmel, Lebanon, and Bashan, the Plain of Sharon was famous for its wild

▲ View of the Plain of Sharon and the Yarkon River from the excavation area at the site of Aphek.

vegetation and natural grazing land (cp. 1 Chron. 27:29). The biblical writers used the fertility of the Sharon to signal God's blessing on a renewed earth (Isa. 35:1-2; 65:10; cp. Isa. 33:9).

During most of the biblical period, no sizable towns or harbors of any consequence bent the international highway to the shore as it traversed the Plain of Sharon. Only in the first century did Herod the Great begin to build the magnificent port city of Caesarea there (Acts 10:1-8; 23:23-24,31-33), destined by late Roman times to become the largest port in the eastern Mediterranean.

Herod's port at Caesarea was intended to show the world that the King of Judea could do the impossible. Using huge wooden frames weighted and sunk by stone, then secured by cement that could harden underwater, Herod's workmen built a massive harbor extending 650 feet from the stiff coastline into the sea. Herod's choice of the northern Sharon coast for a harbor may have been a mirror of his megalomania, but it was also a stroke of genius; for from this spot he was able to control international traffic into both Judea and Galilee.

Because of its sandy swamps and stiff coastline, the Plain of Sharon did not figure prominently in the Old Testament story. By the time of the New Testament, however, the port of Caesarea had taken hold of the coast, and from here the apostle Paul launched the gospel to the Mediterranean world.

Mount Carmel

The Mount Carmel range is one of the most prominent topographical features of Palestine. The range rises abruptly from the coastal plain and Jezreel Valley, jutting dramatically into the Mediterranean; its promontory gives the coastline its characteristic hook shape. Oriented sharply northwest-southeast, the Carmel range slows international traffic which is forced to cross the range through three well-defined natural passes, the

 Mount Carmel range.

most important of which is controlled by Megiddo.

The Mediterranean Sea as seen through the arches of the Herodian aquaduct at Caesarea. From this port Paul launched the gospel to the Greco-Roman world.

The name *Carmel* means "plantation," or "gardenland," and is quite appropriate for the verdant Carmel range. The natural fertility, beauty, and strength of Carmel were admired by the biblical poets (Song 7:5; Isa. 35:1-2; Jer. 50:19). With powerful imagery they often compared God's withering judgment to the summit of Carmel drying up, a sign of doom indeed (Isa. 33:9; Amos 1:2; Nah. 1:4)!

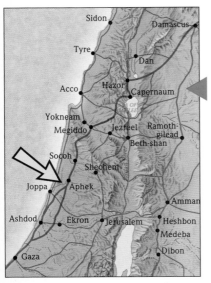

Northeast of the Mount Carmel range, it is more proper to speak simply of the International Highway rather than the International Coastal Highway, since from here the route no longer follows the coast.

Because of its inaccessibility, Mount Carmel proper has tended to be a place of refuge and escape (cp. Amos 9:3). Its majestic, wooded height is also a natural setting for religious sanctuary. Egyptian records from Thutmose III, Ramesses II, and Ramesses III (15th–12th centuries BC) call Mount Carmel "the Holy Headland," suggesting it was thought to be a place of divine abode from early times. A document from the fourth century BC calls Carmel "the holy mountain of Zeus." Mount Carmel was also held in high esteem by the indigenous nature-based fertility religion of Canaan. When Elijah chose to challenge the prophets of Baal, the Canaanite god of lightning and rain, on Mount Carmel, he deliberately entered Baal's "home court," making his victory all the more decisive (1 Kings 18:16-46). The prophet Elisha frequented Mount Carmel a generation later (2 Kings 2:25; 4:25).

Mount Carmel is a prominent marker on both the physical landscape of Palestine and the religious landscape of the Old Testament story. Here the Lord showed that He is God of all creation and that even places of abundant rainfall will wither at His command.

The Jordan Valley

The Jordan Valley is the portion of the rift valley that lies between the Sea of Galilee and the Dead Sea. The valley itself is only 65 miles long, but the Jordan River, meandering a torturous path to the Dead Sea, is approximately 135 miles in length. The entire valley lies below sea level, dropping gradually from -690 feet at the Sea of Galilee to -1,350 feet at the Dead Sea.

The Jordan Valley varies in width from 2 to 15 miles, with the broadest portion in the south, just above the Dead Sea. Here the Bible speaks of the "plains of Jericho" (Josh. 4:13; 2 Kings 25:5) west of the Jordan, and the "plains of Moab" east of the river (Num. 26:3; Deut. 34:1). In the north, just over ten miles below the Sea of Galilee, the valley also widens considerably to the west. This extension of the

Jordan Valley.

Jordan Valley is commonly called the Beth-shean Valley, after the city of Beth-shean on its northern edge. The Beth-shean Valley provides an important connection with the Jezreel Valley further west.

In speaking of the unique character of the Jordan Valley, the historical geographer George Adam Smith has commented, "There may be something on the surface of another planet to match the Jordan Valley; there is nothing on this" (*The Historical Geography of the Holy Land*, Hodder & Stoughton, 1931, p. 301). Describing the actual trench cut by the Jordan, Smith notes, "the Jordan sweeps to the Dead Sea through unhealthy jungle relieved only by poisonous soil" (p. 313).

 The Jordan River flows south from Mount Hermon through Israel, finally emptying into the Dead Sea.

The climate of the Jordan Valley changes dramatically in its 65-mile course from the Sea of Galilee to the Dead Sea. The north enjoys a Mediterranean climate, with rainfall of 18 inches per year. Fifteen miles south, the valley around Beth-shean has an arid steppe climate (12 inches of rain per year), while the southern Jordan Valley is desert (4 inches of rain annually).

Although natural routes run the length of the Jordan Valley on both sides of the river, the preferred route of antiquity was on the east, following the line of springs at the scarp of the Transjordanian hills. It was this route that Jesus most often traveled on His journeys between Galilee and Jerusalem. The primary fords crossing the Jordan are at Jericho, Adam (the outlet of the Wadi Faria—Josh. 3:16), and points near Beth-shean. These crossings carry important east-west routes that tie western Palestine to Transjordan. In spite of the heat and difficulty of travel, the Jordan Valley has always been a rather permeable border for peoples who live on either side (cp. Gen. 33:16-18; Deut. 9:1; Josh. 3:1-17; 22:1-34; Judg. 3:12-13; 7:24; 12:1-6; 21:8-12; 2 Sam. 17:21-22).

Elisha received the mantle of power and authority from Elijah after both had crossed to the eastern side of the Jordan Valley (2 Kings 2:1-14). Jesus was baptized, receiving power and authority from on high, in the Jordan Valley (Matt. 3:1-17; Mark 1:9-13; Luke 3:21-22). Traditions vary as to whether Jesus was baptized on the east or west bank of the Jordan or in the northern or southern part of the valley. Regardless, His baptism in the Jordan has provided a rich motif for Christian art and hymnody throughout the centuries.

Except for some cities in the north and the oasis of Jericho, few people settled in the Jordan Valley in antiquity. Many biblical characters crossed the valley, however, in spite of its wild and harsh conditions. The Jordan became an important symbol in Christian art and theology, signaling barriers (such as death) that we can only cross with God's help.

The Jordan River just north of the Sea of Galilee.

THE NORTHERN REGIONS
(Galilee)

The northern portion of Palestine, called Galilee in both the Old and New Testaments, is composed of five distinct geographical regions: the Jezreel Valley, Lower Galilee, Upper Galilee, the Sea of Galilee and the Huleh Basin (see map 4, p. 13).

16 ▶ NORTHERN COASTAL PLAINS, JEZREEL VALLEY, GALILEE, AND BASHAN

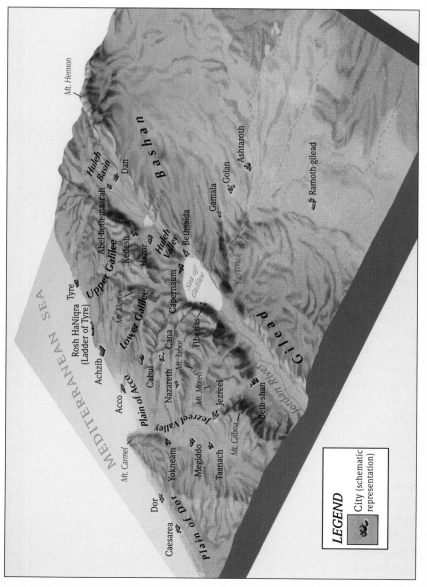

Mt. Hermon

Huleh Basin
Dan
Bashan
Ashtaroth
Abel-beth-maacah
Lake Huleh
Golan
Gamala
Ramoth-gilead
Upper Galilee
Kedesh
Hazor
Huleh Valley
Bethsaida
Tyre
Mt. Meron
Capernaum
Sea of Galilee
Yarmuk River
Rosh HaNiqra
(Ladder of Tyre)
Lower Galilee
Tiberias
Gilead
Achzib
Cabul
Cana
Mt. Tabor
Jordan River
Acco
Nazareth
Mt. Moreh
Jezreel
Beth-shan
Plain of Acco
Jezreel Valley
MEDITERRANEAN SEA
Yokneam
Megiddo
Taanach
Mt. Gilboa
Mt. Carmel
Dor
Plain of Dor
Caesarea

LEGEND
City (schematic representation)

The Jezreel Valley

The Jezreel Valley is the largest and most fertile valley in Palestine. It is shaped roughly like the head of a spear with its point facing northwest toward the Mediterranean. The shaft of the spearhead, the narrow Harod Valley, leads southeast to Beth-shean and the Jordan Valley. Together, the Jezreel and Harod Valleys are the land's most important international crossroads.

The Valley of Jezreel (or Esdraelon or Megiddo) as viewed from the top of the Megiddo tel.

Jezreel means "God sows," which is certainly a fitting name for the valley that is Palestine's breadbasket. Besides the name "Valley of Jezreel" (Josh. 17:16; Judg. 6:33; Hos. 1:5), the Bible also calls this region "the plain of Megiddo" (Zech. 12:11) and, poetically, "the pasturelands of God" (Ps. 83:12). The term *Esdraelon* is a Greek form of *Jezreel* occurring only in extrabiblical literature from the New Testament period. *Armageddon* (Rev. 16:16) is a Greek word that has long been assumed to render the Hebrew phrase *har Megiddo*, "the mountain of Megiddo"; it is usually understood as referring to the entire Jezreel Valley.

Jerome Murphy-O'Connor has characterized Megiddo as "the royal box in one of the great theatres of history. From time immemorial armies have surged from the surrounding valleys to play their parts on the flat stage of the Jezreel valley" (Jerome Murphy-O'Connor, *The Holy Land*, 4th ed., New York: Oxford, 1998, p. 342). The Bible records several military actions that took place in the Jezreel and Harod Valleys. These include the battle of Deborah and Barak against Sisera (Judg. 4–5); the battle of Gideon against the Midianites (Judg. 7); Saul's last stand against the Philistines (1 Sam.

28:4; 31:1-10); Jehu's *coup d'etat* (2 Kings 9:14-37); and Josiah's attempted face-down of Pharaoh Neco (2 Kings 23:28-30).

The mountains that surround the Jezreel Valley contrast sharply with the low, open expanse of the valley itself. The Jezreel is drained toward the Mediterranean by the Nahal Kishon, which collects runoff rainfall from the surrounding hills. Because of the flatness of the Jezreel, the size of its runoff area, and the narrowness of the pass at the foot of Mount Carmel through which the valley drains, a heavy rainstorm will turn the valley floor into a soggy, muddy morass. Wintertime conditions have impeded armies, chariots, and travelers throughout history (cp. Judg. 4:13-15; 5:19-21; 1 Kings 18:45-46). To the east, the valley floor dips below sea level at the point where the Harod Valley joins the Jezreel, then drops gradually into the rift. The Harod is drained by the Nahal Harod. Several powerful springs line the foot of Mount Gilboa along its southern edge (Judg. 7:1).

The rich alluvial soil of the Jezreel Valley is as much as 330 feet deep in places, and the abundance of water ensures excellent crops even in years of limited rainfall. The agriculture possibilities here are so extraordinary compared to the rest of Palestine that Herod the Great claimed the valley as his own royal estate. Today the Jezreel is drained and fertile fields abound.

Because of the muddy wintertime conditions, the Jezreel's natural routes generally follow the perimeter of the valley. The exception is the International Coastal Highway. An underground rise of basalt has slightly raised the level of the valley floor on a line running between Megiddo and Mount Tabor. In antiquity the International Highway followed this low ridge across the Jezreel as it began to pick its way through the natural obstacles of Galilee to Damascus.

The Jezreel Valley has always been the major crossroads of Palestine. Here the main International Highway crosses a second that connects the Plain of Acco to the Jordan Valley and Transjordanian Highway beyond. The ceaseless flow of travelers and armies through the Jezreel via these international highways gave rise to the biblical phrase "Galilee of the Gentiles" (Isa. 9:1; Matt. 4:15).

Because of its superior farmland and strategic highways, the Jezreel Valley has always been one of the most valuable pieces of real estate in Palestine. Overflowing with material blessings, this valley was Israel's testing ground of faith. Perhaps for this reason it figures so prominently in John's Apocalypse (Rev. 16:16).

Lower Galilee

Lower Galilee is an area of relatively open topography that lies north of the Jezreel and Harod Valleys and between the Mediterranean Sea and rift valley. In size Lower Galilee measures 25 miles east-west and between 15 and 30 miles north-south. *Lower Galilee* is not a biblical name but a convenient way to refer to that portion of Galilee that is lower in elevation (below 2,000 feet) and hence more open to travel than the more mountainous region further north.

Lower Galilee can be divided into three distinct geological regions: the Plain of Acco, western Lower Galilee, and eastern Lower Galilee.

The east-west valleys of western Lower Galilee act as a type of wind tunnel, channeling the westerly afternoon breezes off the Mediterranean directly toward the Sea of Galilee. The winds gain strength through these "tunnels" and drop dramatically into the rift, where they bang up against the steep scarp of hills on the eastern side of the sea. If the winds pick up suddenly, they can quickly turn the low, relatively shallow Sea of Galilee into a churning mass of water. This evidently happened to Jesus and His disciples one night as they made their way across the sea in a small boat: "A fierce windstorm arose, and the waves were breaking over the boat, so that the boat was already being swamped" (Mark 4:37). Jesus calmed the sea as He would a baby, and His disciples were understandably incredulous (Mark 4:38-41).

 A storm breaking across the Sea of Galilee.

The relatively low terrain and broad valleys of Lower Galilee make for fairly easy travel. The International Highway enters Lower Galilee from the south at Mount Tabor, then angles to the Sea of Galilee by following a topographical line formed by the seam between the limestone hills of western Lower Galilee and the basalt hills of eastern Lower Galilee. On the way, it skirts the Horns of Hattin, the extinct and eroded volcanic cone that was responsible for the basalt in the region. The International Highway then drops to the Sea of Galilee through the narrow Arbel pass, a sheer cut in the basalt ridge that boarders the sea on the southwest. The top of the cliff above this pass provides a breathtaking sweep of Galilee, from Mount Tabor to snowy Mount Hermon north of Bashan.

The International Highway from Aphek to Damascus.

A second major natural route in Lower Galilee connects Acco/Ptolemais to Tiberius on the western shore of the Sea of Galilee, passing through the broad Valley of Iphtah-el on the way. This route was Galilee's lifeline to the world during the time of the New Testament, tying the mixed population Galilee to the Greco-Roman lands of the Mediterranean.

The capital of Galilee during Jesus' early years was Sepphoris, a Greco-Roman city in the Valley of Iphtah-el just over five miles north of Nazareth. Sepphoris had been captured by Jewish nationalists following the death of Herod the Great in 4 BC, then burned as Roman troops dislodged the Jews from the city. Herod Antipas, son of Herod the Great and his successor as king in Galilee, began to rebuild Sepphoris a year later. Jesus' father, Joseph, a skilled workman in wood and stone (Gk. *tekton*—Mark 6:3), may have helped to rebuild Sepphoris as jobs were probably scarce in his small, poor hometown. Jesus may have honed His skills as a craftsman in Sepphoris as well.

Mount Tabor, located a few miles southeast of Nazareth.

Because of its openness, good soil, and pleasant climate, Lower Galilee has always been a favored region for settlement. This was a prize coveted by the kings of ancient Israel but separated from the Israelite heartland by the wide-open (and militarily dangerous) Jezreel Valley.

Throughout history ancient Israel had trouble holding on to Galilee. Isaiah spoke of "Galilee of the Gentiles" (Isa. 9:1) as all Galilee was being cut off by a ruthless Assyrian army, sweeping down the International Highway from the northeast. Galilee was no less a region of Gentile influence in the first century, when Jesus used Isaiah's words to introduce a kingdom that far surpasses the work of even the greatest armies and kings (Matt. 4:15).

Repeated cultural and military threats by Canaanites, Phoenicians, Syrians, Greeks, and Romans throughout the biblical period caused many Jews living in Galilee in Jesus' day to adopt a strongly nationalistic stance against the world around them. This attitude probably led the men of Nazareth to try to kill Jesus when He preached that God's favor rested also on Galilee's Gentile neighbors (Luke 4:16-30). On another occasion, the Pharisees declared that Jesus couldn't be the Messiah because no prophet had ever come from Galilee (John 7:40-52). They failed to mention that Jonah, the prophet whom God had sent to Israel's worst enemy, the Assyrians, was also from Galilee (2 Kings 14:25). Not insignificantly, Jonah's hometown, Gath-hepher, lay only five miles from Nazareth.

Lower Galilee is blessed with many natural resources: good water and soil, an agreeable climate, important highways, and pleasant vistas. This was the boyhood homeland of Jesus—and here He grew up, hearing the great stories of His peoples' struggles for redemption through the ages. The openness of Galilee provided the stimulating environment in which Jesus first began to preach a new kind of kingdom.

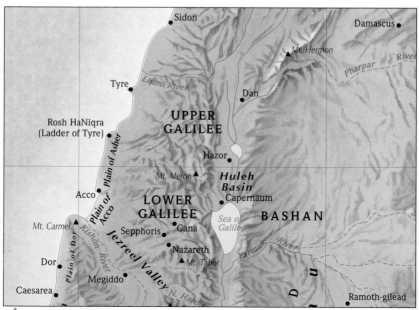

Lower and Upper Galilee.

Upper Galilee

Upper Galilee is the rugged, uplifted limestone region north of Lower Galilee. The eastern boundary is a steep scarp above the Huleh Basin (the upper Jordan Valley), while on the west the hills drop to the Plain of Acco and into the Mediterranean Sea. To the north, Upper Galilee rises gradually to the mountainous Lebanese Range, beyond the Litani River. Hard Cenomanian limestone dominates the western two-thirds of Upper Galilee, while the eastern third is primarily softer Eocene limestone.

Numerous small fault lines have dissected the topography of Upper Galilee, breaking the landform into rugged, uneven blocks. The high point is Mount Meron, slightly southeast of center. At 3,963 feet, Meron is also the highest point in all of western Palestine. Deep wadis cut away from Mount Meron in every direction, adding to the region's rugged topography.

The high elevation and northwestern exposure of Upper Galilee ensures abundant rainfall, up to 40 inches or more annually. The soil is fertile, and natural scrub forests blanket the hills with green throughout the year. For ancient Israel, Upper Galilee was a taste of the richness of Lebanon, so often a symbol of strength and fertility in the biblical texts (e.g., Pss. 29:5-6; 92:12; Song 4:15; 5:15; Isa. 60:13; Jer. 18:14).

Because of its ruggedness, Upper Galilee has never been a region of large cities. Rather, numerous small towns and villages dotted the landscape in antiquity, just as they do today. Natural routes tend to avoid Upper Galilee, adding to its remoteness. Joshua allotted the western portion of Upper Galilee, along with the Plain of Acco, to the tribe of Asher (Josh. 19:24-31), and the higher, eastern portion to Naphtali (Josh. 19:32-39). Here Israel could dwell in safety, away from the strong Canaanite presence in the valleys to the west, south, and east. Archaeological evidence has uncovered the remains of many small settlement villages in Upper Galilee dating to the 13th–11th centuries BC (Iron I), the time of ancient Israel's settlement in the land.

The blessings that Jacob bestowed on his 12 sons are reflected in the actual territories in which the 12 tribes of Israel eventually settled. For instance, Jacob blessed Naphtali by saying, "Naphtali is a doe set free that bears beautiful fawns" (Gen. 49:21). This short blessing evokes vivid images of a wild and beautiful land, where Israel could live in freedom and safety. Moses' blessing on the tribe of Naphtali echoes Jacob's: "Naphtali is abounding with the favor of the LORD and is full of his blessing; he will inherit southward to the lake [i.e., the Sea of Galilee]" (Deut. 33:23).

During the time of the New Testament, Upper Galilee was filled with small, largely conservative farming villages. Jesus no doubt visited some of them on His journey from the Sea of Galilee to Phoenicia (Matt. 15:21-28). In the second century AD, after the Jews had been banished from Jerusalem by Rome, Jewish life flourished in the remote hills of Upper Galilee, away from the hassles and temptations of the valleys and plains below. Zefat (Safed), the primary city of Upper Galilee today, was an important center of Jewish learning in the medieval period.

The rugged limestone hills of Upper Galilee allow a similar lifestyle as is found in the hill country of Judah and Ephraim. Here ancient Israel felt at home, even though separated from the southern tribes by a wide international zone that was usually overrun by Gentiles.

The Sea of Galilee

 The Sea of Galilee as viewed from the northwest.

The Sea of Galilee fills a shallow depression in the rift valley east of Lower Galilee. The Jordan River enters the sea from the northeast and exits to the southwest. The surface of the sea is 690 feet below sea level, and its bottom lies 150 feet below that. The sea measures just 13 by 7 miles, more a lake than a sea.

The Sea of Galilee is known by several names in the Bible: the Sea of Chinnereth (Num. 34:11; Deut. 3:17; Josh. 12:3; 13:27), the Lake of Gennesaret (Luke 5:1), the Sea of Tiberius (John 6:1; 21:1), the Sea of Galilee (Matt. 4:18; 15:29; Mark 1:16; 7:31), and simply the "sea" or "lake" (e.g., Matt. 8:24). Some believe that the name *Chinnereth*, which is perhaps related to the Hebrew word for "harp," derives from the sea's harp shape. More likely, the sea was simply named after the city of Chinnereth, located on its northwestern shore during Old Testament times (Josh. 19:35). Gennesaret is a form of Chinnereth. Today Israelis call the Sea of Galilee "the Kinneret."

The sea is enclosed by basalt hills that rise 1,300 feet above the surface of the water (approximately 600 feet above sea level). To the east and west, the scarp of the rift valley presses close to the sea, while on the north, the remains of a huge flow of basalt (the Rosh Pinna sill) separates the sea from the Huleh Basin. Three plains provide fertile fields for agriculture: the Plain of Bethsaida to the northeast where the Jordan enters the sea, the Plain of Gennesaret on the northwest (cp. Matt. 14:34-36), and a plain formed by the Jordan Valley to the south.

The Sea of Galilee receives less rainfall than the surrounding hills, about 16 inches annually. Temperatures are moderate to hot, and the air is usually humid. Several hot mineral springs enter the Sea of Galilee from its shore and bottom, a result of the gigantic rip in the surface of the earth that formed the rift valley. Fish tend to congregate around these springs in the wintertime. Many fish are also found in the northeast, feeding on the organic matter deposited into the sea by the Jordan River. Fishing and agriculture are excellent, as the Gospel writers did attest.

The New Testament mentions three different kinds of fishing nets that were used in the Sea of Galilee. A cast net was a circular net 25 feet in diameter with sinkers around the edge; it was cast into shallow water by a fisherman standing near shore (Mark 1:16-18). The dragnet or seine was 800–900 feet long, 12–25 feet wide, and weighted along one edge. This net was unrolled by boat into a huge arc and stood upright in the water. It was then drawn ashore by fisherman standing at the water's edge. Because the dragnet pulled everything within its arc to shore (cp. Hab. 1:15), the fish it caught had to be sorted for commercial viability (Matt. 13:47-48). A trammel net consisted of a cross-netting of three nets. Because fish easily caught their gills in its web, trammel nets had to be repaired often (Mark 1:19-20). A fishhook is mentioned only once in the Gospels (Matt. 17:24-27).

Jesus' ministry was focused on the northern shore of the Sea of Galilee. He made His home in Capernaum (Matt. 4:12-17; 9:1) and called His disciples from villages in the vicinity (Matt. 4:18-22). At least three disciples, Philip, Peter, and Andrew, hailed from Bethsaida (John 1:44). Although its exact location remains in doubt, Bethsaida was apparently either in the marshy delta of the Jordan (el-Araj) or on a higher mound slightly north (et-Tell). A third town visited often by Jesus, Chorazin, was located in the basalt hills (the Rosh Pinna sill) above Capernaum (Matt. 11:21). It was probably in these hills that Jesus went in the early mornings to find "a deserted place" to pray (Mark 1:35).

"Its nature is wonderful as well as its beauty. Its soil is so fruitful that all sorts of trees can grow upon it, and the inhabitants accordingly plant all sorts of trees there, for the temper of the air is so well mixed that it agrees very well with all. One may call this place the ambition of nature, where it forces those plants that are naturally enemies to one another to agree together. It supplies men with the principle fruits, with grapes and figs continually, during 10 months in the year and the rest of the fruit as it becomes ripe together, through the whole year, for besides the good temperature of the air, it is also watered from a most fertile spring. The people of the country call it Capernaum" (Josephus, Wars iii.10.8).

The local building material around the Sea of Galilee is hard, black basaltic stone. Archaeological excavations have uncovered square blocks of houses (*insulae*) built of this stone in Capernaum, Bethsaida, Chorazin, and other villages in the region. The rooms in these houses were small and dark, with low doors and narrow windows set high in the wall above. One such *insula* excavated in Capernaum is believed to have belonged to Peter (Mark 1:29-30), where Jesus apparently made His home. The synagogue in Capernaum in Jesus' day was also made of black basaltic stone. The white synagogue that dominates Capernaum today was built in a later century out of Cenomanian limestone brought from the hills of Lower Galilee.

An overview of the third-century synagogue at Capernaum.

Capernaum is often thought of as a sleepy fishing village, but during the first century it had a vibrant, mixed economy. In addition to fishing and agriculture (e.g., Mark 4:1-9), archaeological evidence suggests that Capernaum was also a place where high-quality agricultural implements were manufactured. Many olive presses and grain mills made out of local basalt, a highly durable and abrasive rock, were found in excavations at Capernaum, more, in fact, than the local population would have been expected to use by themselves. Because Capernaum was on a trade route and was the first village that travelers came to in Herod Antipas' Galilee after crossing the Jordan River from the east, Rome made it a tax collection center (cp. Mark 2:14-15). To enforce tax collection, a unit of Roman soldiers was also garrisoned in Capernaum (cp. Luke 7:2-5).

▲ The foundational material of this third-century synagogue may possibly date from the first century.

Three separate political entities bordered the Sea of Galilee in the first century AD (see Map 9). Galilee proper, governed by Herod Antipas, son of Herod the Great, was located west of the sea and Jordan River. The main city on the western Galilee shore was—and still is—Tiberius, founded by Antipas between AD 17 and 20 to honor the new Caesar in Rome. Tiberius is within sight of Capernaum and an easy two-hour walk away, yet the Gospels fail to mention if Jesus ever went there (but cp. John 6:23-24).

The territory lying east of the Jordan River and northeast of the Sea of Galilee was governed by Herod Philip, another son of Herod the Great. Philip's territory was divided into three expansive regions, Gaulanitus, Iturea, and Traconitis (cp. Luke 3:1,19). Philip raised Bethsaida, his main city on the sea, to the status of a Greco-Roman *polis*, renaming it Julius after the daughter of Caesar Augustus.

A confederation of ten Greco-Roman cities called the Decapolis lay south of Philip's territory, stretching from the southeastern shore of the sea deep into Transjordan. This Gentile region was home to the Gergasenes, where Jesus healed a man possessed by demons (Mark 5:1-20). One of the Decapolis cities, Hippus, sat on a prominent hill above the Sea of Galilee within sight of Capernaum (cp. Matt. 5:14).

These various political regions in the New Testament period were closely connected by sea and land. Here people with every competing religious and political ideology and agenda were crowded together under tropical heat and the ever-watchful eye of Rome. In this pressure-cooker setting Jesus chose to minister. Here He could touch the very human needs of influential people and commoners alike, of Jews and Gentiles.

The Sea of Galilee was an ideal setting for the Gospel story. Here Jesus placed Himself in the center of all of the forces competing for power and influence in His day. Here He also met and ministered to regular folk, people who were seeking to live quiet lives that were pleasing to God and man.

17 ► THE MINISTRY OF JESUS AROUND THE SEA OF GALILEE

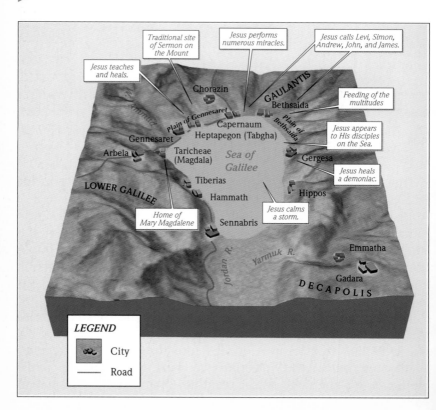

The Huleh Basin

The Huleh Basin is the northernmost extension of the Jordan Valley. The northern point of the basin, the city of Dan, lies 25 miles north of the Sea of Galilee, at the foothills of Mount Hermon. The southern end is plugged by the thick basalt Rosh Pinna sill, a lava flow from Bashan. The floor of the basin lies approximately 240 feet above sea level, requiring the Jordan River to drop considerably on its journey through a narrow cut in the eastern side of the sill to the Sea

The Huleh Basin.

of Galilee (-690 feet). The Cenomanian limestone hills of Upper Galilee tower 1,600 feet above the Huleh to the west, while the basalt slopes of Bashan pull back more gradually to the east.

The Huleh is filled with rich alluvial soil (basaltic and terra rosa) and some peat. In the north, rainfall reaches 25 inches per year. Most of the water in the basin, however, comes from the four tributaries of the Jordan River (Nahal Hermon, Nahal Dan, Nahal Senir, and Nahal Ijon), that produce a combined five thousand gallons of water per second. These tributaries arise from huge karstic springs in the southern end of Mount Hermon and are fed year-round by snowmelt from its heights (cp. Jer. 18:14). Because of the steep sides of the basin, strong winds tend to skip over the top, while sunlight pours down. Together, the soil, water, and heat produce greenhouse-like conditions, and a wide variety of crops are grown year-round. Should one choose to do so, it is possible to get 18 cuttings of alfalfa in the basin per year.

The waters of the Jordan back up at the southern end of the Huleh Basin as they are slowed through the cut of the Rosh Pinna sill. Until the early 1950s these waters formed a small lake, Lake Huleh, with marshes, papyrus, and water birds common to the Nile Delta. Some Bible atlases suggest that this lake was the "Waters of Merom" that figured in Joshua's defeat of Hazor (Josh. 11:5), but others connect this battle with Mount Meron in Upper Galilee. Today Lake Huleh has been drained for agriculture although a lush nature preserve remains.

The Huleh Basin has always been the funnel through which travelers and armies poured into Palestine from the north. During the Old Testament period, the International Highway passed through

Dan (Gen. 14:14; Judg. 18:27-29; 2 Sam. 3:10; 1 Kings 12:29) and skirted the western edge of the Huleh, out of its swampy soil, to Hazor (Josh. 11:1; Judg. 4:2; 1 Kings 9:15). It then crossed the Rosh Pinna sill to Chinnereth on the Sea of Galilee before finding its way through the natural obstacles of Galilee to the coast. In the time of the New Testament, however, the international route dropped down the eastern side of the basin, connecting Caesarea Philippi (Matt. 16:13), at the edge of the foothills of Mount Hermon, with Bethsaida-Julius on the Sea of Galilee.

The city of Hazor is mentioned several times in cuneiform tablets from the middle and late Bronze Ages (20th through 13th centuries BC), testifying to its importance as "the head of all these kingdoms" (Josh. 11:10). Archaeological excavations have corroborated Hazor's importance. On the eve of Joshua's conquest, the city was two hundred acres in size, ten times bigger than other Canaanite cities of the time and of a size rivaling the great cities of Mesopotamia. Recent excavations have uncovered remains of the grand Canaanite palace at Hazor, with rooms paneled in basalt. While a handful of cuneiform tablets have been found at Hazor, the city's full archive, which was probably housed in the palace, remains to be discovered.

 Israelite storehouses dating from the ninth century BC at ancient Hazor in Israel.

Because of its position astride the northern approaches of Palestine, the Huleh Basin is the land's first line of defense from the north. Joshua knew that his conquests in Canaan would not be secure without defeating the coalition headed by Jabin, king of Hazor (Josh. 11:1-23). Deborah and Barak also conquered Hazor when its king sought to reestablish Canaanite control in the Jezreel Valley (Judg. 4:1–5:31). Solomon fortified Hazor along with Gezer and

Megiddo in his attempt to control traffic on the International Highway (1 Kings 9:15). In the early days of the divided monarchy, Ben-hadad, king of Damascus, captured the entire Huleh Basin from Israel (1 Kings 15:20), and the region remained a "land between," coveted by both Syria and Israel, throughout the biblical period.

Eventually larger powers—the Assyrians (2 Kings 15:29), Babylonians, Persians, Greeks, Seleucids, Ptolemies, and Romans—seized the Huleh Basin to secure their position in the area. By New Testament times the Huleh sat in the middle of Jewish and Gentile populations. In offering the wealth and opportunities of the world, this region became a true testing ground of faith.

> From at least the time of Alexander the Great's conquest of Palestine, the area around the springs feeding the eastern-most tributary of the Jordan River was a sanctuary for Pan, the Greco-Roman god of shepherds, hunters, and fertility. This region was called Panias (modern Banyas), in Pan's honor. Herod the Great built a temple here, which he dedicated to Caesar Augustus. Herod Philip made Panias the capital of his realm upon the death of his father, changing its name to Caesarea Philippi. In this region, full in the face of the Greco-Roman world, Jesus challenged His disciples, "Who do you say that I am?" (Matt. 16:15). It was also here that Jesus first mentioned the church (Matt. 16:18).

The Huleh Basin is awash with water and fertility. As the northern gateway into Palestine, its control is critical for anyone who seeks to live securely in the land. Like the coastal plain this basin witnessed the ebb and flow of foreign powers through the Levant, and it remained a region that challenged the efforts of ancient Israel and Judea to control their own destiny.

THE EASTERN REGIONS
(Transjordan)

The eastern regions of Palestine lie east of the rift valley: Bashan, Gilead, Ammon, the Medeba Plateau, Moab, and Edom. While most of the events of the Bible took place west of the Jordan River, the regions of Transjordan were closely tied to the overall sweep of the biblical story. Except for Bashan, each is located today in the Hashemite Kingdom of Jordan.

Bashan

Bashan is an expansive plateau in northern Transjordan stretching from Mount Hermon to south of the Yarmuk River (Num. 21:33; Deut. 3:1-11; 29:7). During the time of the New Testament, the western portion of Bashan—the slopes facing the Huleh Basin—was

Bashan.

called Gaulanitis. The name *Gaulanitis* is a latinized form of *Golan*, the Old Testament city of refuge in the region (Deut. 4:43; Josh. 21:27). Today most of Gaulanitis falls within the borders of the Golan Heights, a narrow buffer between the modern states of Israel and Syria.

The topography of Bashan is relatively flat but drops dramatically into the Huleh Basin in the west. These rocky slopes provide excellent grazing land for cattle, which were renowned in antiquity for their strength (Ps. 22:12) and fatness (Ezek. 39:18; Amos 4:1). In the flatter areas, the basalt boulders have broken down into a dark, rich soil that was farmed extensively for wheat during the Roman period.

Rainfall on the western portions of Bashan is abundant, up to 40 inches annually. The rain gradually tapers, however, toward the vast eastern desert, as it does in all of Transjordan. Most of the rainfall on Bashan drains into the upper tributaries of the Yarmuk River, which curls around the region on the south and east. The large Yarmuk canyon enters the Jordan River south of the Sea of Galilee. To the north, Mount Hermon receives heavy snow each year; one of its Arabic names, *Jebel eth-Thalj,* means "mountain of the snow."

At 9,233 feet Mount Hermon is by far the highest peak in Palestine. If the wintertime skies are exceptionally clear, snowy Hermon can be seen from the hills northwest of Jerusalem, 115 miles away. The Bible sometimes calls Hermon by its Phoenician name, Sirion, or its Amorite name, Senir (Deut. 3:9; Ps. 29:6). The name *Hermon* comes from a Hebrew word that means "devoted," aptly conveying the mountain's sacred character in both Canaanite and Israelite religion (cp. Judg. 3:3; 1 Chron. 5:23). Psalm 48:1-2 combines images of Hermon with Mount Zion in speaking of the holy habitation of God (cp. Ps. 68:15-16).

The Bible speaks glowingly of the fertility of Bashan, as it does the Plain of Sharon, Mount Carmel, Lebanon, and Gilead. "I will bring Israel back to his own pasture and he will graze on Carmel and Bashan" (Jer 50:19), and, "Shepherd your people with your staff, the flock of your inheritance, which lives by itself in a forest, in fertile pasturelands. Let them feed in Bashan and Gilead as in days long ago" (Mic. 7:14). More often, however, the prophets spoke of Bashan's withering up as a sure sign of God's judgment (Isa. 33:9; Nah. 1:4; Zech. 11:2).

Politically Bashan has always been a wide open buffer zone between Syria and Israel, connected to them by international highways yet belonging securely to neither. One branch of the International Highway leaving Damascus skirts Mount Hermon on its way to Galilee and the coast. The other branch, the Transjordanian Highway, takes a southern course through the Old Testament cities of Karnaim (Gen. 14:5), Ashtoroth (Gen. 14:5; Josh. 9:10; 12:4; 13:12,31) and Edrei (Deut. 1:4; 3:1,10), on its way to Ammon, Moab, Edom, and the Arabian Peninsula. These international highways are joined by cross routes bisecting Bashan east to west.

Moses conquered Bashan from the Amorite king Og (Num. 21:33-35; Deut. 3:1-7), giving the region to the tribe of Manasseh (Deut. 3:13; Josh. 13:29-30). During the monarchy the kings of Israel and Syria fought continuously over Bashan (2 Kings 10:32-33; 14:25). Any time a king of Syria appeared within the borders of Israel or Transjordan (e.g., 1 Kings 20:1-3; 22:1-3; 2 Kings 6:24), it can be assumed that Bashan had been taken first. Overrun by the Assyrians in the late eighth century BC, Bashan never again was an integral part of ancient Israel. In New Testament times Bashan belonged to the territory of Philip, son of Herod the Great, yet remained largely a Gentile region.

The fertility of Bashan and its position as a buffer between Israel and Syria underlies its strategic role in the biblical story. Here Israel met Syria face-to-face. Not insignificantly, it was somewhere on Bashan's open expanse that Saul of Tarsus met God visibly and became Christianity's first great missionary to the Gentiles (Acts 9:1-6).

Gilead and Ammon

Three regions, Lower Gilead, the Dome of Gilead, and Ammon, make up the hills of central Transjordan. These lie across the Jordan River from the hill country of Ephraim and Manasseh, the heartland of ancient Israel. The landforms, soils, and water resources of these three regions are quite varied, as were the lifestyle patterns of their inhabitants in antiquity.

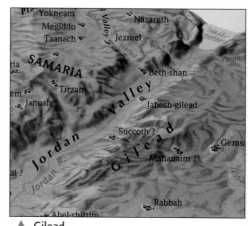

▲ Gilead.

The meaning of the word *Gilead* is unknown. Genesis 31:45-48 connects it to *Galeed*, "a heap of witness," meaning a pile of stones placed as a memorial, but this may be simply a pun on the names. Gilead may also be related to a word meaning "strong" or "sturdy," perhaps reflecting the strength of the hills that dominate the region. The Bible's use of Gilead is also indefinite; sometimes the term is limited to the hills around the Jabbok River; other times it seems to refer to the entire region of Transjordan that was under Israelite control (Josh. 22:13; Ps. 60:7).

Lower Gilead is a relatively level plateau south of the Yarmuk River composed of soft Eocene limestone and Senonian chalk. The elevations of Lower Gilead do not exceed 1,650 feet, and rainfall can reach 24 inches annually. The soils of Lower Gilead are not as rich as those of Bashan, but they are more easily plowed and, like Bashan, well suited for grains.

Lower Gilead fell within the southern portion of the kingdom of Og, and after being conquered by Moses, it was allotted to the tribe of Manasseh (Num. 21:33-35; Deut. 3:1-12). Its biblical name during the time of the judges was Havvoth-jair, "the villages of Jair," after Jair, a descendant of Manasseh (Num. 32:40-41; Judg. 10:3-5). The primary cities in Lower Gilead during the Old Testament period were Jabesh-gilead, which figured prominently in the life of King Saul (1 Sam. 11:1-11; 31:11-13; cp. Judg. 21:6-14), and Ramoth-gilead, the key to military strategy in the entire region. Ancient Ramoth-gilead lay at the juncture of the Transjordanian Highway and the primary route running through the Harod and Jezreel Valleys. Ahab lost his life in an attempt to control this strategic crossroads and thereby check Syria's moves toward Israel (1 Kings 22:1-40; cp. 2 Kings

8:28–9:13). During the time of the New Testament, Gadara and Pella, two cities of the Decapolis, dominated the region.

South of Lower Gilead is a rugged, uplifted dome of hard Cenomanian limestone commonly known as the Dome of Gilead. Elevations here reach 4,091 feet, considerably higher than the hills of Ephraim and Manasseh west of the Jordan. The Dome of Gilead has been deeply cut in two by the Jabbok River, a huge open wedge running east-west and joining the Jordan River midway between the Sea of Galilee and the Dead Sea. Because of its elevation, the Dome of Gilead is generally wetter than the hills west of the Jordan, and snowfall on its heights is not uncommon. The terra rosa soil of Gilead supports the traditional hill country crops (grapes, olives, figs, pomegranates, and almonds), allowing the ancient Israelites to feel at home here.

▲ The rugged hill country of Gilead.

After Moses conquered the Amorite kingdom of Sihon and the kingdom of Og in Bashan, he allowed the tribes of Reuben, Gad, and a portion of Manasseh to settle in areas of Transjordan that were not already considered part of the homelands of Ammon, Moab, or Edom (Num. 21:21-35; 32:1-42; 34:13-15; Deut. 2:26–3:17; 29:7-8). Gad settled in the Jordan Valley, on the western slopes of the Lower Gilead and the Dome of Gilead, and at the northern edge of the Medeba Plateau.

The Prophet Jeremiah spoke of balm in Gilead (Jer. 8:22; 46:11) as a metaphor of "medicine" that could cure Israel's sin (cp. Jer. 51:8). Scanty textual evidence suggests that balm is a kind of a spice with medicinal qualities derived from plant resin, although its exact identification is unknown (cp. Gen. 37:25). The value of balm can be seen in Ezekiel 27:17, which notes that Israel exported balm to Tyre, apparently for distribution on Tyre's vast Mediterranean trading network.

Like the remote hills of Upper Galilee, the Dome of Gilead was primarily dotted by farming villages during the Old Testament period. The major cities in the region at the time, Penuel (Gen. 32:30-31; 1 Kings 12:25) and Mahanaim (Gen. 32:2), were located deep in the cleft of the Jabbok, while Succoth (Judg. 8:4-16) guarded the opening of the Jabbok to the Jordan Valley. The main city in the days of the New Testament, Gerasa (modern Jerash, the best-preserved Roman city in the world), belonged to the Decapolis.

Throughout biblical history the Dome of Gilead was a kind of frontier land for Israel, considered part of their homeland but a bit removed from the main line of events. Jacob (Gen. 32:1-32), Gideon (Judg. 8:1-21), and Jephthah (Judg. 10:6–12:7) met adversaries here, while Ish-bosheth (2 Sam. 2:8), Abner (2 Sam 2:24-29), David (2 Sam. 17:24-29), and Jeroboam (1 Kings 12:25) used the rugged hills of Gilead as a place of refuge. During the time of the New Testament, Herod Antipas, ruler of Galilee, governed Perea ("beyond the Jordan"), the western portion of this region (Matt. 4:25).

A relatively small basin of soft Senonian chalk tucked below the southeastern rim of the Dome of Gilead formed the heartland of the Old Testament kingdom of Ammon (Num. 21:24; Judg. 10:6-7; 11:4-6; 2 Sam. 10:1-19). This region separates the fertile agricultural lands of Gilead from the open desert, and both farmers and shepherds have been able to make a living there. Rainfall begins to taper in Ammon, but a few springs and an upper tributary of the Jabbok that bisects the region ensures reasonable supplies of water.

During the Old Testament period, the capital city of Ammon was Rabbah (or Rabbah of the Ammonites—Deut. 3:11; Josh. 13:25). During the time of the New Testament, the name of this city, now a member of the Decapolis, was Philadelphia. From here the Transjordanian Highway splits into two branches. One of these, the King's Highway, drops south to connect Ammon with the ancient capitals of Moab and Edom (Num. 20:17). The other, the "Way of the Wilderness of Moab," bypasses the Arnon and Zered river canyons along the edge of the desert to the east (Deut. 2:8). Today the Ammon basin is filled to overflowing with the city of Amman, the capital of the Hashemite Kingdom of Jordan, while Jordan's main north-south highway follows the line of the eastern branch of the Transjordanian Highway, now called the Desert Highway.

Ezekiel's oracle against the Ammonites speaks of Ammon's tenuous position between the land of the farmer and the land of the shepherd: "Therefore I am going to give you to the people of the East as a possession. They will set up their camps and pitch their tents among you; they will eat your fruit and drink your milk. I will turn

Rabbah into a pasture for camels and Ammon into a resting place for sheep. Then you will know that I am the LORD" (Ezek. 25:4-5).

Israel was attracted to the hills directly east of the Jordan River but found them to be a frontier that was hard to control. The rugged Jabbok canyon served as a place of refuge and escape for Israelites who lived west of the Jordan. The cities of the Decapolis secured Rome's eastern frontier in Transjordan during the time of the New Testament.

Moab and the Medeba Plateau

The heartland of ancient Moab was the high, hilly region lying between the Arnon and Zered river canyons east of the southern half of the Dead Sea, approximately 30 by 30 miles in size. This is a mixed region of Cenomanian limestone and Senonian chalk, with large outcrop-

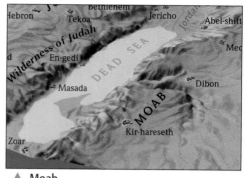
▲ Moab.

pings of basalt on the higher elevations. The highest hills in Moab run about 3,600 feet, but an elevation of 4,282 feet is reached in the south above the Zered.

North of the Arnon is a lower plateau of Senonian chalk (approximately 2,300 feet in elevation) that the Bible calls the *mishor* ("plateau" or "tableland"—Deut. 3:10; Josh. 13:9,16). Cenomanian limestone and reddish Nubian sandstone are exposed on the western scarp of this plateau as it drops into the rift valley and Dead Sea. A common name for this region is the Medeba Plateau, after Medeba (modern Madaba), its most important city today.

The remains of a mosaic floor from the ruins of a sixth-century AD Byzantine church in the city of Madaba depict the oldest known map of Palestine. This beautiful map was originally 77 by 20 feet in size and showed the world of the eastern Mediterranean from Lebanon to the Nile Delta. Unfortunately, only the area from south central Palestine to the Nile, about one third of the original remains. The Medeba map is an invaluable primary source for the geography and settlement of the land of Palestine during the Byzantine period. Of particular note is the map's depiction of Jerusalem, which graphically shows the primary streets, gates, and buildings of the city of that time.

The Arnon (Deut. 2:24) and Zered (Deut. 2:13), like the Yarmuk and Jabbok farther north, are huge water erosion canyons that have cut deeply into the Transjordanian hills, channeling most of the region's rainfall into the rift valley. At 2,300 feet deep, the Arnon is perhaps the most dramatic of all. From rim to rim the Arnon spans over three miles, and the torturous road that crosses this chasm today, close to the ancient route of the King's Highway, can take an hour to traverse by bus.

While rainfall on the Dead Sea scarcely tops four inches per year, these higher hills to the east receive amounts only somewhat less than the hills west of the Jordan—on average 10 inches on the Medeba Plateau and 16 in Moab proper. During the biblical period, this was the land of the shepherd Mesha, king of Moab and contemporary of Ahab, where he "raised sheep, and he had to supply the king of Israel with a hundred thousand lambs and with the wool of a hundred thousand rams" (2 Kings 3:4). Today the level chalk tableland north of the Arnon is one of Jordan's prime grain producing areas.

The tranquil book of Ruth is set in the turbulent period of the judges. The story opens with a famine gripping Bethlehem (Ruth 1:1), a not-too-unusual occurrence for a city whose agricultural lands drop toward the chalk wilderness east of the watershed ridge. Naomi, her husband Elimelech, and their two sons left their ancestral home in Bethlehem to journey to the higher hills of Moab to the east (Ruth 1:2), an area where rainfall was more reliable, if less in overall amounts. Here they tried to piece together an agricultural and shepherding existence like the one they left behind in Judah. Naomi eventually returned home to Bethlehem with only her daughter-in-law Ruth (Ruth 1:6-19).

During the Old Testament period, the major cities on the Medeba Plateau and in Moab were located on the route of the King's Highway. From north to south, these were Heshbon (Num. 21:25-26), Medeba (Num. 21:30) and Dibon (Num. 21:30) north of the Arnon, and Ar (Num. 21:28) and Kir-hareseth (2 Kings 3:25) in Moab proper. Heshbon was the city of Sihon, whose Amorite kingdom Moses and the Israelites conquered on their way to Canaan (Num. 21:21-31; Deut. 2:24-37). Kir-hareseth was the capital of the kingdom of Moab; the remains of the Crusader castle of Kerak dominate the site today.

Of note during the time of the New Testament is Machaerus, Herod the Great's desert fortress east of the rift valley. Machaerus sits on the scarp of the Medeba Plateau east of the Dead Sea. According to Josephus, John the Baptist was beheaded here by Herod Antipas, who ruled the region of Perea which included Machaerus, at the behest of his new wife, Herodias (Mark 6:14-29).

Throughout the biblical period the Medeba Plateau was a frontier zone between the kingdoms of Moab and Israel, and each tried to contain the other by seizing the plateau and its highways. Moses gave the Medeba Plateau to the tribe of Reuben after conquering Sihon (Josh. 13:15-23), but by the time of the judges, the Moabite king Eglon had crossed both the plateau and the Jordan River to set up residence in Jericho, the city of palms (Judg. 3:12-30). Later Moab and, by implication, the Medeba Plateau were subject to both David (2 Sam. 8:2,11-12) and Ahab, king of Israel (2 Kings 1:1). Ahab's claim on the plateau had been anticipated when Hiel of Bethel rebuilt Jericho (1 Kings 16:34), securing that city as a launching pad for Israelite control east of the Jordan. After Ahab's death Mesha king of Moab pushed Moabite influence back onto the Medeba Plateau (2 Kings 3:4-5); the Mesha Stele (Moabite Stone) tells of this expansion from Moab's point of view. Moab remained Israel's eastern nemesis throughout the period of the monarchy and was the object of prophetic wrath by Amos (2:1-3), Isaiah (15:1–16:14), and Jeremiah (48:1-47).

View of the Jordan Valley from the top of Mount Nebo looking toward Jericho.

According to Deuteronomy 34:1-3, Moses viewed the Canaan from Mount Nebo, the top of Pisgah, northeast of the Dead Sea. It is unclear from the biblical texts whether Mount Nebo is a range of hills of which Pisgah is a single peak or vice versa (Num. 21:20; 23:14; Deut. 3:27; 32:49; 34:1). While there is a traditional site of Mount Nebo today, complete with Byzantine church and beautiful mosaics, it is impossible to know which mountain of many in the area Moses actually climbed. The traditional spot provides a breathtaking panorama of Canaan, including spires of the Mount of Olives on a clear day, but it is geographically impossible to see everything that Moses saw from this location without "spiritual eyes."

Like Bashan, the Medeba Plateau was an important "land between" in the biblical story. Here, on its open expanse, Israel met Moab face-to-face. Each struggled to control the plateau as they sought to secure their position in the hills east of the Jordan River.

Edom

Stretching 110 miles from the Zered canyon to the Gulf of Aqaba, Edom is the largest region of Transjordan. The geography of Edom is complex, with limestone plateaus in the north giving way to a rugged and awesome sandstone topography in the south. Most of Edom is true desert. Here the open expanse of the vast Arabian Peninsula

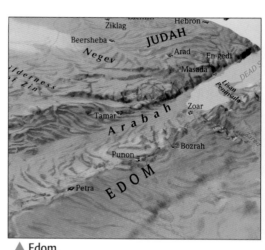

Edom.

encroaches closely onto the settled lands of Palestine.

The word *Edom* is derived from a Hebrew word that means "red," probably reflecting the reddish color of the sandstone cliffs in the region that front the rift valley. Edom is an alternate name for Esau, the brother of Jacob (Israel) and ancestor of the Edomites (Gen. 25:30; 36:19). The name *Esau* is related to Seir, yet another name for Edom (Gen. 14:6; 36:19-20; Deut. 1:2; Josh. 24:4). Both Esau and Seir apparently come from a Hebrew meaning "hairy." It has been

Gulf of Eilat/Gulf of Aqaba.

suggested that the trees that lined the scarp of Edom in antiquity looked "hairy" when viewed from the rift valley below, and hence the name, but this is unlikely.

The narrow gulf of the Red Sea that touches the southern point of Palestine is called the Gulf of Eilat today by Israelis and the Gulf of Aqaba by Jordanians. The former name is more appropriate when discussing the Negev, while the latter is best used in the context of Edom (cp. 1 Kings 9:26).

Geologically, the land of Edom can be divided into three subregions:

• The northernmost subregion, from the Zered to the vicinity of the city of Punion 25 miles south, was the heartland of the Old Testament kingdom of Edom. Elevations reach 5,384 feet, and rainfall averages around 14 inches on the heights overlooking the arid rift below. Limited agriculture is possible along this narrow north-south band, but just to the east the climate of the vast eastern desert overwhelms the land.

• The central subregion is composed of a high limestone plateau that stretches for 50 miles south of Punion. The highest point, near Petra, reaches 5,696 feet. Rainfall averages six to ten inches along the western scarp, and because of its height—which is significantly greater than the hills of the Negev west of the rift—snow is not unusual during the winter. Mountains of red sandstone line the rift valley, and the view through them into the rift from Petra is truly astonishing.

• The central plateau ends abruptly with a dramatic scarp running perpendicular to the rift valley. Below lies a vast expanse of rugged sandstone and granite peaks, a complex maze of sails jutting out of a vast sea of sand. Spectacular vistas are found in the Wadi Rum, the southeastern portion of this subregion. To the southwest, thick bands of copper and iron lace the surface of the hills. Rainfall here averages less than two inches per year. Geologically and culturally, this is the land of Arabia.

The primary cities of Edom during the Old Testament period were the oasis of Bozrah (Gen. 36:33; Isa. 34:6; Amos 1:11-12) and Sela (2 Kings 14:7; Isa. 16:1), both located in the northern subregion. The magnificent remains of the rose-red city of Petra, capital of the vast Nabatean trading network during the New Testament period, are tucked away in the sandstone hills along the western scarp of the central subregion.

Both *Sela* (Hebrew) and *Petra* (Greek) mean "rock," and both are apt names for cities in the bare, rugged hills of Edom. Because of the similarity of name, it is often thought that Old Testament Sela was located at what was to become Petra.

The mountainous landscape of the land of Edom.

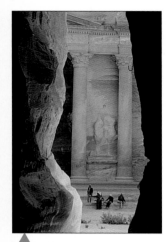

The so-called "Treasury" building of ancient Petra as seen from the only entranceway into the city.

It is more likely, however, that Sela was further north, in the vicinity of Bozrah, the heartland of the Edomite kingdom.

The King's Highway, linking Bozrah and Sela to the capitals of Moab and Ammon, joins its eastern branch, the Desert Highway, just above the scarp that drops into Edom's southern subregion. To the south, this international route connects Transjordan to the Red Sea and the great spice route of Arabia. An important side route links Bozrah to the Negev, funneling international traffic from Edom to Egypt and the Mediterranean.

Unconquered by Moses (Deut. 2:1-7), the Edomites remained the nemesis of Israel and Judah throughout the monarchy. Edom's natural point of expansion was to the west, into the Negev, which brought its people into direct conflict with Judah, who was seeking to expand into the same region (2 Sam. 8:14; 1 Kings 22:47-49; 2 Kings 8:20-22; 14:7; 16:5-6; 2 Chron. 20:1-37). Both wanted to control the lucrative trade flowing out of Arabia and Egypt, and each tried to establish a port on the Gulf of Eilat. When Judah fell to the Babylonians—apparently with Edomite assistance—the Edomites were finally able to pour unchecked into the Negev; this fueled some of the prophetic utterances of Jeremiah (49:7-22) and Obadiah (1-21). By the time of the New Testament, a remnant of the Edomites, now known by their Greek name, Idumeans, had settled in the Judean shephelah. Edom proper—and most of the Negev—came under the control of the powerful trading empire of the Nabateans.

Although the Nabateans are not mentioned in the New Testament, twice persons associated with the Nabateans are. The first-century historian Josephus mentions that the woman Herod Antipas divorced in order to marry Herodias, the wife of his brother Philip, was a Nabatean queen, the daughter of Aretas (cp. Mark 6:17-29; Josephus Ant. xviii.5.2). The apostle Paul writes that when he was in Damascus, the city governor under King Aretas tried to arrest him, but he slipped out of the city by being lowered from a window in the wall in a basket (2 Cor. 11:30-33). In both cases, the Aretas in question was probably Aretas IV, the greatest builder of Petra.

High and majestic, the mountains of Edom tower over the rift valley and Negev. From its secure heights, the Edomites, ancestral brothers of Israel, challenged Judah's claim to the southern approaches of Palestine.

MAPS, CHARTS, AND RECONSTRUCTIONS OF BIBLE LANDS

18▶ THE RISE OF EARLY CIVILIZATIONS

DATE	EGYPT	MESOPOTAMIA	PALESTINE
3300 BC	*Predynastic Period*	Consolidation of cities in Southern Mesopotamia Plain; continued development of cuneiform writing	Expansion of agricultural villages
3200 BC	Development of hieroglyphic writing		
3000 BC	*The Archaic Period* First and Second Dynasties		Development of true urban centers (Arad, Ai, Jericho); massive walled cities; trade with Egypt and the Sinai; some cities (Arad, Ai) abandoned or destroyed about 2750, but others were rebuilt or newly founded (Hazor) in the Early Bronze III era (2750–2200 BC)
		Classical Sumerian Age (ca. 2900–2350 BC)	
2800 BC		Gilgamesh, king of Uruk	
	The Old Kingdom Third through Sixth Dynasties		
2600 BC	*The Pyramid Age* Step Pyramid of Zoser; Great Pyramid of Cheops (Kufu)		
		Royal burials from Ur	
2400 BC		*The Akkadian Period* (ca. 2371–2230 BC)	
		Sargon the Great	
2200 BC		Naram-Sin	Collapse of urban culture; many sites abandoned or destroyed from ca. 2250–2000 BC
		Period of Darkness	
	The First Intermediate Period Seventh through early Eleventh Dynasties	Guti invasion	
	Collapse of centralized authority		
2000 BC		*The Neo-Sumerian Revival;* Ur III (ca. 2113–2006 BC); Ziggurat of Ur-Nammu	

THE DAYS OF NOAH

An artist's rendition of Noah's ark, copyright © Answers in Genesis, www.AnswersInGenesis.org. Used by permission.

Genesis 6–9 tells the story of the flood that covered the whole earth, and of Noah, the man used by God to save the world of men and beasts. The deluge was brought on by sin. The first six verses of Genesis 6 speak of the "sons of God" having relations with the "daughters of men." Some have seen the sons of God as angelic (or demonic) beings, and thus the evil as demons cohabiting with humans. More likely the sons of God were the sons of the godly line of Seth, and the daughters of men were women from the profane line of Cain. The evil then was the righteous being unequally yoked with unbelievers, thus stamping out the remnant on the earth, so that "the earth was corrupt in the sight of God, and the earth was filled with violence" (Gen. 6:11 NASB). Noah was apparently the only remnant left. "But Noah found favor in the eyes of the Lord" (Gen. 6:8). He was a man of faith, whose trust in God "condemned the world" (Heb. 11:7).

The Lord commanded Noah to construct an ark of "gopher wood." Into this ark went 14 ("by sevens") of all clean animals and two each of the unclean animals (Gen. 7:1-5). There were more of the clean animals since they would be needed for food and for sacrifice once the flood was over (8:20-22; 9:2-4). God then sent judgment in the form of rain, which fell on the earth for 40 days (7:17) and prevailed for 150 days (7:24). Finally the ark settled on the mountains of Ararat. Noah sent out doves three times until the last one did not return. He then opened the ark, praised God, offered a sacrifice, and received God's covenant promise not to judge the world by water again (8:21-22).

Over the last 30 years much interest has been focused on photographs which seem to depict a large wooden structure buried atop Mount Ararat in Turkey. It remains to be seen whether this will ever be resolved and whether it actually is the ark. Second, there is much discussion over evidence for the flood. New data pours in seemingly by the week. Not long ago scientists discovered the remnants of a city a hundred feet or more beneath the surface of the Black Sea. It appears that this sea was not always there or not always so expansive. This would be clear evidence of a flood in ancient times. The third issue is whether the flood was local or worldwide. Proponents of a local flood only, some of whom are evangelicals, stand in sometimes vocal opposition to those who believe the flood to have been universal. Both OT and NT texts seem clearly to teach that the flood was universal (Gen. 7:19-24; 2 Pet. 3:6,20). But that does not mean that any one way of arguing for a universal flood, such as the catastrophist approach, for instance, is the last word on the matter. Much work remains to be done. What can be said is that the scientific evidence for a flood, even for a universal flood, is strong and growing daily.

 This mountain in modern Turkey may be part of the Mountains of Ararat where Noah's ark came to rest after the flood.

19 THE TABLE OF NATIONS

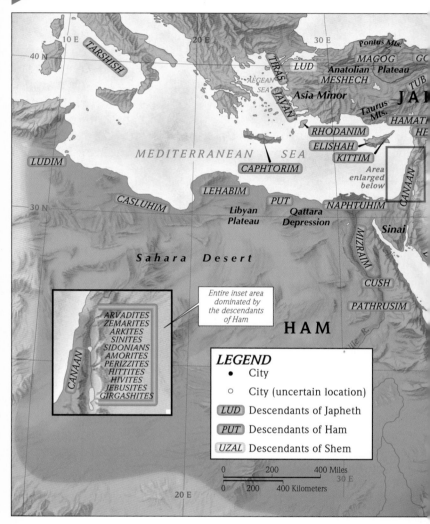

Genesis 10:1

These are the family records of Noah's sons, Shem, Ham, and Japheth. They also had sons after the deluge.

Genesis 10 lists the descendants of Noah's sons to explain the origin of the nations and peoples of the known world. The account is unique for several reasons. First, a new chapter begins in biblical history at this point; humanity has a new beginning through Noah and his three sons. Second, the account highlights the ethnic makeup of the ancient world, listing some 70 different ethnic groups that formed the basis of the known world. Third, despite our lack of knowledge about many of the groups listed in the chapter, Genesis

10 underlines the fact that the Bible is based on historical events. Fourth, Genesis 10 provides the basis for understanding Abraham, introducing his world and his relationship to that world. The account of the Table of Nations, with a few variations, also appears in 1 Chronicles 1:5-23.

The Table of Nations has three basic divisions. The people and lands of the known world fit into one of three families, the family of Shem, Ham, or Japheth. The names which appear in each of the families are names which come from several different categories: racial descent, geographical location, language differences, or political units.

Japheth's descendants (Gen. 10:2-5) inhabited the Aegean region and Anatolia or Asia Minor. The descendants of Ham (Gen. 10:6-20) were located especially in the regions of North Africa and the coastal regions of Canaan and Syria. The descendants of Shem (Gen. 10:21-31) are especially important because Abraham comes from the line of Shem. Thus Abraham is a Shemite or Semite. Because he is also a descendant of Eber, he is called a Hebrew (Gen. 11:14-32). The descendants of Shem were located generally in north Syria, that is, the region of the upper part of the Euphrates River, and Mesopotamia, especially the eastern part.

20 ▶ ANCIENT NUMBER SYSTEMS

AMERICAN	SUMERIAN	EARLY EGYPTIAN (HIEROGLYPHIC)	LATER EGYPTIAN (HIERATIC)	CANAANITE (and PHOENICIAN)	POST-EXILIC HEBREW	EARLY GREEK	LATER GREEK (IONIC)	ANCIENT ROMAN (LATIN)
1	𐤀 (or ˅)	I	I	/	א	I	A	I
2	𐤀𐤀 (or ˅˅)	II	𐞥	//	ב	II	B	II
3	𐤀𐤀𐤀 (or ˅˅˅)	III	𐞥𐞥	///	ג	III	Γ	III
4	𐤀𐤀𐤀𐤀 (or ˅˅˅˅)	IIII	𐞥𐞥𐞥	////	ד	IIII	Δ	III (or IV)
5	(or ˅˅)	IIIII	"/	// ///	ה	Γ	E	V
6	(or ˅˅˅)	III III	"/	/// ///	ו	ΓI	F	VI
7	(or ˅˅˅)	III IIII	⌐	/ /// ///	ז	ΓII	Z	VII
8	(or ˅˅˅˅)	IIII IIII	𐏓	// /// ///	ח	ΓIII	H	VIII
9	(or ˅˅˅˅)	III III III	⸜⸝	/// /// ///	ט	ΓIIII	θ	VIII (or IX)
10	⟨ (or ⟨)	∩	∧	⌒	י	Δ	I	X
20	⟨⟨ (or ⟨⟨)	∩∩	λ	⸠	כ	ΔΔ	K	XX
50			⌐		נ		N	L
100		℮	⌐		ק	H	P	C
200		℮℮			ר	HH	Σ	CC
1,000		𐰃	⌿			X	/A	M

NUMBER SYSTEMS AND NUMBER SYMBOLISM

To understand properly the number systems of the biblical world, one must look to the neighbors of Israel. The Egyptians were already using relatively advanced mathematics by 3000 BC. The construction of such structures as the pyramids required an understanding of complex mathematics. The Egyptian system was decimal. The Sumerians by that same time had developed their own number system. In fact, the Sumerians knew two systems, one based on ten (a decimal system) and one based on six or twelve (usually designated as a duodecimal system). We still make use of remnants of the Sumerian system today in our reckoning of time—12 hours for day and 12 hours for night, 60 minutes and 60 seconds as divisions of time. We also divide a circle into 360 degrees. Our calendar was originally based on the same division with the year having 12 months of 30 days for a total of 360. Even our units of the dozen (12) and gross (144) and inches to the foot may have their origin in the Sumerian mathematical system.

The Hebrews did not develop the symbols to represent numbers until the postexilic period (after 539 BC). In all preexilic inscriptions, small numbers are represented by individual strokes (for example, //// for four). Larger numbers were either represented with Egyptian symbols, or the name of the number was written out ("four" for the number 4). The Arad inscriptions regularly used Egyptian symbols for numbers, individual strokes for the units and hieratic numbers for five, ten, and larger numbers. The Samaria ostraca more frequently wrote out the number. Letters of the Hebrew alphabet are first used to represent numbers on coins minted in the Maccabean period (after 167 BC).

With the coming of the Hellenistic and Roman periods to Palestine, Greek symbols for numbers and Roman numerals appeared. The Greeks used letters of their alphabet to represent numerals, while the Romans used the familiar symbols I,V,X,L,C,M, and so on.

Biblical passages show that the Hebrews were well acquainted with the four basic mathematical operations of addition (Num. 1:20-46), subtraction (Gen. 18:28-33), multiplication (Num. 7:84-86), and division (Num. 31:27). The Hebrews also used fractions such as a half (Gen. 24:22), a third (Num. 15:6), and a fourth (Exod. 29:40).

In addition to their usage to designate specific numbers or quantities, many numbers in the Bible came to have a symbolic meaning. Thus seven came to symbolize completeness and perfection. God's work of creation was both complete and perfect—and it was completed in seven days. All of mankind's existence was related to God's creative activity. The seven-day week reflected God's first creative activity. The Sabbath was that day of rest following the workweek, reflective of God's rest (Gen. 1:1–2:4). Israelites were to remember the land also and give it a sabbath, permitting it to lie fallow in the seventh year (Lev. 25:2-7). Seven was also important in cultic matters beyond the Sabbath: major festivals such as Passover and Tabernacles lasted seven days as did wedding festivals (Judg. 14:12,17). In Pharaoh's dream the seven good years followed by seven years of famine (Gen. 41:1-36) represented a complete cycle of plenty and famine. Jacob worked a complete cycle of years for Rachel; then, when he was given Leah instead, he worked an additional cycle of seven (Gen. 29:15-30).

A major Hebrew word for making an oath or swearing, shava', was closely related to the word "seven," sheva'. The original meaning of "swear an oath" may have been "to declare seven times" or "to bind oneself by seven things."

A similar use of the number seven can be seen in the NT. The seven churches (Rev. 2–3) perhaps symbolized all the churches by their number. Jesus taught that forgiveness is not to be limited, even to a full number or complete number of instances. We are to forgive, not merely seven times (already a generous number of forgivenesses) but 70 times seven (limitless forgiveness, beyond keeping count) (Matt. 18:21-22).

As the last example shows, multiples of seven frequently had symbolic meaning. The year of Jubilee came after the completion of every 49 years. In the year of Jubilee all Jewish bondslaves were released, and land which had been sold reverted to its former owner (Lev. 25:8-55). Another multiple of seven used in the Bible is 70. Seventy elders are mentioned (Exod. 24:1,9). Jesus sent out the 70 (Luke 10:1-17). Seventy years is specified as the length of the exile (Jer. 25:12, 29:10; Dan. 9: 2). The messianic kingdom was to be inaugurated after a period of 70 weeks of years had passed (Dan. 9:24).

After seven the most significant number for the Bible is undoubtedly 12. The Sumerians used 12 as one base for their number system. Both the calendar and the signs of the zodiac reflect this 12-base number system. The tribes of Israel and Jesus' disciples numbered 12. The importance of the number 12 is evident in the effort to maintain that number. When Levi ceased to be counted among the tribes, the Joseph tribes, Ephraim and Manasseh, were counted separately to keep the number 12 intact. Similarly, in the NT when Judas Iscariot committed suicide, the 11 moved quickly to add another to keep their number at 12. Twelve seems to have been especially significant in the book of Revelation. New Jerusalem had 12 gates; its walls had 12 foundations (Rev. 21:12-14). The tree of life yielded 12 kinds of fruit (Rev. 22:2).

Multiples of 12 are also important. There were 24 divisions of priests (1 Chron. 24:4) and 24 elders around the heavenly throne (Rev. 4:4). Seventy-two elders, when one includes Eldad and Medad, were given a portion of God's spirit that rested on Moses, and they prophesied (Num. 11:24-26). An apocryphal tradition holds that 72 Jewish scholars, six from each of the 12 tribes, translated the OT into Greek, to give us the version we call today the Septuagint. The 144,000 servants of God (Rev. 7:4) were made up of 12,000 from each of the 12 tribes of Israel.

Three as a symbolic number often indicated completeness. The created cosmos had three elements: heaven, earth, and underworld. Three Persons make up the Godhead: Father, Son, and Holy Spirit.

Prayer was to be lifted at least three times daily (Dan. 6:10; cp. Ps. 55: 17). The sanctuary had three main parts: vestibule, nave, inner sanctuary (1 Kings 6). Three-year-old animals were mature and were, therefore, prized for special sacrifices (1 Sam. 1:24; Gen. 15:9). Jesus said He would be in the grave for three days and three nights (Matt. 12:40), the same time Jonah was in the great fish (Jon. 1:17). Paul often used triads in his writings, the most famous being "faith, hope, and love" (1 Cor. 13:13). One must also remember Paul's benediction: "The grace of the Lord Jesus Christ, and the love of God, and the communion of the Holy Ghost be with you all" (2 Cor. 13:14).

Four was often used as a sacred number. Significant biblical references to four include the four corners of the earth (Isa. 11:12), the four winds (Jer. 49:36), four rivers which flowed out of Eden to water the world (Gen. 2:10-14), and four living creatures surrounding God (Ezek. 1; Rev. 4:6-7). God sent forth the four horsemen of the Apocalypse (Rev. 6:1-8) to bring devastation to the earth.

The most significant multiple of four is 40, which often represented a large number or a long period of time. Rain flooded the earth for 40 days (Gen. 7:12). For 40 days Jesus withstood Satan's temptations (Mark 1:13). Forty years represented approximately a generation. Thus all the adults who had rebelled against God at Sinai died during the 40 years of the wilderness wandering period. By age 40 a person had reached maturity (Exod. 2:11; Acts 7:23).

A special system of numerology known as gematria developed in later Judaism. Gematria is based on the idea that one may discover hidden meaning in the biblical text from a study of the numerical equivalence of the Hebrew letters. The first letter of the Hebrew alphabet, *aleph*, represented one; *beth*, the second letter, represented two, and so on. With gematria one takes the sum of the letters of a Hebrew word and seeks to find some meaning. For example, the Hebrew letters of the name Eliezer, Abraham's servant, have a numerical value of 318. When Genesis 14:14 states that Abraham took 318 trained men to pursue the kings from the east, some Jewish commentaries interpret this to mean that Abraham had but one helper, Eliezer, since Eliezer has the numerical value of 318. Likewise, the number 666 in Revelation is often taken as a reverse gematria for the emperor Nero. The name Nero Caesar, put in Hebrew characters and added up following gematria, totals 666. Any interpretation based on gematria must be treated with care; such interpretation always remains speculative.

21 ▶ ZIGGURAT

Ziggurats were stepped buildings, usually capped by a temple. The architecture was made popular by the Babylonians. The design consisted of placing smaller levels of brick on top of larger layers. Those so far excavated reveal advanced building techniques used by ancient civilizations. Most biblical scholars believe the tower of Babel was a ziggurat (Gen. 11:3-9).

Babel is the Hebrew word meaning "confusion," derived from a root which means "to mix." It was the name given to the city that the disobedient descendants of Noah built so they would not be scattered over all the earth (Gen. 11:4,9). Babel is also the Hebrew word for Babylon.

The tower and the city which were built were intended to be a monument of human pride, for they sought to "make a name" for themselves (Gen. 11:4). It was also a monument to mankind's continued disobedience. They had been commanded to fill up the earth but were seeking to avoid being scattered abroad (Gen. 9:1; 11:4). Further, it was a monument to human engineering skills, for the techniques of its building described the use of fired clay bricks as a substitute for stone. Bitumen, found in relative abundance in the Mesopotamian Valley, was used to bind the bricks together.

Ruins of numerous ziggurats have been found in the region of Babylon. It is possible that ruins of the great temple-tower to Marduk found in the center of ancient Babylon is the focus of the narrative about the Tower of Babel.

To bring the people's monumental task to an end, God confused their language. The inspired writer apparently considered this to be the basis for the origin of the different human languages. When the builders were no longer able to communicate with one another, they then fled from one another in fear. The city of Babylon became to the OT writers the symbol of utter rebellion against God and remained so even into the NT (Rev. 17:1-5).

▲ Ziggurat at Susa, Iran. Five floors, the top two of which have been destroyed.

22 ▶ ANCIENT NEAR EAST IN THE THIRD MILLENNIUM

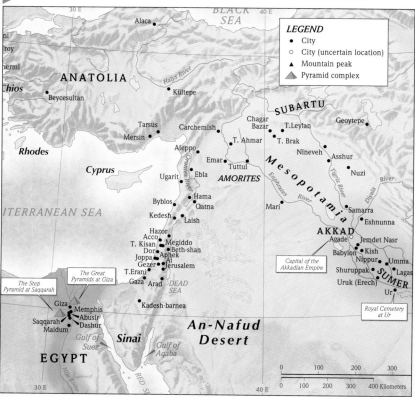

THE PATRIARCHS: ABRAHAM TO JOSEPH

▲ Vista of Haran from Crusader's castle. Haran was home for Abram for a time and remained home for his relatives like Laban.

A major era began with God's call of Abram (Gen. 12), the first Hebrew patriarch. Abram was the son of Terah, a descendant of Noah's son, Shem. (Gen. 11:27). His childhood was spent in Ur of the Chaldees, a prominent Sumerian city. He was known at the beginning as "Abram" ("father is exalted"), but this was changed subsequently to "Abraham" ("father of a multitude"—Gen. 17:5).

About 2092 BC, Terah, his father, moved to Haran with the family (Gen. 11:31) and after some years died there. God called Abram to migrate to Canaan, assuring him that he would father a vast nation. At different times he lived in Shechem, Bethel, Hebron, and Beer-sheba. His wife Sarai's beauty attracted the pharaoh when they moved to Egypt during a famine (Gen. 12:10), but God intervened to save her. The trouble arose partly because Abram had claimed her as his sister rather than his wife, and in fact she was his halfsister (Gen. 20:12). After returning to Palestine, Abram received further covenantal assurances from God (Gen. 15). He decided he could produce offspring by taking Sarai's handmaid Hagar as a concubine. Though the union produced a son, Ishmael, he was not destined to become Abram's promised heir. Even after another covenantal assurance (Gen. 17:1-21) in which the rite of circumcision was made a covenantal sign, Abram and Sarai still questioned God's promise of an heir.

Then Sarai, whose name had been changed to Sarah ("princess"), had her long-promised son, Isaac ("laughter"), when Abraham was 100 years old. Ishmael's presence caused trouble in the family, and he was expelled with his mother Hagar to the wilderness of Paran.

Abraham's faith and obedience were tested by God in Moriah when he was commanded to sacrifice Isaac. God provided an alternative sacrifice, however, saving the boy's life. As a reward for Abraham's faithfulness, God renewed the covenant promises of great blessing and the growth of a mighty nation to father and son.

Isaac had twin sons, Jacob and Esau. Continuing the pattern, the younger of the twins, Jacob, became the child of the promise. His 12 sons became the namesakes for the 12 tribes of Israel, but the child of the promise, Judah, was not the hero of his generation, rather Joseph became the savior of his family.

Joseph's story (Gen. 37–50) accurately reflects the history of Egypt in the 19th century BC. Joseph's story falls into three parts: Joseph and his brothers in Canaan, Joseph alone in Egypt, and Joseph in Egypt with his father Jacob (by this time renamed Israel), his brothers and their families.

One of the younger sons but favored by his father, Joseph was resented deeply by his brothers who sold him into slavery and told his father he was dead. In Egypt he repeatedly overcame great obstacles until he rose to the right hand of Pharaoh. Famine sent his brothers to Egypt for food where they came before Joseph who, after testing them, brought his father's family to live in safety in Egypt about 1875 BC. The Joseph stories exhibit an overwhelmingly Egyptian context that fits well what is known of this period. Joseph's story provides the explanation for why Jacob's family and the tribes of Israel found themselves in Egypt for the next 430 years.

▲ Well at modern Beersheba though by some to be Abraham's well. Abraham and a nearby king, Abimelech, swore to protect Abraham's right to the water of the region (Gen. 21:22-33). Abraham then named the place "Beersheba," meaning "well of the oath" or preferably "well of the seven," referring to seven lambs involved in the agreement.

23 ▶ MIDDLE BRONZE AGE

DATE	MESOPOTAMIA	EGYPT	PALESTINE
2100 BC	*Third Dynasty or Ur* (2113-2006) Ur-Nammu		Emergence of urban centers after two centuries of decline; Abraham, Isaac, and Jacob's migrations
2000 BC		*Middle Kingdom:* Late Eleventh and Twelfth Dynasties (ca. 2000-1786 BC)	
	Increasing domination over Mesopotamia by Amorites		
		Tale of Sinuhe	
1900 BC		Execration Texts	
1800 BC	*Old Babylonian Kingdom* Hammurabi (1792-1750)	*Second Intermediate Period;* Thirteenth through Seventeenth Dynasties	*Classical Canaanite Era;* many heavily fortified cities; introduction of Bronze technology
	(Zimri-lim, king of Mari)	infiltration of Asiatics (Hyksos)	
	Law code of Hammurabi		
	Babylonian Literary Epics: Gilgamesh Epic; Enuma Elish		
1700 BC		Egyptian unity collapses; Hyksos kings rule the Delta and central Egypt from Avaris; native Egyptian kings maintain some control on southern Egypt	
1600 BC		(Descent of Joseph and his brothers into the Delta of Egypt?)	Indication of earliest writing in Palestine
1550 BC	Sack of Babylon by the Hittite King Mursilis I	Kings of the Seventeenth Dynasty (Kamose, Seqenenre, and Ahmose) drive Hyksos from the Delta, attacking Hyksos strongholds in southern Palestine	

PATRIARCHAL PERIOD

The date of the patriarchal period has been much discussed. A time before 2000 BC (early Bronze Age) seems too early and cannot be supported easily by reference to current archaeological evidence. The middle Bronze period (2000–1500 BC) seems more promising because of contemporary archaeological parallels and also because many of the Negev irrigation systems date from that period. Some

24 THE ANCIENT NEAR EAST IN THE TIME OF THE PATRIARCHS

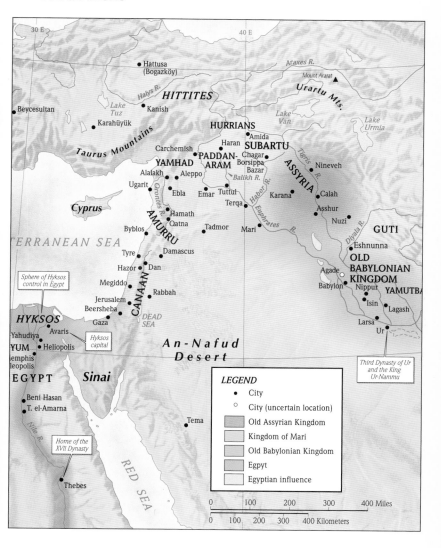

scholars have suggested the Amarna period (1500–1300 BC) as the one in which the patriarchs lived, but this presents problems for any dating for the exodus. The same objection applies to a late Bronze Age (1500–1200 BC) period for the patriarchs. The least likely date is in the judges period or the time of King David. All such dates do not allow time for the patriarchal traditions to have developed and make it impossible for Abraham, Isaac, and Jacob to be fitted realistically into an already known chronology. A date in the middle Bronze Age seems to offer the most suitable solution to a complex problem of dating.

25▶ PALESTINE IN THE MIDDLE BRONZE AGE

LEGEND
- City
- City (uncertain location)
- City (mentioned in Execration texts)

MEDITERRANEAN SEA

"T." typically denotes a modern name for an ancient place. These terms are generally not found in the Bible.

Beq'a

Damascus

Pharpar River

Litani River

Dan (Laish)

Kedesh
Iqrat
Achzib
T. Kabri
Hazor

Acco
T. Kisan

Achshaph
Yokneam
T. Shimron

Sea of Galilee

Dor
T. Burga
T. Zeror
Taanach
Megiddo
T. Rekhesh

Yarmuk River

Beth-shan
Rehob
Pehel (Pella)

Dothan

Gath-padalla

T. Poleg
T. el-Farah (Tirzah)

Jordan River

T. Gerisa
Aphek
Shechem
Shiloh

Jabbok River

Joppa

Yavne Yam
Gibeon
Bethel
Jericho

SHUTU

Gezer
Jerusalem

Ashdod
Timnah
Beth-shemesh

T. Zafit
Ashkelon
Beth-zur
Shaveh-kiriathaim

T. el-Ajjul
T. Nagila
Gerar
Lachish
Hebron

T. Jemmeh
T. Beit Mirsim

Arnon River

T. Malhata
DEAD SEA

T. el-Farah (S)
T. Masos

Zoar
Zered River

W. el-Arish

0 10 20 30 40 50 Miles
0 10 20 30 40 50 Kilometers

35 E

36 E

33 N

32 N

31 N

26▶ FAMILY OF ABRAHAM

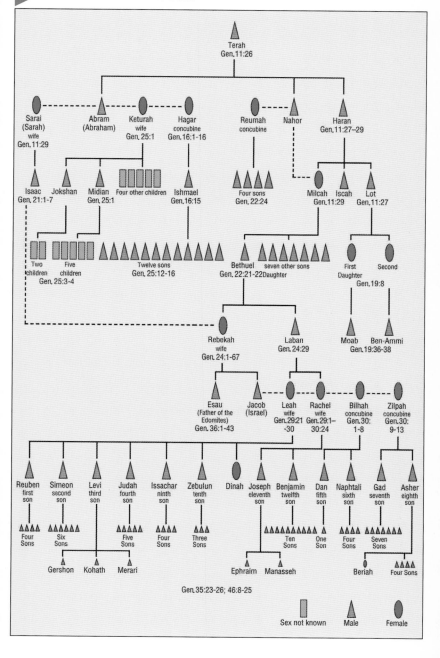

Terah
Gen. 11:26

Sarai (Sarah)
wife
Gen. 11:29

Abram (Abraham)

Keturah
wife
Gen. 25:1

Hagar
concubine
Gen. 16:1-16

Reumah
concubine

Nahor

Haran
Gen. 11:27-29

Isaac
Gen. 21:1-7

Jokshan

Midian
Gen. 25:1

Four other children

Ishmael
Gen. 16:15

Four sons
Gen. 22:24

Milcah
Gen. 11:29

Iscah

Lot
Gen. 11:27

Two children

Five children
Gen. 25:3-4

Twelve sons
Gen. 25:12-16

Bethuel
Gen. 22:21-22

seven other sons
Daughter

First Daughter
Gen. 19:8

Second

Rebekah
wife
Gen. 24:1-67

Laban
Gen. 24:29

Moab
Gen. 19:36-38

Ben-Ammi

Esau
(Father of the Edomites)
Gen. 36:1-43

Jacob
(Israel)

Leah
wife
Gen. 29:21-30

Rachel
wife
Gen. 29:1–30:24

Bilhah
concubine
Gen. 30:1-8

Zilpah
concubine
Gen. 30:9-13

Reuben
first son

Simeon
second son

Levi
third son

Judah
fourth son

Issachar
ninth son

Zebulun
tenth son

Dinah

Joseph
eleventh son

Benjamin
twelfth son

Dan
fifth son

Naphtali
sixth son

Gad
seventh son

Asher
eighth son

Four Sons

Six Sons

Five Sons

Four Sons

Three Sons

Ten Sons

One Son

Four Sons

Seven Sons

Gershon Kohath Merari

Ephraim Manasseh

Beriah Four Sons

Gen. 35:23-26; 46:8-25

Sex not known   Male   Female

27 LIFE OF ABRAHAM

EVENT	OLD TESTAMENT PASSAGE	NEW TESTAMENT REFERENCE
The birth of Abram	Gen. 11:26	
God's call of Abram	Gen. 12:1-3	Heb. 11:8
The entry into Canaan	Gen. 12:4-9	
Abram in Egypt	Gen. 12:10-20	
Lot separates from Abram	Gen. 13:1-18	
Abram rescues Lot	Gen. 14:1-17	
Abram pays tithes to Melchizedek	Gen. 14:18-24	Heb. 7:1-10
God's covenant with Abraham	Gen. 15:1-21 Gal. 3:6-25 Heb. 6:13-20	Rom. 4:1-25
The birth of Ishmael	Gen. 16:1-16	
Abraham promised a son by Sarah	Gen. 17:1-27 Heb. 11:11-12	Rom. 4:18-25
Abraham intercedes for Sodom	Gen. 18:16-33	
Lot saved and Sodom destroyed	Gen. 19:1-38	
The birth of Isaac	Gen. 21:1-7	
Hagar and Ishmael sent away	Gen. 21:8-21	Gal. 4:21-31
Abraham challenged to offer Isaac as sacrifice	Gen. 22:1-19	Heb. 11:17-19 Jas. 2:20-24
The death of Sarah	Gen. 23:1-20	
The death of Abraham	Gen. 25:1-11	

28▶ THE MIGRATION OF ABRAHAM

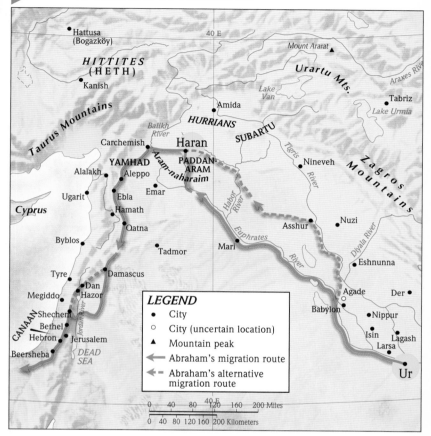

Genesis 11:31

Terah took his son Abram, his grandson Lot (Haran's son), and his daughter-in-law Sarai, his son Abram's wife, and they set out together from Ur of the Chaldeans to go to the land of Canaan. But when they came to Haran, they settled there.

Genesis 12:1,4

The LORD said to Abram: "Go out from your land, your relatives, and your father's house to the land that I will show you." . . .

So Abram went, as the LORD had told him, and Lot went with him. Abram was 75 years old when he left Haran.

29 ► ABRAHAM IN CANAAN

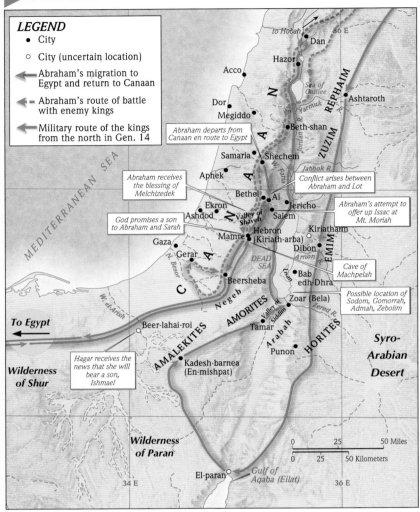

LEGEND
- ● City
- ○ City (uncertain location)
- ◄— Abraham's migration to Egypt and return to Canaan
- ◄ = Abraham's route of battle with enemy kings
- ◄— Military route of the kings from the north in Gen. 14

Abraham departs from Canaan en route to Egypt

Abraham receives the blessing of Melchizedek

Conflict arises between Abraham and Lot

Abraham's attempt to offer up Issac at Mt. Moriah

God promises a son to Abraham and Sarah

Cave of Machpelah

Possible location of Sodom, Gomorrah, Admah, Zeboiim

Hagar receives the news that she will bear a son, Ishmael

to Hobah · Dan · 36 E · Hazor · Acco · Sea of Galilee · Ashtaroth · Dor · Megiddo · Beth-shan · Samaria · Shechem · Jabbok R. · Aphek · Bethel · Ai · Jericho · Ekron · Salem · Ashdod · Valley of Shaveh · Kiriathaim · Mamre · Hebron (Kiriath-arba) · Dibon · Gaza · Arnon · Gerar · DEAD SEA · Beersheba · Bab edh-Dhra · Zoar (Bela) · To Egypt · Beer-lahai-roi · Tamar · Punon · Kadesh-barnea (En-mishpat) · **Syro-Arabian Desert** · **Wilderness of Shur** · **Wilderness of Paran** · El-paran · Gulf of Aqaba (Eilat) · 34 E · 36 E

MEDITERRANEAN SEA · CANAAN · REPHAIM · ZUZIM · EMIM · AMORITES · HORITES · AMALEKITES · Negeb · Arabah

0 · 25 · 50 Miles
0 · 25 · 50 Kilometers

Genesis 12:10
There was a famine in the land, so Abram went down to Egypt to live there for a while because the famine in the land was severe.

30 TRAVELS OF JACOB

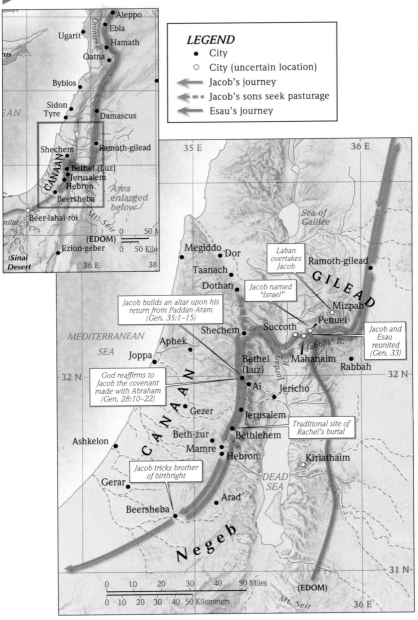

LEGEND
- • City
- ○ City (uncertain location)
- → Jacob's journey
- ⟵--- Jacob's sons seek pasturage
- → Esau's journey

Aleppo
Ebla
Ugarit
Hamath
Qatna
Byblos
Sidon
Tyre
Damascus
Shechem
Ramoth-gilead
Bethel (Luz)
Jerusalem
Hebron
Beersheba
CANAAN
Area enlarged below
Beer-lahai-roi
(EDOM)
Ezion-geber
Sinai Desert
Orontes R.
Mt. Seir
0   50 M
0   50 Kilo
35 E   36 E   38

35 E   36 E

Sea of Galilee

Megiddo Dor
Taanach
Dothan

Laban overtakes Jacob

Ramoth-gilead

G I L E A D

Jacob named "Israel"

Mizpah
Penuel

Jacob builds an altar upon his return from Paddan-Aram (Gen. 35:1–15)

MEDITERRANEAN SEA
Aphek
Joppa

Shechem   Succoth

Jabbok R.

Jacob and Esau reunited (Gen. 33)

Bethel (Luz)   Mahanaim
Rabbah

God reaffirms to Jacob the covenant made with Abraham (Gen. 28:10–22)

Ai   Jericho

32 N   32 N

C A N A A N

Gezer
Beth-zur   Jerusalem
Ashkelon   Bethlehem

Traditional site of Rachel's burial

Mamre   Hebron

Jacob tricks brother of birthright

Gerar   Kiriathaim

DEAD SEA

Beersheba   Arad

N e g e b

31 N

0   10   20   30   40   50 Miles
0   10   20   30   40 50 Kilometers

(EDOM)

Mt. Seir   36 E

Jordan R.

Genesis 28:12-13

And he dreamed: A stairway was set on the ground with its top reaching heaven, and God's angels were going up and down on it.

The LORD was standing there beside him, saying, "I am the LORD, the God of your father Abraham and the God of Isaac. I will give you and your offspring the land that you are now sleeping on."

31▶ THE JOURNEYS OF JOSEPH

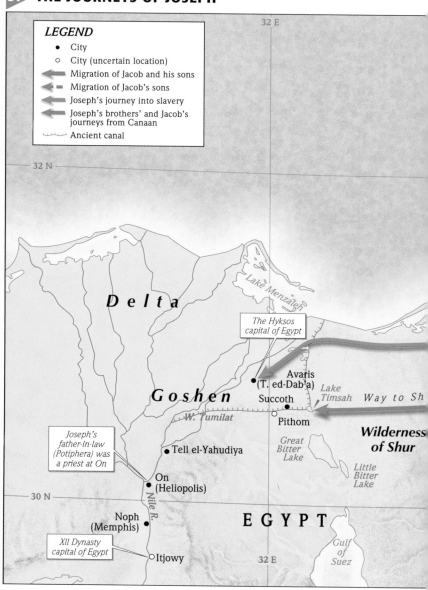

LEGEND
- • City
- ○ City (uncertain location)
- ← Migration of Jacob and his sons
- ←■ Migration of Jacob's sons
- ← Joseph's journey into slavery
- ← Joseph's brothers' and Jacob's journeys from Canaan
- ⌣⌣⌣ Ancient canal

32 E

32 N

Lake Menzaleh

D e l t a

The Hyksos capital of Egypt

G o s h e n

Avaris
(T. ed-Dab'a)

Lake Timsah   *Way to Sh*

Succoth

W. Tumilat

Pithom

Joseph's father-in-law (Potiphera) was a priest at On

Wilderness of Shur

Great Bitter Lake

• Tell el-Yahudiya

Little Bitter Lake

On
(Heliopolis)

30 N

Noph
(Memphis) •

E G Y P T

Nile R.

Gulf of Suez

XII Dynasty capital of Egypt

○ Itjowy

32 E

Genesis 37:3-4

Now Israel loved Joseph more than his other sons because Joseph was a son born to him in his old age, and he made a robe of many colors for him. When his brothers saw that their father loved him more than all his brothers, they hated him and could not bring themselves to speak peaceably to him.

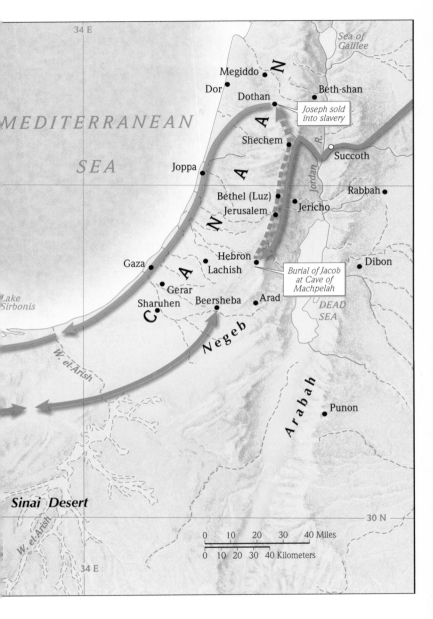

Genesis 46:2-4

That night God spoke to Israel in a vision: "Jacob, Jacob!" He said. And Jacob replied, "Here I am."

God said, "I am God, the God of your father. Do not be afraid to go down to Egypt, for I will make you a great nation there. I will go down with you to Egypt, and I will also bring you back. Joseph will put his hands on your eyes."

THE EXODUS

▲ The Temple of Luxor, Egypt, at night.

The Egyptian Period

Several hundred years of relative silence separate the end of the story of Joseph (Gen. 37–50) from the beginning of the story told in the Book of Exodus. Joseph's story indicates that Israel probably entered Egypt in the middle of the illustrious Twelfth Dynasty (ca. 1875–1850 BC). The Hyksos (Egyptian for "rulers of foreign lands") were an Asiatic people who seized control of Egypt during a time of

Sailboat on the Nile River near Luxor.

political instability, overthrowing native Egyptian dynasties around 1730–1710 BC. The Hyksos established their capital in the Nile River Delta at Avaris and controlled northern Egypt for about 250–260 years. The Hyksos were the people of the king who "knew not Joseph." The Hyksos did not control all Egypt for much of their sojourn but were leaders of a federation of rulers over various parts of Egypt. With their accession the lot of the Israelites worsened. No longer favored by the pharaohs, they instead were reduced to servitude. The Hyksos were expelled from Egypt about 1570 BC.

Moses appeared early in the new kingdom era, born about 1526 BC. His parents, Amram and Jochebed, sought to save his life from Pharaoh's decree, that all male Hebrew infants be killed, by setting him adrift on the Nile in a basket. His basket came to rest at the place where a daughter of Pharaoh bathed. She took the child in and raised him as the grandson of Pharaoh. Educated in the palace of Egypt, Moses received one of the finest educations in the world. Learning a spectrum of languages and a wide variety of subject matter that prepared him well to lead and govern the Israelites after they left Egypt.

View of Giza, Egypt, showing two of three pyramids located here together with the famous Sphinx.

Interior chapel of Hatshepsut's festival hall. Hatshepsut was the wife of Thutmose II and the aunt and stepmother of Thumose III, believed by some to be the pharaoh of the Exodus.

Likely the pharaoh of Moses' infancy was Amenhotep I, and the successor who especially oppressed the Israelites was Thutmose I who reigned 1526–1512 BC. Thutmose II reigned 1512–1504 BC and Thutmose III 1504–1450 BC Moses' foster mother likely was a powerful woman named Hatshepsut, who effectively controlled Egypt while Thutmose III was still a minor after his accession to the throne. Thutmose III fits best the pharaoh who sought Moses' life when he had killed a prominent Egyptian (at about age 40), and his successor Amenhotep II (reigned 1450–1425 BC) was probably the pharaoh of the exodus, which most likely occurred in 1447 or 1446 BC.

The Exodus from Egypt—ca. 1447 BC

The exodus from Egypt was a foundational event in the history of Israel. This is graphically confirmed by the fact that some variation of the formula that Yahweh "brought you (Israel) up out of Egypt and the house of bondage" occurs 125 times in the OT.

Some scholars see the exodus as the miraculous deliverance of the people of God from the grip of Pharaoh's army at the Red Sea. Others see it as an escape across a sprawling wilderness and sweltering desert of a small mixed band of border slaves. Some argue that the military language in the account indicates that the event was a military skirmish. Such language may be the language of holy war.

The Bible stresses that the exodus was the work of God. God brought the plagues on Egypt (Exod. 7:1-5). The miracle at the sea was never treated merely as a natural event or as Israel's victory alone. In the earliest recorded response to the event Miriam sang, "Sing to the Lord, for He is highly exalted; the horse and his rider He has hurled into the sea" (Exod. 15:21 NASB).

Elements of the wonderful and the ordinary contributed to the greatest OT events. The natural and supernatural combined to produce God's deliverance. The exodus was both miraculous and historical. An air of mystery surrounds this event as all miraculous events. Despite the time reference in 1 Kings 6:1 and Judges 11:26, when the exodus occurred is still a hotly contested issue. Rather than this fifteenth-century date, many scholars place the exodus during the thirteenth century when Ramesses II was Pharaoh. We do not know precisely where it happened since the Hebrew term may have meant the Red Sea as we know it, one of its tributaries, or a "sea of reeds" whose location is unknown. We do not know who or how many may have been involved. The record makes clear that God delivered Israel from bondage because of His covenant with the patriarchs and because He desired to redeem His people (Exod. 6:2-8).

▲ Lake Timsah, possibly the place where the Hebrews crossed the Red Sea.

Israel arrived at Mount Sinai around 1447 BC. Though various locations have been suggested, the best option for the location of Mount Sinai is the traditional site Jebel Musa in the southern end of the Sinai Peninsula. At Sinai Israel entered into covenant with Yahweh, received the Ten Commandments, and began her first experience in self-governance.

The Wilderness Period—ca. 1447–1407 BC

About a year later they started for the land of promise but were deterred from entry, first by disobedience and then by God, and did not arrive in Canaan for another 40 years. A remarkable sense of identity and mission emerged during the years in the Sinai wilderness. Also during these years Israel received all the legislation necessary for an orderly society. Good times and bad characterized Israel's wilderness experience. God supernaturally protected and preserved Israel, but the generation that refused to enter the land at God's command died out except for the two faithful spies, Joshua and Caleb.

 The desolate country of the Wilderness of Sin.

The Number Involved in the Exodus

In our English Bibles Exodus 12:37 says, "Now the sons of Israel journeyed from Rameses to Succoth, about six hundred thousand men on foot, aside from children" (NASB). For various reasons (water/food supply in Sinai, evidence of burials, etc.) current scholarship translates the Hebrew word for "thousand" as "clan or military unit." This view results in drastically reducing the numbers of Israelites in the exodus, as well as in the rest of OT. However, they must admit that this translation cannot be used consistently in this manner throughout the OT for some numbers are more specific. Numbers 1:46 states more specifically that God commanded Moses to take a census in the second year after the exodus from Egypt and the men of war numbered–603,550. It is not unusual for round numbers to be used at times both in the Bible and in the Ancient Near East, but this does not mean the rounded numbers lack historicity, or veracity. Just prior to entering the promised land, in Numbers 26, God commanded Moses to take a census after the plague caused by immorality with the Moabite women. The Israelites numbered 601,730 men of war (Num. 26:51) over the age of twenty (Num. 1:3). The differences in the numbers found in Exod. 12 and Num. 26 may be attributed to the death of the older exodus generation through both divine judgment and natural causes as well as the increase through new births in the first 20 of the 40 years of wandering in the

▲ Jebel Musa, the traditional site of Mount Sinai, in the southern Sinai Peninsula.

◄ View from Jebel Musa (the probable location of Mount Sinai) of the surrounding rugged landscape.

wilderness of Sinai. Some scholars try to get around large numbers which are specific by breaking the number into two parts—the thousands being military units/clans and the hundreds standing for the actual number of men, but this method breaks down when we see in Numbers 1:46 [603,550] 603 military units/clans but a total of only 550 men. If the statistics are correct that males over the age of 20 make up approximately 25 percent of the total population, then the Israelites numbered well over two million people at both the beginning and the end of the wilderness wanderings.

The exodus was the work of God. It was a historical event involving a superpower nation and an oppressed people. God acted redemptively in power, freedom, and love. When the kingdom of God did not come, the later prophets began to look for a second exodus. That expectation was fulfilled spiritually in Christ's redemptive act.

32 THE ROUTE OF THE EXODUS

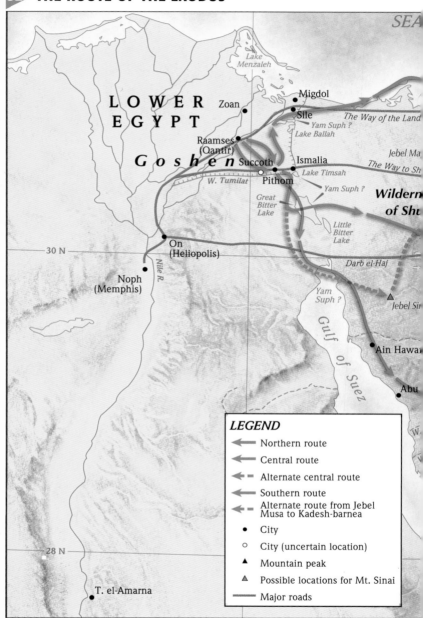

Exodus 14:21-22

Then Moses stretched out his hand over the sea. The LORD drove the sea back with a powerful east wind all that night and turned the sea into dry land. So the waters were divided, and the Israelites went through the sea on dry ground, with the waters like a wall to them on their right and their left.

Exodus 14:29-31

But the Israelites had walked through the sea on dry ground, with the waters like a wall to them on their right and their left. That day the LORD saved Israel from the power of the Egyptians, and Israel saw the Egyptians dead on the seashore. When Israel saw the great power that the LORD used against the Egyptians, the people feared the LORD and believed in Him and in His servant Moses.

33 THE TEN PLAGUES OF EGYPT

PLAGUE	SCRIPTURE
1. WATER TO BLOOD—The waters of the Nile turned to blood.	Exod. 7:14-25
2. FROGS—Frogs infested the land of Egypt.	Exod. 8:1-15
3. GNATS (Mosquitoes)—Small stinging insects infested the land of Egypt.	Exod. 8:16-19
4. FLIES—Swarms of flies, possibly a biting variety, infested the land of Egypt.	Exod. 8:20-32
5. PLAGUE ON THE CATTLE—A serious disease, possibly anthrax, infested the cattle belonging to Egyptians.	Exod. 9:1-7
6. BOILS—A skin disease infected the Egyptians.	Exod. 9:8-12
7. HAIL—A storm that destroyed the grain fields of Egypt but spared the land of Goshen inhabited by the Israelites.	Exod. 9:13-35
8. LOCUSTS—An infestation of locusts stripped the land of Egypt of plant life.	Exod. 10:1-20
9. DARKNESS—A deep darkness covered the land of Egypt for three days.	Exod. 10:21-29
10. DEATH OF THE FIRSTBORN—The firstborn of every Egyptian family died.	Exod. 11:1–12:30

THE SACRIFICIAL SYSTEM

NAME	REFERENCE	ELEMENTS	SIGNIFICANCE
Burnt Offering	Lev. 1; 6:8-13	Bull, ram, male goat, male dove, or young pigeon without blemish. (Always male animals, but species of animal varied according to individual's economic status.)	Voluntary. Signifies propitiation for sin and complete surrender, devotion, and commitment to God.
Grain Offering Also called Meal, or Tribute, Offering	Lev. 2; 6:14-23	Flour, bread, or grain made with olive oil and salt (always unleavened); or incense.	Voluntary. Signifies thanksgiving for firstfruits.
Fellowship Offering Also called Peace Offering: includes (1) Thank Offering, (2) Vow Offering, and (3) Freewill Offering	(1) Lev. 3; 7:11-36; 22:17-30; 27	Any animal without blemish. (Species of animal varied according to individual's economic status.) (1) Can be grain offering.	Voluntary. Symbolizes fellowship with God. (1) Signifies thankfulness for a specific blessing; (2) offers a ritual expression of a vow; and (3) symbolizes general thankfulness (to be brought to one of three required religious services).
Sin Offering	Lev. 4:1–5:13; 6:24-30; 12:6-8	Male or female animal without blemish—as follows: bull for high priest on congregation; male goat for king; female goat or lamb for common person; dove or pigeon for slightly poor; tenth of an ephah of flour for the very poor.	Mandatory. Made by one who had sinned unintentionally or was unclean in order to attain purification.
Guilt Offering	Lev. 5:14–6:7; 7:1-6; 14:12-18	Ram or lamb without blemish.	Mandatory. Made by a person who had either deprived another of his rights or had desecrated something holy. Made by lepers for purification.

35► THE TEN COMMANDMENTS

COMMANDMENT	PASSAGE	RELATED OLD TESTAMENT PASSAGES
You shall have no other gods before me.	Exod. 20:3; Deut. 5:7	Exod. 34:14; Deut. 6:4,13-14; 2 Kings 17:35; Ps. 81:9; Jer. 25:6 35:15
You shall not make for yourself an idol.	Exod. 20:4-6; Deut. 5:8-10	Exod. 20:23; 32:8; 34:17; Lev. 19 26:1; Deut. 4:15-20; 7:25; 32:21; Ps. 115:4-7; Isa. 44:12-20
You shall not misuse the name of the Lord.	Exod. 20:7; Deut. 5:11	Exod. 22:28; Lev. 18:21; 19:12; 22 24:16; Ezek. 39:7
Remember the Sabbath day by keeping it holy.	Exod. 20:8-11; Deut. 5:12-15	Gen. 2:3; Exod. 16:23-30; 31:13- 35:2-3; Lev. 19:30; Isa. 56:2; Jer. 17:21-27
Honor your father and your mother.	Exod. 20:12; Deut. 5:16	Exod. 21:17; Lev. 19:3; Deut. 21: 21; 27:16; Prov. 6:20
You shall not murder.	Exod. 20:13; Deut. 5:17	Gen. 9:6; Lev. 24:17; Num. 35:33
You shall not commit adultery.	Exod. 20:14; Deut. 5:18	Lev. 18:20; 20:10; Deut. 22:22; Num. 5:12-31; Prov. 6:29,32
You shall not steal.	Exod. 20:15; Deut. 5:19	Lev. 19:11,13; Ezek. 18:7
You shall not give false testimony.	Exod. 20:16; Deut. 5:20	Exod. 23:1, 7; Lev .19:11; Pss. 15:2 101:5; Prov. 10:18; Jer. 9:3-5; Zech. 8
You shall not covet.	Exod. 20:17; Deut. 5:21	Deut. 7:25; Job 31:24-28; Ps. 62

RELATED NEW TESTAMENT PASSAGES	JESUS' TEACHINGS
Acts 5:29	Matt. 4:10; 6:33; 22:37-40
Acts 17:29; 1 Cor. 8:4-6, 10-14; 1 John 5:21	Matt. 6:24; Luke 16:13
Rom. 2:23-24; James 5:12	Matt. 5:33-37; 6:9; 23:16-22
Acts 20:7; Heb. 10:25	Matt. 12:1-13; Mark 2:23-27; 3:1-6; Luke 6:1-11; John 5:1-18
Eph. 6:1-3; Col. 3:20	Matt. 15:4-6; 19:19; Mark 7:9-13; Luke 2:51; 18:20; John 19:26-27
Rom. 13:9-10; 1 Pet. 4:15	Matt. 5:21-24; 19:18; Mark 10:19; Luke 18:20
Rom. 13:9-10; 1 Cor. 6:9; Heb. 13:4; James 2:11	Matt. 5:27-30; 19:18; Mark 10:19; Luke 18:20; John 8:1-11
Rom. 13:9-10; Eph. 4:28; James 5:4	Matt. 19:18; Mark 10:19; 12:40; Luke 18:20
Eph. 4:25,31; Col. 3:9; Titus 3:2	Matt. 5:37; 19:18; Mark 10:19; Luke 18:20
Rom. 7:7; 13:9; Eph. 5:3-5; Heb. 13:5; James 4:1-2	Luke 12:15-34

36 ARK OF THE COVENANT

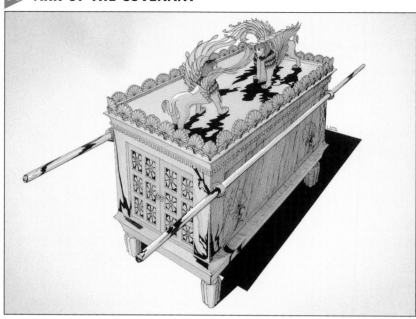

37 THE TABERNACLE

JEWISH FEASTS AND FESTIVALS

NAME	MONTH: DATE	REFERENCE	SIGNIFICANCE
Passover	Nisan (Mar./Apr.): 14-21	Exod. 12:2-20; Lev. 23:5	Commemorates God's deliverence of Israel out of Egypt.
Feast of Unleavened Bread	Nisan (Mar./Apr.): 15-21	Lev. 23:6-8	Commemorates God's deliverence of Israel out of Egypt. Includes a Day of Firstfruits for the barley harvest.
Feast of Weeks, or Harvest (Pentecost)	Sivan (May/June): 6 (seven weeks after Passover)	Exod. 23:16; 34:22; Lev. 23:15-21	Commemorates the giving of the law at Mount Sinai. Includes a Day of Firstfruits for the wheat harvest.
Feast of Trumpets (Rosh Hashanah)	Tishri (Sept./Oct.): 1	Lev. 23:23-25 Num. 29:1-6	Day of the blowing of the trumpets to signal the beginning of the civil new year.
Day of Atonement (Yom Kippur)	Tishri (Sept./Oct.): 10	Lev. 23:26-33; Exod. 30:10	On this day the high priest makes atonement for the nation's sin. Also a day of fasting.
Feast of Booths, or Tabernacles (Sukkot)	Tishri (Sept./Oct.): 15-21	Lev. 23:33-43; Num. 29:12-39; Deut. 16:13	Commemorates the forty years of wilderness wandering.
Feast of Dedication, or Festival of Lights (Hanukkah)	Kislev (Nov./Dec.): 25-30; and Tebeth (Dec./Jan.): 1-2	John 10:22	Commemorates the purification of the temple by Judas Maccabaeus in 164 BC.
Feast of Purim, or Esther	Adar (Feb./Mar.): 14	Esther 9	Commemorates the deliverance of the Jewish people in the days of Esther.

39 JEWISH CALENDAR

YEAR		MONTH	ENGLISH MONTHS (NEARLY)
Sacred 1	Civil 7	Nison/Abib 30 days	April
2	8 29 days	Iyyar/Ziv	May
3	9 30 days	Sivan	June
4	10 29 days	Tammuz	July
5	11 30 days	Ab	August
6	12 29 days	Elul	September
7	1 30 days	Tishri/Ethanim	October
8	2 29 days	Marchesran/Bul	November
9	3 30 days	Chislev	December
10	4 29 days	Tebeth	January
11	5 30 days	Shebat	February
12	6 29 days	Adar	March
13	Leap year Sheni	Veadar/Adar	March/April

FESTIVALS	SEASONS AND PRODUCTIONS
1 New Moon 14 The Passover 15-21 Unleavened Bread	Spring rains (Deut. 11:14) Floods (Josh. 3:15) Barley ripe of Jericho
1 New Moon 14 Second Passover (for those unable to keep first) Summer begins No rain from April to Sept. (1 Sam. 12:17)	Harvest Barley Harvest (Ruth 1:22) Wheat Harvest
1 New Moon 6 Pentecost	
1 New Moon 17 Fast for the taking of Jerusalem	Hot Season Heat increases
1 New Moon 9 Fast for the destruction of Temple	The streams dry up Heat intense Vintage (Lev. 26:5)
1 New Moon (2 Kings 4:19) Grape harvest (Num. 13:23)	Heat intense
1 New Year, Day of Blowing of Trumpet Day of Judgment and Memorial (Num. 29:1) 10 Day of Atonement (Lev. 16) 15 Booths 21 (Lev. 23:24) 22 Solemn Assembly	Seed time Former or early rains begin (Joel 2:23) Plowing and sowing begin
1 New Moon Wheat and barley sown	Rain continues
1 New Moon 25 Dedication (John 10:22,29) Snow on mountains	Winter Winter begins
1 New Moon 10 Fast for the siege of Jerusalem	Coldest month Hail and snow (Josh. 10:11)
1 New Moon	Weather gradually warmer
1 New Moon 13 Fast of Esther 14-15 Purim	Thunder and hail frequent Almond tree blossoms
1 New Moon 13 Fast of Esther 14-15 Purim	Intercalary Month

40 NAMES OF GOD

NAME	REFERENCE	MEANING
Hebrew Names		
Adonai	Ps. 2:4	Lord, Master
El-Shaddai	Gen. 17:1-2	All Powerful God
El-Elyon	Gen. 14:18-20	Most High God/Exalted One
El-Olam	Gen. 21:33	The Eternal God
El-Berith	Judg. 9:46	God of the Covenant
El-Roi	Gen. 16:13	God Who Sees Me
Qedosh Yisra'el	Isa. 1:4	The Holy One of Israel
Shapat	Gen. 18:25	Judge/Ruler
Yahweh-Jireh	Gen. 22:14	Yahweh Provides
Yahweh-Nissi	Exod. 17:15	Yahweh My Banner
Yahweh-Mekaddesh	Exod. 31:13	Yahweh Sanctifies
Yahweh-Shalom	Judg. 6:24	Yahweh My Peace
Yahweh-Sabaoth	1 Sam. 1:3	Yahweh of Armies
Yahweh-Rohi	Ps. 23:1	Yahweh My Shepherd
Yahweh-Shammah	Ezek. 48:35	Yahweh Is There
Yahweh-Tsidkenu	Jer. 23:6	Yahweh Our Righteousness
Aramaic Names		
Attiq yomin	Dan. 7:9	Ancient of Days
Illaya	Dan. 7:25	Most High

41 COVENANTS AND LAW CODES

LAW CODE		COVENANT*
Title	Identifies superior partner.	Title
Prologue	Shows how the superior partner has cared for the subordinate one in the past, thereby inspiring gratitude and obedience within the subordinate partner.	Prologue
Laws	Lists the laws given by the superior partner which are to be obeyed by the subordinate partner.	Stipulations/Laws
Blessings and Curses	Provides for the preservation of the text in the temple of the subordinate partner.	Depositions Reading
	Witnessed and guaranteed by the gods of both partners.	Witnesses
	Pronounces curses on those who disobey and blessings on those who obey.	Blessings and Curses
	Ratified by an oath and a ceremony, and sanctions are pronounced against any person who breaks the covenantal relationship.	Oath Ceremony Sanctions

* Covenants also follow the pattern of an ancient Near Eastern treaty. See the discussion in the introduction to the Book of Deuteronomy.

42 ▶ PRIESTS IN THE OLD TESTAMENT

NAME	REFERENCE	IDENTIFICATION
Aaron	Exod. 28–29	Older brother of Moses; first high priest of Israel
Abiathar	1 Sam. 22:20-23; 2 Sam. 20:25	Son of Ahimelech who escaped the slayings at Nob
Abihu	See Nadab and Abihu	
Ahimelech	1 Sam. 21–22	Led a priestly community at Nob; killed by Saul for befriending David
Amariah	2 Chron. 19:11	High priest during the reign of Jehoshaphat
Amaziah	Amos 7:10-17	Evil priest of Bethel; confronted Amos the prophet
Azariah	2 Chron. 26:16-20	High priest who stood against Uzziah when the ruler began to act as a prophet
Eleazar and Ithamar	Lev. 10:6; Num. 20:26	Godly sons of Aaron; Eleazar—Israel's second high priest
Eli	1 Sam. 1–4	Descendant of Ithamar; raised Samuel at Shiloh
Eliashib	Neh. 3:1; 13:4-5	High priest during the time of Nehemiah
Elishama and Jehoram	2 Chron. 17:7-9	Teaching priests during the reign of Jehoshaphat
Ezra	Ezra 7–10; Neh. 8	Scribe, teacher, and priest during the rebuilding of Jerusalem after the Babylonian captivity
Hilkiah	2 Kings 22–23	High priest during the reign of Josiah
Hophni and Phinehas	1 Sam. 2:12-36	Evil sons of Eli
Ithamar	See Eleazar and Ithamar	Levite who assured Jehoshaphat of deliverance from an enemy
Jahaziel	2 Chron. 20:14-17	High priest who saved Joash from Queen Athaliah's purge
Jehoiada	2 Kings 11–12	
Jehoram	See Eliashama and Jehoram	
Joshua	Hag. 1:1,12; Zech. 3	First high priest after the Babylonian captivity
Nadab and Abihu	Lev. 10:1-2	Evil sons of Aaron
Pashhur	Jer. 20:1-6	False priest who persecuted the prophet Jeremiah
Phinehas	(1) Num. 25:7-13 (2) See Hophni and Phinehas	(1) Son of Eleazar; Israel's third high priest whose zeal for pure worship stopped a plague
Shelemiah	Neh. 13:13	Priest during the time of Nehemiah; was in charge of administrating storehouses
Uriah	2 Kings 16:10-16	Priest who built pagan altar for evil King Ahaz
Zadok	2 Sam. 15; 1 Kings 1	High priest during the reign of David and Solomon

43 JOURNEY OF THE SPIES

LEGEND
- City
- ○ City (uncertain location)
- ◉ Oasis
- ▲ Mountain peak
- ← Journey of the twelve spies
- The promised land

Numbers 13:1–2,32

The LORD spoke to Moses: "Send men to scout out the land of Canaan I am giving to the Israelites. Send one man who is a leader among them from each of their ancestral tribes." . . . So they gave a negative report to the Israelites about the land they had scouted: "The land we passed through to explore is one that devours its inhabitants, and all the people we saw in it are men of great size.

THE CONQUEST OF CANAAN

Transition from Moses to Joshua—ca. 1407–1400 BC

Following its exodus from Egypt, Israel was within eleven days from the land of promise. But the journey that could be made in eleven days stretched out for a total of 40 years. Near the end of this period, Moses died and was buried by the Lord Himself; and Joshua, an Ephraimite, assumed leadership of the nation. Joshua occupies comparatively little space in the record. He is introduced as Moses' successor and as the conqueror of Canaan (Deut. 1:38; 3:21,28; Josh. 1). Outside the book bearing his name, he is mentioned only in Exod. 17:8-16; Judg. 1:1, 2:6-9; 1 Kings 16:34; 1 Chron. 7:27; and Neh. 8:17.

Joshua's Strategy

Ruins of a temple at Hazor destroyed by Joshua in the conquest of Canaan.

Joshua led a three-campaign invasion of Canaan. At the close of the wilderness wanderings, the Israelites arrived on the plains of Moab in the Transjordan ("beyond the Jordan"). There they subdued two local kings, Sihon and Og (Num. 21:21-35). Some of the Israelite tribes—Reuben, Gad, and half of the tribe of Manasseh—chose to settle in this newly conquered territory (Num. 32).

As God instructed him, Joshua led the people across the Jordan River into Canaan. The crossing was made possible by a supernatural separation of the water of the Jordan (Josh. 3–4). After crossing the river, the Israelites camped at Gilgal. From there Joshua led the first military campaign against the Canaanites in the sparsely populated central highlands, northwest of the Dead Sea. The initial object of the attack was the ancient stronghold of Jericho. The Israelite force marched around the city once a day for six days. On the seventh day they marched around it seven times, then blasted trumpets and shouted. In response the walls of Jericho collapsed, allowing the invaders to destroy the city (Josh. 6).

The Israelites then attempted to conquer the nearby city of Ai, where they met with their first defeat. The reason for the failure was that Achan, one of the Israelite soldiers, had kept some booty from the invasion of Jericho —an action which violated God's orders to destroy everything in the city. After Achan was executed, the Israelites were able to destroy Ai (Josh. 7–8).

In the foreground the tel of NT Jericho with the tel of OT Jericho behind.

Not all of the Canaanites tried to resist Israel's invasion. One group, the Gibeonites, avoided destruction by deceiving the Israelites into making a covenant of peace with them (Josh. 9). Alarmed by the defection of the Gibeonites to Israel, a group of southern Canaanite kings, led by Adoni-zedek of Jerusalem, formed a coalition against the invading force. The kings threatened to attack the Gibeonites, causing Joshua to come to the defense of his new allies. Because of supernatural intervention, the Israelites were able to defeat the coalition. Joshua then launched a southern campaign that resulted in the capture of numerous Canaanite cities (Josh. 10).

Joshua's third and last military campaign was in northern Canaan. In that region King Jabin of Hazor formed a coalition of neighboring kings to battle with the Israelites. Joshua made a surprise attack upon them at the waters of Merom, utterly defeating his foe (Josh. 11:1-15).

The invasion of Canaan met with phenomenal success; large portions of the land fell to the Israelites (Josh. 11:16–12:24). However, some areas still remained outside their control, such as the heavily populated land along the coast and several major Canaanite cities like Jerusalem (Josh. 13:1-5; 15:63; Judg. 1). The Israelites struggled for centuries to control these areas.

Israelite Settlement

The Israelite tribes slowly settled Canaan without completely removing the native population. Even though some sections of the land remained to be conquered, God instructed Joshua to apportion Canaan to the tribes which had not yet received territory (Josh. 13:7). Following the land allotments, Israel began to occupy its territory. Judges 1 describes the settlement as a slow process whereby individual tribes struggled to remove the Canaanites. In the final analysis the tribes had limited success in driving out the native population (Judg. 1). As a result, Israel was plagued for centuries by the infiltration of Canaanite elements into its religion (Judg. 2:1-5).

44 ▶ KADESH BARNEA

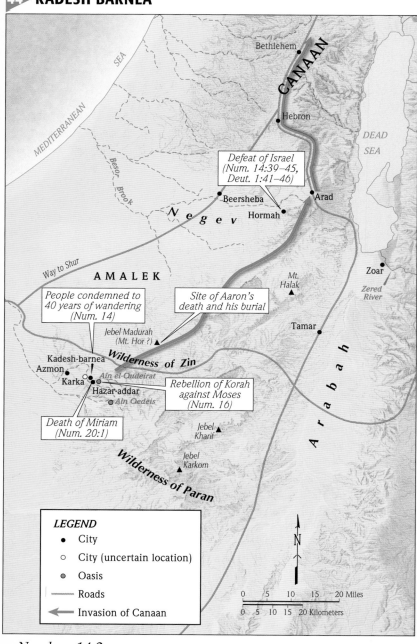

Bethlehem

CANAAN

MEDITERRANEAN SEA

Hebron

DEAD SEA

Defeat of Israel
(Num. 14:39–45,
Deut. 1:41–46)

Beersheba

Arad

N e g e v

Hormah

Way to Shur

A M A L E K

Zoar

Mt.
Halak ▲

Zered
River

People condemned to
40 years of wandering
(Num. 14)

Site of Aaron's
death and his burial

Jebel Madurah
(Mt. Hor ?) ▲

Tamar

Kadesh-barnea

Wilderness of Zin

A
r
a
b
a
h

Azmon

Karka

Ain el-Qudeirat

Hazar-addar

Rebellion of Korah
against Moses
(Num. 16)

Ain Qedeis

Death of Miriam
(Num. 20:1)

Jebel
Kharif ▲

Jebel
Karkom ▲

Wilderness of Paran

LEGEND
- ● City
- ○ City (uncertain location)
- ◉ Oasis
- — — Roads
- ◀— Invasion of Canaan

N

0   5   10   15   20 Miles
0   5 10 15 20 Kilometers

Numbers 14:2
All the Israelites complained about Moses and Aaron, and the
whole community told them, "If only we had died in the land of
Egypt, or if only we had died in this wilderness!"

45 THE JOURNEY FROM KADESH BARNEA TO THE PLAINS OF MOAB

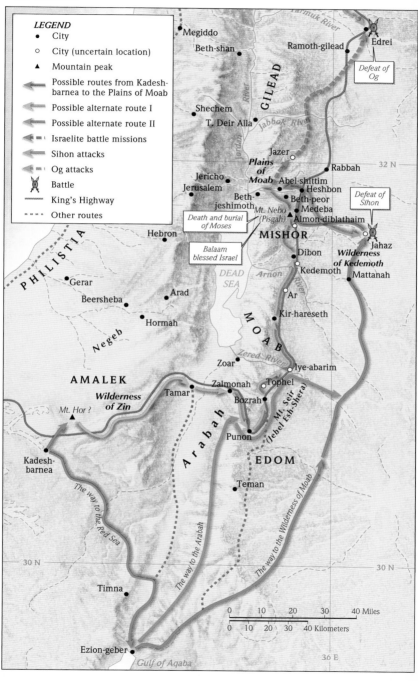

LEGEND

- • City
- ○ City (uncertain location)
- ▲ Mountain peak
- ← Possible routes from Kadesh-barnea to the Plains of Moab
- ← Possible alternate route I
- ← Possible alternate route II
- ← Israelite battle missions
- ← Sihon attacks
- ← Og attacks
- Battle
- — King's Highway
- --- Other routes

Deuteronomy 2:2-3

"The LORD then said to me, 'You've been traveling around this hill country long enough; turn north.'"

46 JOSHUA'S CENTRAL AND SOUTHERN CAMPAIGNS

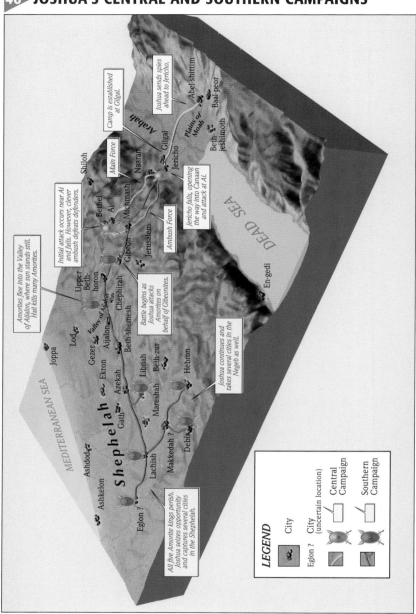

Joshua 10:12-13

On the day the LORD gave the Amorites over to the Israelites, Joshua spoke to the LORD in the presence of Israel: "Sun, stand still over Gibeon, and moon, over the valley of Aijalon." And the sun stood still and the moon stopped, until the nation took vengeance on its enemies. Isn't this written in the Book of Jashar? So the sun stopped in the middle of the sky and delayed its setting almost a full day.

47 ▶ JOSHUA'S NORTHERN CAMPAIGN

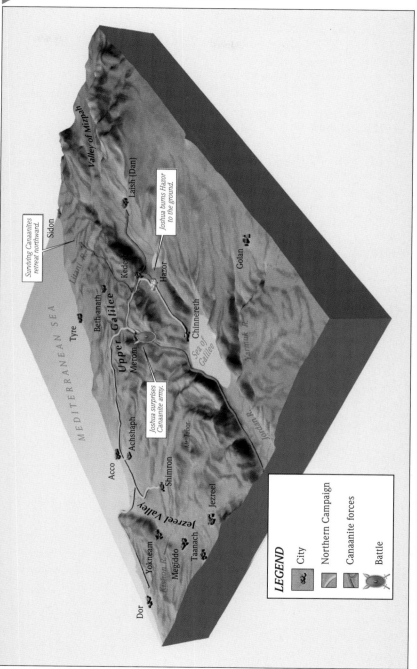

Surviving Canaanites retreat northward.

Joshua burns Hazor to the ground.

Joshua surprises Canaanite army.

Valley of Mizpah

Laish (Dan)

Sidon

Kedesh

Litani R.

Hazor

Golan

Beth-anath

Upper Galilee

Chinnereth

MEDITERRANEAN SEA

Tyre

Merom

Sea of Galilee

Yarmuk R.

Achshaph

Mt. Tabor

Jordan R.

Acco

Shimron

Jezreel

Jezreel Valley

Yokneam

Kishon R.

Megiddo

Taanach

Dor

LEGEND

🐚 City

Northern Campaign

Canaanite forces

⚔ Battle

Joshua 11:10

At that time Joshua turned back, captured Hazor, and struck down its king with the sword, because Hazor had formerly been the leader of all these kingdoms.

48 CITIES OF JOSHUA'S CONQUESTS

CITY	SCRIPTURE	OCCUPANTS
Gilgal	4:19–5:15	Unoccupied?
Jericho	6:1-27	Canaanites
Ai	7:1–8:29	Amorites
Shechem	8:30-35; ch. 24	Hivites (Gen. 38); patriarchs;
Gibeon, Chephirah, Beeroth, Kiriath-jearim	9:1–10:27	Hivites
Jerusalem	10:1-27	Jebusite
Hebron	10:1-27,36-37	Amorite, but in patriarchal times Hittite; also home of Anakim (11:21
Jarmuth	10:1-27	Amorite
Lachish	10:1-27,31-32	Amorite
Eglon	10:1-27,34-35	Amorite
Makkedah	10:16-17,28	?
Libnah	10:29-30	?
Gezer	10:33	Canaanite
Debir	10:38-39	Amorite; home of Anakim (11:21)
Hazor	11:1-15	Canaanite
Madon	11:1	?
Shimron	11:1	?
Achshaph	11:1	?
Geder	12:13	?
Hormah	12:14	?
Arad	12:14	Canaanites
Adullam	12:15	?
Bethel	12:16	?
Tappuah	12:17	?
Hepher	12:17	?
Aphek	12:18	?
Lasharon	12:18	?
Taanach	12:21	Canaanite
Megiddo	12:21	Canaanite
Kedesh	12:22	?
Jokneam	12:22	?
Dor	12:23; compare 11:2	Associated with sea peoples
Goiim in Gilgal	12:23	Name means "nations"
Tirzah	12:24	Canaanite

COMMENTS

COMMENTS
No battle; became worship center
Rahab spared; oldest walled city; Achan sinned
Israel defeated at first for Achan's sin; Ai means "ruin"
Not conquered; became worship center relatives of Israel
Entered covenant with Israel to be servants at worship place
Part of coalition Joshua defeated but city not conquered
Coalition partner whose city was destroyed; patriarchal city (Gen. 13:18); given to Caleb 14:9-13); city of refuge (20:7)
Coalition partner
Coalition partner whose city was destroyed
Coalition partner whose city was destroyed
Scene of battle with coalition
Levitical city (21:13)
Old, large city whose king Joshua defeated; city not occupied (Judg. 1:29); Levitical city (21:21)
Captured by Joshua and Othniel (15:17); levitical city (21:15); name of King of Eglon (10:3)
Largest city in Canaan; ancient history; head of northern coalition; destroyed by Joshua
Northern coalition partner Joshua defeated; Greek Septuagint calls it Meron; compare Waters of Merom
Has various spellings in mss; appears in ancient Egyptian sources
Means "place of sorcery"; mentioned in ancient Egyptian sources
Mystery city unknown elsewhere; sometimes seen as scribe's notation for city of longer name
Southern border city (Num. 14:45); defeated by Simeon and Judah (Judg. 1:1,17)
Defeated by Moses (Num. 21:1-3) and named Hormah; occupied by Kenites (Judg. 1:16-17)
Patriarchal ties (Gen. 38)
Strong patriarchal ties (Gen. 12; 28; 35); means "house of God;" associated with Ai 7:2); Joseph defeated it (Judg. 1:22-25)
Border city between Ephraim and Manasseh (16:8; 17:7-8)
Name of a clan in Manasseh (17:1-2; compare Num. 26:28-37)
In ancient Egyptian sources (compare 1 Sam. 4; 29)
Unusual Hebrew construction; means, "of Sharon;" may modify Aphek
In ancient Egyptian sources; levitical city (21:25); Manasseh could not occupy it (Judg. 1:27)
Major ancient city guarding military pass; in Egyptian sources; Manasseh could not occupy (Judg. 1:27)
City of refuge (20:7); levitical city (21:32); home of Barak (Judg. 4:6)
Also spelled Jokmeam; levitical city (21:34); in Egyptian sources
Manasseh could not occupy (17:11-13; Judg. 1:27) in Egyptian records
Compare Gen. 14:1; uncertain scribal reading in text; appears to be in Galilee
Ancient city; became capital of Israel (1 Kings 14:17); see Song 6:4

49 THE LEVANT FROM 1200 TO 1000 BC

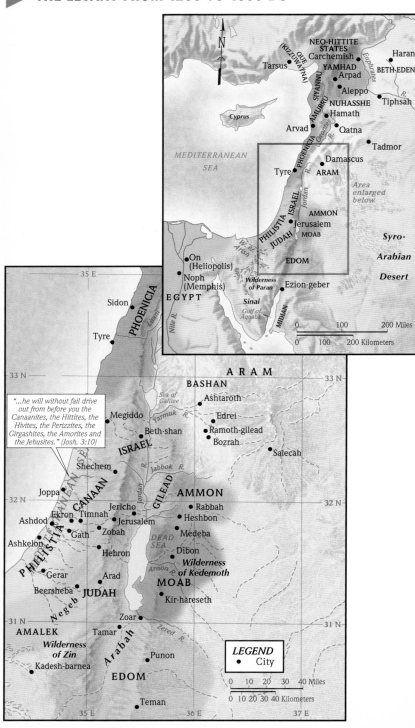

"...he will without fail drive out from before you the Canaanites, the Hittites, the Hivites, the Perizzites, the Girgashites, the Amorites and the Jebusites." (Josh. 3:10)

LEGEND
● City

50 LIMITS OF ISRAELITE SETTLEMENT AND THE LAND TO BE CONQUERED

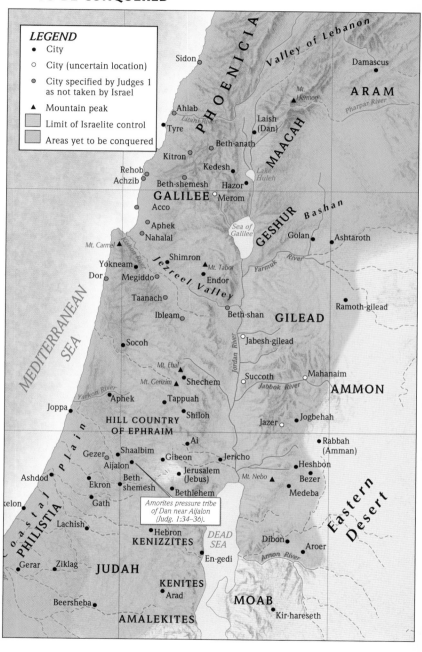

LEGEND
- • City
- ○ City (uncertain location)
- ◉ City specified by Judges 1 as not taken by Israel
- ▲ Mountain peak
- Limit of Israelite control
- Areas yet to be conquered

PHOENICIA

Valley of Lebanon

Sidon

Damascus

Mt. Hermon ▲

ARAM

Pharpar River

Ahlab

Litani River

Laish (Dan)

Tyre

Beth-anath

MAACAH

Kitron

Kedesh

Lake Huleh

Rehob

Achzib

Beth-shemesh

Hazor

GALILEE ○ Merom

Acco

GESHUR

Bashan

Aphek

Sea of Galilee

Golan

Ashtaroth

Nahalal

Mt. Carmel ▲

Shimron

▲ Mt. Tabor

Yarmuk River

Yokneam

Jezreel Valley

Endor

Dor

Megiddo

Taanach

Ibleam

Beth-shan

GILEAD

Ramoth-gilead

MEDITERRANEAN SEA

Socoh

Jabesh-gilead

Jordan River

Mt. Ebal ▲

Mt. Gerizim ▲ Shechem

Succoth

Mahanaim

Jabbok River

AMMON

Joppa

Yarkon River

Aphek

Tappuah

HILL COUNTRY OF EPHRAIM

Shiloh

Jazer

Jogbehah

Ai

Rabbah (Amman)

Gezer

Shaalbim

Gibeon

Jericho

Heshbon

Ashdod

Aijalon

Beth-shemesh

Jerusalem (Jebus)

Mt. Nebo ▲

Bezer

Ekron

Bethlehem

Medeba

...elon

Gath

Amorites pressure tribe of Dan near Aijalon (Judg. 1:34–36).

PHILISTIA

Coastal Plain

Lachish

DEAD SEA

Dibon

Aroer

Eastern Desert

Gerar

Ziklag

Hebron

KENIZZITES

En-gedi

Arnon River

JUDAH

KENITES

Arad

MOAB

Beersheba

AMALEKITES

Kir-hareseth

Joshua 13:1

Joshua was now old, advanced in years, and the LORD said to him, "You have become old, advanced in years, but a great deal of the land remains to be possessed."

51 ▶ THE TRIBAL ALLOTMENTS OF ISRAEL

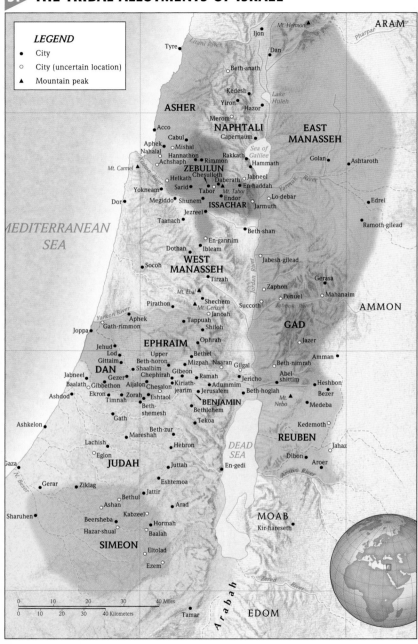

Joshua 19:49-50

When they had finished distributing the land into its territories, the Israelites gave Joshua son of Nun an inheritance among them. By the LORD's command, they gave him the city Timnath-serah in the hill country of Ephraim, which he requested. He rebuilt the city and lived in it.

52 LEVITICAL CITIES AND CITIES OF REFUGE

LEGEND
- ● Levitical city
- ○ Levitical city (uncertain location)
- ▢ City of refuge
- ● Other city
- ▲ Mountain peak

Joshua 21:8
The Israelites gave these cities with their pasturelands around them to the Levites by lot, as the LORD had commanded through Moses.

Joshua 20:1-3
Then the LORD spoke to Joshua, "Tell the Israelites: 'Select your cities of refuge, as I instructed you through Moses, so that a person who kills someone unintentionally or accidentally may flee there. These will be your refuge from the avenger of blood.

THE JUDGES

Period of the Judges—ca. 1360–1084 BC

Judges 1:1-29 forms a literary transition from the life of Joshua to the period of the judges. The downward spiral lasted about 280 years. The judges, shophetim, were more like leaders or rulers than legal functionaries. The reports of the work of the various judges are not strictly chronological and overlapped frequently, explaining how the elapsed time of 280 years is so much shorter than the aggregate total of 410 years for the 15 judges mentioned.

Interpretation of Judges

Scholars and lay readers tend to read Judges differently. Many scholars interpret the book as a political document, demonstrating the need for a king to resolve the problems of Israel during the transitional period between the conquest of Canaan under Joshua and the establishment of the monarchy, and specifically to support the cause of David in opposition to the household of Saul. Taking their cue from Hebrews 11:32, most laypeople read Judges as a book of heroes who demonstrate strength of character in achieving great feats for God.

However, a close reading of Judges suggests that both interpretations miss the author's point. If we read Judges as a prophetic book, we discover that the focus is not on the judges but on God, on whose behalf they served as the nation's deliverers. Specifically, the book describes the Lord's response to the Canaanization of Israelite society during the period of settlement. As 2:6-10 declares, within a generation after the death of Joshua and those who had participated in the conquest, Israel's spiritual problems surfaced. This nation entered the land of promise triumphantly as the redeemed people of the Lord but became more and more like the people they were charged to displace.

This historical introduction is followed by a heavily theological preamble (2:1–3:6). The fundamental problem is Israel's loss of the memory of the Lord's redemptive work on their behalf (2:1-10). This resulted in the sorry truth expressed in a refrain that is repeated seven times in the book: The Israelites did evil (literally "the evil") in the sight of the Lord; they served the Baals and abandoned the Lord their Redeemer (2:11-12; cp. 3:7,12; 4:1; 6:1; 10:6; 13:1). The following narratives of the individual judges, which take up the bulk of the book (3:7–16:31), describe the consequences of this apostasy. This preamble (2:1–3:6) invites the reader to interpret these accounts not merely as cyclical recurrences of the same problem but as illustrative of an intensification of the evil in Israel (2:17-19), offering the reader the key to understanding both the people of Israel and the judges who led them.

Because of the theological nature of the narrative and the author's selective use of data, it is difficult to reconstruct the history of Israel during the period of the judges from the accounts in the heart of the book (3:7–16:31). The events are deliberately arranged so that each judge is presented in a worse light than the previous, beginning with Othniel, an exemplary character (3:7-11), and ending with Samson, who embodies all that is wrong with Israel. Each cycle is structured after a literary pattern signaled by a series of recurring formulas:

(1) "The Israelites did evil in the eyes of the Lord" (2:11; 3:7,12; 4:1; 6:1; 10:6; 13:1).

(2) "The Lord gave/sold the Israelites into the hands of the enemy" (2:14; 6:1; 13:1).

(3) "The Israelites cried out to the Lord" (3:9,15; 4:3; 6:6; 10:10).

(4) "The Lord raised up a deliverer for Israel to save them" (2:16,18; 3:9,15).

(5) "And X [the oppressing nation] was made subject to Israel" (8:28; cp. 3:30; 4:23).

(6) "Then the land was undisturbed for X years" (3:11,30; 5:31; 8:28).

(7) "Then X [the judge] died" (2:19; 3:11; 4:1b; 8:28; 12:7).

From these formulas it is evident that the Lord is the most important character in the book, and the author's attention is fixed on His response to the Canaanization of His people. In judgment He sends in foreign enemies (as Lev. 26 and Deut. 28 predicted), then in mercy He hears their cry, raises up a deliverer and provides victory over the enemy. But the Israelites do not learn the lesson; on the contrary the spiritual rot goes deeper and deeper into the very soul of the nation so that in the end Gideon acts like an oriental despot (8:18-32). Like the pagans around him, Jephthah tried to win the good will of God by sacrificing his daughter (11:30-40) and Samson's life and death looked more like that of a Philistine than one of the people of the Lord (chaps. 14–16).

Toward the end of this period, hope emerged in the heroic saga of Naomi, Ruth, and Boaz, who demonstrate that faithful Israelites remained loyal to their covenant Lord. From this family would come the great King David.

The last of the judges was the greatest: Samuel, a Benjaminite whose mother dedicated him to the service of the Lord. Raised by the priest Eli, Samuel became priest and judge when God excised the family of Eli for its unfaithfulness. Samuel administered the nation wisely and fairly, and stability prevailed during the time of his stewardship. However, the people longed to be like the other nations and asked for a king.

53 JUDGES OF THE OLD TESTAMENT

NAME	REFERENCE	IDENTIFICATION
Othniel	Judg. 1:12-13; 3:7-11	Conquered a Canaanite city
Ehud	Judg. 3:12-30	Killed Eglon, king of Moab, and defeated Moabites
Shamgar	Judg. 3:31	Killed 600 Philistines with an oxgoad
Deborah	Judg. 4–5	Convinced Barak to lead an army to victory against Sisera's troops
Gideon	Judg. 6–8	Led 300 men to victory against 135,000 Midianites
Tola	Judg. 10:1-2	Judged for 23 years
Jair	Judg. 10:3-5	Judged for 22 years
Jephthah	Judg. 11:1–12:7	Defeated the Ammonites after making a promise to the Lord
Ibzan	Judg. 12:8-10	Judged for 7 years
Elon	Judg. 12:11-12	Judged for 10 years
Abdon	Judg. 12:13-15	Judged for 8 years
Samson	Judg. 13–16	Killed 1,000 Philistines with a donkey's jawbone; was deceived by Delilah; destroyed a Philistine temple; judged 20 years
Samuel	1 and 2 Sam.	Was the last of the judges and the first of the prophets

54▶ THE JUDGES OF ISRAEL

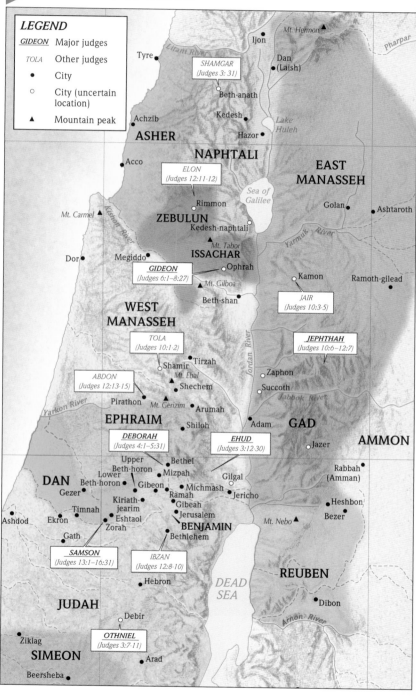

LEGEND

GIDEON	Major judges
TOLA	Other judges
•	City
○	City (uncertain location)
▲	Mountain peak

SHAMGAR
(Judges 3: 31)

ELON
(Judges 12:11-12)

GIDEON
(Judges 6:1–8:27)

JAIR
(Judges 10:3-5)

TOLA
(Judges 10:1-2)

JEPHTHAH
(Judges 10:6–12:7)

ABDON
(Judges 12:13-15)

DEBORAH
(Judges 4:1–5:31)

EHUD
(Judges 3:12-30)

SAMSON
(Judges 13:1–16:31)

IBZAN
(Judges 12:8-10)

OTHNIEL
(Judges 3:7-11)

ASHER
NAPHTALI
EAST MANASSEH
ZEBULUN
ISSACHAR
WEST MANASSEH
EPHRAIM
DAN
BENJAMIN
GAD
AMMON
REUBEN
JUDAH
SIMEON
DEAD SEA

Ijon
Mt. Hermon ▲
Tyre
Dan (Laish)
Litani River
Pharpar
Beth-anath
Kedesh
Achzib
Hazor
Lake Huleh
Acco
Rimmon
Sea of Galilee
Golan
Ashtaroth
Mt. Carmel ▲
Kedesh-naphtali
Kishon River
Yarmuk River
Dor
Megiddo
Mt. Tabor ▲
Ophrah
Kamon
Ramoth-gilead
Mt. Gilboa ▲
Beth-shan
Shamir
Tirzah
Zaphon
Mt. Ebal ▲
Shechem
Succoth
Jabbok River
Pirathon
Mt. Gerizim ▲
Arumah
Adam
Yarkon River
Shiloh
Jordan River
Jazer
Rabbah (Amman)
Upper Beth-horon
Bethel
Mizpah
Gilgal
Lower Beth-horon
Gibeon
Michmash
Jericho
Gezer
Ramah
Heshbon
Timnah
Kiriath-jearim
Gibeah
Bezer
Ekron
Eshtaol
Jerusalem
Mt. Nebo ▲
Ashdod
Zorah
Gath
Bethlehem
Hebron
Dibon
Debir
Arnon River
Ziklag
Arad
Beersheba

Judges 21:25

In those days there was no king in Israel; everyone did whatever he wanted.

55 ▶ EHUD AND THE OPPRESSION OF THE MOABITES

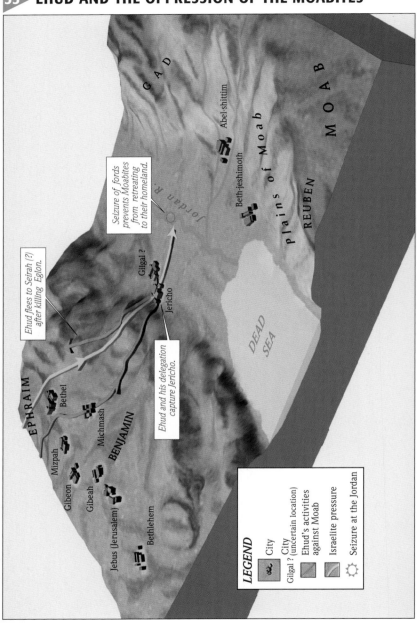

Seizure of fords prevents Moabites from retreating to their homeland.

Ehud flees to Seirah (?) after killing Eglon.

Ehud and his delegation capture Jericho.

Gilgal ?

Jericho

Abel-shittim

Beth-jeshimoth

Plains of Moab

G A D

R E U B E N

M O A B

DEAD SEA

EPHRAIM

Bethel

Michmash

BENJAMIN

Mizpah

Gibeon

Gibeah

Jebus (Jerusalem)

Bethlehem

LEGEND

City

City
Gilgal ? (uncertain location)

Ehud's activities against Moab

Israelite pressure

Seizure at the Jordan

Judges 3:14-16

The Israelites served Eglon king of Moab 18 years.

Then the Israelites cried out to the LORD, and He raised up Ehud son of Gera, a left-handed Benjaminite, as a deliverer for them. The Israelites sent him to Eglon king of Moab with tribute money.

Ehud made himself a double-edged sword 18 inches long. He strapped it to his right thigh under his clothes.

56 DEBORAH'S VICTORY OVER THE CANAANITES

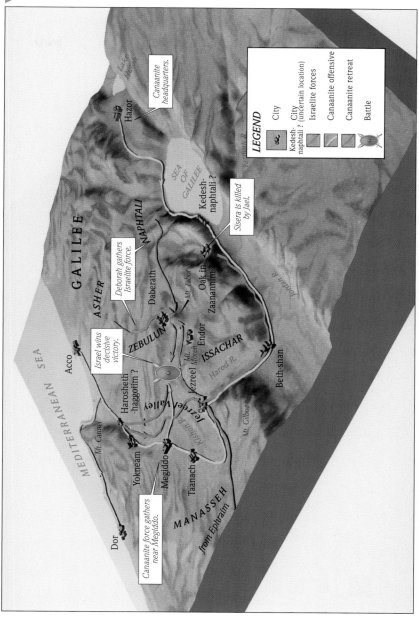

Judges 4:8-9

Barak said to her, "If you will go with me, I will go. But if you will not go with me, I will not go."

"I will go with you," she said, "but you will receive no honor on the road you are about to take, because the LORD will sell Sisera into a woman's hand." So Deborah got up and went with Barak to Kedesh.

57 ▷ GIDEON'S BATTLES WITH THE AMALEKITES

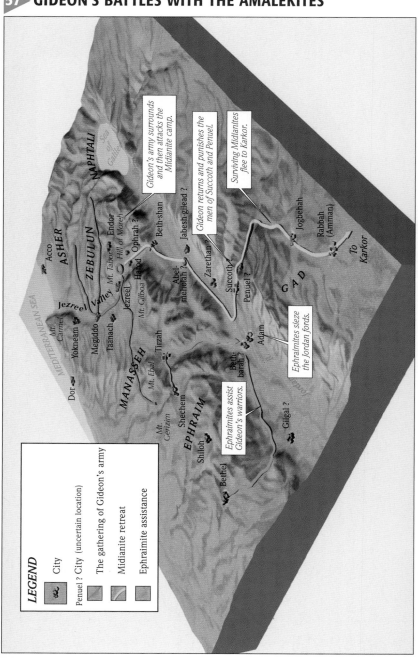

Judges 8:28

So Midian was subdued before the Israelites, and they were no longer a threat. The land was peaceful 40 years during the days of Gideon.

58 ▶ SAMSON AND THE PHILISTINES

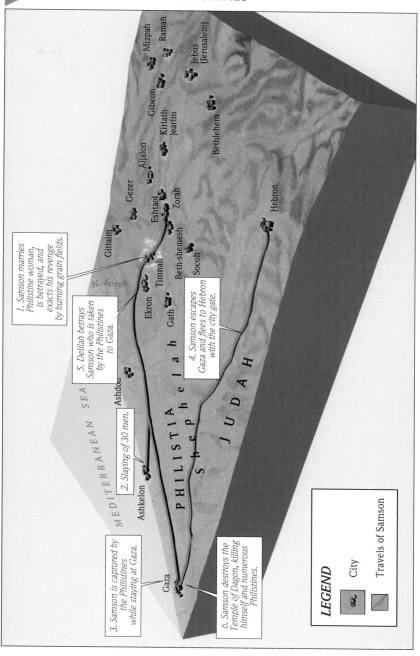

1. Samson marries Philistine woman, is betrayed, and exacts his revenge by burning grain fields.

5. Delilah betrays Samson who is taken by the Philistines to Gaza.

4. Samson escapes Gaza and flees to Hebron with the city gate.

2. Slaying of 30 men.

3. Samson is captured by the Philistines while staying at Gaza.

6. Samson destroys the Temple of Dagon, killing himself and numerous Philistines.

LEGEND

City

Travels of Samson

Mizpah · Ramah · Jebus (Jerusalem) · Gibeon · Kiriath-jearim · Bethlehem · Ajalon · Gezer · Eshtaol · Zorah · Hebron · Gittaim · Timnah · Beth-shemesh · Socoh · N. Sorek · Ekron · Gath · Ashdod · Ashkelon · Gaza

MEDITERRANEAN SEA

PHILISTIA · Shephelah · JUDAH

Judges 16:23

Now the Philistine leaders gathered together to offer a great sacrifice to their god Dagon. They rejoiced and said: "Our god has handed over our enemy Samson to us."

59 ▶ JEPHTHAH AND THE AMMONITES

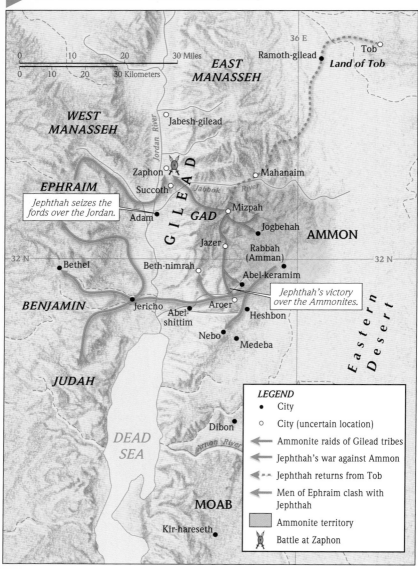

Judges 11:4-6

Some time later, the Ammonites fought against Israel. When the Ammonites made war with Israel, the elders of Gilead went to get Jephthah from the land of Tob. They said to him, "Come, be our commander, and let's fight against the Ammonites."

60▶ THE BATTLE AT EBENEZER

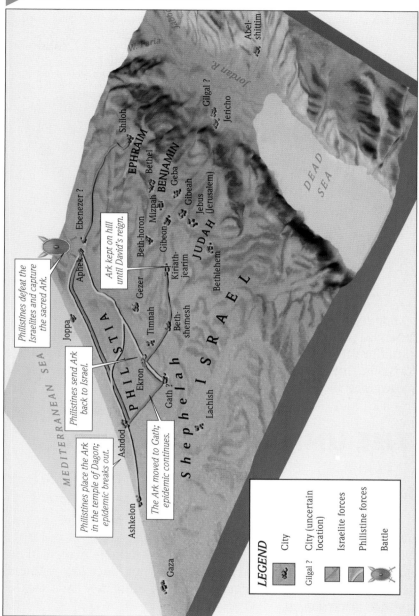

Abel-shittim

Gilgal ?

Jericho

Shiloh

EPHRAIM

Bethel

BENJAMIN

Geba

Mizpah

Gibeah

Gibeon

Jebus (Jerusalem)

JUDAH

Ebenezer ?

Beth-horon

Kiriath-jearim

Bethlehem

Aphek

Ark kept on hill until David's reign.

Gezer

Timnah

Beth-shemesh

I S R A E L

Joppa

Philistines defeat the Israelites and capture the sacred Ark.

Philistines send Ark back to Israel.

P H I L I S T I A

Ekron

S h e p h e l a h

Gath ?

Lachish

Philistines place the Ark in the temple of Dagon; epidemic breaks out.

Ashdod

The Ark moved to Gath; epidemic continues.

M E D I T E R R A N E A N   S E A

Ashkelon

Gaza

Jordan R.

DEAD SEA

LEGEND

City

Gilgal ?   City (uncertain location)

Israelite forces

Philistine forces

Battle

1 Samuel 4:2-3

The Philistines lined up in battle formation against Israel, and as the battle intensified, Israel was defeated by the Philistines, who struck down about 4,000 men on the battlefield. When the troops returned to the camp, the elders of Israel asked, "Why did the LORD let us be defeated today by the Philistines? Let's bring the ark of the LORD's covenant from Shiloh. Then it will go with us and save us from the hand of our enemies."

61 ▶ MINISTRY OF SAMUEL AND ANOINTING OF SAUL

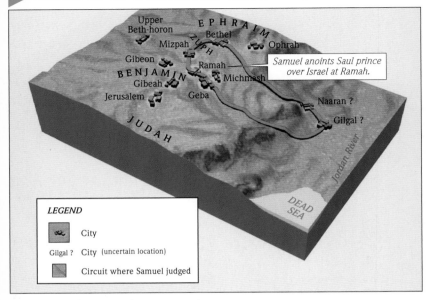

Samuel anoints Saul prince over Israel at Ramah.

LEGEND

City

Gilgal ? City (uncertain location)

Circuit where Samuel judged

1 Samuel 7:15-17

Samuel judged Israel throughout his life. Every year he would go on a circuit to Bethel, Gilgal, and Mizpah and would judge Israel at all these locations. Then he would return to Ramah because his home was there, he judged Israel there, and he had built an altar to the LORD there.

THE UNITED MONARCHY

Saul

Samuel was provoked, but God commanded him to give the people what they asked for, a king of their desire, Saul, son of Kish, a wealthy Benjaminite. A tall, handsome, and humble man, Saul did not seek power and accepted it reluctantly. But, once in command, Saul demonstrated poor judgment and an ultimately fatal lack of spiritual discernment.

Saul made a good beginning by defeating the Philistines with the intervention of young David who killed the Philistine champion Goliath foreshadowing things to come. Almost immediately Saul became suspicious and resentful of David and kept him close by giving David his daughter Michal in marriage and by making David a commander of troops who reported to Saul (1 Sam. 18). Saul was determined to pass the throne to his son Jonathan and neglected the kingdom to pursue David for years, his reign lasting about 40 years.

David

David was the youngest son of Jesse of Bethlehem. He served his father as a shepherd. Samuel anointed David years before his accession to the throne, and David consistently honored the king and repeatedly passed up opportunities to kill Saul. Rather than attack Saul, David

A view of the excavations of the City of David led by Kathleen Kenyon.

ran from him for years. As Saul's kingdom disintegrated, David grew stronger and gained a significant following.

Ultimately Saul and Jonathan were slain in battle, and David reigned over his tribe of Judah for seven years in Hebron, while the remaining tribes were led by Saul's son, Ish-Bosheth. After Ish-Bosheth's brutal assassination, David acceded to the throne of all Israel for an additional 33 years, establishing his capital in Jerusalem. He defeated Israel's enemies and established peace for his people. David was Israel's greatest king, described by God as "a man after My heart" (Acts 13:22; 1 Sam. 13:14), but failed morally and spent years in personal and family turmoil as a result. David not only had an affair with the wife of one of his most loyal subordinates, but when threatened with exposure, he engineered Uriah's death. His household never knew peace again, ultimately costing the lives of some of his children. David developed the plans for the temple and gathered the resources, but because of David's own sins, God did not allow him to complete the project.

Solomon

At the end of David's life, the accession of his son Solomon to the throne was a bloody interfamily struggle. Solomon made a marvelous beginning, building and dedicating a magnificent temple. Genuinely humble, God prospered him beyond his fondest hopes. Solomon was revered for his wisdom and maintained a kingdom expanded to five times the size of the land God promised to Abraham, extending south to the Sinai and north to the Euphrates River. Solomon became one of the most significant monarchs of his era. By the end of his 40-year reign, his kingdom was strong, but his commitment to the Lord had waned, and his latter years were troubled by internal problems. Soon after his death, the united monarchy ended.

62 THE KINGDOM OF SAUL AND HIS WARS

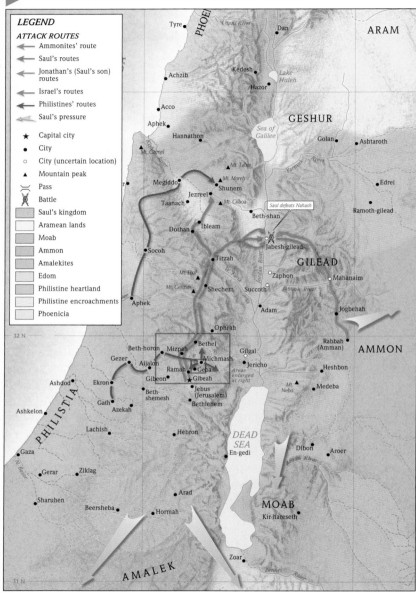

1 Samuel 13:5-7

The Philistines also gathered to fight against Israel: 3,000 chariots, 6,000 horsemen, and troops as numerous as the sand on the seashore. They went up and camped at Michmash, east of Beth-aven. The men of Israel saw that they were in trouble because the troops were in a difficult situation. They hid in caves, thickets, among rocks, and in holes and cisterns. Some Hebrews even crossed the Jordan to the land of Gad and Gilead. Saul, however, was still at Gilgal, and all his troops were gripped with fear.

63 DAVID'S FLIGHT FROM SAUL

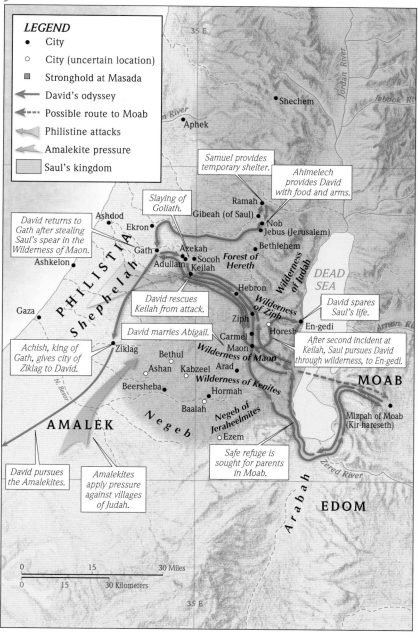

LEGEND
- City
- ○ City (uncertain location)
- ■ Stronghold at Masada
- ← David's odyssey
- ◄--- Possible route to Moab
- ← Philistine attacks
- ← Amalekite pressure
- Saul's kingdom

Samuel provides temporary shelter.

Ahimelech provides David with food and arms.

Slaying of Goliath.

David returns to Gath after stealing Saul's spear in the Wilderness of Maon.

David rescues Keilah from attack.

David marries Abigail.

Achish, king of Gath, gives city of Ziklag to David.

David spares Saul's life.

After second incident at Keilah, Saul pursues David through wilderness, to En-gedi.

David pursues the Amalekites.

Amalekites apply pressure against villages of Judah.

Safe refuge is sought for parents in Moab.

Shechem
Aphek
Ramah
Gibeah (of Saul)
Ashdod
Ekron
Nob
Jebus (Jerusalem)
Bethlehem
Gath
Azekah
Socoh *Forest of Hereth*
Adullam *Keilah*
Ashkelon
Hebron
Gaza
Ziph
Horesh *En-gedi*
Ziklag
Bethul
Carmel
Maon
Ashan *Kabzeel* *Arad*
Beersheba
Hormah
Baalah
Ezem
Mizpah of Moab (Kir-hareseth)

PHILISTIA
Shephelah
Wilderness of Judah
DEAD SEA
Wilderness of Ziph
Wilderness of Maon
Wilderness of Kenites
Negeb of Jeraheelmites
AMALEK
Negeb
MOAB
EDOM
Arabah
Jordan River
Jabbok Ri
River
N. Besor
Arnon R
Zered River
35 E
35 E

0   15   30 Miles
0   15   30 Kilometers

1 Samuel 24:1-2

When Saul returned from pursuing the Philistines, he was told, "David is in the wilderness near En-gedi." So Saul took 3,000 of Israel's choice men and went to look for David and his men in front of the Rocks of the Wild Goats.

64 ► DAVID'S RISE TO POWER

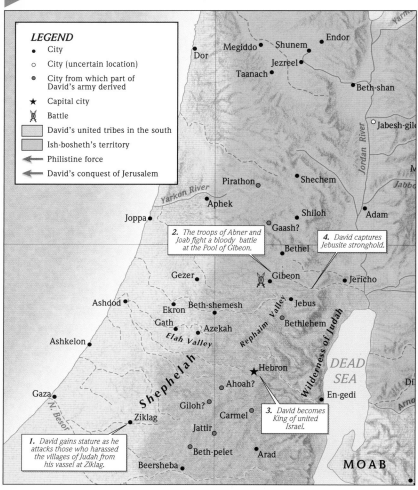

LEGEND
- • City
- ○ City (uncertain location)
- ● City from which part of David's army derived
- ★ Capital city
- ✗ Battle
- ▢ David's united tribes in the south
- ▢ Ish-bosheth's territory
- ◄── Philistine force
- ◄── David's conquest of Jerusalem

2. *The troops of Abner and Joab fight a bloody battle at the Pool of Gibeon.*

4. *David captures Jebusite stronghold.*

3. *David becomes King of united Israel.*

1. *David gains stature as he attacks those who harassed the villages of Judah from his vassal at Ziklag.*

2 Samuel 5:6-10

The king and his men marched to Jerusalem against the Jebusites who inhabited the land. The Jebusites had said to David: "You will never get in here. Even the blind and lame can repel you," thinking, "David can't get in here."

Yet David did capture the stronghold of Zion, the city of David. He said that day, "Whoever attacks the Jebusites must go through the water shaft to reach the lame and the blind who are despised by David." For this reason it is said, "The blind and the lame will never enter the house."

David took up residence in the stronghold, which he named the city of David. He built it up all the way around from the supporting terraces inward. David became more and more powerful, and the LORD God of Hosts was with him.

65 ▶ DAVID'S WARS OF CONQUEST

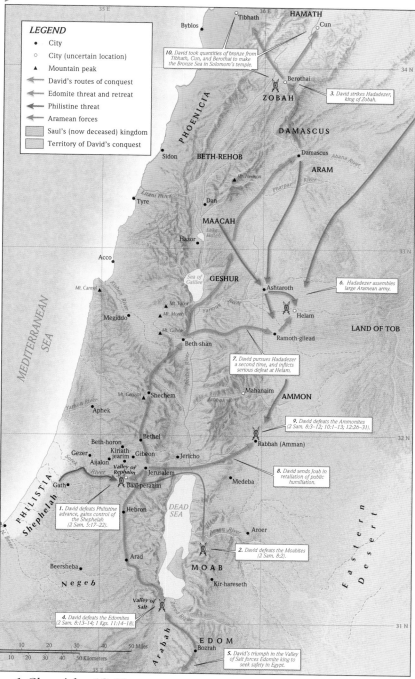

LEGEND

- • City
- ○ City (uncertain location)
- ▲ Mountain peak
- ← David's routes of conquest
- ← Edomite threat and retreat
- ← Philistine threat
- ← Aramean forces
-   Saul's (now deceased) kingdom
-   Territory of David's conquest

10. David took quantities of bronze from Tibhath, Cun, and Berothai to make the Bronze Sea in Solomom's temple.

3. David strikes Hadadezer, king of Zobah.

6. Hadadezer assembles large Aramean army.

7. David pursues Hadadezer a second time, and inflicts serious defeat at Helam.

9. David defeats the Ammonites (2 Sam. 8:3–12; 10:1–13; 12:26–31).

8. David sends Joab in retaliation of public humiliation.

1. David defeats Philistine advance, gains control of the Shephelah (2 Sam. 5:17–22).

2. David defeats the Moabites (2 Sam. 8:2).

4. David defeats the Edomites (2 Sam. 8:13–14; 1 Kgs. 11:14–18).

5. David's triumph in the Valley of Salt forces Edomite king to seek safety in Egypt.

HAMATH · Tibhath · Cun · Byblos · Berothai · ZOBAH · DAMASCUS · Damascus · Abana River · ARAM · PHOENICIA · BETH-REHOB · Sidon · Mt. Hermon · Pharpar River · Litani River · Tyre · Dan · MAACAH · Hazor · Lake Huleh · Acco · Sea of Galilee · GESHUR · Ashtaroth · Helam · LAND OF TOB · Mt. Carmel · Kishon River · Mt. Tabor · Mt. Moreh · Yarmuk River · Megiddo · Mt. Gilboa · Ramoth-gilead · Beth-shan · MEDITERRANEAN SEA · Mt. Gerizim · Shechem · Jabbok River · Mahanaim · AMMON · Aphek · Jordan River · Yarkon River · Bethel · Rabbah (Amman) · Gezer · Beth-horon · Kiriath-jearim · Gibeon · Jericho · Aijalon · Sorek River · Valley of Rephaim · Jerusalem · Gath · Baal-perazim · Medeba · PHILISTIA · Shephelah · Hebron · DEAD SEA · N. Besor · Aroer · Arad · Eastern Desert · Beersheba · MOAB · Kir-haresheth · Negeb · Arnon River · Valley of Salt · Arabah · Zered River · EDOM · Bozrah

10 20 30 40 50 Miles
10 20 30 40 50 Kilometers

35 E   36 E   34 N   33 N   32 N   31 N   35 E

1 Chronicles 18:13

He put garrisons in Edom, and all the Edomites were subject to David. The LORD made David victorious wherever he went.

66 ▶ THE FAMILY OF DAVID

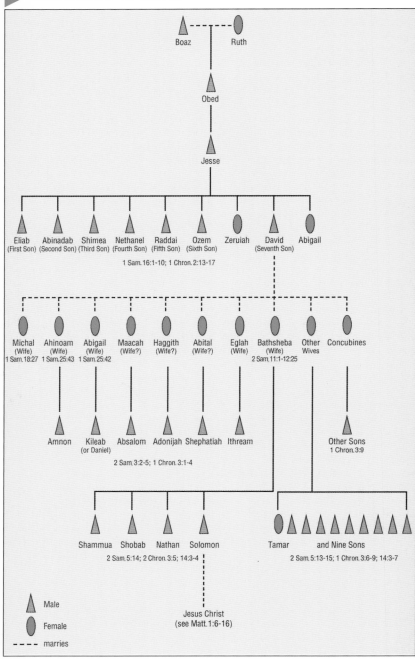

Boaz — Ruth

Obed

Jesse

Eliab (First Son) Abinadab (Second Son) Shimea (Third Son) Nethanel (Fourth Son) Raddai (Fifth Son) Ozem (Sixth Son) Zeruiah David (Seventh Son) Abigail

1 Sam. 16:1-10; 1 Chron. 2:13-17

Michal (Wife) 1 Sam. 18:27 Ahinoam (Wife) 1 Sam. 25:43 Abigail (Wife) 1 Sam. 25:42 Maacah (Wife?) Haggith (Wife?) Abital (Wife?) Eglah (Wife) Bathsheba (Wife) 2 Sam. 11:1–12:25 Other Wives Concubines

Amnon Kileab (or Daniel) Absalom Adonijah Shephatiah Ithream

Other Sons 1 Chron. 3:9

2 Sam. 3:2-5; 1 Chron. 3:1-4

Shammua Shobab Nathan Solomon

2 Sam. 5:14; 2 Chron. 3:5; 14:3-4

Tamar and Nine Sons

2 Sam. 5:13-15; 1 Chron. 3:6-9; 14:3-7

▲ Male

⬤ Female

- - - - marries

Jesus Christ (see Matt. 1:6-16)

67▶ JERUSALEM IN THE TIME OF DAVID AND SOLOMON

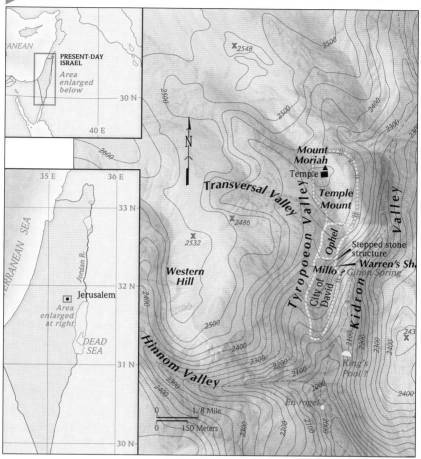

2 Chronicles 3:1-2

Then Solomon began to build the LORD's temple in Jerusalem on Mount Moriah where the LORD had appeared to his father David, at the site David had prepared on the threshing floor of Ornan the Jebusite. He began to build on the second day of the second month in the fourth year of his reign.

JERUSALEM

Jerusalem is a city set high on a plateau in the hills of Judah, considered sacred by Judaism, Christianity, and Islam. Its biblical-theological significance lies in its status as Yahweh's chosen center of his divine kingship and of the human kingship of David and his sons, Yahweh's vice-regents. Besides the name "Jerusalem," the city is also called "the City of David" and "Zion" (originally referring to a part of the city, the "stronghold of Zion" that David captured from the Jebusites; see 2 Sam. 5:6-10).

In the Pentateuch, the city of Jerusalem is not directly mentioned. Moriah (Gen. 22:2; associated with the site of Solomon's temple in 2 Chron. 3:1) and Salem (Gen. 14:18; associated with Zion in Ps. 76:2) apparently refer to the same site and establish a link between the city and the patriarch Abraham. The city (known earlier as Jebus; see Judg. 19:10-11) was captured in Joshua's time (Judg. 1:8), but the Jebusites were not driven out (Josh. 15:63; Judg. 1:21). After David captured it and made it Israel's capital (2 Sam. 5:6-10, 1 Chron. 11:4-9), David brought the ark of the covenant into Jerusalem (2 Sam. 6:17) and made it the seat not only of his own but also of God's monarchy (cp. 1 Kings 11:36; 14:21; and Ps. 132; which emphasize that it is Yahweh's own chosen/desired habitation). Jerusalem came to be "the city of our God," "the city of the great King," "the city of Yahweh of hosts" (Ps. 48). Under Solomon, the temple was constructed (2 Chron. 3-7) and the nation reached its political and economic zenith with Jerusalem at the center (2 Chron. 9).

David and his men may have captured Jerusalem through Warren's Shaft that runs form the Gihon Spring up to the old city of Jerusalem.

In the prophets, besides literal references to the city, "Jerusalem" appears as a corporate representative of the entire community

▲ Stairway from city of David up western hill.

in speeches of judgment and of future salvation. The theological centrality of Jerusalem and events such as God's historical deliverance of the city from the hands of Sennacherib (2 Kings 19) led the people to a mistaken belief in the city's invincibility. This view is denounced by prophets such as Jeremiah (Jer. 7:1-15) and Micah (Mic. 3:11-12) as it abetted the people's apostasy from Yahweh. Since the people had abandoned Yahweh, Yahweh eventually abandoned His chosen city to the Babylonians in 586 BC (2 Kings 23:26-27).

Yet judgment was not Yahweh's final word. The Persian king Cyrus (decree in 538 BC) was Yahweh's servant in facilitating the return of many exiles and the rebuilding of the city and the temple (Isa. 44:26-28; 45:13; Ezra 6; Neh. 1–6). Moreover, the future salvation of Jerusalem would exceed the temporal restoration of the postexilic community. All peoples would come to it (Isa. 2:2-4; Jer. 3:17). God's new work for Jerusalem would usher in nothing less than a new age (Isa. 65:18-25; Zech. 14:8-21).

68 ► RECONSTRUCTION OF DAVID'S JERUSALEM

69 ▶ KINGDOM OF DAVID AND SOLOMON

1 Kings 2:12
Solomon sat on the throne of his father David, and his kingship was firmly established.

70 ▶ SOLOMON'S BUILDING ACTIVITIES

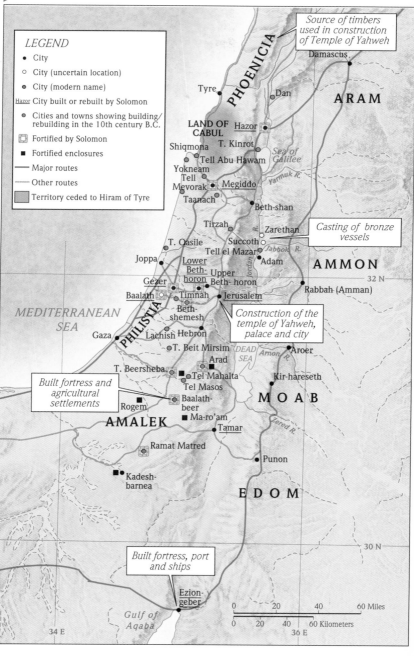

LEGEND

- • City
- ○ City (uncertain location)
- ● City (modern name)
- Hazor City built or rebuilt by Solomon
- ● Cities and towns showing building/ rebuilding in the 10th century B.C.
- ▣ Fortified by Solomon
- ■ Fortified enclosures
- — Major routes
- — Other routes
- Territory ceded to Hiram of Tyre

Source of timbers used in construction of Temple of Yahweh

Damascus

PHOENICIA

Tyre

Dan

ARAM

LAND OF CABUL

Hazor

Shiqmona

T. Kinrot

Sea of Galilee

Tell Abu Hawam

Yokneam

Yarmuk R.

Tell Mevorak

Megiddo

Taanach

Beth-shan

Tirzah

Zarethan

Casting of bronze vessels

Succoth

T. Qasile

Tell el Mazar

Jabbok R.

Joppa

Adam

AMMON

Lower Beth-horon

Upper Beth-horon

32 N

Gezer

Jerusalem

Rabbah (Amman)

Baalath

Timnah

MEDITERRANEAN SEA

Beth-shemesh

Construction of the temple of Yahweh, palace and city

Gaza

Lachish

Hebron

PHILISTIA

T. Beit Mirsim

(DEAD SEA)

Arad

Amon R.

Aroer

T. Beersheba

Tel Mahalta

Kir-hareseth

Built fortress and agricultural settlements

Tel Masos

Rogem

Baalath-beer

M O A B

Ma-ro'am

Tamar

AMALEK

Zered R.

Ramat Matred

Punon

Kadesh-barnea

E D O M

30 N

Built fortress, port and ships

Ezion-geber

0   20   40   60 Miles

0   20   40   60 Kilometers

Gulf of Aqaba

34 E

36 E

1 Kings 6:1

Solomon began to build the temple for the LORD in the four hundred eightieth year after the Israelites came out from the land of Egypt, in the fourth year of his reign over Israel, in the second month, in the month of Ziv.

SOLOMON'S TEMPLE

71 ▶ **RECONSTRUCTION OF SOLOMON'S TEMPLE**

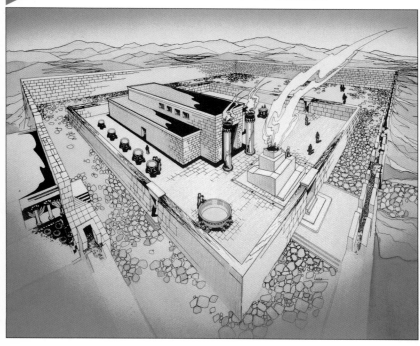

Chronicles makes clear that King David planned the temple and accumulated great wealth and gifts for it, though Solomon was the one who actually built it. We have the detailed literary account of its building preserved in Kings (1 Kings 5:1–9:10) and Chronicles (2 Chron. 2–7).

Solomon's temple was shaped as a "long house" of three successive rooms from east to west, a vestibule of only 15-feet depth, a nave (the holy place) of 60 feet and an inner sanctuary (the most holy place) of 30 feet (1 Kings 6:2-3,16-17). It was approximately 30 feet wide and 45 feet high by its interior measurements for the "house" proper, not counting the porch, which was sort of an open entryway. This is similar to, though not precisely the same as, the shape of several Syrian and Canaanite temples excavated in the past few decades (at Hazor, Lachish, Tell Tainat). There is even one Israelite "temple" at the southeast border of Judah in the iron age fortress of Arad which some have compared with Solomon's temple. None was so symmetrical or ornately decorated, or even as large as the Jerusalem temple, even though Solomon's palace complex of which the temple was only a part (1 Kings 7:1-12) was much larger and took longer to build

(Tell Tainat, in northern Syria, is the closest analogy). Around the outside of the house proper was constructed three stories of side chambers for temple storehouses, above which were recessed windows in the walls of the holy place (1 Kings 6:4-6,8-10).

The inside of the house proper was paneled with cedar, floored with cypress, and inlaid with gold throughout. It was decorated with well-known Phoenician artistic ornamentation, floral designs with cherubim, flowers, and palm trees. The most holy place, a windowless cube of about 30 feet, housed the ark of the covenant and was dominated by two guardian cherubim 15 feet tall with outstretched wings spanning 15 feet to touch in the middle and at each side wall (1 Kings 6:15-28). One of the interesting results of archaeological research is the recovery of the form of these ancient cherubim. They are Egyptian-type sphinxes (human-headed winged lions) such as are pictured as the arms of a throne chair of a Canaanite king on one of the Megiddo ivories. The ark, the mercy-seat lid of which had its own guardian cherubim (Exod. 25:18-20), was Yahweh's "footstool." Beneath these awesome cherubim, God was invisibly enthroned.

The double doors of the inner sanctuary and the nave were similarly carved and inlaid of finest wood and gold (1 Kings 6:31-35). The arrangement prescribed for the wall of the inner court, "three rows of cut stone and a row of cedar beams" (NASB) was followed in Solomonic buildings excavated at Megiddo (1 Kings 6:36; 7:12). This arrangement is also known from the Tell Tainat temple. This exquisite sanctuary took seven years to build (about 960 BC—1 Kings 6:37-38). The marvelous furnishings of the holy place and the courtyard require another chapter to describe (1 Kings 7:9-51).

The most mysterious creations were two huge free-standing bronze pillars about 35 feet tall, including their beautifully ornamented capitals of lily-work netting and rows of pomegranates (1 Kings 7:15-20). They were nearly six feet in diameter, hollow, with a thickness of bronze about three inches. The pillars were named Jachin ("He shall establish") and Boaz ("in the strength of"), perhaps to signify the visible symbolism of the temple as a testimony to the stability of the Davidic dynasty to which it was intimately related.

The reader at this point expects an account of the bronze altar, included in Chronicles (2 Chron. 4:1), but only presumed in Kings (1 Kings 8:22,54,64; 9:25). This altar is large, 35 feet square and 15 feet tall, presumably with steps.

The molten sea, which may have had some kind of cosmic symbolism, stood in the south-central quadrant of the inner courtyard opposite the bronze altar. It was round with a cup-shaped brim, 15 feet in diameter, 7½ feet tall, with a circumference of 45 feet. It was cast of heavy bronze, ornately decorated, and resting on the back of 12 bronze oxen in four sets of three, facing each point of the compass.

Since it held about 10,000 gallons of water, it must have been for supplying water to the lavers by some sort of siphoning mechanism.

The third great engineering feat was the crafting of ten ornate, rolling stands for ten lavers, five on either side of the courtyard. These were six feet square and four and a half feet tall, each containing some two hundred gallons of water, quite heavy objects to be rolled about on chariot wheels. Chronicles says they were used to wash the utensils for sacrificial worship (2 Chron. 4:6).

At the Feast of Tabernacles, Solomon conducted an elaborate dedication festival for the temple (1 Kings 8:1–9:9). The story begins with a procession of the ark containing the two tables of the Decalogue; God's glory in the shining cloud of His presence filled the sanctuary (1 Kings 8:1-11). Then the king blessed the assembly, praised God for His covenant mercies in fulfilling Nathan's promise to David, and gave a long, fervent prayer on behalf of seven different situations in which the prayers of His people should arise to the heavenly throne of God from His earthly temple, closing with a benediction. Solomon provided myriads of sacrifices for the seven days of the great dedication festival. God had consecrated this house of prayer, but He required covenant obedience of Solomon and each of his successors, lest He have to destroy this magnificent sanctuary because of the apostasy of His people (1 Kings 9:1-9). The consistent emphasis of Solomon's prayer and God's answer is the awareness of sin and the necessity for wholehearted repentance to keep the temple a ceremonial and meaningful symbol of worship and devotion (2 Chron. 7:13-14). The great prophets preached that, in their temple worship, Israel was not able to avoid syncretism with pagan religious impulses or the hypocritical irrelevance of meaningless overemphasis upon ritual without righteous obedience to their sovereign overlord (Isa. 1:10-17; Mic. 6:6-8; Jer. 7:1-26).

The history of Solomon's temple has many ups and downs through its almost four hundred years of existence. Its treasures of gold were often plundered by foreign invaders like Shishak of Egypt (1 Kings 14:25-26). At the division of the kingdoms, Jeroboam set up rival sanctuaries at Bethel and Dan that drew worshipers away from Jerusalem for two hundred years. King Asa plundered his own temple treasuries to buy a military ally, Ben-hadad of Syria against Baasha, king of North Israel (1 Kings 15:18-19), though he had previously repaired the temple altar and carried out limited worship reforms (2 Chron. 15:8-18). Temple repairs were carried out by Jehoash (Joash) of Judah after the murder of wicked Queen Athaliah, but even he had to strip the temple treasuries to buy off Hazael, king of Syria (2 Kings 12). Jehoash (Joash), king of Israel, when foolishly challenged to battle by Amaziah, king of Judah, not only defeated him but also came to Jerusalem and plundered the temple (1 Kings

72 CUTAWAY VIEW OF SOLOMON'S TEMPLE

14:12-14). King Ahaz plundered his own temple for tribute to Assyria during the Syro-Ephraimitic war of 735 BC, even stripping some of the bronze furnishings in the courtyard (2 Kings 16:8-9,17). Good King Hezekiah raised a huge tribute for Sennacherib, king of Assyria, in his 701 BC invasion, even stripping gold off the temple doors (2 Kings 18:13-16). During the long and disastrous reign of King Manasseh many abominable idols and pagan cult objects were placed in the temple which good King Josiah had to remove during his reform (2 Kings 23:4-6,11-12). Both Hezekiah and Josiah were able to centralize worship in the Jerusalem temple during their reforms and even recover some worshipers from the north for the Jerusalem sanctuary, but Josiah's successor, Jehoiakim, reversed all of Josiah's reforms and filled up the temple with pagan abominations (Ezek. 8). Despite the warnings of Jeremiah and Ezekiel, the people refused to repent of their political and religious folly, and their temple and holy city were first plundered by Nebuchadnezzar in 597 BC, then burned by Nebuzaradan, his general, in 587/586 BC.

For both groups of Judah, those in Babylon and those still in Jerusalem, the loss of the temple and city were a grievous blow (Ps. 137; Lam. 1–5). But Jeremiah and Ezekiel had prepared a remnant in their prophecies for a return and rebuilding of the temple.

73 ▶ SOLOMON'S ECONOMIC ENTERPRISES

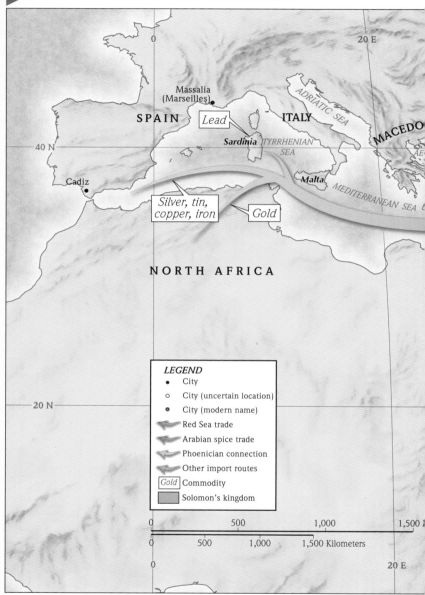

Massalia
(Marseilles)

SPAIN

Lead

ITALY

MACEDO

ADRIATIC SEA

Sardinia

TYRRHENIAN
SEA

40 N

Cadiz

Malta

MEDITERRANEAN SEA

Silver, tin,
copper, iron

Gold

NORTH AFRICA

20 N

LEGEND

- ● City
- ○ City (uncertain location)
- ● City (modern name)
- ◄ Red Sea trade
- ◄ Arabian spice trade
- ◄ Phoenician connection
- ◄ Other import routes
- *Gold* Commodity
- ▨ Solomon's kingdom

0   500   1,000   1,500

0   500   1,000   1,500 Kilometers

20 E

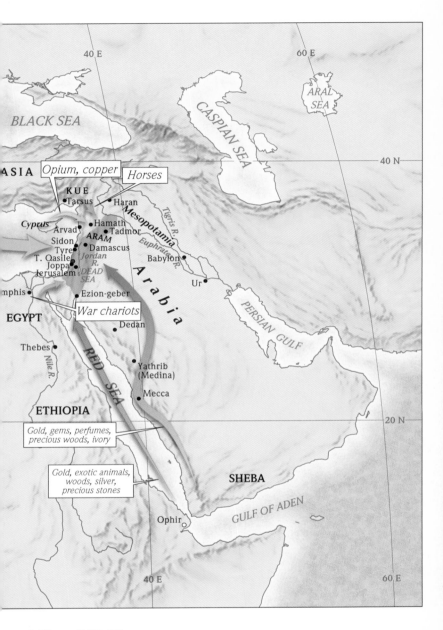

1 Kings 5:10-11

So Hiram provided Solomon with all the cedar and cypress timber he wanted, and Solomon provided Hiram with 100,000 bushels of wheat as food for his household and 110,000 gallons of beaten oil. Solomon did this for Hiram year after year.

THE DIVIDED MONARCHY

The Divided Monarchy—ca. 931–586 BC

The united kingdom of the 12 tribes suddenly divided in 931/930 BC. The ten tribes in the north would henceforth be known as Israel or Ephraim (its most influential tribe). The two southern tribes, Judah and Benjamin, remained loyal to the house of David and were known as Judah. Even before the united kingdom was founded, the unity of Israel was fragile. Petty rivalries and jealousies were common during the period of the judges. The division between Judah and Israel was apparent even during Samuel's lifetime, but David achieved a high degree of national unity. The heavy taxes of Solomon and the forced periods of labor imposed on the people under Solomon and Rehoboam brought the matter to a head.

Sedition boiled toward the surface late in the reign of Solomon. Jeroboam, son of Nebat, was a successful supervisor of civilian labor in Ephraim for Solomon (1 Kings 11:27-28). The prophet Ahijah from Shiloh met Jeroboam one day and tore his (Ahijah's) garment into 12 pieces, handed Jeroboam 10 of them, and announced that Jeroboam would become ruler over Israel (1 Kings 11:31). The rumor of this prophecy spread quickly, and Jeroboam fled to Egypt where he found refuge with Pharaoh Shishak, a political oppor-tunist. Peace was preserved until the death of Solomon, but then trouble arose quickly and Rehoboam was not wise enough to sal-vage the tenuous situation.

Interior of Bubastite portal with inscription of Shishak's campaign in Palestine.

Rather than easing the onerous governmental burdens on the people, Rehoboam threatened to increase them, and ten tribes rebelled, leaving the southern kingdom of Rehoboam containing only the tribes of Judah and Benjamin. Jeroboam, son of Nebat, became the first king of the northern kingdom and immediately led the people into idolatry. In order to make up for the loss of religious ties to Jerusalem, Jeroboam had two golden calves fashioned for the two sites of Dan and Bethel. Because of his apostasy Jeroboam's family forfeited the kingship. His name became a refrain and a stereotype for the evil in the reigns of the rulers of the northern kingdom.

▲ The altar and worship area established by Jeroboam I at Dan.

Rehoboam was attacked by Jeroboam's ally, Pharaoh Shishak (Shosenq I, ca. 945–924 BC), who looted the temple and then moved further into the territory of Israel, Gilead, and Edom. An inscription left by Shishak at Karnak claimed the defeat of 150 cities in the region. Oddly Shishak did not consolidate his gains of territory but returned to Egypt where he soon died. Rehoboam secured his kingdom and turned over a stable nation to his son Abijah, who reigned only two years. He failed in an attempt to reunite the tribes. Abijah's son Asa reigned 41 years in Judah. He partially, but not entirely, reversed the religious deterioration of Judah.

In the entire subsequent history of the two nations, there were nine overlapping reigns or coregencies, which makes the chronology in Kings and Chronicles hard to establish. The north also was divided once into two factions, which further confuses the issue. During the divided kingdom era each nation had 19 kings. The kings of the north came from nine dynasties (families), while all the kings of Judah were descended from David. The 19 kings of the north ruled from 930 to 722 BC; the average length of each reign was relatively brief. The kings of the south served from 930 to 586 BC, demonstrating the greater stability and continuity of life in Judah. All the kings of the north are evaluated in Kings and Chronicles as bad, while the kings of Judah were partly bad and partly good kings. Ironically, the worst of the kings was from Judah: Manasseh, who sacrificed one of his own children as a pagan sacrifice.

A key figure in this era is Elijah. He challenged Baalism one of many expressions of fertility religion that weakened both Israel and Judah during the years following the division in the kingdom. Jezebel, daughter of Ethbaal, king of Sidon and Tyre (1 Kings 16:31), was Ahab's wife and Israel's queen. She brought the worship of her god Baal into Ahab's kingdom. Even "Ahab served Baal a little" (2 Kings 10:18). The contest on Carmel showed a contrast between the contesting deities. Yahweh's power and Baal's impotence were further revealed through the drought. Jezebel planned revenge toward Elijah for ordering the false prophets slain, so Elijah retreated to Judah and finally Mount Horeb. There he observed the power of the wind, earthquake, and fire; but the Lord was not seen in these forces. In a small voice the Lord commanded him to go anoint Hazael king of Syria, Jehu king of Israel, and Elisha as his own successor (1 Kings 19:1-17).

Mount Carmel (vineyard of God) where Elijah held a contest with 450 prophets of Baal.

Elijah statue on Mount Carmel.

Statue of Baal, the Canaanite weather god from Minet-el-beida.

SURREXIT ELIAS
PROPHETA QUASI
IGNIS ET VERBUM
IPSIUS QUASI FACULA

Vistas from Mount Carmel.

During the Israelite monarchies, great nations came across the biblical stage as their affairs intersected those of Judah and Israel. Because the focus of the biblical record is on God's people, only vignettes and brief glimpses are provided of the larger history of the era. The details provided in the Bible are confirmed repeatedly by the archives and artifacts of various kinds left by other ancient kingdoms.

The relationship between Israel and Judah fluctuated from hostile to civil to fraternal over the life of the northern kingdom. Sometimes they were allied and at other times involved in competing alliances. Overall both kingdoms enjoyed periods of peace and prosperity. An ominous development was the emergence of Syria as a major power about the time of the division of the Israelite kingdom (ca. 930 BC). By about 850 BC Damascus was the capital of the most powerful state in the region. Assyria was in a time of domestic turmoil, which allowed more autonomy for other nations. After about a century of weakness, however, an Assyrian resurgence (ca. 745 BC) changed the geopolitical balance and foreshadowed future trouble for the Israelite kingdoms.

Syria became isolated and surrounded by territory under Assyrian control. With Syria thus preoccupied with problems of her own, Judah prospered most notably under the long reign of the good king Hezekiah. However, the end of Israel was just around the corner.

The last century of the northern kingdom (eighth century BC) was marked by the ministry of four great prophets: Amos, Hosea, Micah, and Isaiah, as well as Jonah. With perfect clarity they saw the demise of Israel and eventually Judah. Yet both nations believed themselves to be invincible because of their relationship with Yahweh. Most of the people ignored the prophets and clung to delusions of grandeur and safety.

Tragically the Assyrians swept Israel away after the fall of Samaria in 722 BC. Twice, perhaps, Assyria came against Judah (701 and 688 BC) but was unable to conquer her because of divine intervention. Judah continued for another 135 years, often as a vassal state of Assyria. Jerusalem ultimately fell in 587–586 BC to the Babylonians under Nebuchadnezzar, who displaced Assyria as the dominant world power late in the seventh century BC (ca. 612–609).

74 THE DIVIDED MONARCHY

DATE	JUDAH	ISRAEL	PROPHETS	ARAM-DAMASCUS	ASSYRIA
922	Split of Solomon's kingdom				
	Rehoboam II (922-915)	Jeroboam I (922-901)			
	Campaign of Shishak (918)				
900	Asa appealed to Ben-hadad I.			Ben-hadad I attacked Judah.	
		Omri (876-869)			Ashurnasirpal II (883-859)
875		Ahab (869-850)	Elijah	Ben-hadad II (Hadadezer) besieged Samaria, fought Ahab; joined coalition at Qarqar.	Shalmaneser III (859-824)
					Battle at Qarqar (853)
850		Jehu paid tribute to Shalmaneser III.	Elisha	Hazael: frequently oppressed Israel from ca. 843-806.	Received tribute from Israel (841)
825					Assyrian weakness (824-745)
		Jehoash (802-786)		Ben-hadad III oppressed Israel, but was attacked by Adad-nirari III.	Adad-nirari III (810-783) attacked Damascus; relieved pressure on Israel.
800	Amaziah (800-783)				
	Uzziah (783-742)	Jeroboam II (786-746)			
	Period of prosperity for both Judah and Israel				
775			Amos		
750			Isaiah		
			Hosea		
735	Ahaz (735-715)	Pekah (736-732)		Rezin: with Pekah tried to force Judah to join anti-Assyrian coalition.	Tiglath-pileser III (Assyrian Empire) took tribute from Menachen (738); attacked Israel (733).
	Syro-Ephraimite War (735)	Israel attacked by Tiglath-pileser. Hoshea rebelled against Assyria.			Shalmaneser V (727-722) Siege of Samaria
722		Destruction of Israel	Micah		Sargon II (722/1-705) deported 27,000 Israelites.

75 KINGS OF THE DIVIDED MONARCHY

JUDAH	(Bright)[1]	(Miller/Hays)[2]	ISRAEL	(Bright)[1]	(Miller/Hays)[2]
Rehoboam	922-915	924-907	⌐ Jeroboam I	922-901	924-903
Abijam	915-913	907-906	*Nadab	901-900	903-902
Asa	913-873	905-874	⌐		
			⌐ Baasha	900-877	902-886
			└ *Elah	877-876	886-885
			⌐ Zimri (suicide)	876	
			The Omrides	876-842	885-843
Jehoshaphat	873-849	874-850	⌐ Omri	876-869	885-873
			Ahab	869-850	873-851
			Ahaziah	850-849	851-849
Jehoram	849-843	850-843	└ *Jehoram	849-842	849-843
Ahaziah	843-842	843	Dynasty of Jehu	842-746	843-745
Athaliah (upsurper)	842-837	843-837	⌐ Jehu	843/2-815	843-816
Joash	837-800	837-?	Jehoahaz	815-802	816-800
Amaziah	800-783	?-?	Jehoash (Joash)	802-786	800-785
Uzziah (Azariah)	783-742	?-?	Jeroboam II	786-746	785-745
Jotham	742-735	?-742	└ *Zechariah	746-745	745
			⌐ *Shallum	745	745
Ahaz	735-715	742-727	⌐ Menahem	745-737	745-736
			└ *Pekahiah	737-736	736-735
			⌐ *Pekah	736-732	735-732
			⌐ Hoshea	732-724	732-723
			Fall of Samaria	722	722
Hezekiah	715-687/6	727-698			
Manasseh	687/6-642	697-642			
Amon	642-640				
Josiah	640-609	639-609			
Jehoahaz	609	609			
Jehoiakim	609-598	608-598			
Jehoiachin	598/7	598/7			
Zedekiah	597-587	597-586			
Destruction of Jerusalem and the temple: 586					

Asterisk (*) indicates assassination
[1]Dates preferred by John Bright, *A History of Israel,* 3rd ed.
[2]Dates preferred by J. Maxwell Miller and John H. Hayes, *A History of Ancient Israel and Judah.*
Brackets ([) indicate dynasties

76 QUEENS OF THE OLD TESTAMENT

NAME	REFERENCE	IDENTIFICATION
Abijah	2 Kings 18:2	Mother of King Hezekiah of Judah
Athaliah	2 Kings 11	Evil daughter of Ahab and Jezebel; mother of King Ahaziah of Judah (only woman to rule Judah in her own right)
Azubah	1 Kings 22:42	Mother of King Jehoshaphat of Judah
Bathsheba	2 Sam. 11–12; 1 Kings 1–2	Wife of Uriah, then wife of David and mother of Solomon
Esther	Esther 2–9	Jewish wife of King Ahasuerus of Persia
Hamutal	2 Kings 23:31; 24:18	Mother of King Jehoahaz and King Zedekiah of Judah
Hephzibah	2 Kings 21:1	Mother of King Manasseh of Judah
Jecoliah	2 Kings 15:2	Mother of King Azariah of Judah
Jedidah	2 Kings 22:1	Mother of King Josiah of Judah
Jehoaddin	2 Kings 14:2	Mother of King Amaziah of Judah
Jezebel	1 Kings 16:31; 18:13,19; 19:1-2;21:1-25; 2 Kings 9:30-37	Evil wife of King Ahab of Israel (who promoted Baal worship, persecuted God's prophets, and planned Naboth's murder)
Maacah	1 Kings 15:10; 2 Chron. 15:16	Mother of King Abijah and grandmother of King Asa of Judah
Meshullemeth	2 Kings 21:19	Mother of King Amon of Judah
Michal	1 Sam. 18:20-28; 26:44; 2 Sam. 3:13-16; 6:20-23	Daughter of Saul and first wife of David
Naamah	1 Kings 14:21,31	Mother of King Rehoboam of Judah
Nehushta	2 Kings 24:8	Mother of King Jehoiachin of Judah
Queen of Sheba	1 Kings 10:1-13	Foreign queen who visited Solomon
Zebidah	2 Kings 23:36	Mother of King Jehoiakim of Judah

77 THE KINGDOMS OF ISRAEL AND JUDAH

LEGEND
- • City
- ★ Capital city
- ○ City (uncertain location)
- ▲ Mountain peak
- Israel
- Judah
- —— International roads
- —— Local roads

Jeroboam built a sanctuary

Political capital of Israel from Omri onward

Jeroboam built a sanctuary

MEDITERRANEAN SEA

GESHUR

ISRAEL

JUDAH

PHILISTIA

MOAB

EDOM

DEAD SEA

Negeb

1 Kings 12:26-27

Jeroboam said to himself, "The way things are going now, the kingdom might return to the house of David. If these people regularly go to offer sacrifices in the LORD's temple in Jerusalem, the heart of these people will return to their lord, Rehoboam king of Judah. They will murder me and go back to the king of Judah."

78 THE CAMPAIGN OF SHISHAK AND REHOBOAM'S DEFENSE LINES

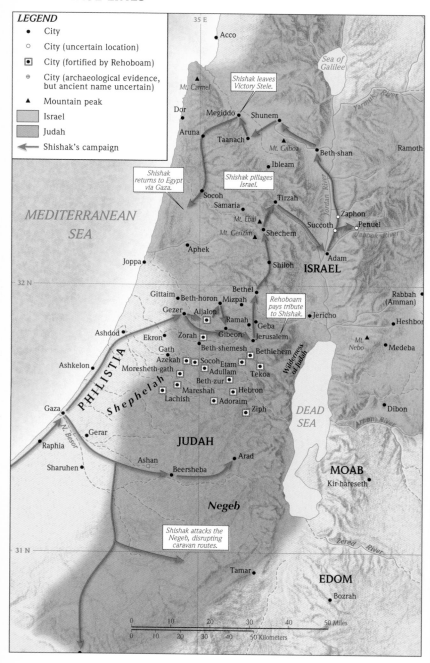

2 Chronicles 12:2
Because they were unfaithful to the LORD, in the fifth year of King Rehoboam, Shishak king of Egypt went to war against Jerusalem.

79 CONFLICTS BETWEEN ISRAEL AND ARAM-DAMASCUS

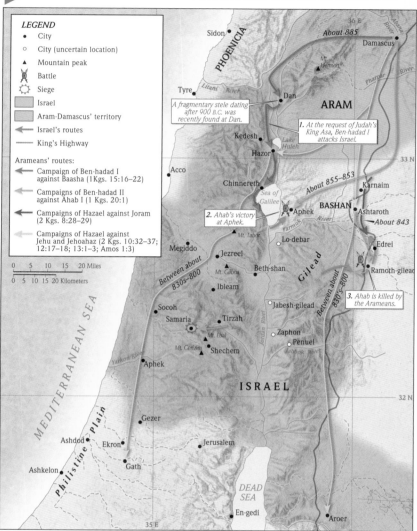

LEGEND
- • City
- ○ City (uncertain location)
- ▲ Mountain peak
- Battle
- Siege
- Israel
- Aram-Damascus' territory
- ← Israel's routes
- — King's Highway

Arameans' routes:
- ← Campaign of Ben-hadad I against Baasha (1 Kgs. 15:16–22)
- ← Campaigns of Ben-hadad II against Ahab I (1 Kgs. 20:1)
- ← Campaigns of Hazael against Joram (2 Kgs. 8:28–29)
- ← Campaigns of Hazael against Jehu and Jehoahaz (2 Kgs. 10:32–37; 12:17–18; 13:1–3; Amos 1:3)

A fragmentary stele dating after 900 B.C. was recently found at Dan.

1. At the request of Judah's King Asa, Ben-hadad I attacks Israel.

2. Ahab's victory at Aphek.

3. Ahab is killed by the Arameans.

Map labels: Sidon, Damascus, PHOENICIA, Mt. Hermon, Tyre, Litani River, Dan, ARAM, Pharpar River, About 885, 36 E, Kedesh, Lake Huleh, Hazor, 33 N, Acco, Chinnereth, Sea of Galilee, Aphek, Karnaim, About 855–853, BASHAN, Ashtaroth, About 843, Yarmuk River, Mt. Tabor, Lo-debar, Edrei, Megiddo, Jezreel, Mt. Gilboa, Beth-shan, Gilead, Ramoth-gilead, Ibleam, Jabesh-gilead, Between about 830s–800, Socoh, Samaria, Tirzah, Zaphon, Penuel, Mt. Ebal, Mt. Gerizim, Shechem, MEDITERRANEAN SEA, Aphek, ISRAEL, 32 N, Gezer, Ashdod, Ekron, Jerusalem, Ashkelon, Gath, Philistine Plain, Yarkon River, Jordan River, Jabbok River, DEAD SEA, En-gedi, Aroer, 35 E

Scale: 0 5 10 15 20 Miles / 0 5 10 15 20 Kilometers

2 Kings 8:28

Ahaziah went with Joram son of Ahab to fight against Hazael king of Aram in Ramoth-gilead, and the Arameans wounded Joram.

80 KINGS OF ARAM-DAMASCUS

NAME	OLD TESTAMENT REFERENCE	KEY OLD TESTAMENT PASSAGE
Rezon	Contemporary of Solomon; seized Damascus and became an adversary of Israel. Some scholars identify Rezon with Hezion (1 Kings 15:18)	1 Kings 11:23-25
Tabrimmon	Father of Ben-hadad I	1 Kings 15:18
Ben-hadad I	Son of Tabrimmon. Attacked Israel at Asa's request in the reign of Baasha.	1 Kings 15:18-22; 2 Chron. 16:1-6
Ben-hadad II, known as Hadad-ezer in Assyrian sources	Contemporary of Ahab. Besieged Samaria. Fought Ahab at Aphek east of the Sea of Chinnereth. Fought Israel at Ramoth-gilead. Joined Ahab in an anti-Assyrian coalition that fought Shalmaneser III at Qarqar in 853 BC.	1 Kings 20:1-34; 22:1-40; 2 Kings 6:24–7:20, 8:7-15; 2 Chron. 18:1-34
Hazael	Usurper who seized the throne of Damascus ca. 843 BC. Assyrian records call him "a son of nobody," i.e., a commoner. Besieged Ramoth-gilead in the days of Joram. During the late ninth century in the reigns of Jehu and Jehoahaz, Hazael frequently oppressed Israel, Judah, and the Philistine cities as well. Most able of kings of Damascus.	1 Kings 19:15; 2 Kings 8:7-15; 8:28-29; 10:32; 12:17-18; 13:1-9; 13:25
Ben-hadad III	Son of Hazael. Contemporary of Jehoahaz. Continued to oppress Israel. Joash fought Ben-hadad, temporarily throwing off the Aramean yoke; Adad-nirari III attacked Damascus (either in 805 or 796). Ben-hadad lost much of the kingdom built by his father, Hazael.	2 Kings 13:3-8
Rezin	Probably a usurper; led an anti-Assyrian coalition, including Israel, Philistia, and Phoenician cities ca. 737–735. With Israel, attacked Judah to force Ahaz to join coalition ca. 735 (Syro-Ephraimite War). Last king of an independent Aram-Damascus. Killed by the Assyrians ca. 732 BC.	2 Kings 15-16; Isa. 7

81 THE OMRIDE DYNASTY

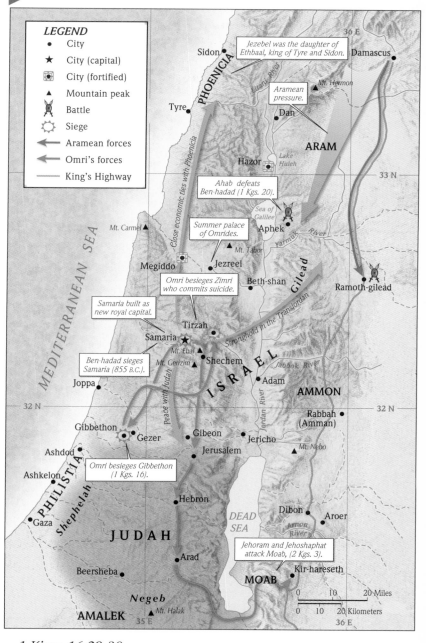

LEGEND
- • City
- ★ City (capital)
- ▣ City (fortified)
- ▲ Mountain peak
- ✖ Battle
- ⚙ Siege
- ← Aramean forces
- ← Omri's forces
- — King's Highway

Jezebel was the daughter of Ethbaal, king of Tyre and Sidon.

Aramean pressure.

Ahab defeats Ben-hadad (1 Kgs. 20).

Summer palace of Omrides.

Omri besieges Zimri who commits suicide.

Samaria built as new royal capital.

Ben-hadad sieges Samaria (855 B.C.).

Omri besieges Gibbethon (1 Kgs. 16).

Jehoram and Jehoshaphat attack Moab, (2 Kgs. 3).

PHOENICIA
ARAM
ISRAEL
JUDAH
AMMON
MOAB
PHILISTIA
AMALEK
MEDITERRANEAN SEA
DEAD SEA
Negeb
Shephelah
Gilead
Stronghold in the Transjordan
Close economic ties with Phoenicia
Peace with Judah
Litani River
Yarmuk River
Jabbok River
Jordan River
Arnon River

Sidon
Damascus
Tyre
Dan
Mt. Hermon
Hazor
Lake Huleh
Mt. Carmel
Aphek
Sea of Galilee
Mt. Tabor
Megiddo
Jezreel
Beth-shan
Ramoth-gilead
Tirzah
Samaria
Mt. Ebal
Mt. Gerizim
Shechem
Adam
Joppa
Gibeon
Jericho
Rabbah (Amman)
Mt. Nebo
Gibbethon
Gezer
Jerusalem
Ashdod
Ashkelon
Hebron
Dibon
Aroer
Gaza
Arad
Kir-hareseth
Beersheba
Mt. Halak

36 E
33 N
32 N
35 E
36 E

0   10   20 Miles
0   10   20 Kilometers

1 Kings 16:29-30

Ahab son of Omri became king over Israel in the thirty-eighth year of Judah's King Asa; Ahab son of Omri reigned over Israel in Samaria 22 years. But Ahab son of Omri did what was evil in the LORD's sight more than all who were before him.

82 ELIJAH AND ELISHA

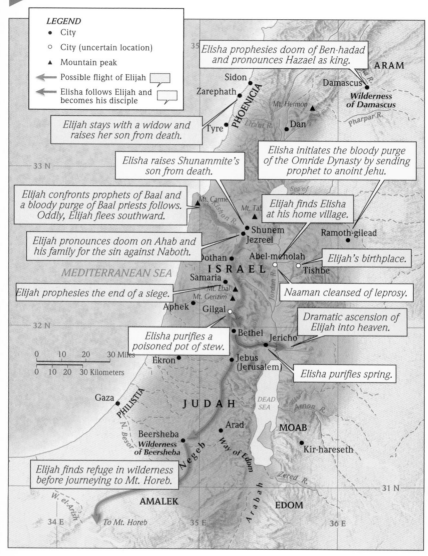

LEGEND
- ● City
- ○ City (uncertain location)
- ▲ Mountain peak
- ← Possible flight of Elijah
- ← Elisha follows Elijah and becomes his disciple

Elisha prophesies doom of Ben-hadad and pronounces Hazael as king.

Elijah stays with a widow and raises her son from death.

Elisha raises Shunammite's son from death.

Elijah confronts prophets of Baal and a bloody purge of Baal priests follows. Oddly, Elijah flees southward.

Elisha initiates the bloody purge of the Omride Dynasty by sending prophet to anoint Jehu.

Elijah finds Elisha at his home village.

Elijah pronounces doom on Ahab and his family for the sin against Naboth.

Elijah's birthplace.

Elijah prophesies the end of a siege.

Naaman cleansed of leprosy.

Elisha purifies a poisoned pot of stew.

Dramatic ascension of Elijah into heaven.

Elisha purifies spring.

Elijah finds refuge in wilderness before journeying to Mt. Horeb.

ARAM · Sidon · Damascus · Zarephath · PHOENICIA · Mt. Hermon · Wilderness of Damascus · Pharpar R. · Tyre · Dan · Litani R. · Sea of · Mt. Carmel · Mt. Tab · Kishon R. · Shunem · Jezreel · Ramoth-gilead · Dothan · Abel-meholah · ISRAEL · Tishbe · MEDITERRANEAN SEA · Samaria · Mt. Ebal · Mt. Gerizim · Jordan R. · Aphek · Gilgal · Bethel · Jericho · Ekron · Jebus (Jerusalem) · Gaza · PHILISTIA · JUDAH · DEAD SEA · Amon R. · N. Besor · Arad · MOAB · Beersheba · Wilderness of Beersheba · Kir-haresth · Negeb · Way of Edom · Zered R. · W. el-Arish · AMALEK · Arabah · EDOM · To Mt. Horeb · 33 N · 32 N · 31 N · 34 E · 35 E · 36 E

0 10 20 30 Miles
0 10 20 30 Kilometers

2 Kings 2:1-2

The time had come for the LORD to take Elijah up to heaven in a whirlwind. Elijah and Elisha were traveling from Gilgal, and Elijah said to Elisha, "Stay here; the LORD is sending me on to Bethel." But Elisha replied, "As the LORD lives and as you yourself live, I will not leave you." So they went down to Bethel.

83 ▶ THE REVOLT OF JEHU

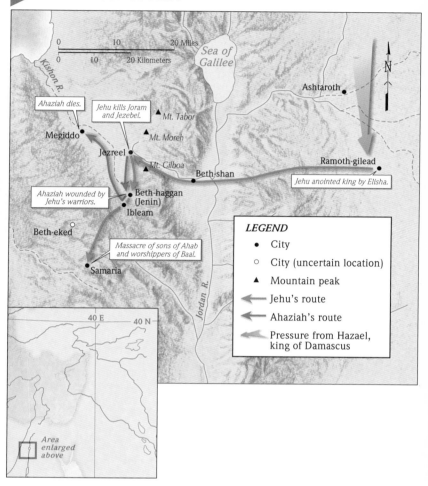

Sea of Galilee

Kishon R.

Ashtaroth

Ahaziah dies.

Jehu kills Joram and Jezebel.

▲ Mt. Tabor

▲ Mt. Moreh

Megiddo

Jezreel

▲ Mt. Gilboa

Beth-shan

Ramoth-gilead

Jehu anointed king by Elisha.

Ahaziah wounded by Jehu's warriors.

Beth-haggan (Jenin)

Ibleam

Beth-eked

Massacre of sons of Ahab and worshippers of Baal.

Samaria

Jordan R.

LEGEND

● City

○ City (uncertain location)

▲ Mountain peak

← Jehu's route

← Ahaziah's route

← Pressure from Hazael, king of Damascus

40 E   40 N

Area enlarged above

2 Kings 10:17
When Jehu came to Samaria, he struck down all who remained from the house of Ahab in Samaria until he had annihilated his house, according to the word of the LORD spoken to Elijah.

ASSYRIA

Less than a century after Solomon's death, Assyria, a nation of northern Mesopotamia became an empire. Assyrian expansion into the region of Palestine (ca. 855–625 BC) had enormous impact on the Hebrew kingdoms of Israel and Judah.

Assyria lay north of the region of Babylonia along the banks of the Tigris River (Gen. 2:14) in northern Mesopotamia. The name Assyria (Hb., *Ashshur*) is from Asshur, its first capital, founded about 2000 BC. The foundation of other Assyrian cities, notably Calah and Nineveh, appears in Genesis 10:11-12.

The history of Assyria is well documented in royal Assyrian annals, building inscriptions, king lists, correspondence, and other archaeological evidence. By 1900 BC these cities were vigorously trading as far away as Cappadocia in eastern Asia Minor. An expanded Assyria warred with the famous King Hammurabi of Babylon shortly before breaking up into smaller city-states about 1700 BC.

Beginning about 1300 BC, a reunited Assyria made rapid territorial advances and soon became an international power. Expanding westward, Tiglath-pileser I (1115–1077 BC) became the first Assyrian monarch to march his army to the shores of the Mediterranean. With his murder, however, Assyria entered a 166-year period of decline.

Assyria awoke from its dark ages under Adad-nirari II (911–891 BC), who reestablished the nation as a power to be reckoned with in Mesopotamia. His grandson, Ashurnasirpal II (883–859 BC) moved Assyria toward the status of an empire. Ashurnasirpal II used a well-deserved reputation for cruelty to

▲ Replica of the black obelisk of Shalmaneser III, kin of Assyria from 858 to 824 BC. The obelisk was discovered at Nimrud.

extort tribute and taxes from states within the reach of his army in predatory campaigns. He also rebuilt the city of Calah as the new military and administrative capital. Carved stone panels in Ashurnasirpal's palace there show violent scenes of the king's vicious campaigns against unsubmissive enemies.

Unusual pottery vessel from Assyrian trading colony period.

Ashurnasirpal's son Shalmaneser III (858–824 BC) continued a policy of Assyrian expansion through his annual campaigns in all directions. These were no longer mere predatory raids. Rather, they demonstrated a systematic economic exploitation of subject states. As always, failure to submit to Assyria brought vicious military action. The results, however, were not always a complete victory for Assyria. In such a context Assyria first encountered the Hebrew kingdoms of the Bible. In 853 BC at Qarqar in north Syria, Shalmaneser fought a coalition of 12 kings including Hadad-ezer (Ben-Hadad; 1 Kings 20:26,34) of Aram-Damascus and Ahab of Israel. This confrontation is not mentioned in the Bible, but it may have taken place during a three-year period of peace between Israel and Aram-Damascus (1 Kings 22:1). In his official inscriptions Shalmaneser claims victory, but the battle was inconclusive. In 841 BC he finally defeated Hazael of Damascus and on Mount Carmel received tribute from Tyre, Sidon, and King Jehu of Israel. A scene carved in relief on the Black Obelisk of Shalmaneser, unearthed at Calah, shows Jehu groveling before Shalmaneser, the only known depiction of an Israelite king.

Recarved fragment of Assyrian soldiers shooting at a town.

With the death of Shalmaneser, Assyria entered another period of decline during which she was occupied with the nearby kingdom of Urartu. For the next century only one Assyrian king seriously affected affairs in Palestine. Adad-nirari III (810–783 BC) entered Damascus, taking extensive tribute from Ben-hadad III. He is probably the "savior" of 2 Kings 13:5, who allowed Israel to escape domination by Aram-Damascus. Nevertheless, Adad-nirari also collected tribute from Jehoash of Israel.

Assyrian preoccupation with Urartu ended with the reign of Tiglath-pileser III (744–727 BC). The true founder of the Assyrian Empire, he made changes in the administration of conquered territories. Nations close to the Assyrian homeland were incorporated as provinces. Others were left with native rule but subject to an Assyrian overseer. Tiglath-pileser also instituted a policy of mass deportations to reduce local nationalistic feelings. He took conquered people into exile to live in lands vacated by other conquered exiles (cp. 2 Kings 17:24).

As Tiglath-pileser, also called Pul, arrived on the coast of Phoenicia, Menahem of Israel (2 Kings 15:19) and Rezin of Aram-Damascus brought tribute and became vassals of Assyria. An anti-Assyrian alliance quickly formed. Israel and Aram-Damascus attacked Jerusalem about 735 BC in an attempt to replace King Ahaz of Judah with a man loyal to the anti-Assyrian alliance (2 Kings 16:2-6; Isa. 7:1-6) and thus force Judah's participation. Against the protests of Isaiah (Isa. 7:4,16-17; 8:4-8), Ahaz appealed to Tiglath-pileser for assistance (2 Kings 16:7-9). Tiglath-pileser, in response, campaigned against Philistia (734 BC), reduced Israel to the area immediately around Samaria (2 Kings 15:29; 733 BC), and annexed Aram-Damascus (732 BC), deporting the population. Ahaz, for his part, became an Assyrian vassal (2 Kings 16:10; 2 Chron. 28:16,20-22).

Little is known of the reign of Tiglath-pileser's successor, Shalmaneser V (726–722 BC), except that he besieged Samaria for three years in response to Hoshea's failure to pay tribute (2 Kings 17:3-5). The city finally fell to Shalmaneser (2 Kings 17:6; 18:9-12), who apparently died in the same year. His successor, Sargon II (722–705 BC), took credit in Assyrian royal inscriptions for deporting 27,290 inhabitants of Samaria.

Sargon campaigned in the region to counter rebellions in Gaza in 720 BC and Ashdod in 712 (Isa. 20:1). Hezekiah of Judah was tempted to join in the Ashdod rebellion, but Isaiah warned against such action (Isa. 18). Meanwhile, unrest smoldered in other parts of the empire. A rebellious king of Babylon, Merodach-baladan, found support from Elam, Assyria's enemy to the east. Though forced to flee Babylon in 710 BC,

▲ Sargon, king of Assyria, with vizier and royal functionary from Sargon's palace.

Merodach-baladan returned some years later to reclaim the throne. He sent emissaries to Hezekiah in Jerusalem (2 Kings 20:12-19; Isa. 39), apparently as part of preparations for a concerted anti-Assyrian revolt.

From the late Assyrian period a human headed winged-apron sphinx.

News of Sargon's death in battle served as a signal to anti-Assyrian forces. Sennacherib (704–681 BC) ascended the throne in the midst of widespread revolt. Merodach-baladan of Babylon, supported by the Elamites, had inspired the rebellion of all southern Mesopotamia. A number of states in Phoenicia and Palestine were also in rebellion, led by Hezekiah of Judah. After subduing Babylon, Sennacherib turned his attentions westward. In 701 BC, he reasserted control over the city-states of Phoenicia, sacked Joppa and Ashkelon, and invaded Judah where Hezekiah had made considerable military preparations (2 Kings 20:20; 2 Chron. 32:1-8,30; Isa. 22:8b-11). Sennacherib's own account of the invasion provides a remarkable supplement to the biblical version (2 Kings 18:13–19:36). He claims to have destroyed 46 walled cities (2 Kings 18:13) and to have taken 200,150 captives. Sennacherib's conquest of Lachish is shown in graphic detail in carved panels from his palace at Nineveh. During the siege of Lachish, an Assyrian army was sent against Jerusalem where Hezekiah was "made a prisoner . . . like a bird in a cage." Three of Sennacherib's dignitaries attempted to negotiate the surrender of Jerusalem (2 Kings 18:17-37), but Hezekiah continued to hold out with the encouragement of Isaiah (2 Kings 19:1-7,20-35). In the end the Assyrian army withdrew, and Hezekiah paid an enormous tribute (2 Kings 18:14-16). The Assyrian account claims a victory over the Egyptian army and mentions Hezekiah's tribute but is rather vague about the end of the campaign. The Bible mentions the approach of the Egyptian army (2 Kings 19:9) and tells of a miraculous defeat of the Assyrians by the angel of the Lord (2 Kings 19:35-36). The fifth-century BC Greek historian Herodotus relates that the Assyrians suffered defeat because a plague of field mice destroyed their equipment. It is not certain whether these accounts can be combined to infer an outbreak of the plague. Certainly, Sennacherib suffered a major setback, for Hezekiah was the only ruler of the revolt to keep his throne.

 Basalt relief orthostats belonging to a doorway. They portray the classes of the Assyrian army. From the neo-Assyrian period during the reign of Tiglath-pileser (744–727 BC).

On a more peaceful front, Sennacherib conducted some major building projects in Assyria. The ancient city of Nineveh was rebuilt as the new royal residence and Assyrian capital. War continued, however, with Elam, which also influenced Babylon to rebel again. An enraged Sennacherib razed the sacred city in 689 BC. His murder, at the hands of his own sons (2 Kings 19:37) in 681 BC, was interpreted by Babylonians as divine judgment for destroying their city.

Esarhaddon (681–669 BC) emerged as the new king and immediately began the rebuilding of Babylon, an act which won the allegiance of the local populace. He warred with nomadic tribes to the north and quelled a rebellion in Phoenicia, while Manasseh of Judah remained a loyal vassal. His greatest military adventure, however, was an invasion of Egypt conducted in 671 BC. Pharaoh Taharqa fled south as Memphis fell to the Assyrians, but returned and fomented rebellion two years later. Esarhaddon died in 669 BC on his way back to subjugate Egypt.

After conducting a brief expedition against eastern tribes, Esarhaddon's son, Ashurbanipal (668–627 BC), set out to reconquer Egypt. Assisted by 22 subject kings, including Manasseh of Judah, he invaded in 667 BC. He defeated Pharaoh Taharqa and took the ancient capital of Thebes. Some 1,300 miles from home, Ashurbanipal had no choice but to reinstall the local rulers his father had appointed in Egypt and hope for the best. Plans for revolt began immediately; but Assyrian officers got wind of the plot, captured the rebels, and sent them to Nineveh. Egypt rebelled again in 665 BC. This time Ashurbanipal destroyed Thebes, also called No-Amon (Nah. 3:8, NASB). Phoenician attempts at revolt were also crushed.

Ashurbanipal ruled at Assyria's zenith but also saw the beginning of her swift collapse. Ten years after the destruction of Thebes, Egypt rebelled yet again. Assyria could do nothing because of a war with Elam. In 651 BC Ashurbanipal's brother, the king of Babylon, organized a widespread revolt. After three years of continual battles

Babylon was subdued but remained filled with seeds of hatred for Assyria. Action against Arab tribes followed, and the war with Elam continued until a final Assyrian victory in 639 BC. That same year the official annals of Ashurbanipal came to an abrupt end. With Ashurbanipal's death in 627 BC, unrest escalated. By 626, Babylon had fallen into the hands of the Chaldean Nabopolassar. Outlying states, such as Judah under Josiah, were free to rebel without fear. War continued between Assyria and Babylon until, in 614 BC, the old Assyrian capital Asshur was sacked by the Medes. Then, in 612 BC, Calah was destroyed. The combined armies of the Babylonians and the Medes laid siege to Nineveh. After two months the city fell.

An Assyrian general claimed the throne and rallied what was left of the Assyrian army in Haran. An alliance with Egypt brought a few troops to Assyria's aid; but in 610 BC the Babylonians approached, and Haran was abandoned. In 605 BC the last remnants of the battered Assyrian Empire, along with their recent Egyptian allies, were deferred on the Battle of Carchemish. Assyria was no more.

▲ The Gihon Spring in the Kidron Valley. King Hezekiah built a tunnel from the spring to the pool of Siloam which he built to provide water in the event of sieges like that threatened by Assyria's King Sennacherib.

84▶ THE RISE OF ASSYRIA

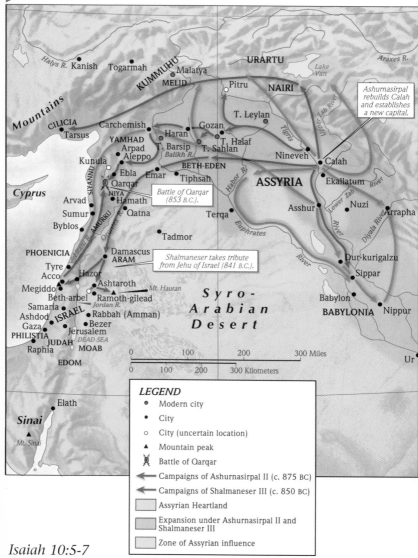

Isaiah 10:5-7

Woe to Assyria, the rod of My anger—
    the staff in their hands is My wrath.
    I will send him against a godless nation;
    I will command him to go
    against a people destined for My rage,
    to take spoils, to plunder,
    and to trample them down like clay in the streets.
    But this is not what he intends;
    this is not what he plans.
    It is his intent to destroy
    and to cut off many nations.

85▶ ISRAEL AND JUDAH IN THE DAYS OF JEROBOAM II AND UZZIAH

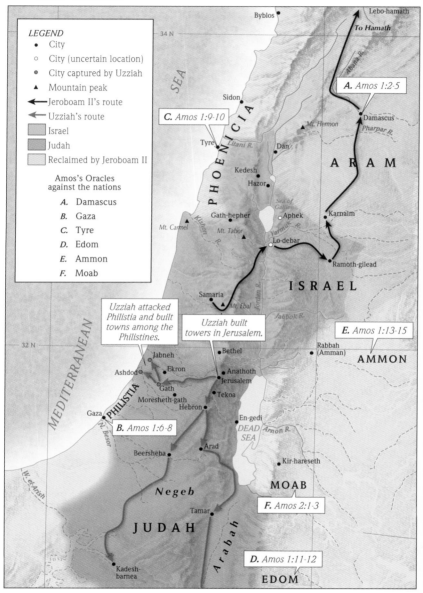

2 Chronicles 26:6-8

Uzziah went out to wage war against the Philistines, and he tore down the wall of Gath, the wall of Jabneh, and the wall of Ashdod. Then he built cities in the vicinity of Ashdod and among the Philistines. God helped him against the Philistines, the Arabs that live in Gur-baal, and the Meunites. The Ammonites gave Uzziah tribute money, and his fame spread as far as the entrance of Egypt, for God made him very powerful.

86 THE NEO-ASSYRIAN EMPIRE

STATE OF ASSYRIAN POWER	KINGS OF ASSYRIA	DATES RULED (BC)
Initial phase of expansion	Ashurnasirpal II	883–859
	Shalmaneser III	859–824
Period of weakness 823–745 BC Reasons for period of weakness: 1. Problems with the kingdom of Urartu 2. Internal unrest 3. Weak central government	Shamshi-adad V	823–811
	Adad-nirari III	810–783
	Shalmaneser IV	782–772
	Ashur-dan III	771–754
	Ashur-nirari V	753–746
Period of imperial expansion	Tiglath-pileser III (Pul)	745–727
	Shalmaneser V	727–722
	Sargon II	722–705
	Sennacherib	705–681
	Esarhaddon	681–669
	Ashurbanipal II	669–627

ACTIVITIES AND ACCOMPLISHMENTS

Utilized tactics of terror to achieve Assyrian goals; rebuilt Calah (Nimrud) and made it his capital; collected tribute from states as far south as Tyre, Sidon, and Byblos

Campaigned six times in the Levant; fought a coalition that included Ahab, king of Israel, at Qarqar in 853 BC; took tribute from Jehu, king of Israel in 841 (Black Obelisk of Shalmaneser)

Campaigned in Syria in late ninth and early eighth centuries (805–796?); Rimnah Stele records an attack on Damascus and tribute collected from Joash "of Samaria"; perhaps the "savior" of 2 Kings 13:5

Dealt with Urartu; centralized the power of the kings; developed policies to expand Assyrian territory west and south of the Euphrates; took tribute from Menahem of Israel in 738 BC (2 Kings 15:19-20); conquered Babylon. Ahaz of Judah appealed to Tiglath-pileser for help during the Syro-Ephraimite War (735 BC; 2 Kings 16:7-9). Tiglath-pileser attacked Israel and Damascus (733-732 BC), significantly reducing Israel's territory (2 Kings 15:29)

Hoshea, king of Israel, initially paid tribute to Shalmaneser V, but finally rebelled with the promise of Egyptian help (2 Kings 17:1-5). Shalmaneser V besieged Samaria for three years, with the city falling in 722 BC

Established a new capital, Dur-Sharrukin (Khorsabad); claimed to be the conqueror of Samaria; converted Samaria into an Assyrian province after putting down additional rebellions backed by Egypt and key Philistine cities in 720 BC; exiled 27,000 Israelites and settled them on the Habor River near Nineveh and settled them in the region of Samaria (2 Kings 17:24); further revolts in 713/712 BC sponsored by Egypt (Shabaku of Twenty-fifth Dynasty) involving Ashdod, Judah, Edom, and Moab provoked additional campaigns in the Levant (see Isa. 20); faced sustained opposition from a Chaldean Elamite coalition led by Merodoch-baladan; led campaigns into Urartu, finally subduing the country; died in battle fighting the Cimmerians in 705

Rebuilt Nineveh for use as the Assyrian capital; subdued further Chaldean troubles in Babylon; led an attack on Judah in 701 BC in which forty-six Judean cities were destroyed; Jerusalem, though besieged, escaped destruction (2 Kings 18-19; Isa. 36-37; 2 Chron. 32); important archaelogical evidence: the Lachish Frieze, the Siloam Inscription, the Prism of Sennacherib

Attacked Egypt in 669 BC

Conquered Thebes in 663 BC; zenith of the Neo-Assyrian Empire; put down revolt in Babylon in 652 led by his brother Shamash-shum-ukin

87 ▶ THE ASSYRIAN EMPIRE UNDER TIGLATH-PILESER III

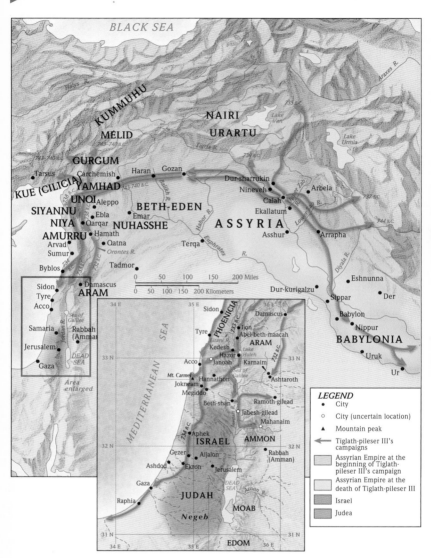

2 Kings 15:19-20
Pul king of Assyria invaded the land, so Menahem gave Pul 75,000 pounds of silver so that Pul would support him to strengthen his grip on the kingdom. Then Menahem exacted 20 ounces of silver from each of the wealthy men of Israel to give to the king of Assyria. So the king of Assyria withdrew and did not stay there in the land.

88 ▶ THE SYRO-EPHRAIMITE WAR

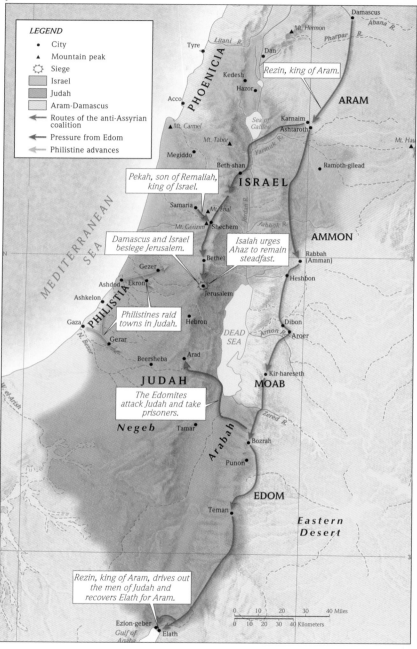

LEGEND
- • City
- ▲ Mountain peak
- ⚙ Siege
- ▨ Israel
- ▨ Judah
- ▨ Aram-Damascus
- ← Routes of the anti-Assyrian coalition
- ← Pressure from Edom
- ← Philistine advances

Rezin, king of Aram.

Pekah, son of Remaliah, king of Israel.

Damascus and Israel besiege Jerusalem.

Isaiah urges Ahaz to remain steadfast.

Philistines raid towns in Judah.

The Edomites attack Judah and take prisoners.

Rezin, king of Aram, drives out the men of Judah and recovers Elath for Aram.

Isaiah 7:1

This took place during the reign of Ahaz, son of Jotham, son of Uzziah king of Judah: Rezin king of Aram, along with Pekah, son of Remaliah, king of Israel, waged war against Jerusalem, but he could not succeed.

89 TIGLATH-PILESER III'S CAMPAIGNS

LEGEND
- City
- ○ City (uncertain location)
- ⊡ City mentioned in 2 Kgs 15:29
- ▲ Mountain peak
- ← Tiglath-pileser III (734 B.C.) (campaign against the Philistines)
- ← Tiglath-pileser III (733 B.C.) (campaign against Israel)
- ← Tiglath-pileser III (732 B.C.) (campaign against Damascus)
- **TYRE** Assyrian province

2 Kings 16:10

King Ahaz went to Damascus to meet Tiglath-pileser king of Assyria. When he saw the altar that was in Damascus, King Ahaz sent a model of the altar and complete plans for its construction to Uriah the priest.

90 ▶ THE FALL OF SAMARIA AND DEPORTATION OF ISRAELITES

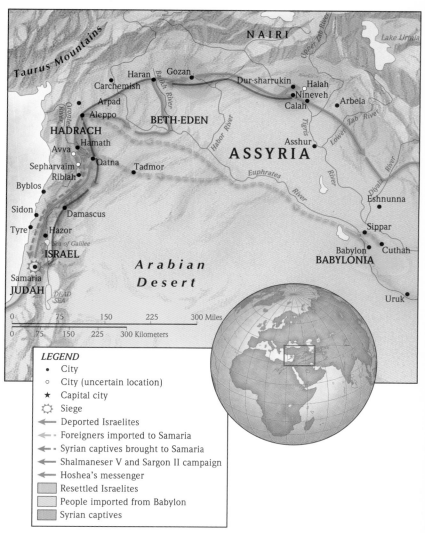

NAIRI

Lake Urmia

Taurus Mountains

Haran · Gozan

Carchemish

Dur-sharrukin · Halah

Nineveh

Arpad

Calah · Arbela

Aleppo

BETH-EDEN

HADRACH

Hamath

Asshur

Avva

ASSYRIA

Sepharvaim · Qatna · Tadmor

Riblah

Euphrates River

Byblos

Eshnunna

Sidon · Damascus

Sippar

Tyre · Hazor

Sea of Galilee

Babylon · Cuthah

ISRAEL

BABYLONIA

Arabian

Samaria

Desert

JUDAH · DEAD SEA

Uruk

Upper Zab River

Halah

Lower Zab River

Tigris

Diyala River

Orontes River

Habor River

Balih River

| 0 | 75 | 150 | 225 | 300 Miles |
| 0 | 75 | 150 | 225 | 300 Kilometers |

LEGEND

- • City
- ○ City (uncertain location)
- ★ Capital city
- ☼ Siege
- ◄— Deported Israelites
- ◄-· Foreigners imported to Samaria
- ◄-■ Syrian captives brought to Samaria
- ◄— Shalmaneser V and Sargon II campaign
- ◄— Hoshea's messenger
- ▭ Resettled Israelites
- ▭ People imported from Babylon
- ▭ Syrian captives

2 Kings 17:5-7

Then the king of Assyria invaded the whole land, marched up to Samaria, and besieged it for three years. In the ninth year of Hoshea, the king of Assyria captured Samaria. He deported the Israelites to Assyria and settled them in Halah and by the Habor, Gozan's river, and in the cities of the Medes. This disaster happened because the people of Israel had sinned against the LORD their God who had brought them out of the land of Egypt from the power of Pharaoh king of Egypt and because they had worshiped other gods.

91 ASSYRIAN DISTRICTS AFTER THE FALL OF SAMARIA

LEGEND
- • City
- • Modern city
- TYRE Assyrian Districts
- Assyrian vassal states
- Semi-independent states

Judah remains loyal to Assyria, while Ahaz permits pagan practices to flourish.

2 Kings 17:24

Then the king of Assyria brought people from Babylon, Cuthah, Avva, Hamath, and Sepharvaim and settled them in place of the Israelites in the cities of Samaria. The settlers took possession of Samaria and lived in its cities.

92 THE PROPHETS IN HISTORY

Prophet	Approx. Dates (BC)	Location/ Home	Basic Bible Passage	Central Teaching	Key Verse
Elijah	875–850	Tishbe	1 Kings 17:1– 2 Kings 2:18	Yahweh, not Baal, is God	1 Kings 18:21
Micaiah	856	Samaria	1 Kings 22; 2 Chron. 18	Judgment on Ahab; proof of prophecy	1 Kings 22:28
Elisha	855–800	Abel Meholah	1 Kings 19:15-21; 2 Kings 2–9; 13	God's miraculous power	2 Kings 5:15
Jonah	786–746	Gath Hepher	2 Kings 14:25; Jonah	God's universal concern	Jon. 4:11
Hosea	786–746	Israel	Hosea	God's unquenchable love	Hos. 11:8-9
Amos	760–750	Tekoa	Amos	God's call for justice and righteousness	Amos 5:24
Isaiah	740–698	Jerusalem	2 Kings 19–20; Isaiah	Hope through repentance & suffering	Isa 1:18; 53:4-6
Micah	735–710	Moresheth Gath Jerusalem	Jer. 26:18; Micah	Call for humble mercy and justice	Mic. 6:8
Oded	733	Samaria	2 Chron. 28:9-11	Do not go beyond God's command	2 Chron. 28:9
Nahum	686–612	Elkosh	Nahum	God's jealousy protects His people	Nah. 1:2-3
Zephaniah	640–621	?	Zephaniah	Hope for the humble humble righteous	Zeph. 2:3
Jeremiah	626–584	Anathoth/ Jerusalem	2 Chron. 36:12; Jeremiah	Faithful prophet points to new covenant	Jer. 31:33-34
Huldah (the prophetess)	621	Jerusalem	2 Kings 22; 2 Chron. 34	God's Book is accurate	2 Kings 22:16
Habakkuk	608–598	?	Habakkuk	God calls for faithfulness	Hab. 2:4
Ezekiel	593–571	Babylon	Ezekiel	Future hope for new community of worship	Ezek. 37:12-13
Obadiah	580	Jerusalem	Obadiah	Doom on Edom to bring God's kingdom	Obad. 21
Joel	539–331	Jerusalem	Joel	Call to repent and experience God's Spirit	Joel 2:28-29
Haggai	520	Jerusalem	Ezra 5:1; 6:14; Haggai	The priority of God's house	Hag. 2:8-9
Zechariah	520–514	Jerusalem	Ezra 5:1; 6:14; Zechariah	Faithfulness will lead to God's universal rule	Zech. 14:9
Malachi	500–450	Jerusalem	Malachi	Honor God and wait for His righteousness	Mal. 4:2

93 ▶ PROPHETS OF THE EIGHTH CENTURY

LEGEND
- • City
- ○ City (uncertain location)
- ▲ Mountain peak

0   10   20   30 Miles
0   10   20   30 Kilometers

Hosea's marriage portrays Israel's faithlessness to Yahweh; predicts Assyria will destroy Israel.

Amos denounces the social sins of Israel and warns of God's impending judgement.

Hosea's homeland ?

Micah condemns corrupt leaders in Jerusalem.

Amos's homeland.

Isaiah advises Ahaz and Hezekiah in attack against Jerusalem.

2 Kings 19:5-7

So the servants of King Hezekiah went to Isaiah, who said to them, "Tell your master this, 'The LORD says: Don't be afraid because of the words you have heard, that the king of Assyria's attendants have blasphemed Me with. I am about to put a spirit in him, and he will hear a rumor and return to his own land where I will cause him to fall by the sword.'"

94▶ EIGHTH-CENTURY BC HEBREW HOME

Houses in the period of the OT usually were built around a central courtyard and entered from the street. They often were two stories high with access to the upper story coming from a staircase or a ladder. The walls of the house consisted of stone foundations with mud bricks placed on the stone layers or courses. They subsequently were plastered. Floors either were paved with small stones or plaster, or they were formed from beaten earth. Large wooden beams laid across the walls composed the supporting structure of the roof. Smaller pieces of wood or reeds were placed in between the beams and then covered with a layer of mud. Rows of columns placed in the house served as supports to the ceiling. Since the roof was flat, people slept on it in the hot seasons and also used it for storage. Sometimes clay or stone pipes that led from the roof to cisterns down below were used to catch rainwater.

The most common type of house was the so-called "four-room" house. This house consisted of a broad room at the rear of the house with three parallel rooms coming out from one side of the broad room. The back room ran the width of the building. Rows of pillars separated the middle parallel room from the other two rooms. This middle room actually was a small, unroofed courtyard and served as the entrance to the house. The courtyard usually contained household items such as silos, cisterns, ovens, and grinding stones and was the place where the cooking was done. The animals could have been kept under a covered section in the courtyard. The other rooms were used for living and storage.

Ovens were constructed with mud bricks and then plastered on the outside. One side of the oven had an air hole. A new oven was created whenever the old one filled up with ashes. By breaking off the top of the old oven and then raising the sides, a new oven was made.

Storage structures were common in the biblical period. Private and public grain silos were round and dug several feet into the ground. The builders usually erected circular mud brick or stone walls around the silo, but sometimes they did nothing to the pit or simply plastered it with mud. Rooms with clay vessels also served as storage space.

While the "four-room" house was the most common plan in Palestine, other arrangements existed. Some homes had a simple plan of a courtyard with one room placed to the side. Other houses had only two or three rooms; still others may have had more than four. The arrangement of the rooms around the open courtyard also varied. The broadroom at the rear of the house seems to be common to all plans.

95 JUDAH ALONE

Date (BC)	Judah	Prophets	Egypt	Assyria	Medes	Babylon
722	Ahaz (735–715): Vassal of Assyria	Isaiah Micah		Sargon II (722–705)		
715	Hezekiah (715–687) Hezekiah's rebellion against Assyria			Sennacherib (705–681) Campaign against Judah		Chaldean chieftain Merodach-baladan
700	Sennacherib's campaign (701) Manasseh (687–642)		Tirhakah (690–664)	Sennacherib destroys Babylon Esarhaddon (681–669) attacks Egypt		
675	Corruption and pagan practices promoted by Manasseh grip Judah		Psammeticus (664–610)	Ashurbanipal II (669–627); sack of Thebes (663)		
650	Josiah (640–609)	Jeremiah (627–582)		Death of Ashurbanipal II (627)		Nabopolassar seized throne of Babylon (626)
625	Josianic reform "Book of the Law" (621)	Nahum		Sin-shar-ushkun	Cyaxares (623–584)	
615	Death of Josiah (609)	Zephaniah Habbakuk	Neco II (610–594)	Asshur sacked (614) Ashur-uballit II; Nineveh destroyed (612) Haran falls (610)		
	Jehoiakim (609–598)					Nebuchadnezzar (605–562) Battle of Carchemish
605	Rebellion against Babylon					
600						
598/97	1st siege of Jerusalem and deportation (Jehoiachin 598–597)	Ezekiel	Apries (Hophra) (589–570)			1st campaign against Judah
587/86	2nd siege of Jerusalem; destruction of temple					2nd campaign against Judah; destruction of the temple

96▶ HEZEKIAH'S PREPARATION FOR REVOLT

2 Kings 18:1-4

In the third year of Israel's King Hoshea son of Elah, Hezekiah son of Ahaz became king of Judah. He was 25 years old when he became king; he reigned 29 years in Jerusalem. His mother's name was Abi daughter of Zechariah. He did what was right in the LORD's sight just as his ancestor David had done. He removed the high places and shattered the sacred pillars and cut down the Asherah poles. He broke into pieces the bronze snake that Moses made, for the Israelites burned incense to it up to that time. He called it Nehushtan.

97 ▶ HEZEKIAH'S JERUSALEM

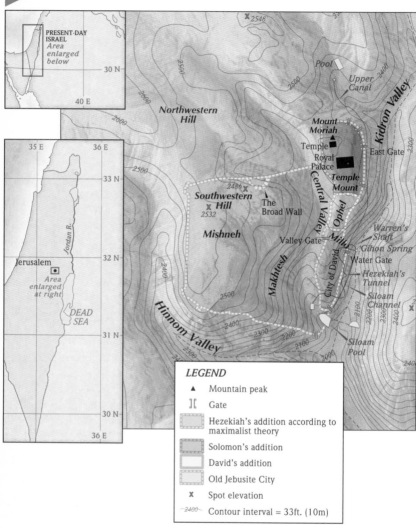

2 Kings 19:32-33

"Therefore, this is what the LORD says about the king of Assyria:

'He will not enter this city
or shoot an arrow there
or come before it with a shield
or build up an assault ramp against it.
He will go back
on the road that he came
and he will not enter this city,
declares the LORD.'"

98 SENNACHERIB'S CAMPAIGN AGAINST JUDAH

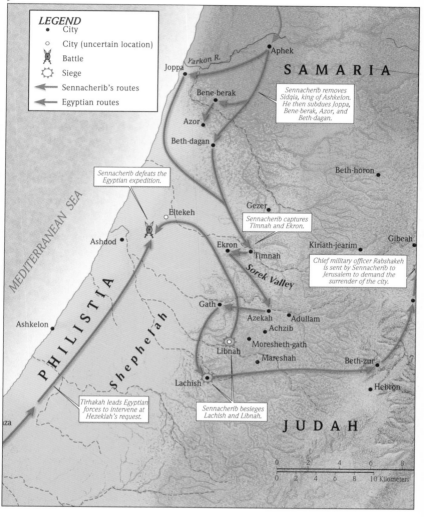

LEGEND
- • City
- ○ City (uncertain location)
- ⚔ Battle
- ⟳ Siege
- ← Sennacherib's routes
- ← Egyptian routes

Sennacherib removes Sidqia, king of Ashkelon. He then subdues Joppa, Bene-berak, Azor, and Beth-dagan.

Sennacherib defeats the Egyptian expedition.

Sennacherib captures Timnah and Ekron.

Chief military officer Rabshakeh is sent by Sennacherib to Jerusalem to demand the surrender of the city.

Tirhakah leads Egyptian forces to intervene at Hezekiah's request.

Sennacherib besieges Lachish and Libnah.

SAMARIA

Aphek
Joppa
Yarkon R.
Bene-berak
Azor
Beth-dagan
Beth-horon
Gezer
Eltekeh
Ashdod
Ekron
Timnah
Kiriath-jearim
Gibeah
Sorek Valley
MEDITERRANEAN SEA
PHILISTIA
Gath
Azekah
Adullam
Achzib
Ashkelon
Shephelah
Moresheth-gath
Libnah
Mareshah
Beth-zur
Lachish
Hebron
...za
JUDAH

0   2   4   6   8
0 2 4 6 8 10 Kilometers

Isaiah 36:1

In the fourteenth year of King Hezekiah, Sennacherib king of Assyria advanced against all the fortified cities of Judah and captured them.

99 ASSYRIAN SUPREMACY IN THE SEVENTH CENTURY

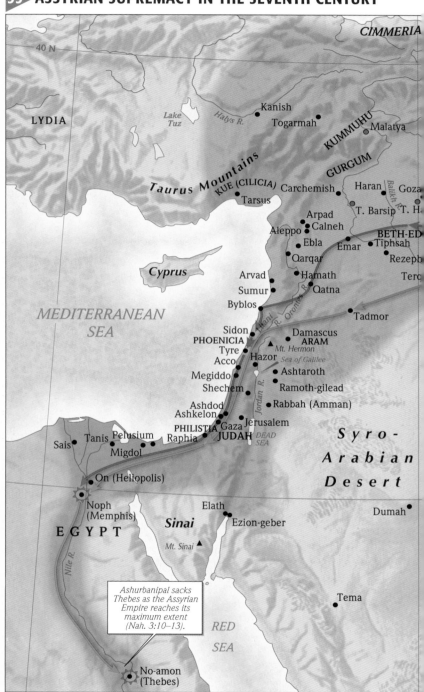

CIMMERIA

40 N

LYDIA

Lake Tuz

Halys R.

Kanish

Togarmah

KUMMUHU

Malatya

Taurus Mountains

GURGUM

KUE (CILICIA)

Carchemish

Haran

Goza

Tarsus

T. Barsip

T. H.

Arpad

Calneh

Aleppo

Ebla

Emar

BETH-ED

Tiphsah

Qarqar

Rezeph

Cyprus

Arvad

Hamath

Terc

Sumur

Qatna

R. Orontes

Byblos

Tadmor

MEDITERRANEAN SEA

Sidon

Damascus

PHOENICIA

ARAM

Tyre

Mt. Hermon

Acco

Hazor

Sea of Galilee

Megiddo

Ashtaroth

Shechem

Ramoth-gilead

Jordan R.

Ashdod

Rabbah (Amman)

Ashkelon

Jerusalem

PHILISTIA

Gaza

Sais

Tanis

Pelusium

Raphia

JUDAH

DEAD SEA

S y r o -

Migdol

A r a b i a n

On (Heliopolis)

D e s e r t

Noph (Memphis)

Elath

Dumah

EGYPT

Sinai

Ezion-geber

Mt. Sinai

Nile R.

Ashurbanipal sacks Thebes as the Assyrian Empire reaches its maximum extent (Nah. 3:10–13).

RED SEA

Tema

No-amon (Thebes)

2 Chronicles 33:10-11

The LORD spoke to Manasseh and his people, but they didn't listen. So He brought against them the military commanders of the king of

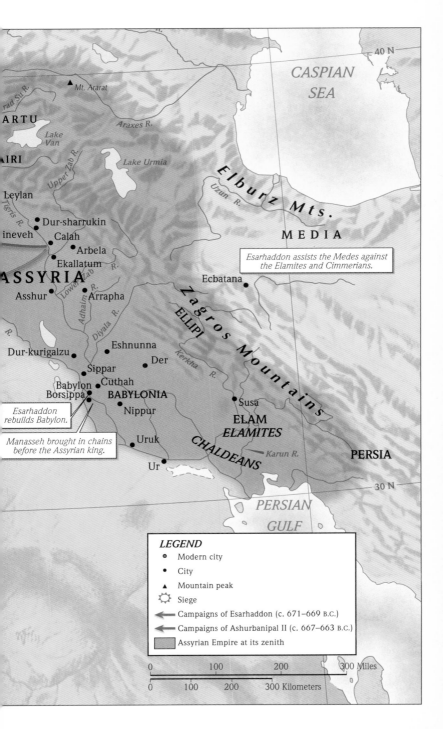

CASPIAN SEA

Mt. Ararat

ARTU

Araxes R.

Lake Van

IRI

Elburz Mts.

MEDIA

Uzun R.

Leylan

Dur-sharrukin

ineveh Calah

Arbela

Ekallatum

ASSYRIA

Ecbatana

Esarhaddon assists the Medes against the Elamites and Cimmerians.

Asshur Arrapha

Zagros Mountains

ELLIPI

Dur-kurigalzu Eshnunna

Der

Sippar

Babylon Cuthah

Kerkha R.

Esarhaddon rebuilds Babylon.

Borsippa BABYLONIA

Nippur

Susa

ELAM
ELAMITES

Manasseh brought in chains before the Assyrian king.

Uruk

CHALDEANS

Karun R.

PERSIA

Ur

30 N

PERSIAN
GULF

LEGEND
- Modern city
- City
- ▲ Mountain peak
- ☼ Siege
- ← Campaigns of Esarhaddon (c. 671–669 B.C.)
- ← Campaigns of Ashurbanipal II (c. 667–663 B.C.)
- Assyrian Empire at its zenith

0   100   200   300 Miles

0   100   200   300 Kilometers

40 N

Lake Urmia

Upper Zab R.

Tigris R.

Lower Zab R.

Adhaim R.

Diyala R.

Assyria. They captured Manasseh with hooks, bound him with bronze shackles, and took him to Babylon.

100▶ THE RISE OF THE NEO-BABYLONIAN EMPIRE

BLACK SEA

Byzantium (Istanbul)

30 E

40 N

Sardis LYDIA

Lake Tuz

Halys R.

Assyrians flee to Haran only to be defeated by coalition forces led by Nabopolassar (610 BC).

IZA

Carchemish Haran

Taurus Mountains KUE (CILICIA)

Tarsus

T. Barsip *Balikh R.*

Egyptian forces led by Necho II are defeated by Nebuchadnezzar, son of Nabopolassar (605 BC).

Arpad

Aleppo

Ebla Rezep

Cyprus

Hamath Qatna

Arvad

Byblos

Orontes R.

Riblah Tadmor

Sidon

Damascus

PHOENICIA

Tyre ▲ Mt. Hermon **ARAM**

LEGEND

- ⦿ Modern city
- ● City
- ▲ Mountain peak
- ⚔ Battle of Carchemish
- ☼ Siege
- ← Medes forces
- ← Chaldean forces
- ← Assyrian forces
- ← Egyptian forces
- ▢ Neo-Babylonian influence

MEDITERRANEAN SEA

Josiah killed in battle with Neco II (609 BC).

Sea of Galilee

Megiddo

Shechem Beth-shan

Joppa **AMMON**

Ashdod *Jordan R.* Rabbah (Amman)

Gaza

Jerusalem

Tanis Raphia **JUDAH**

LIBYA Sais Migdol **MOAB**

EDOM

30 N

On (Heliopolis)

Noph (Memphis)

Syro-Arabian Desert

Duma

Ezion-geber

Sinai

Mt. Sinai ▲

Hermopolis *Nile R.*

E G Y P T

Tema

Sahara RED

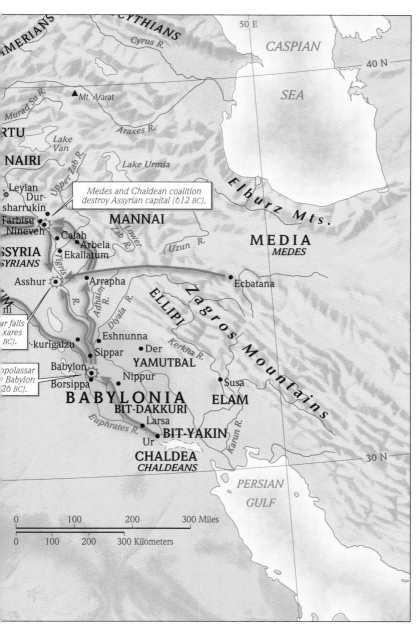

Medes and Chaldean coalition destroy Assyrian capital (612 BC).

Nabopolassar
Babylon
626 BC).

Jeremiah 46:1-2

The word of the LORD that came to Jeremiah the prophet about the nations:

Prophecies against Egypt

About Egypt and the army of Pharaoh Neco, Egypt's king, which was defeated at Carchemish on the Euphrates River by Nebuchadnezzar king of Babylon in the fourth year of Judah's King Jehoiakim son of Josiah.

101▶ THE REIGN OF JOSIAH

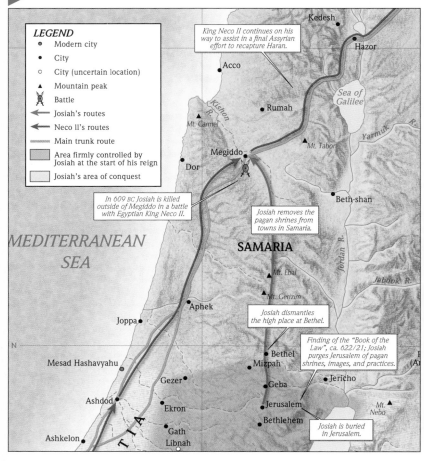

LEGEND
- ● Modern city
- • City
- ○ City (uncertain location)
- ▲ Mountain peak
- ✗ Battle
- ← Josiah's routes
- ← Neco ll's routes
- ▦ Main trunk route
- ▦ Area firmly controlled by Josiah at the start of his reign
- ▢ Josiah's area of conquest

King Neco II continues on his way to assist in a final Assyrian effort to recapture Haran.

In 609 BC Josiah is killed outside of Megiddo in a battle with Egyptian King Neco II.

Josiah removes the pagan shrines from towns in Samaria.

Josiah dismantles the high place at Bethel.

Finding of the "Book of the Law", ca. 622/21; Josiah purges Jerusalem of pagan shrines, images, and practices.

Josiah is buried in Jerusalem.

MEDITERRANEAN SEA

SAMARIA

Kedesh, Hazor, Acco, Sea of Galilee, Rumah, Kishon R., Mt. Carmel, Yarmuk R., Mt. Tabor, Megiddo, Dor, Beth-shan, Jordan R., Jabbok R., Mt. Ebal, Mt. Gerizim, Aphek, Joppa, Bethel, Mizpah, Mesad Hashavyahu, Geba, Jericho, Gezer, Mt. Nebo, Ashdod, Ekron, Jerusalem, Bethlehem, Ashkelon, Gath, Libnah

2 Chronicles 35:20-24

After all this that Josiah had prepared for the temple, Neco king of Egypt marched up to fight at Carchemish by the Euphrates, and Josiah went out to confront him. But Neco sent messengers to him, saying, "What is the issue between you and me, king of Judah? I have not come against you today but to the dynasty I am fighting. God told me to hurry. Stop opposing God who is with me; don't make Him destroy you!"

But Josiah did not turn away from him; instead, in order to fight with him he disguised himself. He did not listen to Neco's words from the mouth of God, but went to the Valley of Megiddo to fight. The archers shot King Josiah, and he said to his servants, "Take me away, for I am severely wounded!" So his servants took him out of the war chariot, carried him in his second chariot, and brought him to Jerusalem. Then he died, and they buried him in the tomb of his fathers. All Judah and Jerusalem mourned for Josiah.

10?> KINGS OF THE NEO-BABYLONIAN EMPIRE

NAME	DATES (BC)	SIGNIFICANT EVENTS
Nabopolassar	626–605	Chaldean chieftain who seized Babylon in 626; established an alliance with Cyaxares the Mede; conquered Nineveh in 612.
Nebuchadnezzar	605–562	Defeated Egypt at Battle of Carchemish in 605; twice besieged Jerusalem (598/97; 587/86).
Evil Merodach (Amel-marduk)	562–560	Son of Nebuchadnezzar; freed Jehoiacahin, king of Judah (2 Kings 25:27-30).
Neriglissar	560–556	Son-in-law of Nebuchadnezzar; likely the Nergal-sharezer who was present at the final siege of Jerusalem (Jer. 39:3).
Labashi-marduk	556 (3-month reign)	Son of Neriglissar; removed by Nabonidus.
Nabonidus	556–539	Spent considerable time outside of Babylon; Belshazzar served as regent in his absence; Babylon surrendered to Cyrus the Great in 539.

103 NEBUCHADNEZZAR'S CAMPAIGNS AGAINST JUDAH

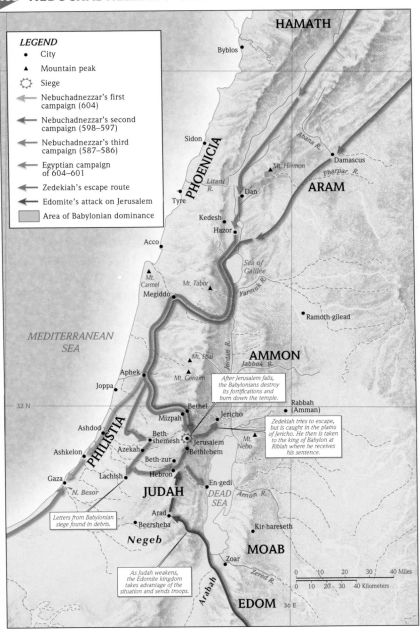

LEGEND
- • City
- ▲ Mountain peak
- ✿ Siege
- Nebuchadnezzar's first campaign (604)
- Nebuchadnezzar's second campaign (598–597)
- Nebuchadnezzar's third campaign (587–586)
- Egyptian campaign of 604–601
- Zedekiah's escape route
- Edomite's attack on Jerusalem
- Area of Babylonian dominance

After Jerusalem falls, the Babylonians destroy its fortifications and burn down the temple.

Zedekiah tries to escape, but is caught in the plains of Jericho. He then is taken to the king of Babylon at Riblah where he receives his sentence.

Letters from Babylonian siege found in debris.

As Judah weakens, the Edomite kingdom takes advantage of the situation and sends troops.

Jeremiah 52:4-5

In the ninth year of Zedekiah's reign, on the tenth day of the tenth month, King Nebuchadnezzar of Babylon advanced against Jerusalem with his entire army. They laid siege to the city and built a siege wall all around it. The city was under siege until King Zedekiah's eleventh year.

104▶ JUDAH DURING THE EXILE

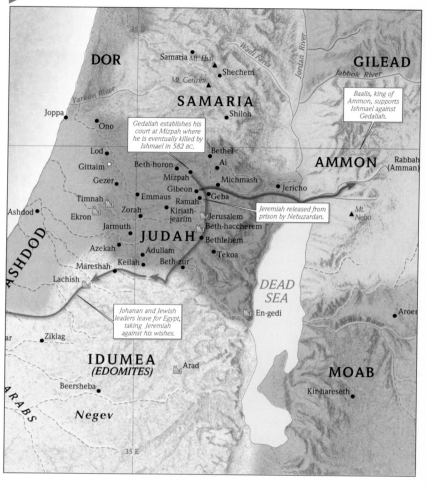

DOR

Samaria *Mt. Ebal*
●Shechem
Mt. Gerizim

Wadi Farah

Jordan River

GILEAD

Jabbok River

SAMARIA
●Shiloh

Joppa●

●Ono

> Gedaliah establishes his court at Mizpah where he is eventually killed by Ishmael in 582 BC.

> Baalis, king of Ammon, supports Ishmael against Gedaliah.

Lod●
Gittaim ○
Gezer●

Beth-horon●

●Bethel
Ai●

Mizpah●
Gibeon●
Emmaus● Ramah●
Timnah● Zorah● Kiriath-
Ekron● jearim●
Jarmuth●

Michmash●

●Geba

AMMON

Rabbah
(Amman)

> Jeremiah released from prison by Nebuzardan.

Mt.
Nebo ▲

Ashdod●

Jerusalem▲
Beth-haccherem●

JUDAH
●Bethlehem

Azekah● Adullam●
Mareshah● Keilah● Beth-zur●
Lachish●

●Tekoa

**DEAD
SEA**

> Johanan and Jewish leaders leave for Egypt, taking Jeremiah against his wishes.

En-gedi●

Aroer●

**A
S
H
D
O
D**

**A
R
A
B
S**

ar●
●Ziklag

**IDUMEA
(EDOMITES)**

●Arad

Beersheba●

Negev

Arnon River

MOAB

Kir-hareseth●

35 E

Jeremiah 42:19

"The LORD has spoken concerning you, remnant of Judah: 'Don't go to Egypt.' Know for certain that I have warned you today!"

BABYLON

▲ Lachish was the last fortress to fall before Jerusalem fell to the Babylonians. The small mound to the right was the siege ramp.

Babylon was founded in unknown antiquity on the river Euphrates, about 50 miles south of modern Baghdad. The English names "Babylon" and "Babel" (Gen. 10:10; 11:9) are translated from the same Hebrew word (*babel*). Babylon may have been an important cultural center during the period of the early Sumerian city-states (before 2000 BC), but the corresponding archaeological levels of the site are below the present water table and remain unexplored.

Babylon emerged from anonymity shortly after 2000 BC, a period roughly contemporary with the Hebrew patriarchs. At that time, an independent kingdom was established in the city under a dynasty of Semitic westerners, or Amorites. Hammurabi (1792–1750 BC), the sixth king of this First Dynasty of Babylon, built a sizable empire through treaties, vassalage, and conquest. From his time forward, Babylon was considered to be the political seat of southern Mesopotamia, the region called Babylonia. The Amorite dynasty of Babylon reached its apex under Hammurabi. Subsequent rulers, however, saw their realm diminished, and in 1595 BC the Hittites sacked Babylon. After their withdrawal, members of the Kassite tribe seized the throne. The Kassite Dynasty ruled for over four centuries, a period of relative peace but also stagnation. Little is known up to about 1350 BC when Babylonian kings corresponded with Egypt and struggled with the growing power of Assyria to the north. After a brief resurgence, the Kassite dynasty was ended by the Elamite invasion in 1160 BC.

When the Elamites withdrew to their Iranian homeland, princes native to the Babylonian city of Isin founded the Fourth Dynasty of Babylon. After a brief period of glory in which Nebuchadnezzar I (about 1124–1103 BC) invaded Elam, Babylon entered a dark age for most of the next two centuries. Floods, famine, widespread settlement of nomadic Aramean tribes, and the arrival of Chaldeans in the south plagued Babylon during this time of confusion.

During the period of the Assyrian Empire, Babylon was dominated by this warlike neighbor to the north. A dynastic dispute in Babylon in 851 BC brought the intervention of the Assyrian king Shalmaneser III. Babylon kings remained independent but nominally subject to Assyrian "protection."

A series of coups in Babylon prompted the Assyrian Tiglath-pileser III to enter Babylon in 728 BC and proclaim himself king under the throne name Pulu (Pul of 2 Kings 15:19; 1 Chron. 5:26). He died the next year. By 721 BC the Chaldean Marduk-apal-iddina, Merodach-baladan of the OT, ruled Babylon. With Elamite support he resisted the advances of the Assyrian Sargon II in 720 BC. Babylon gained momentary independence, but in 710 BC Sargon attacked again. Merodach-baladan was forced to flee to Elam. Sargon, like Tiglath-pileser before him, took the throne of Babylon. As soon as Sargon died in 705 BC, Babylon and other nations, including Judah under King Hezekiah, rebelled from Assyrian domination. Merodach-baladan had returned from Elam to Babylon. It is probably in this context that he sent emissaries to Hezekiah (2 Kings 20:12-19; Isa. 39). In 703 BC the new Assyrian king, Sennacherib, attacked Babylon. He defeated Merodach-baladan, who again fled. He ultimately died in exile. After considerable intrigue in Babylon, another Elamite-sponsored revolt broke out against Assyria. In 689 BC Sennacherib destroyed the sacred city of Babylon in retaliation. His murder, by his own sons (2 Kings 19:37) in 681 BC, was interpreted by Babylonians as divine judgment for this unthinkable act.

▲ The site of the ancient city of Babylon in modern Iraq. The site of this once thriving city was abandoned in AD 200.

Esarhaddon, Sennacherib's son, immediately began the rebuilding of Babylon to win the allegiance of the populace. At his death the crown prince Ashurbanipal ruled over Assyria, while another son ascended the throne of Babylon. All was well until 651 BC when the Babylonian king rebelled against his brother. Ashurbanipal finally prevailed and was crowned king of a resentful Babylon.

Assyrian domination died with Ashurbanipal in 627 BC. In 626 BC Babylon fell into the hands of a Chaldean chief, Nabopolassar, first king of the Neo-Babylonian Empire. In 612, with the help of the Medes, the Babylonians sacked the Assyrian capital Nineveh. The remnants of the Assyrian army rallied at Haran in north Syria, which was abandoned at the approach of the Babylonians in 610 BC. Egypt, however, challenged Babylon for the right to inherit Assyria's empire. Pharaoh Neco II, with the last of the Assyrians (2 Kings 23:29-30), failed in 609 to retake Haran. In 605 BC Babylonian forces under the crown prince Nebuchadnezzar routed the Egyptians at the decisive Battle of Carchemish (Jer. 46:2-12). The Babylonian advance, however, was delayed by Nabopolassar's death that obliged Nebuchadnezzar to return to Babylon and assume power.

In 604 and 603 BC Nebuchadnezzar II (605–562 BC), king of Babylon, campaigned along the Palestinian coast. At this time Jehoiakim, king of Judah, became an unwilling vassal of Babylon. A Babylonian defeat at the border of Egypt in 601 probably encouraged Jehoiakim to rebel. For two years Judah was harassed by Babylonian vassals (2 Kings 24:1-2). Then, in December of 598 BC, Nebuchadnezzar marched on Jerusalem. Jehoiakim died that same month, and his son Jehoiachin surrendered the city to the Babylonians on March 16, 597 BC. Many Judeans, including the royal family, were deported to Babylon (2 Kings 24:6-12). Ultimately released from prison, Jehoiachin was treated as a king in exile (2 Kings 25:27-30; Jer. 52:31-34). Texts excavated in Babylon show that rations were allotted to him and five sons.

Nebuchadnezzar appointed Zedekiah over Judah. Against the protests of Jeremiah, but with promises of Egyptian aid, Zedekiah revolted against Babylon in 589 BC. In the resultant Babylonian campaign, Judah was ravaged and Jerusalem besieged. An abortive campaign by the Pharaoh Hophra gave Jerusalem a short respite, but the attack was renewed (Jer. 37:4-10). The city fell in August of 587 BC. Zedekiah was captured, Jerusalem burned, and the temple destroyed (Jer. 52:12-14). Many more Judeans were taken to their exile in Babylonia (2 Kings 25:1-21; Jer. 52:1-30).

Apart from his military conquests, Nebuchadnezzar is noteworthy for a massive rebuilding program in Babylon itself. The city spanned the Euphrates and was surrounded by an eleven-mile long outer wall that enclosed suburbs and Nebuchadnezzar's summer palace. The inner wall was wide enough to accommodate two chariots abreast. It could be

Tile (glazed brickwork) relief from early 6th-century Babylon. Tile reliefs including this one repeated at regular intervals along the Ishtar Gate and its walls which joined Procession Street, the main highway to the city. The Ishtar Gate was one of Nebuchadnezzar's most impressive architectural achievements.

entered through eight gates, the most famous of which was the northern Ishtar Gate, used in the annual New Year Festival and decorated with reliefs of dragons and bulls in enameled brick. The road to this gate was bordered by high walls decorated by lions in glazed brick behind which were defensive citadels. Inside the gate was the main palace built by Nebuchadnezzar with its huge throne room. A cellar with shafts in part of the palace may have served as the substructure to the famous Hanging Gardens of Babylon, described by classical authors as one of the wonders of the ancient world. Babylon contained many temples, the most important of which was Esagila, the temple of the city's patron god, Marduk. Rebuilt by Nebuchadnezzar, the temple was lavishly decorated with gold. Just north of Esagila lay the huge stepped tower of Babylon, a ziggurat called Etemenanki and its sacred enclosure. Its seven stories perhaps towered some three hundred feet above the city. No doubt Babylon greatly impressed the Jews taken there in captivity and provided them with substantial economic opportunities.

The ruins of the Hanginging Gardens of Babylon (contemporary Iraq), one of the "Seven Wonders of the World."

Nebuchadnezzar was the greatest king of the

Neo-Babylonian Period and the last truly great ruler of Babylon. His successors were insignificant by comparison. He was followed by his son Awel-marduk (561–560 BC), the Evil-Merodach of the OT (2 Kings 25:27-30), Neriglissar (560–558 BC), and Labashi-Marduk (557 BC), murdered as a mere child. The last king of Babylon, Nabonidus (556–539 BC), was an enigmatic figure who seems to have favored the moon god, Sin, over the national god, Marduk. He moved his residence to Tema in the Syro-Arabian Desert for 10 years, leaving his son Belshazzar (Dan. 5:1) as regent in Babylon. Nabonidus returned to a divided capital amid a threat from the united Medes and Persians. In 539 BC the Persian Cyrus II (the Great) entered Babylon without a fight. Thus ended Babylon's dominant role in Near Eastern politics.

Babylon remained an important economic center and provincial capital during the period of Persian rule. The Greek historian Herodotus, who visited the city in 460 BC, could still remark that "it surpasses in splendor any city of the known world." Alexander the Great, conqueror of the Persian Empire, embarked on a program of rebuilding in Babylon that was interrupted by his death in 323 BC. After Alexander, the city declined economically but remained an important religious center until NT times. The site was deserted by AD 200.

105 ▶ RECONSTRUCTION OF ANCIENT BABYLON

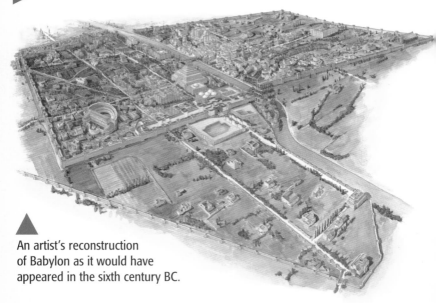

An artist's reconstruction of Babylon as it would have appeared in the sixth century BC.

106▶ WORLD POWERS OF THE SIXTH CENTURY

Daniel 5:25-28;30

"This is the writing that was inscribed:

MENE, MENE, TEKEL, PARSIN

This is the interpretation of the message:

MENE means that God has numbered the days of your kingdom and brought it to an end.

TEKEL means that you have been weighed in the balance and found deficient.

PERES means that your kingdom has been divided and given to the Medes and Persians."

That very night Belshazzar the king of the Chaldeans was killed, and Darius the Mede received the kingdom at the age of 62.

107 ▶ JEWISH EXILES IN BABYLONIA

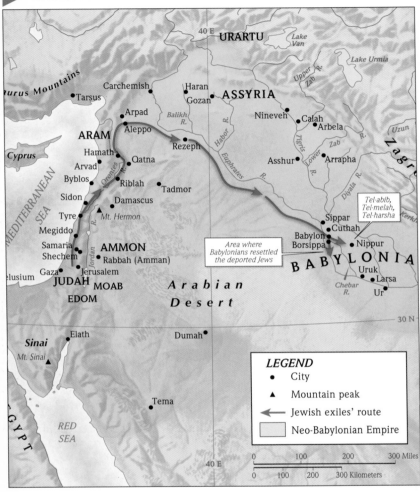

Jeremiah 52:28-30

These are the people Nebuchadnezzar deported: in the seventh year, 3,023 Jews; 29 in his eighteenth year, 832 people from Jerusalem; 30 in Nebuchadnezzar's twenty-third year, Nebuzaradan, the commander of the guards, deported 745 Jews. All together 4,600 people were deported.

108▶ JEWISH REFUGEES IN EGYPT

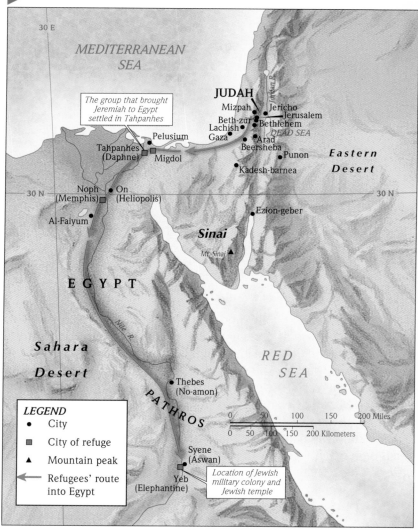

The group that brought Jeremiah to Egypt settled in Tahpanhes

Location of Jewish military colony and Jewish temple

LEGEND
- • City
- ■ City of refuge
- ▲ Mountain peak
- ← Refugees' route into Egypt

2 Kings 25:25-26

In the seventh month, however, Ishmael son of Nethaniah, son of Elishama, of the royal family, came with 10 men and struck down Gedaliah, and he died. Also, they killed the Jews and the Chaldeans who were with him at Mizpah. Then all the people, from the youngest to the oldest, and the commanders of the army, left and went to Egypt, for they were afraid of the Chaldeans.

PERSIA

▲ The great audience hall begun by Darius and completed by Xerxes.

Persia corresponds to the modern state of Iran. As an empire Persia was a vast collection of states and kingdoms reaching from the shores of Asia Minor in the west to the Indus River Valley in the east. It reached northward to southern Russia and in the south included Egypt and the regions bordering the Persian Gulf and the Gulf of Oman. In history the empire defeated the Babylonians and then fell finally to Alexander the Great.

The nation was named for the southernmost region of the area called Parsis or Persis. It was a harsh land of deserts, mountains, plateaus, and valleys. The climate was arid and showed extremes of cold and heat. Gold and silver and wheat and barley were native to the area.

The region was settled shortly after 3000 BC by people from the north. An Elamite culture developed which, at its peak in 1200 BC, dominated the whole Tigris River Valley. It lasted until 1050 BC. After its destruction other northern groups entered the area. Among these groups were tribesmen who formed a small kingdom in the region of Anshan around 700 BC. It was ruled by Achaemenes, the great, great-grandfather of Cyrus II, the Great. (Thus, the period from Achaemenes to Alexander is called the Achaemenid Period.) This small kingdom was the seed of the Persian Empire.

When Cyrus II came to his father's throne in 559 BC, his kingdom was part of a larger Median kingdom. The Medes controlled the territory northeast and east of the Babylonians. In 550 BC Cyrus rebelled against Astyages, the Median king. His rebellion led to the capture of the king and gave Cyrus control over a kingdom stretching from Media to the Halys River in Asia Minor. Soon Cyrus challenged the king of Lydia. Victory there gave Cyrus the western portion of Asia Minor. Then in 539 BC Babylon fell to Cyrus due to his skill and to internal dissension in the Babylonian Empire.

Cyrus died in 530 BC; however, the Persian Empire continued to grow. Cambyses II, Cyrus' son, conquered Egypt in 525 BC. Cambyses' successor Darius I expanded the empire eastward to the Indus and attempted to conquer or control the Greeks. Darius lost to the Greeks at Marathon in 490 BC. This was the greatest extension of the empire. Later emperors did little to expand the empire. They even had difficulty holding such a far-flung empire together.

The Persian Empire is important to the history and development of civilization. It had major effects on religion, law, politics, and economics. The impact came through the Jews, the Bible, contacts with the Greeks, and through Alexander the Great's incorporation of ideas and architecture from the Persians.

Politically the Persian Empire was the best organized the world had ever seen. By the time of Darius I, 522–486 BC, the empire was divided into 20 satrapies (political units of varying size and population). Satrapies were subdivided into provinces. Initially Judah was a province in the satrapy of Babylon. Later Judah was in one named "Beyond the River." The satrapies were governed by Persians who were directly responsible to the emperor. Good administration required good communications that called for good roads. These roads did more than speed administration, though. They encouraged contacts between peoples within the empire. Ideas and goods could move hundreds of miles with little restriction. The empire became wealthy and also gave its inhabitants a sense that they were part of a larger world. A kind of "universal awareness" developed. The use of minted coins and the development of a money economy aided this identification with a larger world. The emperor's coins were handy reminders of the power and privileges of being part of the empire. Also the Persians were committed to rule by law. Instead of imposing an imperial law from above, however, the emperor and his satraps gave their authority and support to local law. For the Jews this meant official support for keeping Jewish law in the land of the Jews.

The Persian Empire affected the Jews and biblical history a great deal. Babylon had conquered Jerusalem and destroyed the temple in 586 BC. When Cyrus conquered

A Persian horse and rider from the late Persian period, the time of Nehemiah.

Babylon, he allowed the Jews to return to Judah and encouraged the rebuilding of the temple (Ezra 1:1-4). The work was begun but not completed. Then, under Darius I, Zerubbabel and the high priest, Joshua, led the restored community with the support and encouragement of the Persians. (Ezra 3–6 tells of some of the events while Haggai's and Zechariah's prophecies were made during the days of the restoration.) Despite some local opposition Darius supported the rebuilding of the temple, which was rededicated in his sixth year (Ezra 6:15). In addition, both Ezra and Nehemiah were official representatives of the Persian government. Ezra was to teach and to appoint judges (Ezra 7). Nehemiah may have been the first governor of the province of Yehud (Judah). He undoubtedly had official support for his rebuilding of the walls of Jerusalem.

The Jews had trouble under Persian rule, too. Although Daniel was taken into exile by the Babylonians (Dan. 1), his ministry continued through the fall of the Babylonians (Dan. 5) into the time of the Persians (Dan. 6). His visions projected even further. Daniel 6 shows a stable government but one in which Jews could still be at risk. His visions in a time of tranquility remind readers that human kingdoms come and go. Esther is a story of God's rescue of His people during the rule of the Persian emperor, Ahasuerus (also known as Xerxes I). The story shows an empire where law was used and misused. Jews were already, apparently, hated by some. Malachi, too, was probably from the Persian period. His book shows an awareness of the world at large and is positive toward the Gentiles and the government.

Throughout the period, the Jews kept looking for the kind of restoration promised by prophets such as Isaiah (chaps. 40–66) and Ezekiel (chaps. 40–48). Prophets such as Haggai and Zechariah and Malachi helped the Jews to hope, but these men of God also reminded their hearers of the importance of present faithfulness and obedience to God.

The second tomb from the left was the tomb of Artaxerxes I. He died in 424 BC of natural causes. His wife is said to have died the same day.

CYRUS

▲ The Cyrus Cylinder, inscribed with the famous Edict of Cyrus the Great in 538 BC (2 Chron. 36:23; Ezra 1:2-3). The Cyrus Cylinder was discovered in 1879 in Nineveh, Iraq by Hormuzd Rassam. It is currently located in the British Museum.

Third king of Anshan, Cyrus (the Great) assumed the throne about 559 BC. According to the best histories Cyrus was reared by a shepherd after his grandfather, Astyages, king of Media, ordered that he be killed. Apparently, Astyages had dreamed that Cyrus would one day succeed him as king before the reigning monarch's death. The officer charged with the execution instead carried the boy into the hills to the shepherds.

As an adult, Cyrus organized the Persians into an army and revolted against his grandfather and father (Cambyses I). He defeated them and claimed their throne.

One of his first acts as king of Medio-Persia was to launch an attack against Lydia, capital of Sardis and storehouse for the riches of its king, Croesus. Turning eastward, Cyrus continued his campaign until he had carved out a vast empire, stretching from the Aegean Sea to India.

The Babylonian Empire next stood in his path, an obstacle that appeared to be insurmountable. Engaging the Babylonian army at Opis, Cyrus's troops routed them and moved on Babylon. The people in the capital welcomed Cyrus with open arms, seeing him as a liberator rather than a conqueror. All that remained was Egypt, which he left for his son, Cambyses II. Cyrus truly was the ruler of the world.

Cyrus's military exploits have become legendary. However, he is best remembered for his policies of peace. His famous decree in 539 BC (2 Chron. 36:22-23; Ezra 1:1-4) set free the captives Babylon had taken during its harsh rule. Among these prisoners were the Jews taken from Jerusalem in 586 BC. They were allowed to return to rebuild the temple and city. Along with this freedom Cyrus restored the valuable treasures of the temple taken during the exile. Since the Jews had done well in Babylon financially, many of them did not want to return to the wastes of Judah. From these people Cyrus exacted a tax to help pay for the trip for those who did wish to rebuild Jerusalem.

An astute politician, Cyrus made it a practice to publicly worship the gods of each kingdom he conquered. In so doing, he won the hearts of his subjects and kept down revolt. He is referred to as Yahweh's shepherd and anointed (Isa. 44:28-45:6) because of his kindness to the Jews and worship of Yahweh.

His last years are obscure. Cyrus was killed while fighting a frontier war with the nomadic Massagetae people. His tomb is in Pasargadae (modern Murghab).

109▶ THE CONQUESTS OF CYRUS THE GREAT

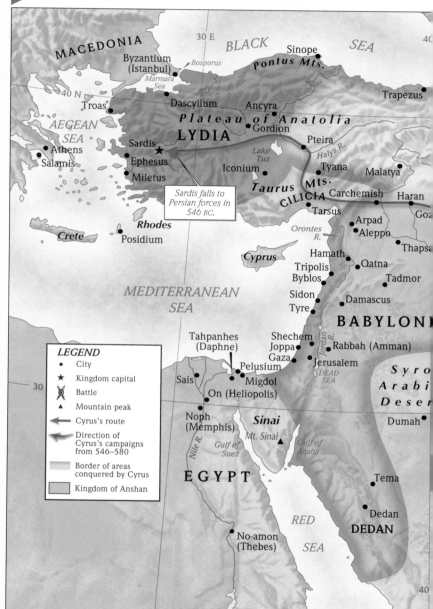

MACEDONIA

BLACK   SEA

Byzantium
(Istanbul)   *Bosporus*

Sinope

Pontus Mts.

Trapezus

Marmara
Sea

40 N

Troas

Dascylium

Ancyra

Plateau of Anatolia

AEGEAN
SEA

LYDIA

Gordion

Pteira

Athens

Sardis ★

Halys R.

Salamis

Ephesus

Lake
Tuz

Tyana

Malatya

Miletus

Iconium

Taurus Mts.

CILICIA Carchemish   Haran

Sardis falls to
Persian forces in
546 BC.

Tarsus

Goz

Arpad

Rhodes

*Orontes
R.*

Aleppo

Crete

Posidium

Cyprus

Hamath

Qatna

Thapsa

Tripolis

MEDITERRANEAN
SEA

Byblos

Tadmor

Sidon

Damascus

Tyre

BABYLON

Tahpanhes
(Daphne)

Shechem

Joppa

Jordan R.

Rabbah (Amman)

Gaza

Pelusium

Jerusalem

Syro

Sais

*DEAD
SEA*

Arabi

On (Heliopolis)

Deser

Noph
(Memphis)

Sinai

Dumah

Nile R.

Mt. Sinai ▲

*Gulf of
Suez*

*Gulf of
Aqaba*

EGYPT

Tema

RED

Dedan

No-amon
(Thebes)

SEA

DEDAN

LEGEND

- • City
- ★ Kingdom capital
- ⚔ Battle
- ▲ Mountain peak
- ⭠ Cyrus's route
- ⬅ Direction of
  Cyrus's campaigns
  from 546–580
- Border of areas
  conquered by Cyrus
- Kingdom of Anshan

Isaiah 44:28
I am the LORD . . . who says to Cyrus: "My shepherd, he will fulfill all My pleasure"

110 THE PERSIAN EMPIRE

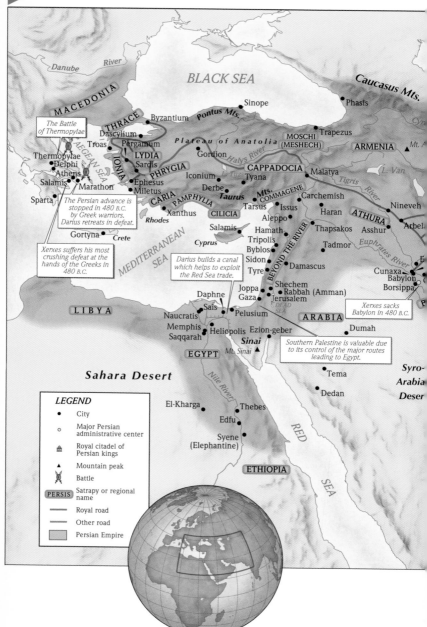

LEGEND

- ● City
- ○ Major Persian administrative center
- ⛩ Royal citadel of Persian kings
- ▲ Mountain peak
- ⚔ Battle
- PERSIS Satrapy or regional name
- ─── Royal road
- ─── Other road
- ▨ Persian Empire

The Battle of Thermopylae

The Persian advance is stopped in 480 B.C. by Greek warriors. Darius retreats in defeat.

Xerxes suffers his most crushing defeat at the hands of the Greeks in 480 B.C.

Darius builds a canal which helps to exploit the Red Sea trade.

Xerxes sacks Babylon in 480 B.C.

Southern Palestine is valuable due to its control of the major routes leading to Egypt.

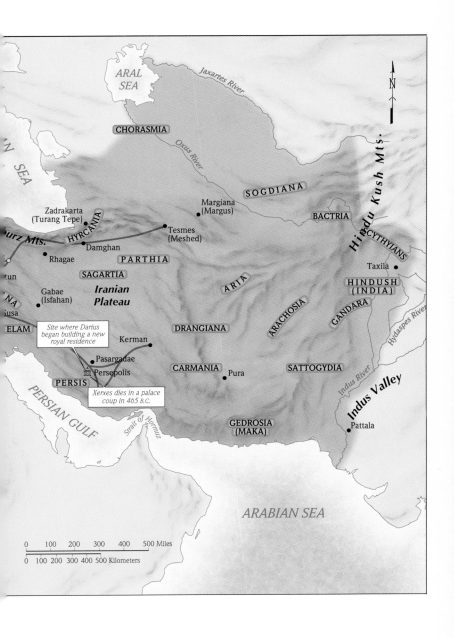

ARAL SEA

Jaxartes River

CHORASMIA

Oxus River

SOGDIANA

N SEA

Margiana
(Margus)

BACTRIA

Hindu Kush Mts.

Zadrakarta
(Turang Tepe)

HYRCANIA

Tesmes
(Meshed)

SCYTHIANS

urz Mts.

Damghan

PARTHIA

Taxila

Rhagae

SAGARTIA

ARIA

HINDUSH
(INDIA)

Gabae
(Isfahan)

Iranian
Plateau

ARACHOSIA

GANDARA

Hydaspes River

NA

Susa

ELAM

*Site where Darius
began building a new
royal residence*

Kerman

DRANGIANA

Indus River

Pasargadae

Persepolis

CARMANIA

Pura

SATTOGYDIA

Indus Valley

PERSIS

*Xerxes dies in a palace
coup in 465 B.C.*

PERSIAN GULF

Strait of Hormuz

GEDROSIA
(MAKA)

Pattala

ARABIAN SEA

0   100   200   300   400   500 Miles

0 100 200 300 400 500 Kilometers

111 KINGS OF PERSIA

PERSIAN KING	DATES (BC)	BIBLICAL CONNECTIONS	EVENTS AND ACCOMPLISHMENTS
Cyrus II (the Great)	559–530	Permitted return of the Jews from exile; facilitated rebuilding of the temple at Jerusalem (Ezra 1:1-4; 6:3-5); the "Anointed One" of Isa. 45:1	King of Anshan, 559 BC, conquered kingdom of Media (550 BC) and Lydian kingdom (546 BC); conquered Babylon, 539 BC
Cambyses II	530–522	Not mentioned in the Bible	Son of Cyrus the Great; conquered Egypt, 525 BC; his death (suicide?) in 522 BC led to two years of fighting between rival claimants to the throne
Darius I Hystaspes	522–486	Haggai and Zechariah preached during the second year of Darius I (520 BC); temple rebuilt and dedicated 515 BC (cf. Ezra 6:13-15)	Member of a collateral royal line; secured the throne ending the unrest following the death of Cambyses; reorganized the Persian Empire into satrapies; established royal postal system; began building Persepolis; invaded Greece and was defeated at Marathon, 490 BC; revolt in Egypt
Xerxes I	486–465	Possibly Ahasuerus of the Book of Esther	Son of Darius I; continued building Persepolis; encountered numerous rebellions at the beginning of his reign (Egypt, Babylon); invaded Greece, sacked Athens (480 BC), but was defeated by the Greeks in a naval engagement (Salamis, 480 BC) and on land (Plataea and Mycale, 479 BC); killed in a palace coup in 465 BC
Artaxerxes I Longimanus	465–425	Nehemiah, cup bearer to Artaxerxes; came to Judah (444 BC, compare Neh. 2:1; 13:6); traditional date of Ezra's mission in the seventh year of his reign (458 BC, cf. Ezra 7:7)	Faced revolt in Egypt; completed major buildings at Persepolis; made peace with the Greeks (Peace of Callias, 449 BC); died of natural causes
Xerxes II	423	Not mentioned in the Bible	Ruled less than two months
Darius II Nothus	423–404	Not mentioned in the Bible; Jews in Egypt (Elephantine) appealed to Samaria and Jerusalem for help in rebuilding their temple about 407 BC	Peloponnesian War, 431-404 BC; Persia recovered several Greek cities in Asia Minor
Artaxerxes II Mnemon	404–359/8	Some scholars place Ezra's mission in the seventh year of Artaxerxes II, about 398 BC	Egypt regained freedom from Persia for a time; revolt of the Satraps, 366-360 BC
Artaxerxes III Ochus	359/8–338/7	Not mentioned in the Bible	Philip II of Macedon; rises to power about 359 BC; Alexander the Great born, 356 BC; Persia reclaims Egypt, 342 BC
Arses		Not mentioned in the Bible	Unknown
Darius III Codomannus	338/7–336 336–330	Alexander subdues the Levant; Tyre and Gaza besieged, 332 BC; conquest of Egypt by Alexander, 332 BC	Philip assassinated, 336 BC; Alexander the Great invades the Persian Empire, 334 BC; Darius III defeated by Alexander at Issus, 333 BC, and Gaugamela, 331 BC; death of Darius, 330 BC

112 THE RETURN FROM EXILE

PHASE	DATE	SCRIPTURE REFERENCE	JEWISH LEADER	PERSIAN RULER	EXTENT OF THE RETURN	EVENTS OF THE RETURN
First	538 BC	Ezra 1–6	Zerubbabel Jeshua	Cyrus	(1) Anyone who wanted to return could go. (2) The temple in Jerusalem was to be rebuilt. (3) Royal treasury provided funding of the temple rebuilding. (4) Gold and silver worship articles taken from temple by Nebuchadnezzar were returned.	(1) Burnt offerings were made. (2) The Feast of Tabernacles was celebrated. (3) The rebuilding of the temple was begun. (4) Persian ruler ordered re-building to be ceased. (5) Darius, King of Persia, ordered rebuilding to be re-sumed in 520 BC. (6) Temple was completed and dedicated in 516 BC.
Second	458 BC	Ezra 7–10	Ezra	Artaxerxes Longimanus	(1) Anyone who wanted to return could go. (2) Royal treasury provided funding. (3) Jewish civil magistrates and judges were allowed.	Men of Israel intermarried with foreign women.
Third	444 BC	Nehemiah 1–13	Nehemiah	Artaxerxes Longimanus	Rebuilding of Jerusalem was allowed.	(1) Rebuilding of wall of Jerusalem was opposed by Sanballat the Horonite, Tobiah the Ammonite and Geshem the Arab. (2) Rebuilding of wall was completed in 52 days. (3) Walls were dedicated. (4) Ezra read the Book of the Law to the people. (5) Nehemiah initiated reforms.

113 THE RETURNS OF JEWISH EXILES TO JUDAH

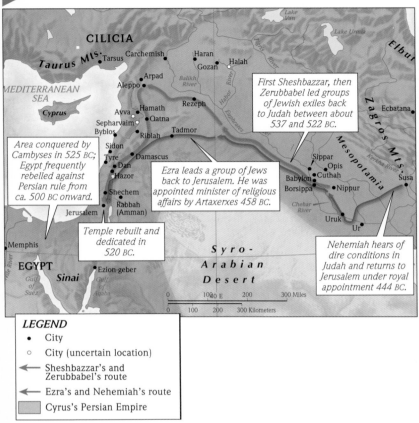

First Sheshbazzar, then Zerubbabel led groups of Jewish exiles back to Judah between about 537 and 522 BC.

Area conquered by Cambyses in 525 BC; Egypt frequently rebelled against Persian rule from ca. 500 BC onward.

Ezra leads a group of Jews back to Jerusalem. He was appointed minister of religious affairs by Artaxerxes 458 BC.

Temple rebuilt and dedicated in 520 BC.

Nehemiah hears of dire conditions in Judah and returns to Jerusalem under royal appointment 444 BC.

LEGEND

- City
- ○ City (uncertain location)
- ← Sheshbazzar's and Zerubbabel's route
- ← Ezra's and Nehemiah's route
- ▢ Cyrus's Persian Empire

Ezra 1:2-4

"This is what King Cyrus of Persia says: 'The LORD, the God of heaven, has given me all the kingdoms of the earth and has appointed me to build Him a house at Jerusalem in Judah. Whoever is among His people, may his God be with him, and may he go to Jerusalem in Judah and build the house of the LORD, the God of Israel, the God who is in Jerusalem. Let every survivor, wherever he lives, be assisted by the men of that region with silver, gold, goods, and livestock, along with a freewill offering for the house of God in Jerusalem.'"

114▶ THE PROVINCE OF JUDAH AND NEHEMIAH'S ENEMIES IN THE FIFTH CENTURY

Given to Sidon about 450 BC.

Nehemiah's enemy Sanballat, governor of Samaria, constantly interferes with Judean efforts to rebuild their homeland.

The wealthy Tobiads meddle in the affairs of Judah for centuries.

Geshem the Arab, one of Nehemiah's enemies, controls trade routes vital to Persian interest.

LEGEND
- • City
- ○ City (uncertain location)
- ★ Possible district capitals
- — Major trade route

Nehemiah 4:6-8
So we rebuilt the wall until the entire wall was joined together up to half its height, for the people had the will to keep working.

When Sanballat, Tobiah, and the Arabs, Ammonites, and Ashdodites heard that the repair to the walls of Jerusalem was progressing and that the gaps were being closed, they became furious. They all plotted together to come and fight against Jerusalem and throw it into confusion.

INTERTESTAMENTAL HISTORY

▲ Acropolis in Athens epitomizes Greek civilization. A process of Hellenization was a part of Alexander the Great's strategy around and beyond the Mediterranean world. The Maccabean revolt sought to reverse this process in Israel.

Shortly after 600 BC the Babylonians captured Jerusalem, destroyed the temple, and took away many of the people as captives. After Cyrus overcame the Babylonian Empire, the Jews who desired were allowed to return. The temple was rebuilt. Under the leadership of Nehemiah and Ezra, the Jewish religious community established itself, and the worship and life of the people continued. Here OT history ends, and the intertestamental period begins.

The history of the intertestamental period can be divided into three sections: The Greek Period, 323–167 BC; the Period of Independence, 167–63 BC; and the Roman Period, 63 BC through the time of the NT.

The Greek Period, 323–167 BC

Philip of Macedon sought to consolidate Greece so as to resist attack by the Persian Empire. When he was murdered in 336 BC, his young son Alexander took up the task. He was only 19 years of age, but he was highly gifted and educated. Within two years he set out to destroy Persia. In a series of battles over the next two years, he gained control of the territory from Asia Minor to Egypt. This included Palestine and the Jews. Josephus, a Jewish historian who lived

Coin bearing the image of Philip of Macedon, father of Alexander the Great.

about AD 37–100, tells of Alexander going to Jerusalem and offering sacrifice in the temple. Many elements of this story are undoubtedly false, but Alexander did treat the Jews well. When he founded the new city of Alexandria in Egypt, he moved many Jews from Palestine to populate one part of that city. In 331 BC Alexander gained full control over the Persian Empire.

Alexander's conquest had three major results. First, he sought to introduce Greek ideas and culture into the conquered territory. This is called Hellenization. He believed that the way to consolidate his empire was for the people to have a common way of life. However, he did not seek to change the religious practices of the Jews. Second, he founded Greek cities and colonies throughout the conquered territory. Third, he spread the Greek language into that entire region so that it became a universal language during the following centuries.

When Alexander died in 323 BC, chaos resulted in his empire. Five of his prominent generals established themselves over different parts of his empire. Ptolemy chose the land of Egypt. Seleucus took control of Babylonia. Antigonus became ruler of Asia Minor and northern Syria. The other two ruled in Europe and did not have direct influence over events in Palestine.

From the beginning, Ptolemy and Antigonus struggled over the control of Palestine. The battle of Ipsus in 301 BC settled the matter for a century. In this battle the other four generals fought against and killed Antigonus. Seleucus was given the territory of Antigonus, including Palestine. However, Ptolemy did not take part in the battle. Instead he took over control of Palestine. The result was that Palestine continued to be a point of contention between the Ptolemies and the Seleucids.

The Jews fared well under the Ptolemies. They had much self-rule.

Head of Alexander the Great.

Their religious practices were not hampered. Greek customs gradually became more common among the people. During this period the translation of the OT into Greek began during the reign of Ptolemy Philadelphus, 285–246 BC. This translation is known as the Septuagint, often abbreviated LXX. The early Christians used the Septuagint, and NT writers often quoted it.

Antiochus III (the Great), 223–187 BC, attempted to take Palestine from the Ptolemies in 217 BC without success. At the battle of Panium, 198 BC, however, he defeated Ptolemy IV, and he and his successors ruled Palestine until 167 BC. The situation of the Jews changed after Antiochus was defeated by the Romans in the battle of Magnesia, 190 BC. Antiochus had supported Hannibal of North Africa, Rome's hated enemy. As a result, Antiochus had to give up all of his territory except the province of Cilicia. He had to pay a large sum of money to the Romans for a period of years, and he had to surrender his navy and elephants. To guarantee his compliance, one of his sons was kept as hostage in Rome. So the tax burden of the Jews increased, as did pressure to Hellenize, that is, to adopt Greek practices.

Antiochus was succeeded by his son Seleucus IV, 187–175 BC. When he was murdered, his younger brother became ruler. Antiochus IV, 175–163 BC, was called Epiphanes ("manifest" or "splendid"), although some called him Epimenes ("mad"). He was the son who had been a hostage in Rome. During the early years of his reign, the situation of the Jews became worse. Part of it was due to their being divided. Some of their leaders, especially the priests, encouraged Hellenism.

Up to the time of Antiochus IV, the office of high priest had been hereditary and held for life. However, Jason, the brother of the high priest, offered the king a large sum of money to be appointed high priest. Antiochus needed the money and made the appointment. Jason also offered an additional sum to receive permission to build a gymnasium near the temple. This shows the pressure toward Hellenism. Within a few years, Menelaus, a priest but not of the high priestly line, offered the king more money to be named high priest in place of Jason. He stole vessels from the temple to pay what he had promised.

Antiochus sought to add Egypt to his territory. He was proclaimed king of Egypt, but when he returned the following year to take control of the

Tetradrachm of Antichochus IV Epiphanes.

land, the Romans confronted him and told him to leave Egypt. Knowing the power of Rome, he returned home. When he reached Jerusalem, he found that Jason had driven Menelaus out of the city. He saw this as full revolt. He allowed his troops to kill many of the Jews and determined to put an end to the Jewish religion. He sacrificed a pig on the altar of the temple. Parents were forbidden to circumcise their children, the Sabbath was not to be observed, and all copies of the law were to be burned. It was a capital offense to be found with a copy of the law. The zeal of Antiochus to destroy Judaism was a major factor in its salvation.

Jewish Independence, 167–63 BC

Resistance was passive at first; but when the Seleucids sent officers throughout the land to compel leading citizens to offer sacrifice to Zeus, open conflict flared. It broke out first at the village of Modein, about halfway between Jerusalem and Joppa. An aged priest named Mattathias was chosen to offer the sacrifice. He refused, but a young Jew volunteered to do it. This angered Mattathias, and he killed both the Jew and the officer. Then he fled to the hills with his five sons and others who supported his action. The revolt had begun.

Leadership fell to Judas, the third son of Mattathias. He was nicknamed Maccabeus, the hammerer. He probably received this title because of his success in battle. He was the ideal guerrilla leader. He fought successful battles against much larger forces. A group called the Hasidim made up the major part of his army. These men were devoutly committed to religious freedom. They were dedicated to obedience to the law and to the worship of God.

Antiochus IV was more concerned with affairs in the eastern part of his empire than with what was taking place in Palestine. Therefore, he did not commit many troops to the revolt at first. Judas was able to gain control of Jerusalem within three years. The temple was cleansed and rededicated exactly three years after it had been polluted by the king, 164 BC. (Dates through this period are uncertain and may be a year earlier than indicated.) This is still commemorated by the Jewish feast of Hanukkah. The Hasidim had gained what they were seeking and left the army. Judas had larger goals in mind. He wanted political freedom. He rescued mistreated Jews from Galilee and Gilead and made a treaty of friendship and mutual support with Rome. In 160 BC at Elasa, with a force of eight hundred men, he fought a vastly superior Seleucid army and was killed.

Jonathan, another son of Mattathias, took the lead in the quest for independence. He was weak militarily. He was driven out of the cities and only gradually established himself in the countryside. Constant struggle engaged those seeking the Seleucid throne. The rivals offered him gifts to gain his support. In 152 BC he gave his support to Alexander Balas, who claimed to be the son of Antiochus IV. In return Jonathan was appointed high priest. For the first time, Jewish religious and civil rule were centered in one person. Jonathan was taken prisoner and killed in 143 BC.

Simon, the last surviving son of Mattathias, ruled until he was murdered by his son-in-law in 134 BC. He secured freedom from taxation for the Jews by 141 BC. At last they had achieved political freedom. Simon was acclaimed by the people as their leader and high priest forever. The high priesthood was made hereditary with him and his descendants. The Hasmonean dynasty, named after an ancestor of Mattathias, had its beginning.

When Simon was murdered, his son John Hyrcanus became the high priest and civil ruler (134–104 BC). For a brief time the Seleucids exercised some power over the Jews, but Hyrcanus broke free and began to expand the territory of the Jews. In the north he destroyed the temple of the Samaritans on Mount Gerizim. He moved southeast and conquered the land of the Idumeans, the ancient kingdom of Edom. The residents were forced to emigrate or convert to Judaism. This had great significance for the Jews, for it was from this people that Herod the Great was to come.

The oldest son of Hyrcanus, Aristobulus I (104–103 BC), succeeded him. He had his mother and three brothers put in prison. One brother was allowed to remain free, but he was later murdered. He allowed his mother to starve to death in prison. He extended his rule to include part of the territory of Iturea, north of Galilee. He was the first to take the title of king.

Salome Alexandra was the wife of Aristobulus. When he died, she released his brothers from prison and married the oldest of them, Alexander Jannaeus. He became high priest and king (103–76 BC). He made many enemies by marrying the widow of his brother. The OT stated that a high priest must marry a virgin (Lev. 21:14). He was an ambitious warrior and conducted campaigns by which he enlarged his kingdom to about the size of the

▲ Terracotta woman with Grecian dress and hairstyle, dating from the second to first century BC.

kingdom of David. He used foreign soldiers because he could not trust Jews in his army. As high priest, he did not always follow prescribed ritual. On one occasion the people reacted to his improper actions by throwing citrons at him. He allowed his soldiers to kill six thousand of them. At another time he had eigth hundred of his enemies crucified. As they hung on the crosses, he had their wives and children brought out and slain before their eyes.

Alexandra succeeded her husband as ruler (76–67 BC). Of course, she could not serve as high priest, so the two functions were separated. Her oldest son, Hyrcanus II, became high priest. He was not ambitious. Her younger son, Aristobulus II, was just the opposite. He was waiting for his mother to die so he could become king and high priest.

When Salome died, civil war broke out and lasted until 63 BC. Aristobulus easily defeated Hyrcanus, who was content to retire. This might have been the end of the story were it not for Antipater, an Idumean. He persuaded Hyrcanus to seek the help of the king of Nabatea to regain his position. Aristobulus was driven back to Jerusalem. At this point Rome arrived on the scene. Both Aristobulus and Hyrcanus appealed to Scaurus, the Roman general charged with the administration of Palestine. He sided with Aristobulus. When the Roman commander Pompey arrived later, both appealed to him. Aristobulus ended up trying to fight against the Romans. He was defeated and taken as a prisoner to Rome. The Romans took control over Palestine.

The Roman Period, 63 BC–AD 70

Under the Romans the Jews paid heavy taxes, but their religious practices were not changed. Roman power was exercised through Antipater, who was named governor of Palestine. Hyrcanus was made high priest. The situation in Palestine was confused due to the efforts of Aristobulus and his sons to lead revolts against Rome. While Palestine was successively under the control of various Roman officials, Antipater was the stabilizing force. He had one son, Phasael, named governor of Judea, and a second son, Herod, made governor of Galilee. Herod sought to bring order to his area. He arrested Hezekiah, a Jewish robber or rebel, and had him executed. The Sanhedrin in Jerusalem summoned Herod to give an account of his action. He went, dressed in royal purple and with a bodyguard. The Sanhedrin could do nothing.

Antipater was murdered in 43 BC. Antony became the Roman commander in the East in 42 BC. In 40 BC the Parthians invaded Palestine and made Antigonus, the last surviving son of Aristobulus, king of Palestine. Hyrcanus was mutilated by having his ears cut or bitten off so he could not serve as high priest again. Phasael was captured and committed suicide in prison. Herod barely escaped with his family. He went to Rome to have his future brother-in-law, Aristobulus, made king, hoping to rule through him as his father had ruled through Antipater. However, the Roman Senate, at the urging of Antony and Octavian (Augustus), made Herod king (40 BC). It took him three years to drive the Parthians out of the country and establish his rule. He was king until his death in 4 BC.

The years of Herod's rule were a time of turmoil for the Jewish people. He was an Idumean. Of course, his ancestors had been forced to convert to Judaism, but the people never accepted him. He was the representative of a foreign power. No matter how well he served Rome, he could never satisfy the Jews. Even his marriage to Mariamne, the granddaughter of Aristobulus II, gave no legitimacy to his rule in their sight. The most spectacular of his building achievements, the rebuilding of the Jerusalem temple, did not win the loyalty of the Jews.

Herod had many problems that grew out of his jealousy and fears. He had Aristobulus, his brother-in-law, executed. Later Mariamne, her mother, and her two sons were killed. Just five days before his own death, Herod had his oldest son, Antipater, put to death. His relations with Rome were sometimes troubled due to the unsettled conditions in the empire. Herod was a strong supporter of Antony even though he could not tolerate Cleopatra with whom Antony had become enamored. When Antony was defeated by Octavian in 31 BC, Herod went to Octavian and pledged his full support. This support was accepted. Herod proved himself an efficient administrator on behalf of Rome. He kept the peace among a people who were hard to rule. To be sure, he was a cruel and merciless man. Yet he was generous, using his own funds to feed the people during a time of famine. He never got over the execution of Mariamne, the wife he loved above all others. His grief led to mental and emotional problems.

During the reign of Herod, Jesus was born (Matt. 2:1-18; Luke 1:5). Herod was the king who ordered the execution of the male babies in Bethlehem (Matt. 2:16-18).

At his death Herod left a will leaving his kingdom to three of his sons. Antipas was to be tetrarch (ruler of a fourth) of Galilee and Perea (4 BC–AD 39). Philip was to be tetrarch of Gentile regions to the northeast of the Sea of Galilee (4 BC–AD 34). Archelaus was to be king of Judea and Samaria. Rome honored the will except that Archelaus was not given the title of king. He was ethnarch (ruler of the people) of these two territories. He proved to be a poor ruler and was deposed in AD 6. His territories were placed under the direct rule of Roman procurators who were under the control of the governor of Syria.

Literature

The Jews produced many writings during the intertestamental period. These writings can be divided into three groups. The Apocrypha are writings that were included, for the most part, in the Greek translation of the OT, the Septuagint. They were translated into Latin and became a part of the Latin Vulgate, the authoritative Latin Bible. Some are historical books. First Maccabees is our chief source for the history of the period from Antiochus Epiphanes to John Hyrcanus. Other books are Wisdom Literature. Others can be classified as historical romances. One is apocalyptic, giving attention to the end of time and God's intervention in history. One writing is devotional in nature. A second group of writings is the Pseudepigrapha. It is a larger collection than the Apocrypha, but there is no final agreement as to which writings should be included in it. Fifty-two writings are included in the two volumes, The Old Testament Pseudepigrapha, edited by James H. Charlesworth. These cover the range of Jewish thought from apocalyptic to wisdom to devotional. Their title indicates that they are attributed to noted people of ancient times, such as Adam, Abraham, Enoch, Ezra, and Baruch. For the most part they were written in the last centuries before the birth of Jesus, although some of them are from the first century AD.

DEAD SEA SCROLLS

The final group of writings from this period is the Qumran scrolls, popularly known as the Dead Sea Scrolls. The Scrolls were discovered between 1947 and 1960 in a cave on the western Dead Sea shore near a ruin called Khirbet Qumran. Eleven caves from the Qumran area have since yielded manuscripts, mostly in small fragments. About 60 percent of the scrolls have so far been published. These were composed or copied between 200 BC and AD 70, mostly around the lifetime of Jesus, by a small community living at Qumran.

Dead Sea Scroll fragment.

The Dead Sea Scrolls and the Old Testament Text

Prior to the discovery of these scrolls, the oldest complete or almost complete manuscripts of the Hebrew Old Testament were the Leningrad Codex (AD 1009) and the Aleppo Codex (AD 930). The discovery of the Dead Sea Scrolls has extended our knowledge of the Hebrew text back one thousand years. The most important lesson to be learned from this is how carefully the Jewish scribes preserved the integrity of the text during that time. Moreover, among the recovered manuscripts was the early textual tradition that later became the standard text, known as the Masoretic Text (MT). This discovery indicated that the Jewish Masoretes were not creating a text but were faithfully preserving an ancient form of the Hebrew Old Testament.

The Dead Sea Scrolls and Christianity

Soon after the discovery of the first of the scrolls, certain scholars posited the idea that some of the ideology of early Christianity may have had its origins in the theology of the Qumran sectarians. Self-identifying phrases such as the "Called-out Ones" (*ekklesia*), "the Way," "the Poor," "the Elects," and "the Saints" were common to both groups, as well as their general identities as messianic communities.

Both groups held to a "new covenant" theology and saw their founders and leaders as the fulfillment of the prophetic promise of the OT. Both groups held that the religious leadership in Jerusalem had become corrupt and was in need of divine intervention to bring correction. Communal meals and property sharing in the early church were paralleled with those at Qumran, and both were seen as practicing forms of baptismal ritual. However these might appear as parallel upon a surface reading of the text, there are notable differences. At the core of the distinctiveness is the personal identity, teaching, and work of Jesus of Nazareth. Qumran sectarians were looking for possibly two messiahs, one of the lineage of Aaron (priestly) and one of the branch of David (royal), whereas for Christianity the Messiah had come and fulfilled the Law and the Prophets and would return in the eschatological future for the saints.

Caves at Qumran in which the Dead Sea Scrolls were discovered.

115 QUMRAN AND THE DEAD SEA SCROLLS

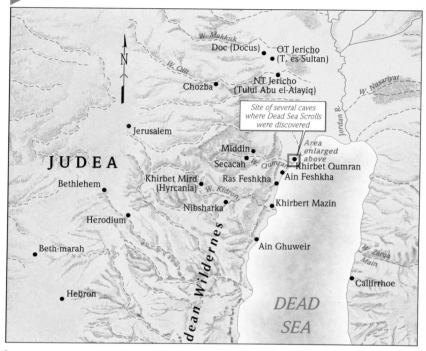

W. Makkuk

Doc (Docus) • OT Jericho
• (T. es-Sultan)

Chozba • NT Jericho
(Tulul Abu el-Alayiq)

W. Qilt

W. Nusariyat

N

Site of several caves
where Dead Sea Scrolls
were discovered

• Jerusalem

Middin •

Area
enlarged
above

JUDEA

Secacah • W. Qumran Khirbet Qumran

Khirbet Mird Ras Feshkha • Ain Feshkha
(Hyrcania) W. Kidron

• Bethlehem

Nibsharka •

• Khirbert Mazin

• Herodium

Ain Ghuweir •

• Beth-marah

W. Zarqa
Main

• Hebron

• Callirrhoe

DEAD
SEA

Judean Wilderness

Jordan R.

116 QUMRAN CAVES

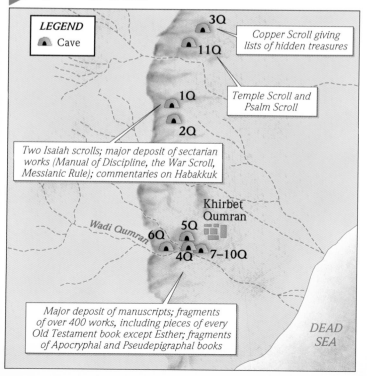

LEGEND
🔺 Cave

3Q

11Q

Copper Scroll giving
lists of hidden treasures

1Q

Temple Scroll and
Psalm Scroll

2Q

Two Isaiah scrolls; major deposit of sectarian
works (Manual of Discipline, the War Scroll,
Messianic Rule); commentaries on Habakkuk

Khirbet
Qumran

5Q

Wadi Qumran 6Q

7–10Q

4Q

Major deposit of manuscripts; fragments
of over 400 works, including pieces of every
Old Testament book except Esther; fragments
of Apocryphal and Pseudepigraphal books

DEAD
SEA

117▶ ALEXANDER THE GREAT'S EMPIRE

Battle of Granicus River

Alexander wins major victory over Darius III (333 BC).

Alexander decisively defeats Darius III (331 BC).

Alexander captures ports vital to the Persian fleet.

Alexander dies at the age of 33 (323 BC).

Alexander visits the oracle of Zeus Ammon.

Alexander secures Egypt and assumes the title of Pharaoh (332 BC).

LEGEND

- ● Modern city
- ● City
- ▲ Mountain peak
- ⚔ Battle
- ⛉ Siege
- ← Alexander's route
- ▨ Alexander's Empire

| 0 | 100 | 200 | 300 | 400 | 500 Miles |

| 0 | 100 | 200 | 300 | 400 | 500 Kilometers |

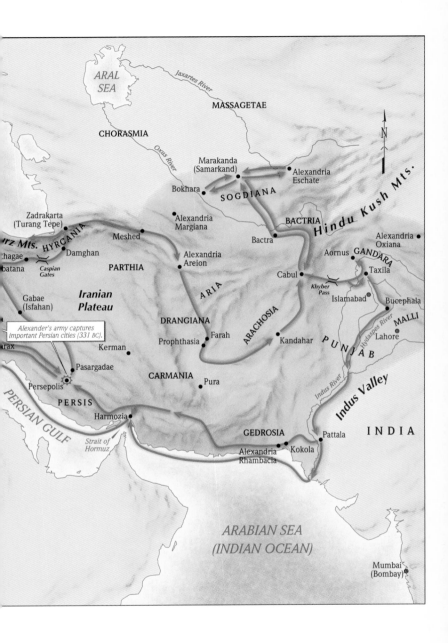

ARAL
SEA

MASSAGETAE

CHORASMIA

Jaxartes River

Oxus River

Marakanda
(Samarkand)

Alexandria
Eschate

Bokhara

SOGDIANA

BACTRIA

Hindu Kush Mts.

Zadrakarta
(Turang Tepe)

rz Mts. HYRCANIA

Meshed

Alexandria
Margiana

Bactra

Alexandria
Oxiana

hagae

Damghan

*Caspian
Gates*

Alexandria
Areion

Aornus GANDARA

Cabul

Taxila

batana

PARTHIA

*Iranian
Plateau*

ARIA

Khyber
Pass

Islamabad

Bucephala

Gabae
(Isfahan)

DRANGIANA

ARACHOSIA

PUNJAB

Lahore

Hydaspes River

MALLI

Alexander's army captures
important Persian cities (331 BC).

Prophthasia

Farah

Kandahar

rax

Kerman

Pasargadae

CARMANIA

Pura

Indus River

Indus Valley

Persepolis

PERSIS

Harmozia

GEDROSIA

Pattala

INDIA

PERSIAN GULF

*Strait of
Hormuz*

Alexandria
Rhambacia

Kokola

ARABIAN SEA
(INDIAN OCEAN)

Mumbai
(Bombay)

N

118 THE DIVISION OF ALEXANDER'S EMPIRE

Ptolemy and Seleucus are victorious at the battle of Ipsus, resulting in the death of Antigonus (301 BC).

Seleucus allied with Ptolemy against Antigonus' fighting many battles in the eastern Mediterranean.

Antigonus initiates conflicts by attacking Ptolemy.

Antigonus forces Seleucus to abandon Babylon.

LEGEND
- Modern city
- City
- ▲ Mountain peak
- Battle
- Seleucid kingdom
- Antigonid kingdom
- Ptolemaic kingdom
- Hellenistic province

Daniel 11:2-4

Now I will tell you the truth. "Three more kings will arise in Persia, and the fourth will be far richer than the others. By the power he gains through his riches, he will stir up everyone against the kingdom of Greece. Then a warrior king will arise; he will rule a vast realm and do whatever he wants. But as soon as he is established, his kingdom will be broken up and divided to the four winds of heaven, but not to his descendants; it will not be the same kingdom that he ruled, because his kingdom will be uprooted and will go to others besides them."

119 THE PTOLEMIES AND THE SELUCIDS

PTOLEMAIC RULERS	KEY EVENTS	SELEUCID RULERS	KEY EVENTS
Ptolemy I Soter (323–285 BC)	Established Ptolemaic line; founded great library of Alexandria; resettled many Jews in Alexandria	Seleucid I (312–280 BC)	Founded Seleucid line of rulers; founded Antioch in 300 BC
Ptolemy II Philadelphus (285–246 BC)	First and Second Wars with Seleucids; Septuagint (LXX) begun in Alexandria	Antiochus I (280–261 BC)	
Ptolemy III Euregetes (246–221 BC)	Third War with Seleucids	Antiochus II (261–246 BC)	
Ptolemy IV Philopator (221–203 BC)	Defeated Antiochus III at Raphia	Seleucus II (246–223 BC)	
Ptolemy V Epiphanes (203–181 BC)	Lost Palestine to Seleucids in 200 BC	Antiochus III (223–187 BC)	Secured Palestine for Seleucid rule at Panias in 200; defeated by Rome in Asia Minor at Magnesia in 190
Ptolemy VI Philometor (181–146 BC)		Seleucus IV (187–175 BC)	Heliodorus tries to plunder the temple at Jerusalem
		Antiochus IV (175–163 BC)	Corrupted the high priesthood in Jerusalem; invaded Egypt but was forced to withdraw by Romans; policies provoked the Maccabean Revolt; profaned the temple in Jerusalem

120 PALESTINE UNDER THE PTOLEMIES

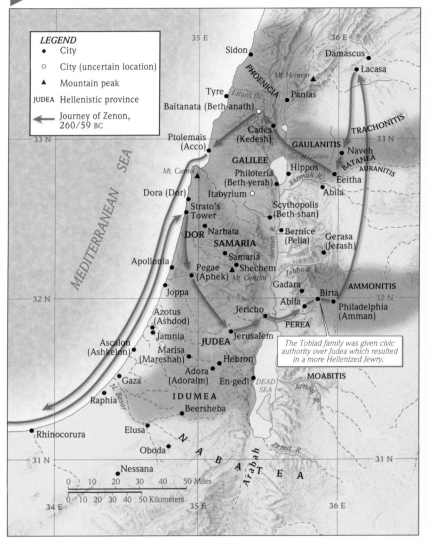

LEGEND
- • City
- ○ City (uncertain location)
- ▲ Mountain peak
- JUDEA Hellenistic province
- ← Journey of Zenon, 260/59 BC

35 E
36 E

Sidon
Damascus
Lacasa
PHOENICIA
Mt. Hermon ▲
Tyre
Panias
Litani R.
Baitanata (Beth-anath)
TRACHONITIS
Cades (Kedesh)
33 N
Ptolemais (Acco)
GAULANITIS
Naveh
Sea of Galilee
GALILEE
Hippos
BATANEA
Eeitha
AURANITIS
Mt. Carmel
Philoteria (Beth-yerah)
Yarmuk R.
Abila
Dora (Dor)
Itabyrium ○
Strato's Tower
Scythopolis (Beth-shan)
DOR
Narbata
Jordan R.
Bernice (Pella)
Gerasa (Jerash)
SAMARIA
Apollonia
Samaria
Pegae (Aphek)
Shechem
Mt. Gerizim
Jabbok R.
Gadara
Birta
AMMONITIS
Joppa
Abila
Philadelphia (Amman)
32 N
Azotus (Ashdod)
Jericho
PEREA
Jamnia
Jerusalem
Ascalon (Ashkelon)
Marisa (Mareshah)
JUDEA
Hebron
The Tobiad family was given civic authority over Judea which resulted in a more Hellenized Jewry.
Adora (Adoraim)
En-gedi
DEAD SEA
MOABITIS
Gaza
IDUMEA
Arnon R.
Raphia
Beersheba
N. Besor
Rhinocorura
Elusa
Zered R.
31 N
Oboda
Arabah
NABATEA
Nessana
0 10 20 30 40 50 Miles
0 10 20 30 40 50 Kilometers
34 E
35 E
36 E

MEDITERRANEAN SEA

121 ▶ THE SELEUCID EMPIRE AND ANTIOCHUS III

Romans decisively beat Antiochus III and demand forfeiture of all Seleucid claims in Asia Minor as well as a large sum of money (190 BC).

Antiochus III defeats Ptolemaic army which results in Seleucid control over Palestine (200 BC).

Antiochus III defeats by Ptolemy IV (217 BC).

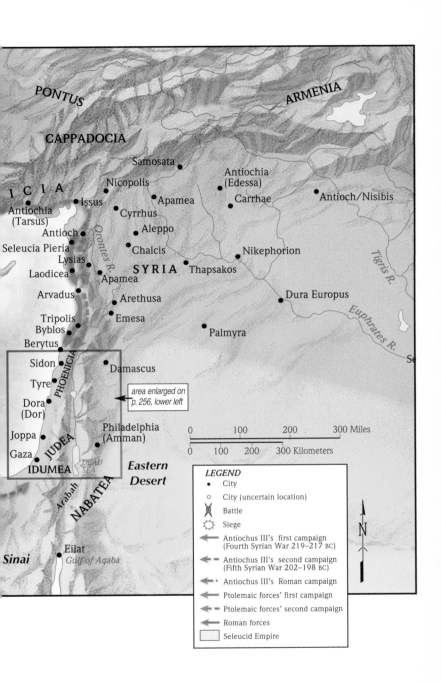

PONTUS

CAPPADOCIA

ARMENIA

Samosata

Antiochia
(Edessa)

Nicopolis

I C I A

Apamea

Carrhae

Antioch/Nisibis

Issus

Antiochia
(Tarsus)

Cyrrhus

Antioch

Aleppo

Seleucia Pieria

Chalcis

Nikephorion

Lysias

Orontes R.

SYRIA

Thapsakos

Tigris R.

Laodicea

Apamea

Arvadus

Arethusa

Dura Europus

Tripolis

Emesa

Euphrates R.

Byblos

Berytus

Palmyra

Sidon

Damascus

Tyre

PHOENICIA

area enlarged on
p. 256, lower left

Dora
(Dor)

Joppa

Philadelphia
(Amman)

JUDEA

| 0 | 100 | 200 | 300 Miles |

| 0 | 100 | 200 | 300 Kilometers |

Gaza

IDUMEA

*DEAD
SEA*

Eastern
Desert

Arabah

NABATEA

LEGEND

• City

○ City (uncertain location)

⊗ Battle

⌗ Siege

← Antiochus III's first campaign
(Fourth Syrian War 219–217 BC)

← Antiochus III's second campaign
(Fifth Syrian War 202–198 BC)

← Antiochus III's Roman campaign

← Ptolemaic forces' first campaign

← Ptolemaic forces' second campaign

← Roman forces

☐ Seleucid Empire

Sinai

Eilat
Gulf of Aqaba

N

122 CAMPAIGN OF ANTIOCHUS AGAINST EGYPT

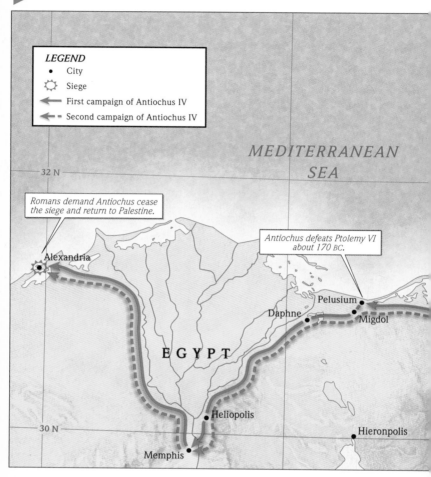

LEGEND
- City
- Siege
- First campaign of Antiochus IV
- Second campaign of Antiochus IV

MEDITERRANEAN SEA

32 N

Romans demand Antiochus cease the siege and return to Palestine.

Alexandria

Antiochus defeats Ptolemy VI about 170 BC.

Pelusium

Daphne

Migdol

EGYPT

Heliopolis

30 N

Hieronpolis

Memphis

123 LIGHTHOUSE IN THE HARBOR AT ALEXANDRIA, EGYPT

Alexandria was capital of Egypt from 330 BC, founded by Alexander the Great as an outstanding Greek cultural and academic center. Alexandria was designed to act as the principal port of Egypt located on the western edge of the Nile Delta. Built on a peninsula, it separated the Mediterranean Sea and Lake Mareotis. A causeway (Heptastadion, or "seven stadia") connected the peninsula with Pharos Island and divided the harbor. The Pharos lighthouse was visible for miles at a height of over four hundred feet and is remembered today as one of the "Seven Wonders of the World."

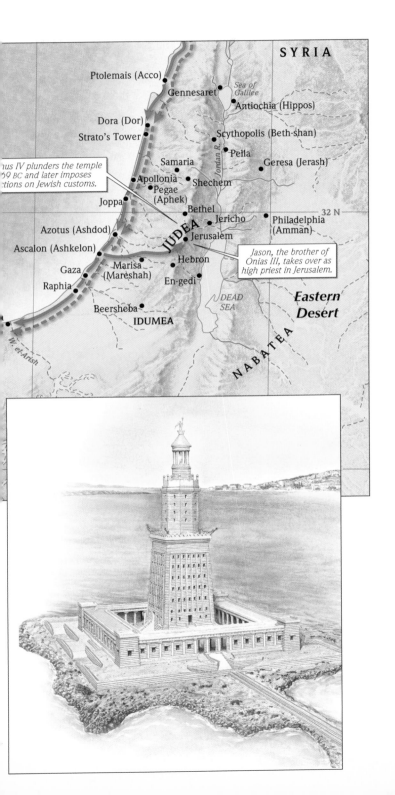

SYRIA

Ptolemais (Acco)

Gennesaret

Sea of Galilee

Antiochia (Hippos)

Dora (Dor)

Strato's Tower

Scythopolis (Beth-shan)

Pella

Geresa (Jerash)

Samaria

...us IV plunders the temple
...9 BC and later imposes
...tions on Jewish customs.

Apollonia

Shechem

Pegae (Aphek)

Joppa

Bethel

Jericho

Philadelphia (Amman)

32 N

JUDEA

Jerusalem

Azotus (Ashdod)

Ascalon (Ashkelon)

Hebron

Jason, the brother of Onias III, takes over as high priest in Jerusalem.

Gaza

Marisa (Mareshah)

En-gedi

Raphia

DEAD SEA

Eastern Desert

Beersheba

IDUMEA

NABATEA

W. el-Arish

Jordan R.

124 FAMILY OF MATTATHIAS AND THE MACCABEAN REVOLT

NAME	DATES OF RULE	SIGNIFICANT EVENTS
Mattathias	167–166 BC	Aged priest living at Modein; died in 166 BC; defied the order to offer a sacrifice in homage to Antiochus IV
Judas "Maccabeus"	166–160 BC	Third son of Mattathias; led revolt from 166 to 160 BC; won victories over Seleucid troops at Beth-horon, Samaria, Emmaus, and Beth-zur; reclaimed and cleansed the temple at Jerusalem in 164 BC; gained religious freedom for the Jews in 162 BC; died fighting at Elasa
Jonathan	160–142 BC	Youngest son of Mattathias; led a guerilla war from the Judean deserts; eventually established a base at Michmash; appointed as High Priest in 152 BC; taken prisoner and executed by the Seleucid Trypho in 143 BC
Simon	412–134 BC	Second eldest son of Mattathias; gained political concessions from Seleucid rulers that led to an independent Jewish state in 142 BC; died in coup in 135 BC

125▶ SELECTED EVENTS IN THE MACCABEAN REVOLT

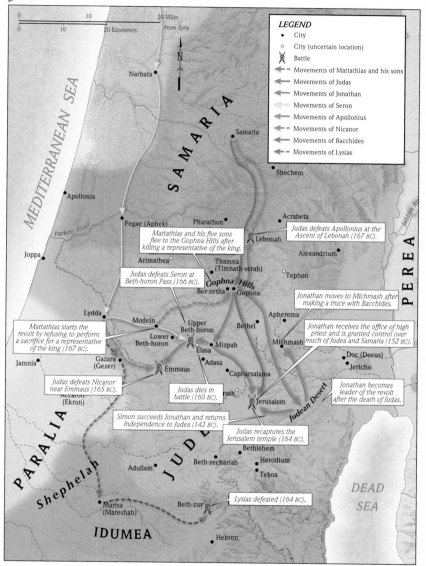

0   10   20 Miles
0   10   20 Kilometers

From Syria

LEGEND
- • City
- ○ City (uncertain location)
- ⚔ Battle
- ◀— Movements of Mattathias and his sons
- ◀— Movements of Judas
- ◀— Movements of Jonathan
- ◀— Movements of Seron
- ◀— Movements of Apollonius
- ◀— Movements of Nicanor
- ◀— Movements of Bacchides
- ◀— Movements of Lysias

MEDITERRANEAN SEA

SAMARIA

PEREA

PARALIA

JUDEA

IDUMEA

Shephelah

Judean Desert

DEAD SEA

Jabbok River

Jordan

Yarkon River

Narbata

Samaria

Shechem

Apollonia

Pegae (Aphek)   Pharathon   Acrabeta

Lebonah

Alexandrium

Joppa

Arimathea

Thamna (Timnath-serah)

Tephon

Gophna Hills

Ber-zetha   Gophna

Apherema

Lydda   Modein   Upper Beth-horon   Bethel

Lower Beth-horon   Mizpah   Michmash

Elasa   Doc (Docus)

Jamnia   Gazara (Gezer)   Adasa   Jericho

Emmaus   Capharsalama

Accaron (Ekron)   roth   Jerusalem

Bethlehem   Herodium

Adullam   Beth-zechariah   Tekoa

Marisa (Mareshah)   Beth-zur

Hebron

Judas defeats Apollonius at the Ascent of Lebonah (167 BC).

Mattathias and his five sons flee to the Gophna Hills after killing a representative of the king.

Judas defeats Seron at Beth-horon Pass (166 BC).

Jonathan moves to Michmash after making a truce with Bacchides.

Jonathan receives the office of high priest and is granted control over much of Judea and Samaria (152 BC).

Mattathias starts the revolt by refusing to perform a sacrifice for a representative of the king (167 BC).

Judas defeats Nicanor near Emmaus (165 BC).

Judas dies in battle (160 BC).

Jonathan becomes leader of the revolt after the death of Judas.

Simon succeeds Jonathan and returns independence to Judea (142 BC).

Judas recaptures the Jerusalem temple (164 BC).

Lysias defeated (164 BC).

126 HASMONEAN RULERS

NAME	DATES OF RULE	SIGNIFICANT EVENTS
John Hyrcanus	135–104 BC	Son of Simon, last of the Maccabean brothers; conquered Medeba, Idumea, Samaria, and Joppa; Pharisees and Sadducees first appear in his reign
Aristobulus	104–103 BC	Oldest son of John Hyrcanus; eliminated all but one of his brothers in securing his rule; Upper Galilee conquered during his reign; first Hasmonean to use the title "king"
Alexander Janneus	103–76 BC	Brother of Aristobulus who married his widow, Salome Alexandra; added territories along the coast (Gaza, Dora, Anthedon, Raphia, Strato's Tower); extended Jewish rule in the Transjordan; civil war between Janneus and the Pharisees and their supporters
Salome Alexandra	76–67 BC	Widow of Alexander Janneus; assumed civil authority; appointed her eldest son Hyrcanus II high priest; favored the Pharisees
Hyrcanus II and Aristobulus II	67–63 BC	Rival sons of Salome Alexandra; Aristobulus, supported by Sadducees, seized power from Hyrcanus II; the Idumean governor Antipater used the Nabateans in an attempt to restore Hyrcanus to power in 63 BC. Pompeii intervened in the dispute.

127 JEWISH EXPANSION UNDER THE HASMONEAN DYNASTY

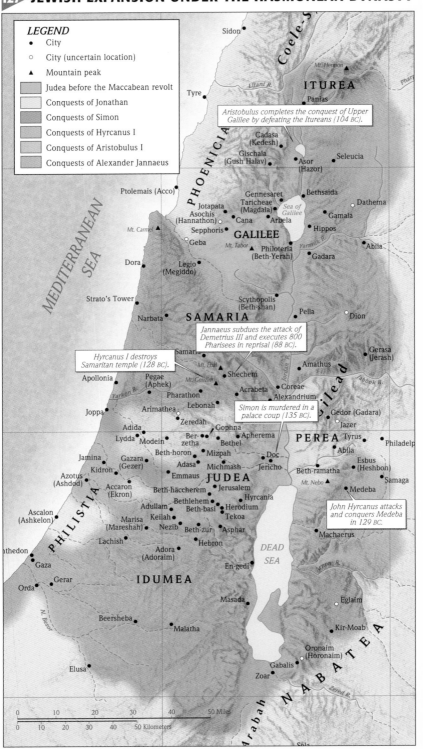

LEGEND
- • City
- ○ City (uncertain location)
- ▲ Mountain peak
- Judea before the Maccabean revolt
- Conquests of Jonathan
- Conquests of Simon
- Conquests of Hyrcanus I
- Conquests of Aristobulus I
- Conquests of Alexander Jannaeus

Aristobulus completes the conquest of Upper Galilee by defeating the Itureans (104 BC).

Hyrcanus I destroys Samaritan temple (128 BC).

Jannaeus subdues the attack of Demetrius III and executes 800 Pharisees in reprisal (88 BC).

Simon is murdered in a palace coup (135 BC).

John Hyrcanus attacks and conquers Medeba in 129 BC.

Sidon
Coele-S
Mt. Hermon
ITUREA
Litani R.
Panias
Tyre
Pharp
Cadasa (Kedesh)
Gischala (Gush Halav)
Asor (Hazor)
Seleucia
PHOENICIA
Ptolemais (Acco)
Gennesaret
Bethsaida
Dathema
Jotapata
Taricheae (Magdala)
Sea of Galilee
Asochis (Hannathon)
Cana
Arbela
Gamala
Sepphoris
GALILEE
Hippos
Mt. Carmel
Geba
Mt. Tabor
Philoteria (Beth-Yerah)
Yarmuk R.
Abila
Gadara
MEDITERRANEAN SEA
Dora
Legio (Megiddo)
Strato's Tower
Scythopolis (Beth-shan)
Pella
Dion
Narbata
SAMARIA
Samar
Gerasa (Jerash)
Mt. Ebal
Amathus
Apollonia
Pegae (Aphek)
Mt. Gerizim
Shechem
Gilead
Jabbok R.
Yarkon R.
Pharathon
Acrabeta
Coreae
Joppa
Lebonah
Alexandrium
Arimathea
Zeredah
Gophna
Gedor (Gadara)
Adida
Ber-zetha
Apherema
Jazer
Lydda
Modein
Bethel
PEREA
Tyrus
Philadelp
Jamina
Gazara (Gezer)
Beth-horon
Mizpah
Doc
Abila
Kidron
Adasa
Michmash
Jericho
Esbus (Heshbon)
Azotus (Ashdod)
Emmaus
Beth-ramatha
Samaga
Accaron (Ekron)
JUDEA
Jerusalem
Mt. Nebo
Medeba
PHILISTIA
Beth-haccherem
Hyrcania
Ascalon (Ashkelon)
Adullam
Bethlehem
Herodium
Marisa (Mareshah)
Beth-basi
Tekoa
Keilah
Nezib
Beth-zur
Asphar
Machaerus
Lachish
Adora (Adoraim)
Hebron
DEAD SEA
Arnon R.
athedon
Gaza
En-gedi
Orda
Gerar
IDUMEA
Masada
Eglaim
N. Besor
Beersheba
Kir-Moab
Malatha
NABATEA
Oronaim (Horonaim)
Elusa
Gabalis
Zoar
Zered R.
Arabah
Sela

0 10 20 30 40 50 Miles
0 10 20 30 40 50 Kilometers

LEGEND
- Etruscan city-state
- Latin settlement
- Other important colonies
- City allied with Sparta
- City allied with Athens
- Roman republic
- Area of Latin tribes
- Etruscan influence
- → Gallic invasion

CELTS

Po R.

Felsina
(Bononia)

Marzabotto

Umbro R.
Faesulae
Arno R.

ETRURIA

Volaterrae
Arretium
Cortona

Murlo
Populonia
Perusia

Vetulonia
Rusellae
Clusium
ITALIA

Sovana
Volsinii (Bolsena)
Telamon
Acquarossa
Volci
Tuscania
Norchia
Falera
Tarquinia
Capena
Pyrgi
Caere
Veii

Rubicon R.

Tiber R.

ADRIATIC SEA

Rome
Tibur
Collatia
Praeneste
Lavinium
Anagnia
LATIUM
Cora
Ferentinum
Ardea
Norba
Satricum
CAMPANIA
Circeii

Cannae

Gauls sack Rome (390 BC).

According to Roman tradition, Romulus founded Rome in 753 B.C.; Roman Republic established in 509 BC.

Early settlements of Latin tribes, 950 BC?

Cumae
Neapolis

TYRRHENIAN SEA

MAGNA GRAECIA

Lipara
Messana
Locri
Rhegium

Segesta
Himera
Strait of Messina

Selinus
Catana

Sicily

Strait of Sicily

Syracuse

Carthage
Gela

MEDITERRANEAN SEA

0   50   100   150 Miles
0 50 100 150 Kilometers

16 E

129 THE RISE OF ROME

DATES (BC)	EVENTS
1000–900?	Early settlement of Latin tribes on hills near Tiber River crossing
753	Traditional date of the founding of Rome; seven kings of Rome; increasing influence and dominance of Etruscans over Rome
509	Expulsion of the Etruscan king Tarquin II (534–509 BC) and establishment of the Roman Republic
390	Sack of Rome by Gauls
312	Construction of the Via Appia, first of the great Roman roads
264–241	Roman colonization and conquest of the Italian Peninsula (334–264 BC); First Punic war (Carthage); annexation of Sicily (241 BC), Sardinia (238 BC), and Corsica (238 BC)
218–202	Second Punic War; Hannibal's campaign in Italy; defeat of Carthage; Rome occupies Spain; First Macedonian War (214–205 BC)
200–197/6	Second Macedonian War; Philip V defeated; Rome invades Asia and defeats Antiochus III at Magnesia in 190 BC
171–168/7	Third Macedonian War; Macedonia divided up into four districts
150-148	Fourth Macedonian War; Macedonia annexed as a province
146	Rome destroys Corinthn after a Greek uprising; Third Punic war (149–146 BC); Carthage destroyed; Rome annexes the province of Africa
133	Attalus III bequeaths the Attalid kingdom centered on Pergamum to Rome

130 ROMAN EXPANSION IN THE THIRD AND SECOND CENTURIES BC

GALLIA

Loire R.

ATLANTIC
OCEAN

Rhone R.

Rhine R.

GALLIA
CISALPINA Verona

Vienna

Rome cor
Peninsula

Rome expands
westward into Spain.

NARBONENSIS Aquae Trebbia Cremona
Tolosa   Sextiae   Genua
Narbo   Massalia   Po R.   Ar
Pisae Tiber ITALIA A
R.

Numantia

Douro R.

Aleria Rome ITALIA
Corsica

Tarraco   Capua

Segovia HISPANIA
CITERIOR   Balearic   Mago   Tharros
Tagus R.   Is.   Sardinia TYRRHENI
Saguntum   SEA
HISPANIA   Nora
ULTERIOR   Corduba Valentia   Panormus
Gibraltar   Carthago Nova   Eryx Si
Sexi   Utica   SICIL
Gades   Abdera   Cirta   Carthage
(Cadiz) Malaca   NUMIDIA AFRICA Zama

MAURETANIA

The Roman Gene
Scipio Africanus de
Hannibal in 202

LEGEND
- • City
- ○ City (uncertain location)
- — Territory under Roman control
- Conquered by 200 B.C.
- Conquered between 200–148 B.C.
- Conquered or bequeathed to Rome between 147–100 B.C.

0   250   5
0   250   500   750

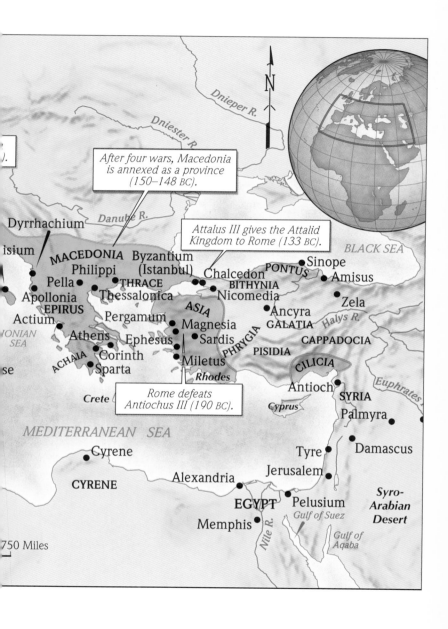

N

After four wars, Macedonia
is annexed as a province
(150–148 BC).

Attalus III gives the Attalid
Kingdom to Rome (133 BC).

Rome defeats
Antiochus III (190 BC).

Dnieper R.

Dniester R.

Danube R.

BLACK SEA

Dyrrhachium

isium

MACEDONIA Byzantium
Philippi (Istanbul) Chalcedon PONTUS Sinope
Pella THRACE BITHYNIA Amisus
Apollonia Thessalonica Nicomedia Zela
EPIRUS ASIA Ancyra
Actium Pergamum Magnesia GALATIA Halys R.
IONIAN Athens Ephesus Sardis PHRYGIA CAPPADOCIA
SEA Corinth Miletus PISIDIA
se ACHAIA Sparta CILICIA
Rhodes Antioch Euphrates

Crete Rome defeats Cyprus SYRIA Palmyra
Antiochus III (190 BC).

MEDITERRANEAN SEA
Cyrene Tyre Damascus
Jerusalem
CYRENE Syro-
Alexandria Arabian
EGYPT Pelusium Desert
Memphis Gulf of Suez

Nile R. Gulf of
Aqaba

750 Miles

131 ▶ CIVIL WARS AND THE EXPANSION OF ROME IN THE FIRST CENTURY BC

BRITANNIA

Julius Caesar conquers Gaul (58–51 BC).

● Boulogne

● Reims

GALLIA (GAUL)

Rhine R.

Loire R.

Besancon

Rhone R.

Geneva
Vienna

GALLIA CISALPINA

Verona

Julius Caesar assassinated (44 BC).

ATLANTIC OCEAN

Trebbia ● Cremona

ILLYRICUM

Aquae Sextiae

NARBONENSIS

Pisae

Po R.

Ancona

Tolosa ●

Massalia

Tiber R.

ADRIATIC SEA

Narbo ●

Aleria

Rome

ITALIA

Brund

Douro R.

Tarraco ●

Corsica

Capua

Cannae

HISPANIA CITERIOR

Tharros

Tarentum

Tagus R.

Saguntum ●

Balearic Is.

● Mago

Sardinia

TYRRHENIAN SEA

HISPANIA ULTERIOR

Corduba ●

Valentia

Nora

Panormus

Locri

Gibraltar

Munda

Carthago Nova

Eryx

Sicily

Mylae

Gades (Cadiz)

Sexi

Abdera

Utica

SICILIA

Syracu

Malaca

Cirta ●

Carthage

Zama

Malta

MAURETANIA

NUMIDIA

AFRICA

MEDITERRANEA SEA

| 0 | 250 | 500 | 750 Miles |

| 0 | 250 | 500 | 750 Kilometers |

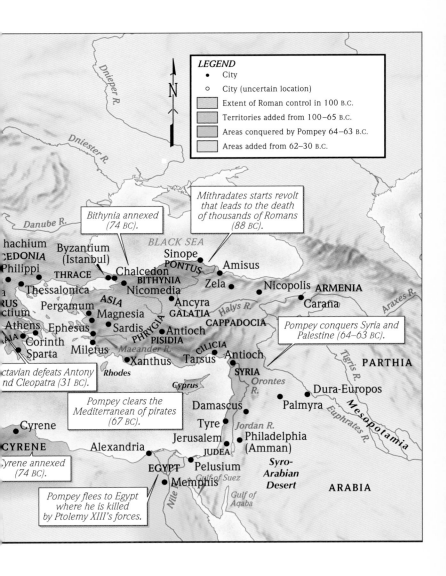

LEGEND
- City
○ City (uncertain location)
Extent of Roman control in 100 B.C.
Territories added from 100–65 B.C.
Areas conquered by Pompey 64–63 B.C.
Areas added from 62–30 B.C.

Mithradates starts revolt
that leads to the death
of thousands of Romans
(88 BC).

Bithynia annexed
(74 BC).

Pompey conquers Syria and
Palestine (64–63 BC).

Pompey clears the
Mediterranean of pirates
(67 BC).

Octavian defeats Antony
and Cleopatra (31 BC).

Cyrene annexed
(74 BC).

Pompey flees to Egypt
where he is killed
by Ptolemy XIII's forces.

Dnieper R.
Dniester R.
Danube R.
BLACK SEA
Byzantium (Istanbul)
chachium
CEDONIA
Philippi
THRACE
RUS
ctium
Thessalonica
a
Athens
Ephesus
AIA
Corinth
Sparta
Miletus
Rhodes
Chalcedon
Nicomedia
ASIA
Pergamum
Magnesia
Sardis
PHRYGIA
Maeander R.
Xanthus
PONTUS
Sinope
Amisus
Zela
Nicopolis
ARMENIA
Carana
Ancyra
GALATIA
Halys R.
CAPPADOCIA
Antioch
PISIDIA
CILICIA
Tarsus
Antioch
SYRIA
Orontes R.
Cyprus
Damascus
Tyre
Jerusalem
JUDEA
Pelusium
Memphis
EGYPT
Gulf of Suez
Nile
Gulf of Aqaba
Araxes R.
PARTHIA
Tigris R.
Dura-Europos
Palmyra
Euphrates R.
Mesopotamia
Jordan R.
Philadelphia (Amman)
Syro-
Arabian
Desert
ARABIA
Cyrene
CYRENE
Alexandria

EVENTS AND PERSONALITIES OF ROME, 133–27 BC

DATES (BC)	EVENTS
133–122	Land reforms proposed by Gaius and Tiberius Gracchus' increasing social tensions
112–105	First war with Jugurtha, king of Numidia; Marius and his professional army threatens the power of the Roman Senate
88–84	Wars against Mithradates, king of Pontus; Sulla sent to deal with Mithradates
74	Annexation of the provinces of Bithynia and Cyrene
73–71	Slave revolt of Spartacus
66–63	Pompeii conquers Syria (64 BC) and Palestine (63 BC) as part of the "Eastern Settlement"
60	First Triumvirate—60–53 BC (Julius Caesar, Pompey, and Crassus)
58–51	Julius Caesar conquers Gaul
49–45	Civil war between Pompey and Caesar
48	Death of Pompey
46	Julius Caesar declared dictator of Rome
44	Julius Caesar murdered by conservative elements of the Senate on March 15, 44 BC
42	Battle of Philippi; Mark antony and Octavian, grandnephew of Julius Caesar, defeat Caesar's assassins
42–31	Years of conflict between Octavian and Antony for ultimate power; Octavian, with command of Italy and the West, struggled with Antony and his consort Cleopatra, with their power base in the East, for control of Rome
31	Octavian defeats Antony and Cleopatra at Actium on the coast of Greece
27	Octavian given the honorific title "Augustus"; the beginning of the Roman Imperial Period

133▶ THE EMPERORS OF ROME

NAME	DYNASTY	DATES	SIGNIFICANT NT EVENTS
Caesar Augustus (Octavian)	Julio-Claudian	27 BC– AD 14	Birth of Jesus; death of Herod the Great and division of his kingdom; first procuratorship established in AD 6
Tiberius	Julio-Claudian	AD 14–37	Public ministry of Jesus; Day of Pentecost; Paul's conversion
Gaius (Caligula)	Julio-Claudian	AD 37–41	Kingdom of Herod Agrippa I
Claudius	Julio-Claudian	AD 41–54	Agrippa I, king of all Palestine, AD 41–44; martyrdom of James; famine in Judea; Paul's first missionary journey (AD 46–48); the Jerusalem Conference (AD 49); Claudius issued an edict expelling the Jews from Rome (see Acts 18:1); Paul's second missionary journey (AD 50–52); Zealot disturbances
Nero	Julio-Claudian	AD 54–68	Paul's third missionary journey (ca. AD 53–57); increasing Zealot pressure; Paul imprisoned at Caesarea (AD 57–59); Paul's voyage to Rome and imprisonment (AD 60–62) likely setting for writing prison letters (Ephesians, Colossians, Philemon, Philippians); great fire in Rome, AD 64; brief but intense persecution of Christians in Rome; outbreak of Jewish Revolt, AD 66; Paul's second Roman imprisonment? AD 66–67; martyrdom of Paul and Peter, AD 65 or 67?; Rome conquers Galilee; suicide of Nero in June, AD 68
The Year of the Four Emperors: Galba, Otho, Vitellius, Vespasian	Flavian	AD 68–69	The uncertainty about Nero's successor temporarily interrupted Rome's suppression of the Jewish Revolt
Vespasian	Flavian	AD 69–79	Jerusalem besieged and destroyed by Titus, April–August AD 70; Masada falls, AD 73 or 74
Titus	Flavian	AD 79–81	Rome again burns, AD 80; dedication of the Flavian Amphitheater (the Colosseum); Arch of Titus dedicated, AD 81
Domitian		AD 81–96	Dacian Wars, AD 86–87, 89, 92; persecutions against leading philosophers and Roman senators, AD 93–94; persecution of Christians, about AD 95; Domitian assassinated, AD 96; John's Revelation
Nerva		AD 96–98	
Trajan		AD 98– 117	Annexation of Nabatean kingdom, AD 106; persecution of Christians in Bithynia-Pontus, AD 113, and Syria, AD 114; Parthian Wars and conquests in the East, AD 114–117; Second Jewish Revolt in Cyrene, Egypt, and Mesopotamia, AD 115–117
Hadrian		AD 117– 138	Bar Kokhba Rebellion in Palestine, AD 132–135; Jerusalem rebuilt as a Roman colony, Aelia Capitolina; continuation of intermittent persecution of Christians in the province

134 ▶ POMPEY'S SIEGE OF JERUSALEM

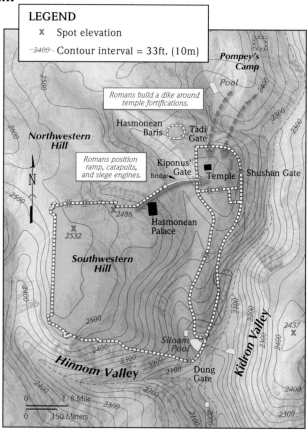

LEGEND

✕   Spot elevation

~2400~ Contour interval = 33ft. (10m)

Pompey's Camp

Pool

Romans build a dike around temple fortifications.

Hasmonean Baris — Tadi Gate

Northwestern Hill

Romans position ramp, catapults, and siege engines.

Kiponus' Gate

Bridge

Temple

Shushan Gate

✕ 2486

Hasmonean Palace

✕ 2532

Southwestern Hill

Kidron Valley

2437 ✕

Siloam Pool

Hinnom Valley

Dung Gate

0   1/8 Mile

0   150 Meters

In chapter 7 of *The Wars of the Jews*, the Jewish historian Josephus says that Pompey, the Roman general, admired the courage of the Jews as their city was being attacked. He was impressed that they continued their worship services while missiles were flying at them from all directions. It was as if Jerusalem were wrapped in peace in the midst of this violence. Even when the Romans entered the city and took the temple, the people continued to worship and die beside the altar.

LEGEND

●   City

○   City (uncertain location)

▲   Mountain peak

✺   Siege of Jerusalem

◀—   Pompey's campaign

◀---   The Romans break through the walls into Jerusalem

◀—   Aristobulus's route

   Jewish state after Pompey's settlement

   Jewish territories ceded to Iturea and Ptolemais

   Samaritan state

●○   Cities of the Decapolis

135> POMPEY'S CAMPAIGN AGAINST JERUSALEM

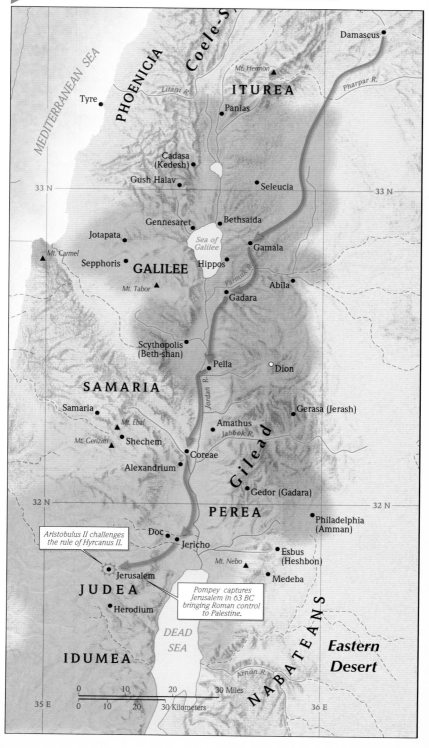

MEDITERRANEAN SEA

PHOENICIA

Coele-S

Damascus

Mt. Hermon ▲

Litani R.

ITUREA

Pharpar R.

Tyre ●

Panias ●

Cadasa
(Kedesh) ●

Gush Halav ●

33 N

Seleucia ●

33 N

Gennesaret ●

Bethsaida ●

*Sea of
Galilee*

Jotapata ●

Gamala ●

▲ *Mt. Carmel*

Sepphoris ●

GALILEE

Hippos ●

Mt. Tabor ▲

Yarmuk R.

Abila ●

Gadara ●

Scythopolis
(Beth-shan) ●

Pella ●

○ Dion

Jordan R.

SAMARIA

Samaria ●

Gerasa (Jerash) ●

▲ *Mt. Ebal*

Amathus ●

Mt. Gerizim ▲   Shechem ●

Jabbok R.

Coreae ●

Gilead

Alexandrium ●

Gedor (Gadara) ●

32 N

PEREA

32 N

Philadelphia
(Amman) ●

Doc ●

*Aristobulus II challenges
the rule of Hyrcanus II.*

Jericho ●

Esbus
(Heshbon) ●

Mt. Nebo ▲

Medeba ●

Jerusalem ⊛

*Pompey captures
Jerusalem in 63 BC
bringing Roman control
to Palestine.*

JUDEA

Herodium ●

NABATEANS

*DEAD
SEA*

**Eastern
Desert**

IDUMEA

Arnon R.

0   10   20   30 Miles

0   10   20   30 Kilometers

35 E   36 E

136 THE ROMAN EMPIRE IN THE AGE OF AUGUSTUS

HIBERNIA

NORTH SEA

BRITANNIA

London

BALTIC S

GERMANIA

BELGICA
Trier

SLA
STA

Lutetia

GALLIA
(GAUL)

Loire R.

Rhine R.

LYONS

RAETIA

NORICUM

PANNONIA

ATLANTIC
OCEAN

AQUITANIA

Lyons

Rhone R.

Alps Mts.

Mediolanum

ILLYRICUM
(DALMATIA)

Bordeaux

Vercellae

Po R.

Pola

Salona

TARRACONENSIS

NARBONENSIS

Massalia

Tiber R.

ITALIA

ADRIATIC
SEA

Corsica

Rome

Canna

Douro R.

LUSITANIA

Balearic Is.

Sardinia

Pompeii

TYRRHENIAN
SEA

Tagus R.

Merida

Nora

Cagliari

IC

Seville

Corduba

BAETICA

Cadiz
(Gades)

Gibraltar

Sicily

SICILIA

Syracu

Hippo (Bone)

Carthage

Malta

Hadrumetum

MAURETANIA

NUMIDIA

AFRICA

MED

Leptis Ma

LEGEND
- • City
- ─── Territory under Roman control
- Senatorial provinces
- Imperial provinces
- Principal client states
- Unconquered territory
- ----- Provincial boundaries

Sahara

D

Luke 2:1-3

In those days a decree went out from Caesar Augustus that the whole empire should be registered. This first registration took place while Quirinius was governing Syria. So everyone went to be registered, each to his own town.

137 ROMAN RULE IN PALESTINE

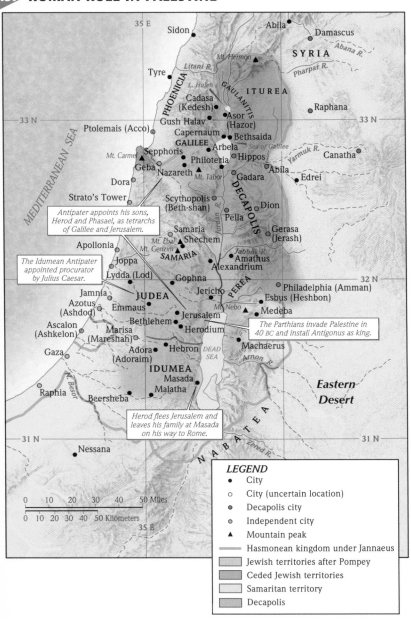

Antipater appoints his sons, Herod and Phasael, as tetrarchs of Galilee and Jerusalem.

The Idumean Antipater appointed procurator by Julius Caesar.

The Parthians invade Palestine in 40 BC and install Antigonus as king.

Herod flees Jerusalem and leaves his family at Masada on his way to Rome.

LEGEND

- ● City
- ○ City (uncertain location)
- ◗ Decapolis city
- ◗ Independent city
- ▲ Mountain peak
- ── Hasmonean kingdom under Jannaeus
- Jewish territories after Pompey
- Ceded Jewish territories
- Samaritan territory
- Decapolis

138▶ THE KINGDOM OF HEROD THE GREAT

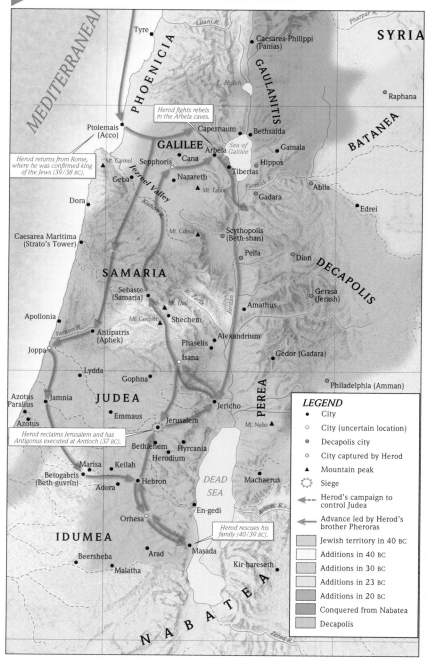

Herod fights rebels in the Arbela caves.

Herod returns from Rome, where he was confirmed king of the Jews (39/38 BC).

Herod reclaims Jerusalem and has Antigonus executed at Antioch (37 BC).

Herod rescues his family (40/39 BC).

LEGEND

- • City
- ○ City (uncertain location)
- ◉ Decapolis city
- ◌ City captured by Herod
- ▲ Mountain peak
- ✵ Siege
- - - - ▶ Herod's campaign to control Judea
- ——▶ Advance led by Herod's brother Pheroras
- Jewish territory in 40 BC
- Additions in 40 BC
- Additions in 30 BC
- Additions in 23 BC
- Additions in 20 BC
- Conquered from Nabatea
- Decapolis

Matthew 2:1-2

After Jesus was born in Bethlehem of Judea in the days of King Herod, wise men from the east arrived unexpectedly in Jerusalem, saying, "Where is He who has been born King of the Jews? For we saw His star in the east and have come to worship Him."

139▶ HEROD'S BUILDING PROGRAM

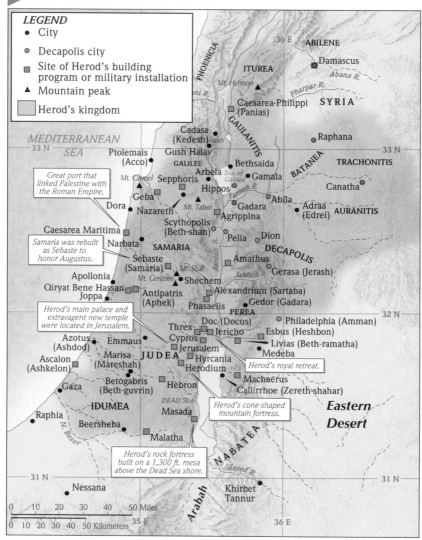

LEGEND
- City
- Decapolis city
- Site of Herod's building program or military installation
- ▲ Mountain peak
- Herod's kingdom

Great port that linked Palestine with the Roman Empire.

Samaria was rebuilt as Sebaste to honor Augustus.

Herod's main palace and extravagent new temple were located in Jerusalem.

Herod's royal retreat.

Herod's cone-shaped mountain fortress.

Herod's rock fortress built on a 1,300 ft. mesa above the Dead Sea shore.

Herod the Great determined that he would please his Jewish subjects and show off his style of kingship to the Romans by making the Jerusalem temple bigger and better than it had ever been. His most notable contribution was the magnificent stonework of the temple platform that was greatly enlarged. The descriptions in Josephus and the Mishnah have been fleshed out by recent archaeological discoveries.

Another of his impressive projects was the Herodium, a fortress-palace built about four miles southeast of Bethlehem. Herod was buried there. The fortress, captured in AD 72, was one of the last strongholds of Jewish resistance in the war with Rome. The Herodium served as a supply depot in the unsuccessful revolt of AD 132–135. Herod also built the fortress at Masada.

140▶ RECONSTRUCTION OF NT JERICHO

Jericho means "moon." Apparently the oldest city in the world and the first city Israel conquered under Joshua.

New Testament Jericho, founded by Herod the Great, was about one and one-half miles southward in the magnificent Wadi Qelt. The spring, Ain es-Sultan, issues some 30,000 cubit feet of water daily which falls about 160 feet in the first mile of its course down many channels to the Jordan River six miles away, irrigating about 2,500 acres.

The combination of rich alluvial soil, the perennial spring, and constant sunshine made Jericho an attractive place for settlement. Jericho could be called "city of palms" (Deut. 34:3; Judg. 1:16; 3:13; 2 Chron. 28:15) and has plenty of palm trees today. Only about 6.4 inches of rain fall there per year (mostly between November and February), and the average temperature in January is 59°F, while it is 88°F in August. Jericho is about 740 feet below sea level (accounting for its warm climate) but well above the Dead Sea, eight miles southward, which at 1,300 feet below sea level marks the earth's lowest point.

In NT times Jericho was famous for its balm (an aromatic gum known for its medicinal qualities). This, along with its being the winter capital, made it a wealthy city. When Jesus was hosted by Zacchaeus (Luke 19:1-10), it was probably in one of Jericho's finest houses. Its sycamore trees were quite valuable. Such a city could expect to have its share of beggars, as the Gospels tell us (Matt. 20:29-34; Mark 10:46-52; Luke 18:35-43).

141 HERODIAN JERICHO

THE HERODIAN RULERS

RULER	FAMILY RELATIONSHIP	REALM OF RESPONSIBILITY	DATES OF REIGN	BIBLICAL REFERENCE
Herod I (the Great)	Son of Antipater	King of Judea	37–4 BC	Matt. 2:1-22; Luke 1:5
Herod Archelaus	Oldest son of Herod the Great	Ethanarch of Judea, Samaria, and Idumea	4 BC–AD 6	Matt. 2:22
Philip*	Son of Herod the Great and Cleopatra of Jerusalem	Tetrarch of territories north and east of the Sea of Galilee	4 BC–AD 34	Luke 3:1
Herod Antipas	Youngest son of Herod the Great; second husband of Herodias	Tetrarch of Galilee and Perea	4 BC–AD 39	Matt. 14:1-11; Mark 6:14-29; Luke 3:1, 19; 13:31-33; 23:7-12
Herod Agrippa I	Grandson of Herod the Great	King of Judea	AD 37–44	Acts 12
Herod Agrippa II	Great-grandson of Herod the Great	Tetrarch and king of Chalcis	AD 44–100 (became king in AD 48)	Acts 25:13-26:32

*Not to be confused with Herod Philip also mentioned in the New Testament. Herod Philip was the son of Herod the Great and Mariamne and was the first husband of Herodias. (See Matt. 14:3; Mark 6:17; and Luke 3:19.)

 ROMAN GOVERNORS OF THE FIRST PROCURATORSHIP (AD 6–41)

NAME	DATES (AD)	APPOINTED BY	SELECTED REFERENCES IN THE WORKS OF JOSEPHUS TO THE PROCURATOR
Coponius	6–9	Augustus	*ANT* 18.1.1 § 2; 18.2.2§29-31 *JW* 2.8.1§117-118
Marcus Ambibulus	9–12	Augustus	*ANT* 18.2.2§31
Annius Rufus	12–15	Augustus	*ANT* 18.2.2§32
Valerius Gratus	15–26	Tiberius	*ANT* 18.2.2§33-35
Pontius Pilate	26–36	Tiberius	*ANT* 18.3.1§55-62; 18.4.1-2 §85-89; *JW* 2.9.2-4§169-177
Marcellus	37	Vitellius, Legate of Syria	*ANT* 18.4.2§89
Marullus	37–41	Caligula	*ANT* 18.6.10§237

144 THE DIVISION OF HEROD'S KINGDOM

LEGEND
- City
- Decapolis city
- Decapolis city (uncertain location)
- ▲ Mountain peak
- To Antipas
- To Archelaus
- To Philip
- To Salome
- Syrian province

Sidon

ITUREA

Mt. Hermon ▲

Pharpar

PHOENICIA

Litani R.

Tyre

Caesarea-Philippi (Panias)

GAULANITIS

Cadasa (Kedesh)

Gischala (Gush Halav)

L. Huleh

Ptolemais (Acco)

Capernaum

Bethsaida

BATANEA

Taricheae

Jotapata Gabara

GALILEE

Arbela

Sea of Galilee

Gamala

Hippos

MEDITERRANEAN SEA

Mt. Carmel ▲

Geba

Sepphoris

Nazareth

Mt. Tabor ▲

Tiberias

Philoteria (Beth-Yerah)

Yarmuk R.

Abila

Gadara

Adraa (Edrei)

Dora

Caesarea Maritima (Strato's Tower)

Narbata

SAMARIA

Ginae (Jenin)

Scythopolis (Beth-shan)

Pella

Dion

DECAPOLIS

Sebaste (Samaria)

Mt. Ebal ▲

Mt. Gerizim ▲

Neapolis (Shechem)

Amathus

Jordan R.

Gerasa (Jerash)

Apollonia

Antipatris (Aphek)

Alexandrium (Sartaba)

Jabbok R.

Joppa

Phasaelis

Gedor (Gadara)

Aphairema (Ophrah)

Archelais

PEREA

Lydda

Gophna

Doc (Docus)

Philadelphia (Amman)

Jamnia

JUDEA

Threx

Jericho

Esbus (Heshbon)

Azotus (Ashdod)

Emmaus (Nicopolis)

Cypros

Livias (Beth-ramatha)

Mt. Nebo ▲

Jerusalem

Medeba

Hyrcania

lon (on)

Herodium

Marisa (Mareshah)

Machaerus

edon

Betogabris (Beth-guvrin)

Hebron

DEAD SEA

Callirrhoe (Zereth-shahar)

aza

IDUMEA

Arnon R.

Masada

Arad

Beersheba

Malatha

N. Besor

NABATEA

Sunset over the Sea of Galilee at Tiberias.

145 PALESTINE IN THE TIME OF JESUS

LEGEND
- • City
- ○ City (uncertain location)
- ◉ Decapolis city
- ○ Decapolis city (uncertain location)
- ★ Administrative capital
- ▲ Mountain peak
- — Major roads
- — Other roads
- ▢ First procuratorship
- ▢ Territory of Antipas
- ▢ Territory of Philip
- ▢ Syrian territory

Coponius was named the first prefect and established the administrative capital at Caesarea Maritima.

Sidon

ITUREA

Mt. Hermon ▲

PHOENICIA (TYRE)

GAULANITIS

Tyre

Caesarea-Philippi (Panias)

King's Highway

TRACH

Cadasa (Kedesh)
Gischala (Gush Halav)

L. Huleh

Rap

Ptolemais (Acco)

Capernaum   Bethsaida

GALILEE   Sea of Galilee   Gergesa (Kursi)

BATANEA

Jotapata

Hippos   Gamala

Sepphoris   Geba

Nazareth   Tiberias

Mt. Carmel ▲

Abila

Adraa (Edrei)

Xaloth (Chesulloth)   Mt. Tabor ▲   Gadara

AURA

Dora

Legio (Megiddo)

Esdraelon Valley

Kison R.

Yarmuk R.

Scythopolis (Beth-shan)

Caesarea Maritima (Strato's Tower) ★

Ginae (Jenin)

Pella   Dion

DECAPOLIS

MEDITERRANEAN SEA

SAMARIA

Aenon
Salim

Gerasa (Jerash)

Apollonia

Sebaste (Samaria)

Mt. Ebal ▲
Neapolis (Shechem)
Mt. Gerizim ▲

Amathus

Jordan R.

Yarkon R.

Antipatris (Aphek)

Joppa

Coreae

Alexandrium

Lydda

Ephraim (Ophrah)

Gedor (Gadara)

Philadelphia (Amma

Jamnia

Emmaus (Nicopolis)

Archelais

PEREA

Azotus (Ashdod)

JUDEA

Jericho

Cypros

Esbus (Heshbon)

Ascalon
(Ashkelon)

Jerusalem   Bethany

Hyrcania

Medeba

Mt. Nebo ▲

Easte
Dese

Betogabris (Beth-guvrin)

Hebron

En-gedi

DEAD SEA

Mesad Hasidim (Qumran)

Machaerus

Callirrhoe (Zereth-shahar)

za

IDUMEA

Masada

Arnon R.

King's Highway

Beersheba   Malatha   Arad

NABATEA

Khirbet Tannur

THE LIFE AND MINISTRY OF JESUS OF NAZARETH

▲ View of Bethlehem, the place of Jesus' birth.

Perhaps the earliest account (Gospel of Mark) of Jesus begins abruptly when He presented Himself at the Jordan River to the desert prophet John the Baptist as a candidate for baptism. All that is said about His origin is that He came to the river "from Nazareth" (Mark 1:9). "Jesus of Nazareth" was a designation that followed Him to the day of His death (John 19:19).

His Origins

Matthew's Gospel demonstrates that although Nazareth was Jesus' home when He came to John for baptism, He was not born there. Rather, He was born (as the Jewish Messiah must be) in Bethlehem, the "city of David," as a descendant of David's royal line (Matt. 1:1-17; 2:1-6). This Child born in Bethlehem ended up as an adult in Nazareth, described sarcastically by his enemies as a "Nazarene" (literally, "Nazarite" 2:23). The play on words seems intended to poke fun simultaneously at Jesus' obscure origins and at the stark contrast (in the eyes of many) between His supposed holiness (like the Nazirites of the OT) and His practice of keeping company with sinners, prostitutes, and tax collectors (Mark 2:17). The Gospel of Luke supplies background information on John the Baptist, showing how the families of John and Jesus were related both by kinship and by circumstances (Luke 1:5-80). Luke added that Nazareth was the family home of Jesus' parents all along (Luke 1:26-27). Yet he confirmed Matthew's testimony that the family was of the line of David.

Luke introduced the Roman census as the reason for their return to the ancestral city of Bethlehem just before Jesus' birth (Luke 2:1-7). More of a biographer than either Mark or Matthew, Luke provided glimpses of Jesus as an eight-day-old infant (2:21-39), a boy of 12 years (2:40-52), and a man of 30 beginning His ministry (3:21-23). Only when this brief biographical sketch was complete did Luke append His genealogy (3:23-38), which confirms in passing Jesus' Davidic ancestry (3:31; cp. 1:32-33), while emphasizing above all His solidarity with the entire human race in its descent from "Adam, son of God" (3:38). The reflection on Jesus' baptism in the Gospel of John centers on John the Baptist's acknowledgement that Jesus "surpassed me, because He existed before me" (John 1:30; cp. v. 15). This pronouncement allowed the Gospel writer to turn the story of Jesus' origins into a theological confession by tracing Jesus' existence back to the creation of the world and before (John 1:1-5).

Despite His royal ancestry and despite His heavenly preexistence as the eternal Word and Son of God, Jesus was of humble origins humanly speaking and was viewed as such by the people of His day. When He taught in Nazareth, the townspeople asked, "Isn't this the carpenter, the son of Mary, and the brother of James, Joses, Judas, and Simon? And aren't His sisters here with us?" (Mark 6:3; cp. Luke 4:22). When He taught in Capernaum, they asked, "Isn't this Jesus the son of Joseph, whose father and mother we know? How can He now say, 'I have come down from heaven'?" (John 6:42). Though two Gospels, Matthew and Luke, tell of His mother Mary's miraculous conception and of Jesus' virgin birth, these matters were not public knowledge during His time on earth, for "Mary was treasuring up all these things in her heart and meditating on them" (Luke 2:19; cp. v. 51).

 An overview of Nazareth from the southwest.

▲ The traditional site on the Jordan River where Jesus was baptized.

Jesus and the God of Israel

Even after the momentous events associated with Jesus' baptism in the Jordan River—the descent of God's Spirit on Him like a dove and the voice from heaven announcing "You are My beloved Son; in You I take delight!" (Mark 1:10-11)—His identity as Son of God remained hidden from those around Him. We have no evidence that anyone except Jesus, and possibly John the Baptist, either heard the voice or saw the dove. Ironically, the first intimation after the baptism that He was more than simply "Jesus of Nazareth" came not from His family or friends or from the religious leaders of Israel but from the devil!

Twice the devil challenged him: "If You are the Son of God, tell this stone to become bread" (Luke 4:3), and (on the pinnacle of the temple in Jerusalem), "If You are the Son of God, throw Yourself down from here" (Luke 4:9). Jesus made no attempt to defend or make use of His divine sonship but appealed instead to an authority to which any devout Jew of His day might have appealed—the holy Scriptures—and through them to the God of Israel. Citing three passages from Deuteronomy, Jesus called attention not to Himself, but to "the Lord your God" (Luke 4:8; cp. Mark 10:18; 12:29-30). Jesus apparently used this story out of His personal experience to teach His disciples that they, too, must "live . . . on every word that comes from the mouth of God," (Matt. 4:4), must "not tempt the Lord your God" (Luke 4:12), and must "worship the Lord your God, and Him alone you shall serve" (Luke 4:8).

Two things about this temptation story have a special bearing on the ministry of Jesus as a whole. First, the God-centered character of His message continued in the proclamation He began in Galilee when He returned home from the desert: "The time is fulfilled, and the kingdom of God has come near. Repent and believe in the good news!" (Mark 1:15; cp. Matt. 4:17). Mark called this proclamation "the good news of God" (Mark 1:14). John's Gospel presented Jesus as reminding His hearers again and again that He had come not to glorify or proclaim Himself but solely to make known "the Father," or "Him who sent me" (John 4:34; 5:19, 30; 6:38; 7:16-18,28; 8:28,42,50; 14:10,28). Second, the issue of Jesus' own identity continued to be raised first by the powers of evil. Just as the devil challenged Jesus in the desert as "Son of God," so in the course of His ministry the demons (or the demon-possessed) confronted Him with such words as "What do You have to do with us, Jesus—Nazarene? . . . I know who You are—the Holy One of God" (Mark 1:24), or "What do You have to do with me, Jesus, Son of the Most High God?" (Mark 5:7).

▲ Telephoto close-up of the rugged wilderness terrain on the east face of the Mount of Temptation.

The mystery of Jesus' person emerged in pronouncements of this kind, but Jesus seemed not to want the question of His identity raised prematurely. He silenced the demons (Mark 1:25,34; 3:12); and when He healed the sick, He frequently told the people who were cured not to speak of it to anyone (Mark 1:43-44; 7:36a). The more He urged silence, however, the faster the word of His healing power spread (Mark 1:45; 7:36b). The crowds appear to have concluded that He must be the Messiah, the anointed King of David's line expected to come and deliver the Jews from Roman rule. If Jesus was playing out the role of Messiah, the Gospels present Him as a strangely reluctant Messiah. At one point, when the crowds tried to "take Him by force to make Him king, He withdrew again to the mountain by Himself" (John 6:15). Seldom, if ever, did He apply to Himself the customary terms "Messiah" or "Son of God." He had instead a way of using the emphatic "I" when it was not grammatically necessary and a habit sometimes of referring to Himself indirectly and mysteriously as "Son of man." In the Aramaic language Jesus spoke, "Son of man" meant simply "a certain man," or "someone." Though He made no explicit messianic claims and avoided the ready-made titles of honor that the Jews customarily applied to the Messiah, Jesus spoke and acted with the authority of God Himself. He gave sight to the blind and hearing to the deaf; He enabled the lame to walk. When He touched the unclean, He made them clean. He even raised the dead to life. In teaching the crowds that gathered around Him, He did not hesitate to say boldly, "You have heard that it was said . . . but I tell you" (Matt. 5:21-22,27-28,31-34,38-39,43-44). So radical was He toward the accepted traditions that He found it necessary to state at the outset: "Don't assume that I came to destroy the Law, or the Prophets. I did not come to destroy but to fulfill" (Matt. 5:17).

Such speech and behavior inevitably raised questions about Jesus' identity. The crowds who heard Him "were astonished at His teaching. For He was teaching them like one who had authority, and not like their scribes" (Matt. 7:28-29). Despite His reluctance (or perhaps because of it), His following in the early days of His ministry was enormous. He had to get up before daylight to find time and a place for private prayer (Mark 1:35). So pressed was He by the crowds that He taught them on one occasion while sitting in a boat offshore on the lake of Galilee (Mark 4:1). Once when a group of people desired healing for a paralyzed man, the huge mob around the house where Jesus was staying forced them to lower the man through a hole in the roof (Mark 2:4). Everyone needed what he or she knew Jesus had to give. There was no way He could meet all their needs at once.

The Sea of Galilee as viewed from the northwest.

Jesus' Mission

Jesus' primary mission was to reach the lost sheep of Israel. Through their carelessness about the law, the religious leaders had become the enemies of God; but God loved His enemies. Jesus' conviction was that both He and His disciples must love them, too (Matt. 5:38-48). Jesus was challenged on one occasion for enjoying table fellowship with social outcasts (known to the religious Jews as "sinners") in the house of Levi, the tax collector in Capernaum. He replied to criticism: "Those who are well don't need a doctor, but the sick do need one. I didn't come to call the righteous, but sinners" (Mark 2:17). Another time, when the religious authorities murmured that "this man welcomes sinners and eats with them" (Luke 15:2), Jesus told three parables of God's inexhaustible love for those who are "lost" and of God's unbridled joy when the lost are found (the parables of the lost sheep, the lost coin, and the lost son—Luke 15:3-32). He claimed that God's joy at the recovery of all such sinners (tax collectors, prostitutes, shepherds, soldiers, and others despised by the pious in Israel) was greater than any joy "over 99 righteous people who don't need repentance" (Luke 15:7; cp. vv. 25-32). Such an exuberant celebration of divine mercy, whether expressed in Jesus' actions or in the stories He told, must have seemed to religious leaders both in Galilee and Jerusalem a serious lowering of ancient ethical standards and a damaging compromise of the holiness of God.

We have little evidence that Jesus included non-Jews among the "sinners" to whom He was sent. Despite the reference in Luke 4:25-27 to Elijah and Elisha and their ministry to foreigners, Jesus explicitly denied that He was sent to Gentiles or Samaritans (Matt. 15:24; 10:5-6). Yet the principle, "not to the righteous, but to sinners," made the extension of the good news of the kingdom of God to the Gentiles after Jesus' resurrection a natural one. Even during Jesus' lifetime, He responded to the initiatives of Gentiles seeking His help (Matt. 8:5-13; Luke 7:1-10; Mark 7:24-30; Matt 15:21-28), sometimes in such a way as to put Israel to shame (Matt. 8:10). Twice He traveled through Samaria (Luke 9:51-56; John 4:4); once He stayed in a Samaritan village for two days, calling a Samaritan woman and a number of other townspeople to faith (John 4:5-42), and once He made a Samaritan the hero of one of His parables (Luke 10:29-37).

None of this was calculated to win Him friends among the priests in Jerusalem or the Pharisees throughout Israel. He described visions that many would "come from east and west, and recline at the table with Abraham, and Isaac, and Jacob in the kingdom of heaven. But the sons of the kingdom will be thrown into the outer darkness" (Matt. 8:11-12). He predicted that 12 uneducated Galileans would one day "sit on 12 thrones, judging the 12 tribes of Israel" (Matt. 19:28; cp. Luke 22:28-29). He warned the religious leaders sternly that they were in danger of "blasphemy against the Spirit" by attributing the Spirit's ministry through Him to the power of the devil (Matt. 12:31). The whole affair was complicated by the concern of Jesus' relatives over his safety and sanity (Mark 3:21) and by His consequent affirmation of His disciples as a new family based on obedience to the will of God (Mark 3:31-35).

The so-called "Beel-zebub controversy," triggered by his healing and saving activity, set a grim precedent for Jesus' relationship with the Jerusalem authorities and made His eventual arrest, trial, and execution almost inevitable (Mark 3:20-30). From that time Jesus began to speak in parables to make the truth about God's kingdom clear to His followers while hiding it from those blind to its beauty and deaf to its call (Mark 4:10-12; notice that Jesus is first said to have spoken in parables in Mark 3:23, in immediate response to the charge of demon possession). He also began to intimate, sometimes in analogy or parable (Mark 10:38; Luke 12:49-50; John 3:14; 12:24,32) and sometimes in explicit language (Mark 8:31; 9:31; 10:33-34), that He would be arrested and tried by the religious leadership in Jerusalem, die on the cross, and rise from the dead after three days. From the start He had defined His mission, at least in part, as that of the "Servant of the Lord" (see, for example the citation of Isa. 61:1-2 in Luke 4:18-19). As His ministry moved toward its completion, the vicarious suffering of the Servant (Isa. 52:13–53:12) came into sharper and sharper focus for Jesus (Mark 10:45; 12:1-11). He also saw Himself as the stricken Shepherd of Zechariah 13:7 (Mark 14:27) and, at the very end, in the role of the righteous Sufferer of the biblical Psalms (for example Mark 15:34; Luke 23:46; John 19:28). Before His arrest He dramatized for the disciples His

▲ Olive trees in the traditional site of the Garden of Gethsemane.

impending death by sharing with them in the bread and the cup of the Passover with the explanation that the bread was His body to be broken for them and that the cup of wine was His blood to be shed for their salvation. Only His death could guarantee the coming of the kingdom He had proclaimed (Matt. 26:26-29; Mark 14:22-25; Luke 22:14-20; cp. 1 Cor. 11:23-26).

Jesus' Death and Resurrection

The Gospel accounts of Jesus' last days in Jerusalem correspond in broad outline to the predictions attributed to Him earlier. He seems to have come to Jerusalem for the last time in the knowledge that He would die there. Though He received a royal welcome from crowds who looked to Him as the long-expected Messiah (Matt 21:9-11; Mark 11:9-10; John 12:13), no evidence points to this as the reason for His arrest. Rather His action in driving the money changers out of the Jerusalem temple (Matt 21:12-16; Mark 11:15-17; cp. John 2:13-22) as well as certain of His pronouncements about the temple aroused the authorities to act decisively against Him.

During His last week in Jerusalem, Jesus had predicted the temple's destruction (Matt. 24:1-2; Mark 13:1-2; Luke 21:5-6) and claimed that "I will demolish this sanctuary made by hands, and in three days I will build another not made by hands" (Mark 14:58; cp. Matt. 26:61). Jesus' intention to establish a new community as a "temple," or dwelling place of God (see Matt. 16:18; John 2:19; 1 Cor. 3:16-17), was perceived as a very real threat to the old community of Judaism and to the temple that stood as its embodiment. On this basis He was arrested and charged as a deceiver of the people.

During a hearing before the Sanhedrin, or Jewish ruling council, Jesus spoke of Himself as "Son of Man seated at the right hand of the Power and coming with the clouds of heaven" (Mark 14:62; cp. Matt. 26:64; Luke 22:69). Though the high priest called this blasphemy and the Sanhedrin agreed that such behavior deserved death, the results of the hearing seem to have been inconclusive. If Jesus had been formally tried and convicted by the Sanhedrin, He would have been stoned to death like Stephen in Acts 7, or like the attempted stoning of the woman caught in adultery in a story reported in some manuscripts of John 8:1-11. For whatever reason the high priest and his cohorts apparently found no formal charges they could make stick. If Jesus were stoned to death without a formal conviction, it would be murder, a sin the Ten Commandments forbid. (John 18:31 refers to what was forbidden to the Jews by their own law, not to what was forbidden by the Romans.) The Sanhedrin decided, therefore, to send Jesus to Pontius Pilate, the Roman governor, with charges against Him that the Romans would take seriously: "We found this man subverting our nation, opposing payment of taxes to Caesar, and saying that He

Himself is the Messiah, a King" (Luke 23:2). Jesus' execution is therefore attributable neither to the Jewish people as a whole, nor to the Sanhedrin, but rather to a small group of priests who manipulated the Romans into doing what they were not able to accomplish within the framework of their law. Though Pilate pronounced Jesus innocent three times (Luke 23:4,14,22; cp. John 18:38; 19:4,6), he was maneuvered into sentencing Jesus with the thinly veiled threat, "If you release this man, you are not Caesar's friend. Anyone who makes himself a king opposes Caesar!" (John 19:12). Consequently, Jesus was crucified between two thieves, fulfilling His own prediction that "as Moses lifted up the serpent in the wilderness, so the Son of Man must be lifted up" (John 3:14). Most of His disciples fled at His arrest; only a group of women and one disciple, called the disciple whom He loved, were present at the cross when He died (John 19:25-27; cp. Matt. 27:55-56; Mark 15:40; Luke 23:49).

The story did not end with the death of Jesus. His body was placed in a new tomb that belonged to a secret disciple named Joseph of Arimathea (Luke 23:50-56; John 19:38-42). The Gospels agree that two days later, the morning after the Sabbath, some of the women who had remained faithful to Jesus came to the tomb. They discovered the stone over the entrance to the tomb rolled away and the body of Jesus gone. According to Mark, a young man was there (Mark 16:5; tradition calls him an angel) and told the women to send word to the rest of the disciples to go and meet Jesus in Galilee, just as He had promised them (16:7; 14:28). The most reliable manuscripts of Mark's Gospel end the story there, leaving the rest to the reader's imagination.

According to Matthew, the young man's word was confirmed to the women by the risen Jesus Himself. When they brought word to the 11 disciples (the Twelve minus Judas, the betrayer), the disciples went to a mountain in Galilee, where the risen Jesus appeared to them as a group. He commanded them to make more disciples, teaching and baptizing among the Gentiles (Matt. 28:16-20). According to Luke, the risen Jesus appeared to the gathered disciples already in Jerusalem on the same day He was raised and before that to two disciples walking to the neighboring town of Emmaus. According to John, there was an appearance in Jerusalem on Easter day to one of the women, Mary Magdalene, another on the same day to the gathered disciples, another a week later (still in Jerusalem) to the same group plus Thomas, and a fourth appearance, at an unstated time, by the lake of Galilee, in which Jesus reenacted the initial call of the disciples by providing them miraculously with an enormous catch of fish. Luke adds in the Book of Acts that the appearances of the risen Jesus went on over a period of 40 days in which He continued to instruct them about the kingdom of God. Whatever the

Emmaus (Imwas). According to the Sinai manuscript Emmaus is thought to be the site of the house of Cleopas.

precise order of the facts, the disciples' experience of the living Jesus transformed them from a scattered and cowardly band of disillusioned visionaries into the nucleus of a coherent movement able to challenge and change forever the Roman Empire within a few short decades.

Though the physical resurrection of Jesus cannot be proven, alternate "naturalistic" explanations of the disciples' experience and of the empty tomb require without exception more credulity than the traditional confession of the Christian church that on the third day He rose from the dead. The unanimous witness of the Gospels is that the story goes on. Mark does it with the promise that Jesus will bring together His scattered flock and lead them into Galilee (Mark 16:7). Matthew does it more explicitly with Jesus' concluding words, "And remember, I am with you always, to the end of the age" (Matt. 28:20). Luke does it with the entire Book of Acts, which traces the spread of the message of the kingdom of God and the risen Jesus from Jerusalem all the way to Rome. John does it with his vivid picture of the Holy Spirit being given to the disciples directly from the mouth of Jesus Himself (John 20:21-22). Each Gospel makes the point differently, but the point is always the same. The story of Jesus is not over; He continues to fulfill His mission wherever His name is confessed and His teaching is obeyed, and the faith of Christians is that He will do so until He comes again.

146 MESSIANIC PROPHECIES OF THE OLD TESTAMENT

PROPHECY	OT REF.	NT FULFILLMENT
Spirit of the Lord on Him	Isa. 11:2; 42:1 1:32; 3:34	Matt. 3:16; Mark 1:10; Luke 3:22; John
Full of wisdom and power	Isa. 11:1-10	Rom. 15:12; 1 Cor. 1:30; Eph. 1:17; Col. 2:3
Reigning in mercy	Isa. 16:4-5	Luke 1:31-33
Key of David	Isa. 22:21-25	Rev. 3:7
Death swallowed up in victory	Isa. 25:6-12	1 Cor. 15:54
A stone in Zion	Isa. 28:16	Rom. 9:33; 1 Pet. 2:6
The deaf hear, the blind see	Isa. 29:18-19	Matt. 11:5; Mark 7:37; John 9:39
Healing for the needy	Isa. 35:4-10	Matt. 9:30; 11:5; 12:22; 20:34; 21:14; Mark 7:31-35; John 9:1-7
Make ready the way of the Lord	Isa. 40:3-5	Matt. 3:3; Mark 1:3; Luke 3:4-5; John 1:23
The Shepherd tends His sheep	Isa. 40:10-11	John 10:11; Heb. 13:20; 1 Pet. 2:25
The meek Servant	Isa. 42:1-4	Matt. 12:17-21; Phil. 2:7
A light to the Gentiles	Isa. 49:6	Luke 2:32; Acts 13:47; 26:23
Scourged and spat upon	Isa. 50:6	Matt. 26:67; 27:26,30; Mark 14:65; 15:15,19; Luke 22:63-65; John 19:1
Rejected and insulted	Isa. 53:3	Matt. 27:1-2,12-14,39; Luke 18:31-33; John 1:10-11
Suffered vicariously	Isa. 53:4-5	Matt. 8:17; Mark 15:3-4,27-28; Luke 23:1-25,32-34
Pierced for our transgressions	Isa. 53:5	Rom. 4:25; 5:6,8; 1 Cor. 15:3; 2 Cor. 5:21
Lamb slaughtered for us	Isa. 53:7	John 1:29,36; Acts 8:28-35; 1 Pet. 1:19; Rev. 5:6; 13:8
Silent when accused	Isa. 53:7	Matt. 26:63; 27:12,14; Mark 14:61; 15:5; Luke 23:9; John 19:9
Buried with the rich	Isa. 53:9	Matt. 27:57-60
Bear Iniquities and give forgivness	Isa. 53:11	Acts 10:43; 13:38-39; 1 Cor. 15:3; Eph. 1:7; 1 Pet. 2:21-25; 1 John 1:7,9
Crucified with transgressors	Isa. 53:12	Mark 15:27-28; Luke 22:37
Calling of Gentiles	Isa. 55:4-5	Rom. 9:25-26; Rev. 1:5
Deliver out of Zion	Isa. 59:16-20	Rom. 11:26-27
Nations walk in the light	Isa. 60:1-3	Luke 2:32
Anointed to preach liberty	Isa. 61:1-3	Luke 4:17-19; Acts 10:38
Called by a new name	Isa. 62:1-2	Rev. 2:17; 3:12
The King cometh	Isa. 62:11	Matt. 21:5; Rev. 22:12
A vesture dipped in blood	Isa. 63:1-3	Rev. 19:13
Afflicted with the afflicted	Isa. 63:8-9	Matt. 25:34-40
New heavens and a new earth	Isa. 65:17-25	2 Pet. 3:13; Rev. 21:1
The Lord our righteousness	Jer. 23:5-6; 33:16	Rom. 3:22; 1 Cor. 1:30; 2 Cor. 5:21; Phil. 3:9
Born a King	Jer. 30:9	Luke 1:69; John 18:37; Acts 13:23; Rev. 1:5
Massacre of infants	Jer. 31:15	Matt. 2:17-18

PROPHECY	OT REF.	NT FULFILLMENT
A New Covenant	Jer. 31:31-34	Matt. 26:27-29; Mark 14:22-24; Luke 22:15-20; 1 Cor. 11:25; Heb. 8:8-12; 10:15-17; 12:24; 13:20
A tree planted by God	Ezek. 17:22-24	Matt. 13:31-32
The humble exalted	Ezek. 21:26-27	Luke 1:52
The good Shepherd	Ezek. 34:23-24	John 10:11
His kingdom triumphant	Dan. 2:44-45	Luke 1:33; 1 Cor. 15:24; 2 Pet. 1:11; Rev. 11:15
Son of man in power	Dan. 7:13-14	Matt. 24:30; 25:31; 26:64; Mark 13:26; 14:61-62; Luke 21:27; Acts 1:9-11; Rev. 1:7
Kingdom for the saints	Dan. 7:27	Luke 1:33; 1 Cor. 15:24; Rev. 11:15; 20:4; 22:5
Israel restored	Hos. 3:5	Rom. 11:25-27
Flight into Egypt	Hos. 11:1	Matt. 2:15
Promise of the Spirit	Joel 2:28-32	Acts 2:17-21;
The sun darkened	Amos 8:9	Matt. 24:29; Acts 2:20; Rev. 6:12
Restoration of David's house	Amos 9:11-12	Acts 15:16-18
The kingdom established	Isa. 2:1-4; Mic. 4:1-8	Luke 1:33
Born in Bethlehem	Mic. 5:1-5	Matt. 2:1-6; Luke 2:4,10-11
Earth filled with knowledge of the glory of the Lord	Hab. 2:14	Rev. 21:23-26
God living among His people	Zech. 2:10-13	Rev. 21:3,24
A new priesthood	Zech. 3:8	Eph. 2:20-21; 1 Pet. 2:5
Enthroned High Priest	Zech. 6:12-13	Heb. 5:5-10; 7:11-28; 8:1-2
Triumphal entry	Zech. 9:9-10	Matt. 21:4-5; Mark 11:1-10; Luke 19:28-38; John 12:13-15
Sold for thirty pieces of silver	Zech. 11:12-13	Matt. 26:14-15
Money buys potter's field	Zech. 11:12-13	Matt. 27:9-10
Piercing of His body	Zech. 12:10	John 19:34,37
Shepherd smitten, sheep scattered	Zech. 13:1,6-7	Matt. 26:31; John 16:32
Preceded by Forerunner	Mal. 3:1	Matt. 11:10; Mark 1:2; Luke 7:27
The sun of righteousness	Mal. 4:2-3	Luke 1:78; Eph. 5:14; 2 Pet. 1:19; Rev. 2:28; 19:11-12; 22:16
The coming of Elijah	Mal. 4:5-6	Matt. 11:14; 17:10-12; Mark 9:11-13; Luke 1:17
Seed of the woman	Gen. 3:15	Gal. 4:4; Heb. 2:14
Nations blessed through Abraham	Gen. 12:3; 18:18; 22:18; 26:4; 28:14	Matt. 1:1; Acts 3:25; Gal. 3:8
Seed of Abraham	Gen. 12:7; 13:15; 15:18; 17:7-10; 23:7	Acts 7:5; Rom. 4:13,16; 9:8; Gal. 3:16,29
Seed of Isaac	Gen. 17:19; 21:12; 26:3-4	Rom. 9:7; Heb. 11:18

146 MESSIANIC PROPHECIES OF THE OLD TESTAMENT (cont.)

PROPHECY	OT REF.	NT FULFILLMENT
Of the tribe of Judah	Gen. 49:10	Heb. 7:14; Rev. 5:5
Lamb slain for us	Exod. 12:1-11; Isa. 53:7	John 1:29-36; 19:36; 1 Cor. 5:7-8; Rev. 5:6-14; 7:14; 21:22-27; 22:1-4
No bone broken	Exod. 12:46; Num. 9:12; Ps. 34:20	John 19:36
Firstborn son sanctified	Exod. 13:2; Num. 3:13; 8:17	Luke 2:23
Serpent in wilderness	Num. 21:8-9	John 3:14-15
A star out of Jacob	Num. 24:17-19	Matt. 2:2
Prophet like Moses	Deut. 18:15, 18-19	Matt. 21:11; Luke 7:16,39; 24:19; John 1:21,25; 6:14; 7:40; Acts 3:22-23
Cursed on the tree	Deut. 21:23	Gal. 3:13
The throne of David established forever	2 Sam. 7:12-13, 16,25-26; 1 Kings 11:36; 1 Chron. 17:11-14, 23-27; 2 Chron. 21:7; Pss. 89:3-4,36-37; 132:10-12; Isa. 9:7	Matt. 19:28; 25:31; Luke 1:32; Acts 2:30; 13:23; Rom. 1:3; 2 Tim. 2:8; Heb. 1:8; 8:1; 12:2; Rev. 22:1
A promised Redeemer	Job 19:25-27	Gal. 4:4-5
Raise Gentile opposition	Ps. 2:1-2	Acts 4:25-26
Declared to be the Son of God	Ps. 2:7; Prov. 30:4	Matt. 3:17; Mark 1:11; Luke 1:35; Acts 13:33; Heb. 1:5; 5:5; 2 Pet. 1:17
Break Gentiles with rod	Ps. 2:9	Rev. 2:26-27; 12:5; 19:15-16
His resurrection	Pss. 16:8-10; 49:15; 86:13	Acts 2:27; 13:35
Felt forsaken by God	Ps. 22:1	Matt. 27:46; Mark 15:34
Mocked and insulted	Ps. 22:7-8, 17	Matt. 27:39-43; Mark 15:29-32; Luke 23:35-39
Thirsty	Pss. 22:15; 69:21	John 19:28
Hands and feet pierced	Ps. 22:16	Matt. 27:31,35-36
Soldiers cast lots for coat	Ps. 22:18	Matt. 27:35; Mark 15:20,24; Luke 23:34; John 19:23-24
Accused by false witnesses	Pss. 27:12; 35:11	Matt. 26:60-61; Mark 14:55-61
He commits His spirit	Ps. 31:5	Luke 23:46
No broken bone	Ps. 34:20	John 19:36
Hated without reason	Pss. 35:19; 69:4	John 15:24-25
Friends stand afar off	Pss. 38:11; 88:18	Matt. 27:55; Mark 15:40; Luke 23:49
"I come to do Thy will"	Ps. 40:6-8	Heb. 10:5-9
Betrayed by a friend	Pss. 41:9; 55:12-14	Matt. 26:14-16,23,47-50; Mark 14:17-21; Luke 22:19-23; John 13:18-19
King known for righteousness	Ps. 45:1-7	Heb. 1:8-9
Blessed by nations	Ps. 72:17	Luke 1:48

PROPHECY	OT REF.	NT FULFILLMENT
His ascension	Ps. 68:18	Eph. 4:8
Stung by reproaches	Ps. 69:9	Rom. 15:3
Zeal for God's house	Ps. 69:9	John 2:17
Given gall and vinegar	Ps. 69:21	Matt. 27:34,48; Mark 15:23,36; Luke 23:36; John 19:29
Care for needy	Ps. 72:13	Luke 10:33
He speaks in parables	Ps. 78:2	Matt. 13:34-35
Make Him my firstborn	Ps. 89:27	Rom. 8:29; Col. 1:15,18; Heb. 1:6
"Thou remainest"	Ps. 102:24-27	Heb. 1:10-12
Prays for His enemies	Ps. 109:4	Matt. 5:44; Luke 23:34
Another to succeed Judas	Ps. 109:7-8	Acts 1:16-20
David's Lord at God's right hand	Ps. 110:1	Matt. 22:41-45; 26:64; Mark 12:35-37; 16:19; Acts 7:56; Eph. 1:20; Col. 3:1; Heb. 1:3,13; 8:1; 10:12; 12:2
A priest like Melchizedek	Ps. 110:4	Heb. 5:6,10; 6:20; 7:1-22; 8:1; 10:11-13
The chief cornerstone	Ps. 118:22-23	Matt. 21:42; Mark 12:10-11; Luke 20:17; Acts 4:11; Eph. 2:20; 1 Pet. 2:4-7
The King comes in the name of the Lord	Ps. 118:26	Matt. 21:9; 23:39; Mark 11:9; Luke 13:35; 19:38; John 12:13
Repentance for the nations	Isa. 2:2-4	Luke 24:47
Hearts are hardened	Isa. 6:9-10	Matt. 13:14-15; John 12:39-40; Acts 28:25-27
Born of a virgin	Isa. 7:14	Matt. 1:22-23; Luke 1:27-35
A rock of offense	Isa. 8:14,15	Rom. 9:33; 1 Pet. 2:8
Light out of darkness	Isa. 9:1-2	Matt. 4:14-16; Luke 2:32
Immanuel, God with us	Isa. 7:14; 8:8,10	Matt. 1:21,23; John 14:8-10; 14:19; Col. 2:9
Son to be given	Isa. 9:6	John 3:16
Government on His shoulders	Isa. 9:6	Matt. 28:18; 1 Cor. 15:24-25

147▶ MAJOR JEWISH SECTS IN THE NEW TESTAMENT

DATES OF EXISTENCE	NAME	ORIGIN	SEGMENTS OF SOCIETY
PHARISEES			
Existed under Jonathan (160–143 BC) Declined in power under John Hyrcanus (134–104 BC) Began resurgence under Salome Alexandra (76 BC)	Pharisees = "the Separated Ones" with three possible meanings: (1) to their separating themselves *from* people (2) to their separating themselves *to* the study of the law ("dividing" or "separating" the truth) (3) to their separating themselves from pagan practices	Probably spiritual descendants of the Hasidim (religious freedom fighters of the time of Judas Maccabeus)	Most numerous of the Jewish parties (or sects) Probably descendants of the Hasidim—scribes and lawyers Members of the middle class—mostly businessmen (merchants and tradesmen)
SADDUCEES			
Probably began about 200 BC Demise occured in AD 70 (with the destruction of the temple)	Sadducees = Three possible translations: (1) "the Righteous Ones"—based on the Hebrew consonants for the word righteous (2) "ones who sympathize with Zadok," or "Zadokites"—based on their possible link to Zadok the high priest (3) "syndics," "judges," or "fiscal controllers"—based on the Greek word syndikoi	Unknown origin Claimed to be descendants of Zadok—high priest under David (see 2 Sam. 8:17; 15:24) and Solomon (see 1 Kings 1:34-35; 1 Chron. 12:28) Had a possible link to Aaron Were probably formed into a group about 200 BC as the high priest's party	Aristocracy—the rich descendants of the high-priestly line (however, not all priests were Sadducees) Possible descendants of the Hasmonean priesthood Probably not as refined as their economic position in life would suggest

BELIEFS	SELECTED BIBLICAL REFERENCES	ACTIVITIES
Monotheistic Viewed entirety of the Old Testament (Torah, Prophets, and Writings) as authoritative Believed that the study of the law was true worship Accepted both the written and oral law More liberal in interpreting the law than were the Sadducees Quite concerned with the proper keeping of the Sabbath, tithing, and purification rituals Believed in life after death and the resurrection of the body (with divine retribution and reward) Believed in the reality of demons and angels Revered humanity and human equality Missionary minded regarding the conversion of Gentiles Believed that individuals were responsible for how they lived	Matt. 3:7-10; 5:20; 9:14; 16:1,6-12; 22:15-22,34-46; 23:2-36 Mark 3:6; 7:3–5; 8:15; 12:13-17 Luke 6:7; 7:36-39; 11:37-44; 18:9-14 John 3:1; 9:13-16; 11:46-47; 12:19 Acts 23:6-10 Phil. 3:4b-6	Developers of oral tradition Taught that the way to God was through obedience to the law Changed Judaism from a religion of sacrifice to a religion of law Progressive thinkers regarding the adaptation of the law to situations Opposed Jesus because He would not accept the teachings of the oral law as binding Established and controlled synagogues Exercised great control over general population Served as religious authorities for most Jews Took several ceremonies from the temple to the home Emphasized ethical as opposed to theological action Legalistic and socially exclusive (shunned non-Pharisees as unclean) Tended to have a self-sufficient and haughty attitude
Accepted only the Torah (Gen. through Deut.—the written law of Moses) as authoritative Practiced literal interpretation of the law Rigidly conservative toward the law Stressed strict observance of the law Observed past beliefs and tradition Opposed oral law as obligatory or binding Believed in the absolute freedom of human will—that people could do as they wished without attention from God Denied divine providence Denied the concept of life after death and the resurrection of the body Denied the concept of reward and punishment after death Denied the existence of angels and demons Materialistic	2 Sam 8:17; 15:24 1 Kings 1:34 1 Chron. 12:26-28 Ezek. 40:45-46; 43:19; 44:15-16 Matt. 3:7-10; 16:1,6-12; 22:23-34 Mark 12:18-27 Luke 20:27-40 John 11:47 Acts 4:1-2; 5:17-18; 23: 6-10	In charge of the temple and its services Politically active Exercised great political control through the Sanhedrin, of which many were members Supported the ruling power and the status quo Leaned toward Hellenism (the spreading of Greek influence)—and were thus despised by the Jewish populace Opposed both the Pharisees and Jesus because these lived by a larger canon (The Pharisees and Jesus both considered more than only Genesis through Deuteronomy as authoritative.) Opposed Jesus specifically for fear their wealth/position would be threatened if they supported Him

147 ▶ MAJOR JEWISH SECTS IN THE NEW TESTAMENT (cont.)

DATES OF EXISTENCE	NAME	ORIGIN	SEGMENTS OF SOCIETY
ZEALOTS			
Three possibilities for their beginning: (1) during the reign of Herod the Great (about 37 BC) (2) during the revolt against Rome (AD 6) (3) traced back to the Hassidim or the Maccabees (about 168 BC) Their certain demise occured around AD 70–73 with Rome's conquering of Jerusalem.	Refers to their religious zeal Josephus used the term in referring to those involved in the Jewish revolt against Rome in AD 6—led by Judas of Galilee	(According to Josephus) The Zealots began with Judas (the Galilean), son of Ezekias, who led a revolt in AD 6 because of a census done for tax purposes	The extreme wing of the Pharisees
HERODIANS			
Existed during the time of the Herodian dynasty (which began with Herod the Great in 37 BC) Uncertain demise	Based on their support of the Herodian rulers (Herod the Great or his dynasty)	Exact origin uncertain	Wealthy, politically influential Jews who supported Herod Antipas (or any descendant of Herod the Great) as ruler over Palestine (Judea and Samaria were under Roman governors at this time.)
ESSENES			
Probably began during Maccabean times (about 168 BC)—around the same time as the Pharisees and the Sadducees began to form Uncertain demise—possibly in AD 68–70 with the collapse of Jerusalem	Unknown origin	Possibly developed as a reaction to the corrupt Sadducean priesthood Have been identified with various groups: Hasidim, Zealots, Greek influence, or Iranian influence	Scattered throughout the villages of Judea (possibly including the community of Qumran) (According to Philo and Josephus) About 4,000 in Palestinian Syria

BELIEFS	SELECTED BIBLICAL REFERENCES	ACTIVITIES
Similar to the Pharisees with this exception: believed strongly that only God had the right to rule over the Jews. Patriotism and religion became inseparable. Believed that total obedience (supported by drastic physical measures) must be apparent before God would bring in the Messianic Age Were fanatical in their Jewish faith and in their devotion to the law—to the point of martyrdom	Matt. 10:4 Matt. 10:4 Luke 6:15 Acts 1:13	Extremely opposed to Roman rule over Palestine Extremely opposed to peace with Rome Refused to pay taxes Demonstrated against the use of the Greek language in Palestine Engaged in terrorism against Rome and others with whom they disagreed politically (Sicarii [or Assassins] were an extremist Zealot group who carried out acts of terrorism against Rome.)
Not a religious group—but a political one Membership probably was comprised of representatives of varied theological perspectives	Matt. 22:5-22 Mark 3:6; 8:15; 12:13-17	Supported Herod and the Herodian dynasty Accepted Hellenization Accepted foreign rule
Very strict ascetics Monastic: most took vow of celibacy (adopting male children in order to perpetuate the group), but some did marry (for the purpose of procreation) Rigidly adherent to the law (including a strict rendering of the ethical teachings) Considered other literature as authoritative (in addition to the Hebrew Scripture) Believed and lived as pacifists Rejected temple worship and temple offerings as corrupted Believed in the immortality of the soul with no bodily resurrection Apocalyptically oriented	None	Devoted to the copying and studying of the manuscripts of the law Lived in a community sense with communal property Required a long probationary period and ritual baptisms of those wishing to join Were highly virtuous and righteous Were extremely self-disciplined Were diligent manual laborers Gave great importance to daily worship Upheld rigid Sabbath laws Maintained a non-Levitical priesthood Rejected worldly pleasures as evil Rejected matrimony but did not forbid others to marry

148 HARMONY OF THE GOSPELS

	MATT.	MARK	LUKE	JOHN
PART I. INTRODUCTORY STATEMENTS				
1. Luke's historical introduction			1:1-4	
2. John's theological introduction				1:1-18
3. Matthew's and Luke's genealogical introductions	1:1-17		3:23-38	
PART II. THE BIRTH AND YOUTH OF JOHN THE BAPTIST AND JESUS				
4. The annunciation to Zacharias Place: Jerusalem			1:5-25	
5. The annunciation to the Virgin Mary Place: Nazareth			1:26-38	
6. Songs of Elizabeth and Mary Place: Judea			1:39-56	
7. Birth and youth of John the Baptist Place: Judea			1:57-80	
8. The annunciation to Joseph Place: Nazareth	1:18-25			
9. The birth of Jesus Place: Bethlehem			2:1-7	
10. The shepherds and angels Place: Near Bethlehem			2:8-20	
11. Circumcision and naming of Jesus Place: Bethlehem			2:21	
12. The presentation in the temple Place: Jerusalem			2:22-38	
13. The visit of the wise men Places: Jerusalem, Bethlehem	2:1-12			
14. Flight into Egypt and return to Nazareth Places: Nazareth, Egypt	2:13-23			2:39
15. Jesus' childhood in Nazareth and visit to Jerusalem Places: Nazareth, Jerusalem			2:40-52	
PART III. MINISTRY OF JOHN THE BAPTIST				
16. The coming of the Word Place: Wilderness		1:1	3:1-2	
17. Response of John in the wilderness Place: Wilderness	3:1-6	1:2-6	3:3-6	
18. The boldness of John's preaching Place: Wilderness	3:7-10		3:7-14	
19. John's idea of the Messiah	3:11-12	1:7-8	3:15-18	

	MATT.	MARK	LUKE	JOHN
PART IV. EARLY MINISTRY OF JESUS				
20. The baptism of Jesus in the Jordan Place: Jordan	3:13-17	1:9-11	3: 21-23	
21. The temptation of Jesus (by Satan) Place: Judean Wilderness	4:1-11	1:12-13	4:1-13	
22. Testimony of John and disciples Place: Bethany				1:19-51
23. The first miracle Place: Cana				2:1-11
24. The first stay in Capernaum Place: Capernaum				2:12
25. First Passover and temple complex cleansing Place: Jerusalem				2:13–3:21
26. Closing ministry and arrest of John Place: Aenon			3:19-20	4:1-3
27. Jesus at Sychar at Jacob's Well Place: Samaria				4:4-42
28. Jesus returns to Galilee Place: Galilee	4:12	1:14	4:14	4:43-45
PART V. THE MINISTRY IN GALILEE				
29. The message of Jesus: repentance Place: Galilee	4:17	1:14-15	4:14-15	
30. Healing an official's son Place: Capernaum				4:46-54
31. Jesus rejected by the people Place: Nazareth	4:13-16		4:16-31	
32. Calling the four fishermen Place: Capernaum	4:18-22	1:16-20	5:1-11	
33. A busy Sabbath in Capernaum Place: Capernaum	8:5-17	1:21-34	4:31-41	
34. The first tour of Galilee Place: Galilee	4:23-25	1:35-39	4:42-44	
35. Cleansing a leper Place: Galilee	8:2-4	1:40-45	5:12-16	
36. Healing a paralytic in Peter's home Place: Capernaum	9:1-8	2:1-2	5:17-26	
37. The call of Matthew (Levi) Place: Sea of Galilee	9:9-13	2:13-17	5:27-32	
38. A question about fasting Place: The seaside	9:14-17	2:18-22	5:33-39	

▶ 148 HARMONY OF THE GOSPELS (cont.)

	MATT.	MARK	LUKE	JOHN
39. First Sabbath controversy in Jerusalem Place: Jerusalem				5:1-47
40. Further controversies in Galilee Place: Galilee	12:1-14	2:23–3:6	6:1-11	
41. Choosing the Twelve and Sermon on the Mount Place: Near Capernaum	10:1-5	5:1–8:1	3:14-19	6:12-49
42. Healing the centurion's servant Place: Capernaum	8:5-13		7:1-10	
43. Raising a widow's son to life Place: Nain			7:11-17	
44. Doubt of John and praise of Jesus Place: Nain	11:2-19		7:18-35	
45. Denouncing the unrepentant towns Place: Capernaum	11:20-30			
46. The sinful woman in the house of Simon Place: Capernaum			7:36-50	
47. Jesus and the disciples go to towns and villages			8:1-3	
48. Jesus accused of blasphemy Place: Galilee	12:15-45	3:19-30		
49. The mother of Jesus calls Him	12:46-50	3:31-35	8:19-21	
50. First extended group of parables Place: Sea of Galilee	13:1-53	4:1-34	8:4-18	
51. Jesus stills the storm and heals demoniac Places: Sea of Galilee, Gadara	8:23-34	4:35–5:20	8:22-39	
52. Healing Jairus' daughter and a bleeding woman Place: Capernaum	9:18-26	5:21-43	8:40-56	
53. Two blind men and a demon-possessed man healed Place: Capernaum	9:27-34			
54. Rejection at Nazareth Place: Nazareth	13:54-58	6:1-6		
55. Commissioning the Twelve Place: Capernaum	10:1-42	6:7-13	9:1-6	
56. John the Baptist beheaded	14:1-12	6:14-29	9:7-9	
PART VI. THE WITHDRAWAL FROM GALILEE				
57. Feeding 5,000	14:13-21	6:30-44	9:10-17	6:1-13
58. Return to Gennesaret Place: Lake of Gennesaret	14:22-36	6:45-56		6:14-21
59. Rejection of Jesus in the synagogue Place: Capernaum				6:22-71

	MATT.	MARK	LUKE	JOHN
60. Pharisee traditions criticized Place: Capernaum	15:1-20	7:1-23		7:1
61. Healing the Canaanite woman's daughter Place: Phoenicia	15:21-28	7:24-30		
62. Jesus departs to Sea of Galilee	15:29-38	7:31–8:9		
63. Pharisees and Sadducees tested Jesus, again asking for a sign Place: Dalmanutha or Magadan	15:39–16:4	8:10-12		
64. Jesus again withdraws to Bethsaida-Julias Place: Bethsaida	16:5-12	8:13-26		
65. Peter's confession of the Messiah Place: Caesarea-Philippi	16:13-20	8:27-30	9:18-21	
66. Jesus' death and resurrection predicted Place: Galilee	16:21-28	8:31-38; 9:1	9:22-27	
67. The transfiguration of Jesus Place: Mount Tabor	17:1-13	9:2-13	9:28-36	
68. The power of faith over a demon	17:14-21	9:14-29	9:37-42	
69. Second prediction of His death and resurrection Place: Galilee	17:22-23	9:30-32	9:42-45	
70. Jesus pays taxes by miracle Place: Capernaum	17:24-27			
71. Disciples contending who is greatest Place: Capernaum	18:1-5	9:33-37	9:46-48	
72. Jesus rebukes the narrowness of John Place: Capernaum	18:6-14	9:38-50	9:49-50	
73. Restoring a brother Place: Capernaum	18:15-35			
74. Following Jesus Place: Capernaum	8:19-22		9:57-62	
75. The unbelief of Jesus brothers Place: Capernaum				7:2-10
76. James and John rebuked for anger Place: Samaria			9:51-56	
PART VII. THE MINISTRY IN JUDEA				
77. Jesus at the Feast of Tabernacles Place: Jerusalem				7:11–8:11
78. Jesus the light of the world Place: Jerusalem				8:12-59
79. Healing a man born blind Place: Jerusalem				9:1-41
80. Jesus is the good shepherd Place: Jerusalem				10:1-21

148 HARMONY OF THE GOSPELS (cont.)

	MATT.	MARK	LUKE	JOHN
81. Sending out the seventy			10:1-24	
82. Parable of the good Samaritan Place: Jerusalem			10:25-37	
83. Jesus received by Martha and Mary Place: Bethany			10:38-42	
84. The disciples are taught the model prayer	6:9-13		11:1-13	
85. Accused of healing through Beelzebub			11:14-36	
86. Religious hypocrisy denounced			11:37-54	
87. Warnings for the disciples			12:1-12	
88. Possessions and the parable of the rich fool				12:13-21
89. Cure for anxiety			12:22-34	
90. Be ready for the Master's return			12:35-48	
91. Christ's eagerness for His baptism of death on the cross			12:49-59	
92. Repentance and parable of fig tree			13:1-9	
93. Healing a daughter of Abraham on the Sabbath			13:10-21	
94. Jesus at Festival of Dedication Place: Jerusalem				10:22-39
PART VIII. THE MINISTRY IN PEREA				
95. Many believe on Jesus Place: Bethany				10:40-42
96. The narrow way Place: Perea			13:22-35	
97. Jesus teaches humility and service Place: Near Jerusalem			14:1-24	
98. The cost of following Jesus Place: Jerusalem			14:25-35	
99. Parables of the lost			15:1-32	
100. Parables concerning stewardship			16:1–17:10	
101. The raising of Lazarus Place: Bethany				11:1-54
102. Jesus travels to Jerusalem for the Passover Places: Samaria, Galilee			17:11-37	
103. Parables on the way to Jerusalem	19:1-2	10:1	18:1-14	
104. Pharisees test Jesus concerning divorce	19:3-12	10:2-12		
105. Jesus blesses the children Place: Perea	19:13-15	10:13-16	18:15-17	
106. Parable of the rich young ruler	19:16-29	10:17-30	18:18-30	

	MATT.	MARK	LUKE	JOHN
107. Parable of the laborers in vineyard	20:1-16	10:31		
108. Jesus' third prediction of His death and resurrection	20:17-19	10:32-34	18:31-34	
109. Selfishness of James and John	20:20-28	10:35-45		
110. Blind Bartimaeus healed	20:29-34	10:46-52	18:35-43	
111. Zacchaeus and parable of the 10 minas Place: Jericho			19:1-28	
PART IX. THE LAST JERUSALEM MINISTRY				
112. The interest in Jesus and Lazarus Place: Bethany				11:55-57; 12:1,9-11
113. The triumphal entry Place: Jerusalem		11:1-11	19:29-44	12:12-19
114. Cursing the fig tree and cleansing the temple complex Place: Jerusalem	21:12-13, 18-19	11:12-18	19:45-48	
115. Jesus predicts His crucifixion Place: Jerusalem				12:20-50
116. The barren fig tree and the power of faith Place: Jerusalem	21:19-22	11:19-26	21:37-38	
117. Sanhedrin questions the authority of Jesus Place: Jerusalem	21:23-46; 22:1-14	11:27–12:12	20:1-19	
118. An attempt to trap Jesus concerning tribute to Caesar Place: Jerusalem	22:15-22	12:13-17	20:20-26	
119. The Sadducees and the resurrection Place: Jerusalem	22:23-33	12:18-27	20:27-40	
120. The primary commandments Place: Jerusalem	22:34-40	12:28-34		
121. Jesus silences enemies by appeal to David Place: Jerusalem	22:41-46	12:35-37	20:41-44	
122. Warning against the Scribes and Pharisees Place: Jerusalem	23:1-39	12:38-40	20:45-47	
123. The widow's gift Place: Jerusalem		12:41-44	21:1-4	
PART X. JESUS COUNSELS HIS DISCIPLES LEADING UP TO HIS SACRIFICE				
124. The great eschatological discourse Place: Jerusalem	24:1–25:46	13:1-37	21:5-36	
125. The plot to kill Jesus Place: Jerusalem	26:1-5	14:1-2	22:1-2	
126. Jesus anointed by Mary at Bethany Place: Bethany	26:6-13	14:3-9		12:2-8
127. Betrayal by Judas Iscariot Place: Jerusalem	26:14-16	14:10-11	22:3-6	

148 ► HARMONY OF THE GOSPELS (cont.)

	MATT.	MARK	LUKE	JOHN
128. Preparation for Passover and jealousy of the disciples Place: Jerusalem	26:17-20	14:12-17	22:7-16, 24-30	
129. Jesus washes His disciples' feet Place: Jerusalem				13:1-20
130. Judas' betrayal predicted Place: Jerusalem	26:21-25	14:18-21	22:21-23	13:21-30
131. Steadfastness of the disciples questioned Place: Jerusalem	26:31-35	14:27-31	22:17-20	13:34-38
132. First Lord's Supper Place: Jerusalem	26:26-29	14:22-25	22:17-20	(1 Cor. 11:23-26)
133. Jesus opens His heart to the disciples concerning His departure Place: Upper room and on way to Gethsemane				14:1– 16:33
134. Jesus' intercessory prayer Place: Near Gethsemane				17:1-26
135. The Agony in Gethsemane	26:36-46	14:32-42	22:39-46	18:1
PART XI. THE CONDEMNATION AND THE CROSS				
136. The betrayal, arrest, and desertion by the disciples Place: Gethsemane	26:47-56	14:43-52	22:47-53	18:2-12
137. Jesus arrested and questioned by Annas Place: Jerusalem			18:13-14, 19-23	
138. Jesus faces the Sanhedrin Place: Jerusalem	26:57-68	14:53-65	22:66-71	18:24
139. Peter's three denials Place: Jerusalem	26:58, 69-75	14:54, 66-72	22:54-62	18:15-18, 25-27
140. An attempt to make the trial legal Place: Jerusalem	27:1	15:1	22:66-71	
141. Judas hangs himself Place: Jerusalem	27:3-10		(see Acts 1:18-19)	
142. Jesus before Pilate the governor Place: Jerusalem	27:2, 11-14	15:1-5	23:1-5	18:28-38
143. Jesus faces Herod Antipas Place: Jerusalem			23:6-12	
144. Herod returns Jesus to Pilate Place: Jerusalem	27:15-26	15:6-15	23:13-25	18:39– 19:16
145. Jesus is mocked by the military Place: Jerusalem	27:27-30	15:16-19		
146. Simon bears the cross Place: On way to Calvary	27:31-34	15:20-23	23:26-33	19:16-17

	MATT.	MARK	LUKE	JOHN
147. Jesus is crucified Place: Calvary	27:35-50	15:24-37	23:33-46	19:18-30
148. The supernatural phenomena Place: Jerusalem	27:51-56	15:38-41	23:45-49	
149. Burial of Jesus in Joseph's tomb Place: Gethsemane	27:57-60	15:42-46	23:50-54	19:31-42
150. The Women by the sepulcher	27:61-66	15:47	23:55-56	
PART XII. THE RESURRECTION AND ASCENSION				
151. Resurrection morning Place: Gethsemane	28:1			
152. Anointing with spices		16:1		24:1
153. The tomb is opened	28:2-4	16:3-4	24:2	20:1
154. Women find the empty tomb and angels	28:5-8	16:2-8		24:1-8
155. The women report to the apostles Place: Jerusalem			24:9-12	20:2-10
156. Jesus appears to Mary Magdalene Place: Jerusalem		16:9-11		20:11-18
157. Other women see Jesus	28:9-10			
158. Soldiers are bribed to lie	28:11-15			
159. Jesus appears to two Place: On the way to Emmaus		16:12-13	24:13-32	
160. Simon Peter sees Jesus			24:33-35	(1 Cor. 15:5)
161. The reality of the risen Lord Place: Jerusalem		16:14	24:36-43	20:19-25
162. Entire group, with Thomas, see Him, finally believing				20:26-31
163. Jesus appears by Sea of Tiberius				21:1-25
164. The Great Commission Place: Galilee	28:16-20	16:15-18	(1 Cor. 15:6)	
165. James the brother of Jesus sees Him			(1 Cor. 15:7)	
166. The ascension Place: The mount called Olive Grove		16:19-20	24:44-53	(Acts 1:9-11)

149 JESUS' BIRTH AND EARLY CHILDHOOD

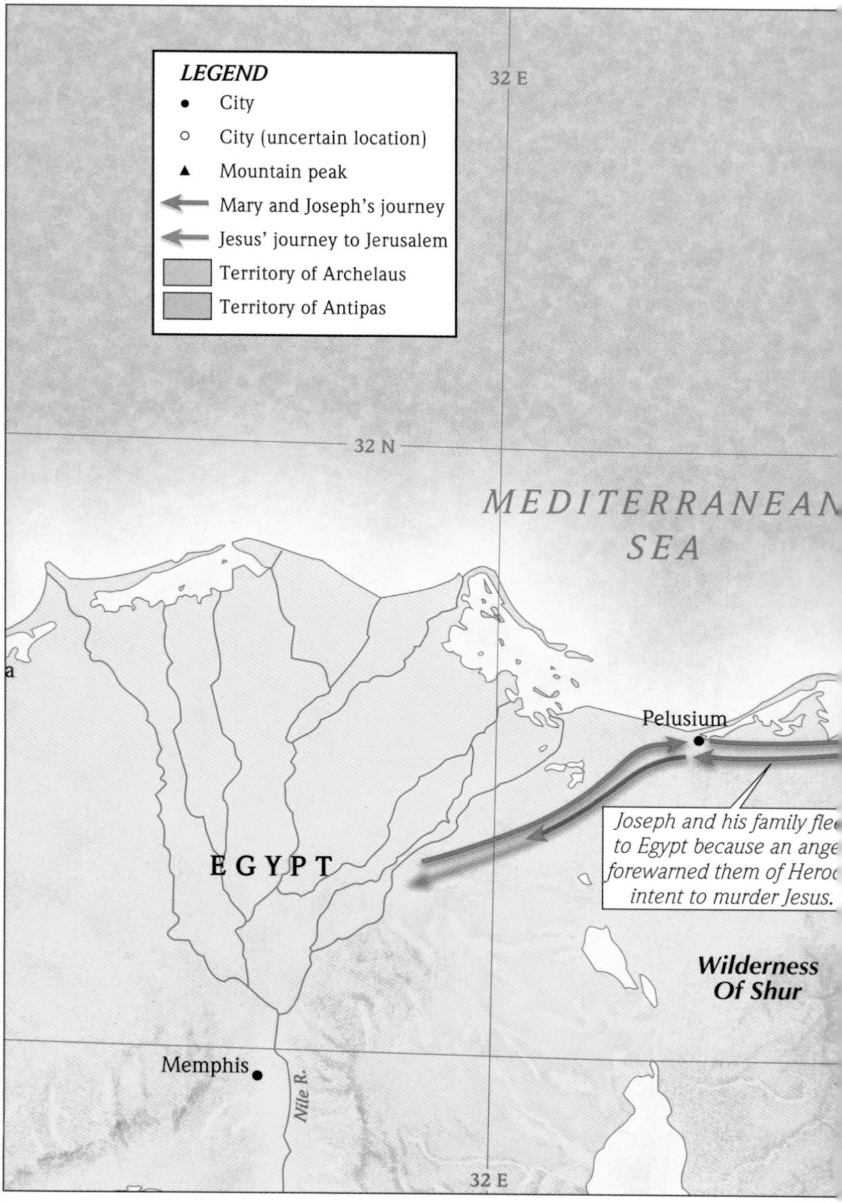

LEGEND
- • City
- ○ City (uncertain location)
- ▲ Mountain peak
- ← Mary and Joseph's journey
- ← Jesus' journey to Jerusalem
- Territory of Archelaus
- Territory of Antipas

32 E

32 N

MEDITERRANEAN
SEA

Pelusium

Joseph and his family flee
to Egypt because an ange[l]
forewarned them of Hero[d's]
intent to murder Jesus.

Wilderness
Of Shur

EGYPT

Memphis

Nile R.

32 E

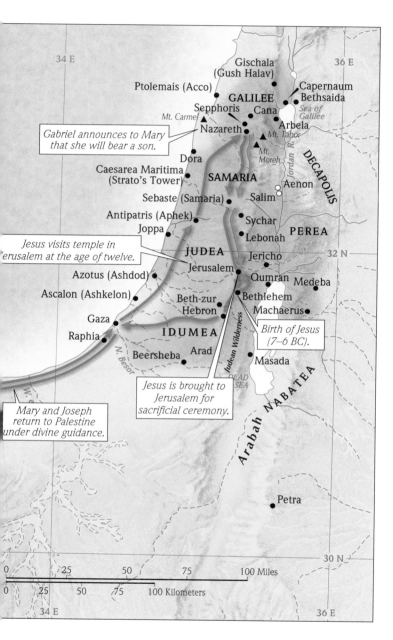

34 E

Gischala
(Gush Halav)

Ptolemais (Acco)

GALILEE

Capernaum
Bethsaida

Sepphoris

Cana

*Sea of
Galilee*

Mt. Carmel

Nazareth

Arbela

36 E

Mt. Tabor

DECAPOLIS

*Gabriel announces to Mary
that she will bear a son.*

Dora

Mt.
Moreh

Caesarea Maritima
(Strato's Tower)

SAMARIA

Aenon

Sebaste (Samaria)

Salim

Antipatris (Aphek)

Sychar

PEREA

Joppa

Lebonah

*Jesus visits temple in
Jerusalem at the age of twelve.*

JUDEA

Jericho

32 N

Jerusalem

Azotus (Ashdod)

Qumran

Medeba

Ascalon (Ashkelon)

Bethlehem

Beth-zur

Gaza

Hebron

Machaerus

Raphia

IDUMEA

*Birth of Jesus
(7–6 BC).*

Beersheba

Arad

Masada

*Jesus is brought to
Jerusalem for
sacrificial ceremony.*

*DEAD
SEA*

NABATEA

*Mary and Joseph
return to Palestine
under divine guidance.*

Arabah

Petra

0   25   50   75   100 Miles

0   25   50   75   100 Kilometers

30 N

34 E

36 E

Luke 2:4-5
And Joseph also went up from the town of Nazareth in
Galilee, to Judea, to the city of David, which is called
Bethlehem, because he was of the house and family line of
David, to be registered along with Mary, who was engaged
to him and was pregnant.

150 **JOHN THE BAPTIZER**

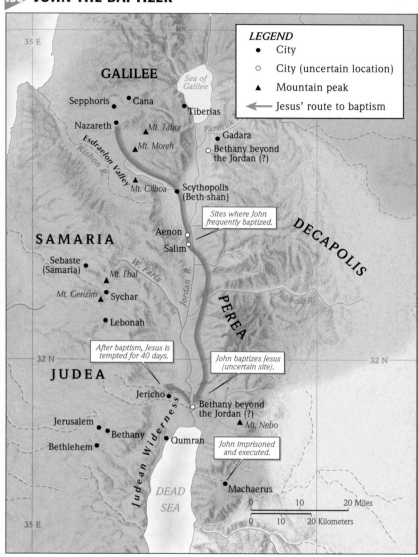

LEGEND
- • City
- ○ City (uncertain location)
- ▲ Mountain peak
- ← Jesus' route to baptism

GALILEE

Sea of Galilee

Sepphoris • • Cana
Tiberias •
Nazareth • ▲ Mt. Tabor
Yarmuk
Esdraelon Valley ▲ Mt. Moreh • Gadara
Kishon R. ○ Bethany beyond
the Jordan (?)
▲ Mt. Gilboa • Scythopolis
(Beth-shan)

DECAPOLIS

Sites where John frequently baptized.

Aenon ○
SAMARIA
Salim ○

Sebaste • W. Farta
(Samaria) ▲ Mt. Ebal

Mt. Gerizim ▲ • Sychar

Jordan R.
PEREA

• Lebonah

Jabbok R.

After baptism, Jesus is tempted for 40 days.

32 N
John baptizes Jesus (uncertain site).
32 N
JUDEA

Jericho ○
Jerusalem • ○ Bethany beyond
• Bethany the Jordan (?)
Judean Wilderness ▲ Mt. Nebo
Bethlehem • • Qumran

John imprisoned and executed.

DEAD SEA
• Machaerus

0   10   20 Miles
0   10   20 Kilometers

35 E

Mark 1:4-5
John came baptizing in the wilderness and preaching a baptism of repentance for the forgiveness of sins. The whole Judean countryside and all the people of Jerusalem were flocking to him, and they were baptized by him in the Jordan River as they confessed their sins.

151 CUTAWAY RECONSTRUCTION OF A FIRST-CENTURY AD ISRAELITE HOUSE

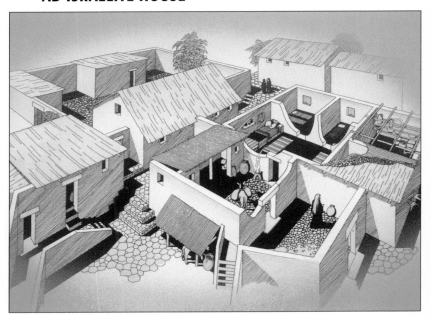

152 A TYPICAL SYNAGOGUE OF THE FIRST CENTURY AD

JESUS' MINISTRY AS FULFILLMENT OF SCRIPTURE IN MATTHEW

ASPECTS OF HIS MINISTRY	FULFILLMENT PASSAGE IN MATTHEW	OT PROPHECY
His virgin birth and role as God with us	Matt. 1:18,22-23	Isa. 7:14
His birth in Bethlehem and shepherd role	Matt. 2:4-6	Mic. 5:2
His refugee years in Egypt and role as God's Son	Matt. 2:14-15	Hos. 11:1
His upbringing in Nazareth and messianic role (the Hebrew term for branch is nezer)	Matt. 2:23	Isa. 11:1
His preaching ministry in Galilee and role as Light to the Gentiles	Matt. 4:12-16	Isa. 9:1-2
His healing ministry and role as God's Servant	Matt. 8:16-17	Isa. 53:4
His reluctance to attract attention and His role as God's chosen and loved Servant	Matt. 12:16-21	Isa. 42:1-4
His teaching in parables and His role in proclaiming God's sovereign rule	Matt. 13:34-35	Ps. 78:2
His humble entry into Jerusalem and role as King	Matt. 21:1-5	Zech. 9:9
His betrayal, arrest, and death and role as Suffering Servant	Matt. 26:50,56	The prophetic writings as a whole

154 CONTROVERSY STORIES IN MARK

CONTROVERSY	REFERENCE IN MARK
Over Jesus' right to forgive sins	2:1-12
Over Jesus' fellowship with tax collectors and "sinners"	2:13-17
Over the disciples' freedom from fasting	2:18-22
Over the disciples' picking grain on the Sabbath	2:23-27
Over Jesus' right to do good on the Sabbath	3:1-6
Over the nature of Jesus' family	3:20-21,31-35
Over the source of Jesus' power to exorcise	3:22-30
Over the disciples' eating with unwashed hands	7:1-5,14-23
Over the Pharisees' and teachers' of the law setting aside the commands of God in order to observe their own tradition	7:6-13
Over the legality of divorce and God's intention for marriage	10:1-12
Over Jesus' authority to cleanse the temple and John's authority to baptize	11:27-33
Over paying taxes to Caesar and giving God His due	12:13-17
Over marriage at the resurrection, the power of God, and the witness of Scripture	12:18-27
Over the most important commandment	12:28-34
Over the nature of the Messiah—son of David or David's Lord	12:35-37

THEMES IN LUKE

THEME	EXAMPLES FROM LUKE	REFERENCE
Theology	Word of God	5:1; 6:47; 8:11,13-15,21; 11:28
	Jesus as Savior	1:69; 2:11; 19:9
	The present kingdom of God	11:20; 19:9
	The Holy Spirit	1:35,41,67; 2:25-27; 3:22; 4:1,14; 11:13; 24:49
Concern for women	Elisabeth	1:5-25,39-45,57-66
	Mary	1:26-56; 2:1-20,41-52
	Anna	2:36-38
	The widow of Nain	7:11-12
	The "sinner" who anoints Jesus' feet	7:36-50
	Women disciples	8:1-3
	The woman searching for her lost coin	15:8-10
	The persistent widow petitioning the unjust judge	18:1-8
	The sorrowful women along the way to the cross	23:27
Concern for the poor/ warnings to the rich	Blessings on the poor	6:20-23
	Woes on the rich	6:24-26
	The rich fool	12:16-20
	The rich man and the beggar Lazarus	16:19-31
	Shepherds	2:8-20
Concern for social outcasts	Samaritans	10:25-37; 17:11-19
	Tax agents and "sinners"	15:1
	Gentiles/all people	2:32; 24:47
	Gratitude and joy	1:46-55,68-79; 2:14; 15:7,10,24,32; 17:16,18; 24:53
	Prayer	3:21; 6:12; 9:18; 11:1-13; 18:1-14
The Christian life	Proper use of material possessions	6:32-36; 10:27-37; 12:32-34;16:1-13
	Changed social behavior in imitation of God	9:3-5,16; 10:2-16,38-42; 12:41-48; 22:24-27
	Repentance/faith	3:7-14; 5:32; 10:13; 11:32; 13:3-5 15:7-10; 24:47

156 THE SEVEN SIGNS IN JOHN

SIGN	REFERENCE	CENTRAL TRUTH
1. Changing water to wine	2:1-11	Points to Jesus as the Source of all the blessings of God's future (see Isa. 25:6-8; Jer. 31:11-12; Amos 9:13-14)
2. Healing the official's son	4:43-54	Points to Jesus as the Giver of life
3. Healing the invalid at Bethesda	5:1-15	Points to Jesus as the Father's coworker
4. Feeding the 5,000	6:1-15, 25-69	Points to Jesus as the life-giving Bread from heaven
5. Walking on water	6:16-21	Points to Jesus as the divine I AM
6. Healing the man born blind	9:1-41	Points to Jesus as the Giver of spiritual sight
7. Raising Lazarus	11:1-44	Points to Jesus as the Resurrection and the Life

157 "I AM" SAYINGS IN JOHN

SAYING	REFERENCE IN JOHN
I am the Bread of Life.	6:35
I am the Light of the World.	8:12
I am the Gate for the Sheep.	10:7
I am the Good Shepherd.	10:11,14
I am the Resurrection and the Life.	11:25
I am the Way, the Truth, and the Life.	14:6
I am the True Vine.	15:1,5
I am a King.	18:37

158 DISCOURSES OF JESUS

WHERE DELIVERED	NATURE OR STYLE	TO WHOM ADDRESSED
1. Jerusalem	Conversation	Nicodemus
2. At Jacob's Well	Conversation	Samaritan Woman
3. At Jacob's Well	Conversation	The Disciples
4. Nazareth	Sermon	Worshipers
5. Mountain of Galilee	Sermon and the People	The Disciples
6. Bethesda—a Pool	Conversation	The Jews
7. Galilee	Conversation	The Pharisees
8. Galilee	Eulogy and Denunciation	The People
9. Galilee	Conversation	The Pharisees
10. Galilee	Conversation	The Disciples
11. Galilee	Conversation	A Messenger
12. Capernaum	Sermon	The Multitude
13. Genessaret	Criticism and Reproof	The Scribes and Pharisees
14. Capernaum	Example	The Disciples
15. Temple–Jerusalem	Instruction	The Jews
16. Temple–Jerusalem	Instruction	The Jews
17. Jerusalem	Instruction	The Jews
18. Capernaum	Charge	The Seventy
19. Unknown	Instruction	The Disciples
20. Unknown	Conversation	The People
21. House of Pharisee	Reproof	The Pharisees
22. Unknown	Exhortation	The Multitude
23. Unknown	Object Lesson	The Disciples
24. Jerusalem	Exhortation	The People
25. Jerusalem	Denunciation	The Pharisees
26. Mount of Olives	Prophecy	The Disciples
27. Jerusalem	Exhortation	The Disciples
28. Jerusalem	Exhortation	The Disciples

THE LESSON TO BE LEARNED	REFERENCES
We must be "born of water and the Spirit" to enter the kingdom	John 3:1-21
"God is spirit" to be worshiped in spirit and truth	John 4:1-30
Our food is to do His will	John 4:31-38
No prophet is welcomed in his own hometown	Luke 4:16-30
The Beatitudes; to let our light shine before men; Christians the light of the world; how to pray; benevolence and humility; heavenly and earthly treasures contrasted; golden rule	Matt. 5–7; Luke 6:17-49
To hear Him and believe on Him is to have everlasting life	John 5:1-47
Works of necessity not wrong on the Sabbath	Matt. 12:1-14; Luke 6:1-11
Greatness of the least in heaven; judged according to the light we have	Matt. 11:2-29; Luke 7:18-35
The unforgivable sin is to sin against the Holy Spirit	Mark 3:19-30; Matt. 12:22-45
The providence of God; nearness of Christ to those who serve Him	Mark 6:6-13; Matt. 10:1-42
Relationship of those doing His will	Matt. 12:46-50; Mark 3:31-35
Christ as the Bread of Life	John 6:22-71
Not outward conditions, but that which proceeds from the heart defiles	Matt. 15:1-20; Mark 7:1-23
Humility the mark of greatness; be not a stumbling block	Matt. 18:1-14; Mark 9:33-50
Judge not according to outward appearance	John 7:11-40
To follow Christ is to walk in the light	John 8:12-59
Christ the door; He knows His sheep; He gives His life for them	John 10:1-21
Need for Christian service; not to despise Christ's ministers	Luke 10:1-24
The efficacy of earnest prayer	Luke 11:1-13
Hear and keep God's will; the state of the backslider	Luke 11:14-36
The meaning of inward purity	Luke 11:37-54
Beware of hypocrisy, covetousness, blasphemy; be watchful	Luke 12:1-21
Watchfulness; the kingdom of God is of first importance	Luke 12:22-34
Death for life; way of eternal life	John 12:20-50
Avoid hypocrisy and pretense	Matt. 23:1-39
Signs of the coming of the Son of man; beware of false prophets	Matt. 24:1-51; Mark 13:1-37
The lesson of humility and service	John 13:1-20
The proof of discipleship; that He will come again	John 14–16

159▷ PARABLES OF JESUS

PARABLE	OCCASION
1. The speck and the log	Sermon on the Mount (Matt.) Sermon on the Plain (Luke)
2. The two houses	Sermon on the Mount, at the close
3. Children in the marketplace	Rejection of John's baptism and Jesus' ministry
4. The two debtors	A Pharisee's self-righteous reflections
5. The unclean spirit	The scribes demand a miracle in the heavens
6. The rich fool	Dispute of two brothers
7. The barren fig tree	Tidings of the execution of certain Galileans
8. The sower	Sermon on the seashore
9. The tares	The same
10. The seed	The same
11. The grain of mustard seed	The same
12. The leaven	The same
13. The lamp	Sermon on the Mount (Matt.) Teaching a large crowd (Mark, Luke)
14. The dragnet	Sermon on the seashore
15. The hidden treasure	The same
16. The pearl of great value	The same
17. The householder	The same
18. The marriage	To the critics who censured the disciples
19. The patched garment	The same
20. The wine bottles	The same
21. The harvest	Spiritual wants of the Jewish people
22. The opponent	Slowness of the people to believe
23. Two insolvent debtors	Peter's question
24. The good Samaritan	The lawyer's question

LESSON TAUGHT	REFERENCES
Do not presume to judge others	Matt. 7:1-6; Luke 6:37-42
Necessity of building life on Jesus' words	Matt. 7:24-27; Luke 6:47-49
Evil of a fault-finding disposition	Matt. 11:16-19; Luke 7:32-34
Love to Christ proportioned to grace received	Luke 7:41-43
Hardening power of unbelief	Matt. 12:43-45; Luke 11:24-26
Folly of reliance upon wealth	Luke 12:16-21
Still time for repentance	Luke 13:6-9
Effects of preaching religious truth	Matt. 13:3-8; Mark 4:3-8; Luke 8:5-8
The severance of good and evil	Matt. 13:24-30
Power of truth	Mark 4:26-29
Small beginnings and growth of Christ's kingdom	Matt. 13:31-32; Mark 4:31-32; Luke 13:19
Dissemination of the knowledge of Christ	Matt. 13:33; Luke 13:21
Effect of good example	Matt. 5:15; Mark 4:21; Luke 8:16; 11:33
Mixed character of the church	Matt. 13:47-48
Value of God's kingdom	Matt. 13:44
The same	Matt. 13;45-46
Varied methods of teaching truth	Matt. 13:52
Joy in Christ's companionship	Matt. 9:15; Mark 2:19-20; Luke 5:34-35
Newness of God's work in Christ, which cannot be impeded by the old	Matt. 9:16; Mark 2:21; Luke 5:36
The same	Matt. 9:17; Mark 2:22; Luke 5:37-38
Need of witness and prayer	Matt. 9:37; Luke 10:2
Need of prompt reconciliation	Matt. 5:25-26; Luke 12:58-59
Duty of forgiveness	Matt. 18:23-35
The golden rule for all	Luke 10:30-37

159▶ **PARABLES OF JESUS** (cont.)

PARABLE	OCCASION
25. The persistent friend	Disciples ask lesson in prayer
26. The good shepherd	Pharisees reject testimony of miracle
27. The narrow, or locked, door	The question, Are there few who can be saved?
28. The two ways	The Sermon on the Mount
29. The guests	Eagerness to take high places
30. The marriage supper	Self-righteous remark of a guest
31. The wedding clothes	Continuation of the same discourse
32. The tower	Multitudes surrounding Christ
33. The king going to war	The same
34. The lost sheep	The disciples' question, Who is the greatest? (Matt.); Pharisees objected to His receiving tax collectors and "sinners"
35. The lost coin	The same
36. The prodigal son	The same
37. The unjust steward	To the disciples
38. The rich man and Lazarus	Derision of the Pharisees
39. The importunate widow	Teaching the disciples
40. The Pharisee and tax gatherer	Teaching the self-righteous
41. The slave's duty	Teaching the disciples
42. Laborers in the vineyard	The same
43. The talents	In Jerusalem (Matt.) at the house of Zaccheus (Luke)
44. The two sons	The chief priests demand His authority
45. The wicked vine growers	The same
46. The fig tree	In prophesying the destruction of Jerusalem
47. The watching householder	The same
48. The watchful slave	The same
49. Character of two slaves	The same
50. The ten virgins	The same
51. The watching slaves	The same
52. The vine and branches	At the last supper

LESSON TAUGHT	REFERENCES
Effect of importunity in prayer	Luke 11:5-8
Christ the only way to God	John 10:1-16
Difficulty of entry into God's Kingdom	Luke 13:24
Difficulty of discipleship	Matt. 7:13-14
Chief places not to be usurped	Luke 14:7-11
Rejection of unbelievers	Matt. 22:2-9; Luke 14:16-24
Necessity of purity	Matt. 22:10-14
Need of counting the cost of discipleship	Luke 14:28-30
The same	Luke 14:31-32
Christ's love for sinners based on God's love for them	Matt. 18:12-13; Luke 15:4-7
The same	Luke 15:8-9
The same	Luke 15:11-32
Prudence in using property	Luke 16:1-9
Salvation not connected with wealth and the adequacy of Scripture	Luke 16:19-31
Perseverance in prayer	Luke 18:2-5
Humility in prayer	Luke 18:10-14
Humble obedience	Luke 17:7-10
God's graciously adequate gift to the unworthy	Matt. 20:1-16
Doom of unfaithful followers	Matt. 25:14-30; Luke 19:11-27
Obedience better than words	Matt. 21:28-30
Rejection of the Jewish people	Matt. 21:33-43; Mark 12:1-9; Luke 20:9-15
Duty of watching for Christ's appearance	Matt. 24:32; Mark 13:28; Luke 21:29-30
The same	Matt. 24:43; Luke 12:39
The same	Mark 13:34-36
Danger of unfaithfulness	Matt. 24:45-51; Luke 12:42-46
Necessity of watchfulness	Matt. 25:1-12
The same	Luke 12:36-38
The need to abide in Christ	John 15:1-6

160 MIRACLES OF JESUS

MIRACLE
Water turned to wine
Many healings
Healing of a leper
Healing of a Roman centurion's servant
Healing of Peter's mother-in-law
Calming of the storm at sea
Healing of the wild men of Gadara
Healing of the lame man
Healing of a woman with a hemorrhage
Raising of Jairus's daughter
Healing of two blind men
Healing of a demon-possessed man
Healing of man with a withered hand
Feeding of 5,000 people
Walking on the sea
Healing of the Syrophoenician's daughter
Feeding of 4,000 people
Healing of an epileptic boy
Healing of two blind men at Jericho
Healing of a man with an unclean spirit
Healing of a deaf, speechless man
Healing of a blind man at Bethesda
Healing of blind Bartimaeus
A miraculous catch of fish
Raising of a widow's son
Healing of a stooped woman
Healing of a man with the dropsy
Healing of ten lepers
Healing of Malchus's ear
Healing of a royal official's son
Healing of a lame man at Bethesda
Healing of a blind man
Raising of Lazarus

BIBLICAL PASSAGES			
			John 2:1
Matt. 4:23	Mark 1:32		
Matt. 8:1	Mark 1:40	Luke 5:12	
Matt. 8:5		Luke 7:1	
Matt. 8:14	Mark 1:29	Luke 4:38	
Matt. 8:23	Mark 4:35	Luke 8:22	
Matt. 8:28	Mark 5:1	Luke 8:26	
Matt. 9:1	Mark 2:1	Luke 5:18	
Matt. 9:20	Mark 5:25	Luke 8:43	
Matt. 9:23	Mark 5:22	Luke 8:41	
Matt. 9:27			
Matt. 9:32			
Matt. 12:10	Mark 3:1	Luke 6:6	
Matt. 14:15	Mark 6:35	Luke 9:12	John 6:1
Matt. 14:22	Mark 6:47		John 6:16
Matt. 15:21	Mark 7:24		
Matt. 15:32	Mark 8:1		
Matt. 17:14	Mark 9:14	Luke 9:37	
Matt. 20:30			
	Mark 1:23	Luke 4:33	
	Mark 7:31		
	Mark 8:22		
	Mark 10:46	Luke 18:35	
		Luke 5:4	John 21:1
		Luke 7:11	
		Luke 13:11	
		Luke 14:1	
		Luke 17:11	
		Luke 22:50	
			John 4:46
			John 5:1
			John 9:1
			John 11:38

161 THE APOSTLES AND THEIR HISTORY

NAME	SURNAME	PARENTS	HOME	BUSINESS
Simon	Peter or Cephas = Rock	Jonah	Early life: Bethsaida; Later: Capernaum	Fisherman
Andrew = manhood or valor		Jonah	Early life: Bethsaida; Later: Capernaum	Fisherman
James the greater or the elder	Boanerges or Sons of Thunder	Zebedee and Salome	Bethsaida, Capernaum, and Jerusalem	Fisherman
John, the beloved disciple	Boanerges or Sons of Thunder	Zebedee and Salome	Bethsaida, Capernaum, and Jerusalem	Fisherman
James the less		Alphaeus and Mary	Galilee	
Jude	Same as Thaddeus and Lebbeus	James	Galilee	
Philip			Bethsaida	
Bartholomew	Nathaniel		Cana of Galilee	
Matthew	Levi		Galilee	Tax Collector
Thomas	Didymus		Galilee	
Simon	The Zealot, lit. Cananaean		Galilee, perhaps Cana	
Judas	Iscariot	Simon Iscariot	Kerioth of Judea	

WRITINGS	BIBLE FACTS
1 & 2 Peter	Confessed Jesus as Messiah (Matt. 16:16); part of Jesus' inner circle (Mark 5:37); walked on water (Matt. 14:29); witnessed Jesus' transfiguration (Luke 9:28); denied Jesus (Luke 22:54-62); restored by Jesus (John 21:15-19); preached at Pentecost (Acts 2:14-40)
	Was a disciple of John the Baptist (John 1:40); introduced his brother, Simon, to Jesus (John 1:40); told Jesus about the boy with loaves and fishes (John 6:8); with Philip told Jesus about the Greeks seeking Him (John 12:20); one of four to hear Jesus' teaching about what would soon happen (Mark 13:3)
	Wanted to call down fire on Samaritans (Luke 9:54); highly ambitious (Mark 10:35-45); went fishing after Jesus' resurrection (John 21:2); first disciple to be martyred (Acts 12:2)
Gospel, three epistles, and Revelation	Highly ambitious (Mark 10:35-45); witnessed Jesus' transfiguration (Luke 9:28); with Peter prepared Passover meal (Luke 22:8); reclined close beside Jesus at the Last Supper (John 13:23); entrusted with the care of Mary, Jesus' mother (John 19:26-27); bold witness (Acts 4:14); exiled on Patmos (Rev. 1:9)
	Was called James the younger; son of Alphaeus and Mary (Mark 3:18; 15:40)
	Asked Jesus how He was going to reveal Himself to the disciples and not to the world (John 14:22)
	Invited Nathanael to come and see Jesus (John 1:43-48); tested by Jesus about how to feed 5000 (John 6:4-7); approached by Greeks who wanted to see Jesus (John 12:20-21); asked Jesus to show the Father to the disciples (John 14: 8)
	In prayer with other disciples following Jesus' ascension (Acts 1:13)
Gospel	Hosts a dinner where his friends could meet Jesus (Mark 2:15)
	Encouraged his fellow disciples to returned to Judea with Jesus and there die with him (John 11:16); asks Jesus where He is going (John 14:5); requires clear evidence that Jesus has been raised from death (John 20:25); Jesus gives Thomas compelling evidence of His resurrection (John 20:27)
	Protested Mary of Bethany's lavish gift to Jesus (John 12:5); stole from the disciples' money bag (John 12:6); Satan entered into him at the Last Supper (John 13:27); betrays Jesus (Luke 22:47-48); was filled with remorse for his betrayal of Jesus (Matt. 27:3); committed suicide (Matt. 27:5)

162 RECONSTRUCTION OF A FIRST-CENTURY WINEPRESS

Making wine has always been a major industry in Syria-Palestine. The ancient Egyptian story of Sinuhe, dating from the time of the middle Bronze Age (about 2200–1550 BC), describes this land as having "more wine than water."

In OT times the presses for making wine were usually cut or hewed out of rock (Isa. 5:2) and were connected by channels to lower rock-cut vats where the juice was allowed to collect and ferment. The juice was squeezed from the grapes by treading over them with the feet (Job 24:11; Amos 9:13). Recent excavations at Tel Aphek have uncovered two unusually large plaster winepresses dating from the late Bronze Age (1550–1200 BC). The presses were connected to large collection pits that still contained the Canaanite jars for the storage of the wine.

After the juice had fermented, it was collected into jars or wine-skins (Matt. 9:17, and parallels). At ancient Gibeon archaeologists discovered a major wine-producing installation dating from about 700 BC. In addition to the presses and fermentation tanks, 63 rock-cut cellars were found with a storage capacity of 25,000 gallons of wine. In these cellars the wine could be kept at a constant cool temperature of 65 degrees Fahrenheit. Both royal presses and cellars are mentioned in 1 Chronicles 27:27 and Zechariah 14:10. Other activities besides the making of wine could go on at a press site (Judg. 6:11; 7:25). By the NT period both beam presses and presses with mosaic pavements were in use.

The harvesting and treading of the grapes was a time of joy and celebration (Isa. 16:10; Jer. 48:33; Deut. 16:13-15), and the image of the abundance of wine is used to speak of God's salvation and blessing (Prov. 3:10; Joel 3:18; Amos 9:13). But God's judgment is also vividly portrayed as the treading of the winepress (Isa. 63:2-3; Rev. 14:19-20).

163 ▷ GALILEE IN THE TIME OF JESUS

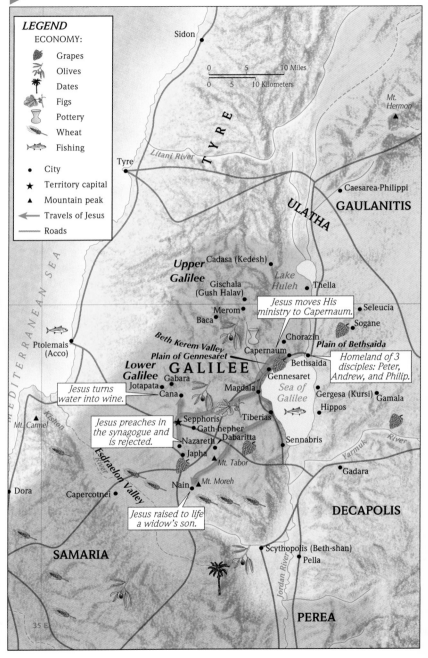

LEGEND
ECONOMY:

- Grapes
- Olives
- Dates
- Figs
- Pottery
- Wheat
- Fishing

- • City
- ★ Territory capital
- ▲ Mountain peak
- ← Travels of Jesus
- — Roads

Sidon

0   5   10 Miles
0   5   10 Kilometers

Mt. Hermon ▲

T Y R E

Litani River

Tyre

U L A T H A

Caesarea-Philippi •

GAULANITIS

M E D I T E R R A N E A N   S E A

Upper Galilee

Cadasa (Kedesh) •

Lake Huleh

Thella •

Gischala (Gush Halav) •

Merom •

Baca •

Jesus moves His ministry to Capernaum.

Seleucia •

Sogane •

Chorazin •

Plain of Bethsaida

Beth Kerem Valley

Plain of Gennesaret

Capernaum •

Ptolemais (Acco) •

Lower Galilee

G A L I L E E

Gabara •

Bethsaida •

Homeland of 3 disciples: Peter, Andrew, and Philip.

Jotapata •

Gennesaret

Cana •

Magdala •

Sea of Galilee

Jesus turns water into wine.

Gergesa (Kursi) •

Gamala •

Mt. Carmel ▲

Sepphoris ★

Gath-hepher •

Tiberias •

Hippos •

Kishon River

Jesus preaches in the synagogue and is rejected.

Nazareth •

Dabaritta •

Japha •

▲ Mt. Tabor

Sennabris •

Yarmuk River

Esdraelon Valley

Dora •

Capercotnei •

Nain •

▲ Mt. Moreh

Gadara •

Jesus raised to life a widow's son.

DECAPOLIS

SAMARIA

Scythopolis (Beth-shan) •

Pella •

35 E

Jordan River

PEREA

John 2:1-2

On the third day a wedding took place in Cana of Galilee. Jesus' mother was there, and Jesus and His disciples were invited to the wedding as well.

 Harbor at Tyre showing ancient Phoenician harbor (facing northwest).

Mark 7:24-30

He got up and departed from there to the region of Tyre and Sidon. He entered a house and did not want anyone to know it, but He could not escape notice. Instead, immediately after hearing about Him, a woman whose little daughter had an unclean spirit came and fell at His feet. Now the woman was Greek, a Syrophoenician by birth, and she kept asking Him to drive the demon out of her daughter. He said to her, "Allow the children to be satisfied first, because it isn't right to take the children's bread and throw it to the dogs." But she replied to Him, "Lord, even the dogs under the table eat the children's crumbs." Then He told her, "Because of this reply, you may go. The demon has gone out of your daughter." When she went back to her home, she found her child lying on the bed, and the demon was gone.

164▶ THE MINISTRY OF JESUS BEYOND GALILEE

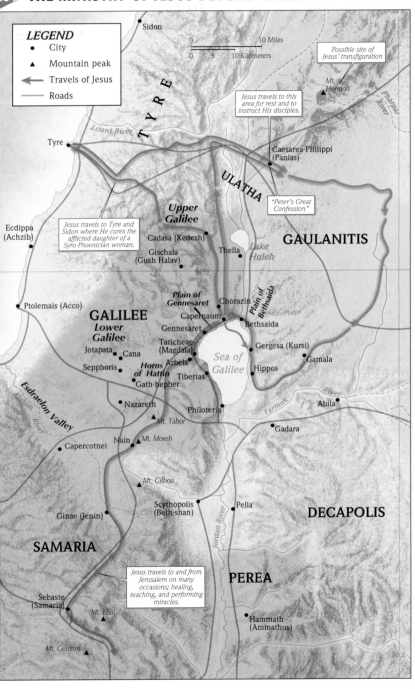

LEGEND
- • City
- ▲ Mountain peak
- ← Travels of Jesus
- — Roads

0   5   10 Miles
0   5   10 Kilometers

Sidon

TYRE

Litani River

Mt. Hermon

Possible site of Jesus' transfiguration

Pharpar River

Jesus travels to this area for rest and to instruct His disciples.

Tyre

Caesarea-Philippi (Panias)

ULATHA

"Peter's Great Confession"

Ecdippa (Achzib)

Upper Galilee

Jesus travels to Tyre and Sidon where He cures the afflicted daughter of a Syro-Phoenician woman.

Cadasa (Kedesh)

GAULANITIS

Gischala (Gush Halav)

Thella

Lake Huleh

Ptolemais (Acco)

GALILEE
Lower Galilee

Plain of Gennesaret

Chorazin

Plain of Bethsaida

Capernaum

Bethsaida

Gennesaret

Jotapata   Cana

Taricheae (Magdala)

Gergesa (Kursi)

Gamala

Sepphoris

Arbela

Horns of Hattin

Sea of Galilee

Hippos

Tiberias

Gath-hepher

Esdraelon Valley

Kishon River

Nazareth

Philoteria

Yarmuk River

Abila

Mt. Tabor

Nain   Mt. Moreh

Capercotnei

Gadara

Mt. Gilboa

DECAPOLIS

Scythopolis (Beth-shan)

Pella

Ginae (Jenin)

Jordan River

SAMARIA

Jesus travels to and from Jerusalem on many occasions; healing, teaching, and performing miracles.

PEREA

Sebaste (Samaria)

Mt. Ebal

Hammath (Ammathus)

Mt. Gerizim

165 JESUS' JOURNEYS FROM GALILEE TO JUDEA

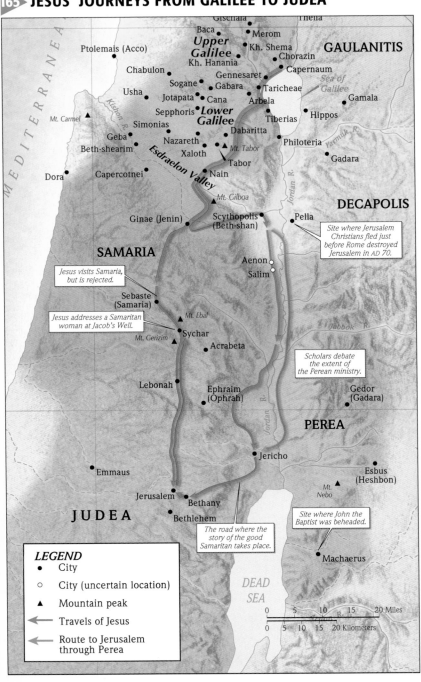

Site where Jerusalem Christians fled just before Rome destroyed Jerusalem in AD 70.

Jesus visits Samaria, but is rejected.

Jesus addresses a Samaritan woman at Jacob's Well.

Scholars debate the extent of the Perean ministry.

The road where the story of the good Samaritan takes place.

Site where John the Baptist was beheaded.

LEGEND
- City
- City (uncertain location)
- ▲ Mountain peak
- ← Travels of Jesus
- ← Route to Jerusalem through Perea

John 4:3-5
He left Judea and went again to Galilee. He had to travel through Samaria, so He came to a town of Samaria called Sychar near the property that Jacob had given his son Joseph.

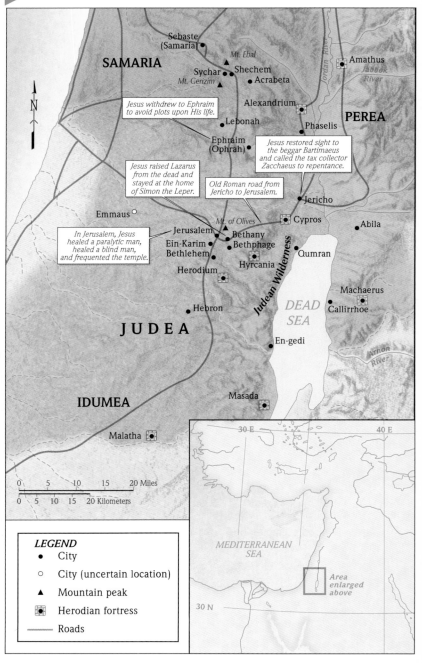

166 JESUS IN JUDEA AND JERUSALEM

SAMARIA

Sebaste (Samaria)

Mt. Ebal

Sychar • • Shechem
Mt. Gerizim • Acrabeta

N

Amathus

Jabbok River

Alexandrium

PEREA

Jesus withdrew to Ephraim
to avoid plots upon His life.

Lebonah

Phaselis

Ephraim (Ophrah) •

Jesus restored sight to
the beggar Bartimaeus
and called the tax collector
Zacchaeus to repentance.

Jesus raised Lazarus
from the dead and
stayed at the home
of Simon the Leper.

Old Roman road from
Jericho to Jerusalem.

Jericho

Emmaus °

Cypros

Mt. of Olives

Abila

In Jerusalem, Jesus
healed a paralytic man,
healed a blind man,
and frequented the temple.

Jerusalem

Bethany

Ein-Karim • • Bethphage
Bethlehem

Hyrcania

Qumran

Herodium

Judean Wilderness

DEAD SEA

Machaerus
Callirrhoe

Hebron

JUDEA

En-gedi

Arnon River

IDUMEA

Masada

Malatha

0   5   10   15   20 Miles
0   5   10   15   20 Kilometers

30 E   40 E

MEDITERRANEAN SEA

Area
enlarged
above

30 N

LEGEND
- • City
- ○ City (uncertain location)
- ▲ Mountain peak
- ⬛ Herodian fortress
- — Roads

Luke 19:1-2

He entered Jericho and was passing through. There was a man
named Zacchaeus who was a chief tax collector, and he was rich.

167 RECONSTRUCTION OF JERUSALEM

KEY

1. The temple (Herod's temple)
2. Women's court
3. The Soreg
4. The Court of the Gentiles
5. Royal Porch
6. Eastern Gate (the present-day Golden Gate)
7. Antonia Fortress
8. The Double Gate (the Western Huldah Gate)
9. The Triple Gate (the Eastern Huldah Gate)
10. Monumental Herodian Staircase (sections still remain today)
11. The City of David (established by David, the oldest part of the city)
12. Earliest defense wall (destroyed and constructed many times)
13. Heroidan outer defense wall around the expanded city
14. Herodian wall separating the Upper City (or affluent district) from the Lower City (or lower economic district)
15. The Second North Wall (possible location)
16. Garden of Gethsemane (the west side of the Mount of Olives)
17. Mount of Olives
18. Kidron Valley
19. Gihon Spring

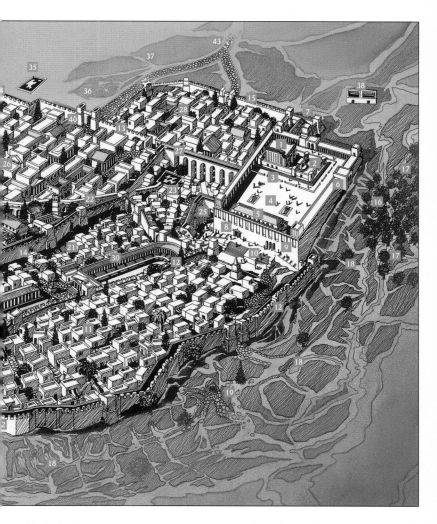

20. Pool of Siloam
21. Tyropoeon Valley (Lower City)
22. Herodian aqueduct (possible location)
23. Shops and marketplace of Jesus' day
24. Additional shops and marketplace (probably added at a later time)
25. Staircase (Robinson's Arch) leading up from the Lower City
26. Upper City
27. Causeway (Wilson's Arch) leading from the Upper City to the Temple
28. Residential houses
29. Roman Theater (structure mentioned by Josephus but whose location remains unverified)

30. Hippodrome (structure mentioned by Josephus but whose location remains unverified)
31. Herod's Palace
32. Phasael Tower
33. Mariamne Tower
34. Hippicus Tower
35. Sheep Pool
36. Traditional Golgotha (Calvary)
37. Traditional tomb of Jesus
38. Pool of Bethesda
39. Hinnon Valley
40. Gennath Gate
41. Serpent's Pool
42. Road to the Dead Sea
43. Road to Sebaste (Samaria)

168▶ JERUSALEM IN THE NEW TESTAMENT PERIOD

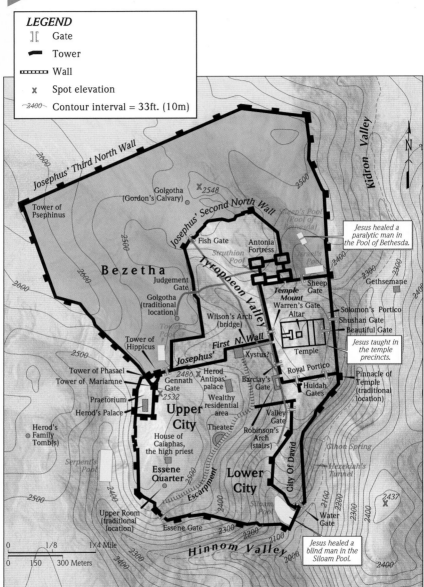

LEGEND

- ⅠⅠ Gate
- ▬ Tower
- ▥▥▥▥ Wall
- x Spot elevation
- ⌒2400⌒ Contour interval = 33ft. (10m)

Josephus' Third North Wall

Tower of Psephinus

Golgotha (Gordon's Calvary)

x 2548

Josephus' Second North Wall

Fish Gate

Antonia Fortress

Struthion Pool

Sheep's Pool (Pool of Bethesda)

Israel's Pool

Jesus healed a paralytic man in the Pool of Bethesda.

Bezetha

Judgement Gate

Golgotha (traditional location)

Tyropoeon Valley

Temple Mount

Warren's Gate

Altar

Sheep Gate

Gethsemane

Solomon's Portico

Shushan Gate

Beautiful Gate

Wilson's Arch (bridge)

Tower of Hippicus

First N. Wall

Josephus'

Xystus?

Temple

Jesus taught in the temple precincts.

Tower of Phasael
Tower of Mariamne

Gennath Gate

x 2486 Herod Antipas' palace

Barclay's Gate

Royal Portico

Pinnacle of Temple (traditional location)

Praetorium

Herod's Palace

x 2532

Wealthy residential area

Huldah Gates

Herod's Family Tomb(s)

Upper City

House of Caiaphas, the high priest

Theater

Valley Gate

Robinson's Arch (stairs)

City Of David

Gihon Spring

Hezekiah's Tunnel

Serpent's Pool

Essene Quarter

Lower City

x 2437

Escarpment

Siloam Pool

Upper Room (traditional location)

Essene Gate

Water Gate

Jesus healed a blind man in the Siloam Pool.

Hinnom Valley

Kidron Valley

N

0 ___ 1/8 ___ 1/4 Mile
0 ___ 150 ___ 300 Meters

169 THE POOL OF BETHESDA AT JERUSALEM

John 5:1-9

After this, a Jewish festival took place, and Jesus went up to Jerusalem. By the Sheep Gate in Jerusalem there is a pool, called Bethesda in Hebrew, which has five colonnades. Within these lay a multitude of the sick—blind, lame, and paralyzed [—waiting for the moving of the water, because an angel would go down into the pool from time to time and stir up the water. Then the first one who got in after the water was stirred up recovered from whatever ailment he had]. One man was there who had been sick for 38 years. When Jesus saw him lying there and knew he had already been there a long time, He said to him, "Do you want to get well?"

"Sir," the sick man answered, "I don't have a man to put me into the pool when the water is stirred up, but while I'm coming, someone goes down ahead of me." "Get up," Jesus told him, "pick up your bedroll and walk!"

Instantly the man got well, picked up his bedroll, and started to walk.

170 ▶ FLOOR PLAN OF HEROD'S TEMPLE

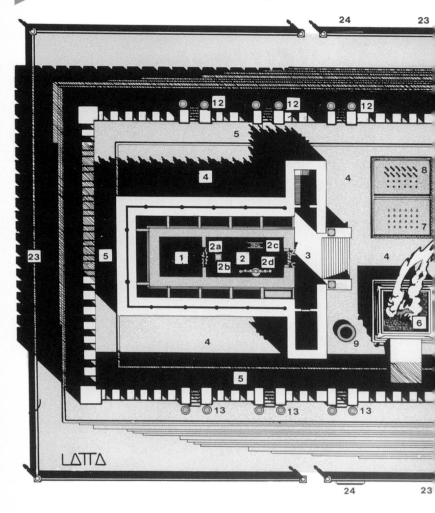

LATTA

Herod's temple (20 BC–AD 70) was begun in the 18th year of King Herod the Great's reign (37–4 BC). According to Josephus, the first-century Jewish historian, Herod's temple was constructed after removing the old foundations. The old edifice, Zerubbabel's temple, was a modest restoration of the temple of Solomon destroyed by the Babylonian conquest. The central building was completed in just two years—without any interruption of the temple services. The surrounding buildings and spacious courts, considerably enlarged, were not completed until AD 64. The temple was destroyed by the Romans under the command of Titus during the second Jewish revolt in AD 70.

KEY

1. Holy of holies (where the ark of the covenant and the giant cherubim were once enshrined)
2. Holy place
2a. Veil (actually two giant tapestries hung before the entrance of the holy of holies to allow the high priest entry between them without exposing the sacred shrine. It was this veil that was "split in two" upon the death of Jesus)

2b. Altar of incense
2c. Table of shewbread
2d. Seven-branched lampstand
(Great Menorah)
3. Temple porch
4. Court of priests
5. Court of Israel (men)
6. Altar of burnt offerings
7. Animal tethering area
8. Slaughtering and skinning area
9. Laver
10. Chamber of Phinehas (storage of vestments)
11. Chamber of the bread maker
12. North gates of the inner courts

13. South gates of the inner courts
14. East (Nicanor) Gate
15. Court of women
16. Court of Nazirites
17. Court of woodshed
18. Lepers' chamber
19. Shemanyah (possible meaning "oil of Yah")
20. Women's balconies (for viewing temple activities)
21. Gate Beautiful (?)
22. Terrace
23. Soreg (three-cubit high partition)
24. Warning inscriptions to Gentiles

171 RECONSTRUCTION OF HEROD'S TEMPLE

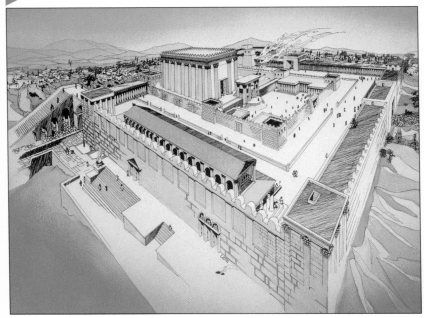

Matthew 24:1-2

As Jesus left and was going out of the temple complex, His disciples came up and called His attention to the temple buildings. Then He replied to them, "Don't you see all these things? I assure you: Not one stone will be left here on another that will not be thrown down!"

There were three historical temples in succession, those of Solomon, Zerubbabel, and Herod in the preexilic, postexilic, and NT periods. Herod's temple was really a massive rebuilding of the Zerubbabel temple, so both are called the "second temple" by Judaism. All three were located on a prominent hill north of David's capital city, which he conquered from the Jebusites (2 Sam. 5:6-7). David had acquired the temple hill from Araunah the Jebusite at the advice of the Prophet Gad to stay a pestilence from the Lord by building an altar and offering sacrifices on the threshing floor (2 Sam. 24:18-25). Chronicles identifies this hill with Mount Moriah, where Abraham had been willing to offer Isaac (2 Chron. 3:1; Gen. 22:1-14). So the temple mount today in Jerusalem is called Mount Moriah, and the threshing floor of Araunah is undoubtedly the large rock enshrined within the Dome of the Rock, center of the Muslim enclosure called Haram es-Sharif (the third holiest place in Islam, after Mecca and Medina). This enclosure is basically what is left of Herod's enlarged temple platform, the masonry of which may best be seen in its Western Wall, the holiest place within Judaism since the Roman destruction of Herod's temple in AD 70.

172► THE PASSION WEEK IN JERUSALEM

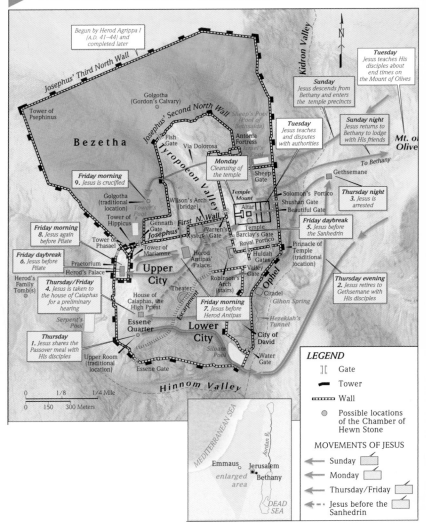

Begun by Herod Agrippa I (A.D. 41–44) and completed later

Josephus' Third North Wall

Kidron Valley

N

Tuesday
Jesus teaches His disciples about end times on the Mount of Olives

Tower of Psephinus

Golgotha (Gordon's Calvary)

Josephus' Second North Wall

Sheep's Pool (Pool of Bethesda)

Sunday
Jesus descends from Bethany and enters the temple precincts

Bezetha

Fish Gate

Via Dolorosa

Antonia Fortress

Israel's Pool

Tuesday
Jesus teaches and disputes with authorities

Sunday night
Jesus returns to Bethany to lodge with His friends

Mt. of Olives

Friday morning
9. Jesus is crucified

Golgotha (traditional location)

Tyropoeon Valley

Monday
Cleansing of the temple

Sheep Gate

To Bethany

Gethsemane

Tower's

Wilson's Arch (bridge)

Temple Mount

Altar

Solomon's Portico
Shushan Gate
Beautiful Gate

Thursday night
3. Jesus is arrested

Tower of Hippicus

Gennath Gate

First N. Wall

Josephus'

Xystus

Warren's Gate

Temple

Barclay's Gate

Royal Portico

Friday daybreak
5. Jesus before the Sanhedrin

Friday morning
8. Jesus again before Pilate

Tower of Phasael

Tower of Marianne

Herod Antipas' Palace

Huldah Gates

Pinnacle of Temple (traditional location)

Friday daybreak
6. Jesus before Pilate

Praetorium

Herod's Palace

Upper City

Valley Gate

Ophel

Thursday evening
2. Jesus retires to Gethsemane with His disciples

Herod's Family Tomb(s)

Thursday/Friday
4. Jesus is taken to the house of Caiaphas for a preliminary hearing

Theater

Robinson's Arch (stairs)

Citadel

Gihon Spring

Serpent's Pool

Friday morning
7. Jesus before Herod Antipas

Escarpment

Hezekiah's Tunnel

Thursday
1. Jesus shares the Passover meal with His disciples

House of Caiaphas, the High Priest

Essene Quarter

Lower City

City of David

Upper Room (traditional location)

Essene Gate

Siloam Pool

Water Gate

Hinnom Valley

0   1/8   1/4 Mile
0   150   300 Meters

LEGEND

Ⅱ Gate

▬ Tower

⬚⬚⬚ Wall

◉ Possible locations of the Chamber of Hewn Stone

MOVEMENTS OF JESUS

◄— Sunday

◄— Monday

◄— Thursday/Friday

◄- - Jesus before the Sanhedrin

MEDITERRANEAN SEA

Jordan R.

Emmaus Jerusalem

enlarged area

Bethany

DEAD SEA

Luke 19:41-44

As He approached and saw the city, He wept over it, saying, "If you knew this day what leads to peace—but now it is hidden from your eyes. For the days will come upon you when your enemies will build an embankment against you, surround you, and hem you in on every side. They will crush you and your children within you to the ground, and they will not leave one stone on another in you, because you did not recognize the time of your visitation.

173 ▶ PENTECOST AND THE JEWISH DIASPORA

Acts 2:1-13

When the day of Pentecost had arrived, they were all together in one place. Suddenly a sound like that of a violent rushing wind came from heaven, and it filled the whole house where they were staying. And tongues, like flames of fire that were divided, appeared to them and rested on each one of them. Then they were all filled with the Holy Spirit and began to speak in different languages, as the Spirit gave them ability for speech. There were Jews living in Jerusalem, devout men from every nation under heaven. When this sound occurred, the multitude came together and was confused because each one heard them speaking in his own language. And they were

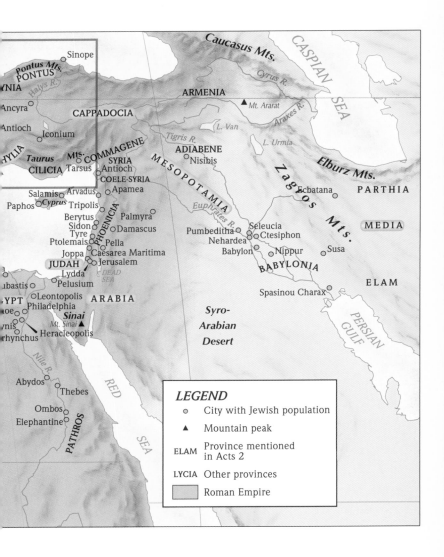

LEGEND

- ○ City with Jewish population
- ▲ Mountain peak
- **ELAM** Province mentioned in Acts 2
- **LYCIA** Other provinces
- Roman Empire

astounded and amazed, saying, "Look, aren't all these who are speaking Galileans?

"How is it that we hear, each of us, in our own native language? Parthians, Medes, Elamites; those who live in Mesopotamia, in Judea and Cappadocia, Pontus and Asia, Phrygia and Pamphylia, Egypt and the parts of Libya near Cyrene; visitors from Rome, both Jews and proselytes, Cretans and Arabs—we hear them speaking in our own languages the magnificent acts of God."

And they were all astounded and perplexed, saying to one another, "What could this be?"

174▶ SECOND PROCURATORSHIP AND THE KINGDOM OF AGRIPPA II

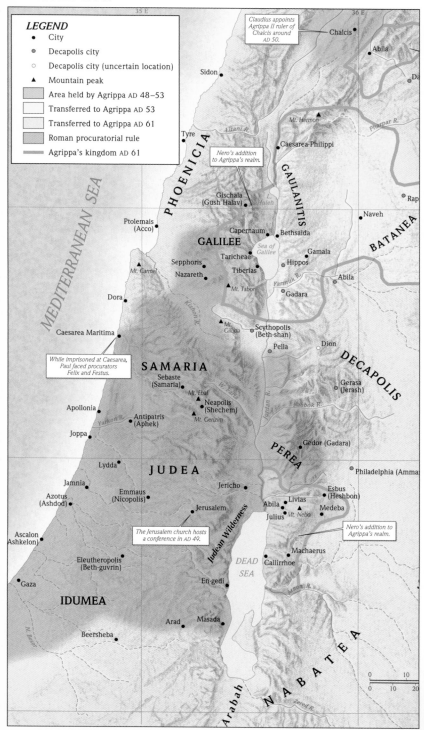

LEGEND
- City
- Decapolis city
- Decapolis city (uncertain location)
- ▲ Mountain peak
- Area held by Agrippa AD 48–53
- Transferred to Agrippa AD 53
- Transferred to Agrippa AD 61
- Roman procuratorial rule
- Agrippa's kingdom AD 61

Claudius appoints Agrippa II ruler of Chalcis around AD 50.

Nero's addition to Agrippa's realm.

While imprisoned at Caesarea, Paul faced procurators Felix and Festus.

The Jerusalem church hosts a conference in AD 49.

Nero's addition to Agrippa's realm.

MEDITERRANEAN SEA

PHOENICIA
GAULANITIS
BATANEA
GALILEE
SAMARIA
DECAPOLIS
JUDEA
PEREA
IDUMEA
NABATEA
DEAD SEA

Chalcis · Abila · Da
Sidon
Mt. Hermon
Caesarea-Philippi
Tyre
Gischala (Gush Halav) · Huleh · Rap
Naveh
Ptolemais (Acco)
Capernaum · Bethsaida
Taricheae · Gamala
Sepphoris · Sea of Galilee · Hippos
Nazareth · Tiberias · Abila
Mt. Carmel · Mt. Tabor · Gadara
Dora · Scythopolis (Beth-shan) · Dion
Caesarea Maritima · Mt. Gilboa · Pella
Sebaste (Samaria) · Gerasa (Jerash)
Apollonia · Mt. Ebal · Neapolis (Shechem) · Mt. Gerizim
Antipatris (Aphek)
Joppa
Lydda · Gedor (Gadara)
Jamnia · Jericho · Esbus (Heshbon)
Azotus (Ashdod) · Emmaus (Nicopolis) · Abila · Livias · Medeba
Jerusalem · Julius · Mt. Nebo
Ascalon (Ashkelon) · Machaerus
Eleutheropolis (Beth-guvrin) · Callirrhoe
Gaza · En-gedi
Arad · Masada
Beersheba

175 ▶ EXPANSION OF THE EARLY CHURCH IN PALESTINE

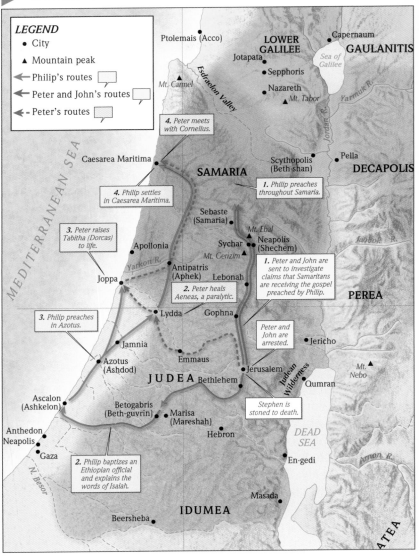

LEGEND
- • City
- ▲ Mountain peak
- ← Philip's routes
- ← Peter and John's routes
- ◄- Peter's routes

4. Peter meets with Cornelius.

4. Philip settles in Caesarea Maritima.

3. Peter raises Tabitha (Dorcas) to life.

1. Philip preaches throughout Samaria.

1. Peter and John are sent to investigate claims that Samaritans are receiving the gospel preached by Philip.

2. Peter heals Aeneas, a paralytic.

3. Philip preaches in Azotus.

Peter and John are arrested.

2. Philip baptizes an Ethiopian official and explains the words of Isaiah.

Stephen is stoned to death.

Ptolemais (Acco) — LOWER GALILEE — Capernaum — GAULANITIS — Jotapata — Sea of Galilee — Sepphoris — Mt. Carmel — Esdraelon Valley — Nazareth — Mt. Tabor — Yarmuk R. — Jordan R. — Scythopolis (Beth-shan) — Pella — DECAPOLIS — Caesarea Maritima — SAMARIA — Sebaste (Samaria) — Mt. Ebal — Jabbok R. — Apollonia — Sychar — Neapolis (Shechem) — Mt. Gerizim — Antipatris (Aphek) — Lebonah — PEREA — Yarkon R. — Joppa — Lydda — Gophna — Jamnia — Emmaus — Jericho — Mt. Nebo — Azotus (Ashdod) — JUDEA — Bethlehem — Jerusalem — Judean Wilderness — Qumran — Ascalon (Ashkelon) — Betogabris (Beth-guvrin) — Marisa (Mareshah) — DEAD SEA — Anthedon Neapolis — Hebron — Gaza — En-gedi — Arnon R. — N. Besor — Masada — IDUMEA — Beersheba — MEDITERRANEAN SEA

Acts 8:1-5

Saul agreed with putting him to death.

On that day a severe persecution broke out against the church in Jerusalem, and all except the apostles were scattered throughout the land of Judea and Samaria. But devout men buried Stephen and mourned deeply over him. Saul, however, was ravaging the church, and he would enter house after house, drag off men and women, and put them in prison.

So those who were scattered went on their way proclaiming the message of good news. Philip went down to a city in Samaria and preached the Messiah to them.

PAUL THE APOSTLE

It would be difficult to overstate the importance of Paul (Saul of Tarsus) to the development of Christianity in the first century. He wrote 13 epistles that comprise almost one-fourth of the NT. Approximately 16 chapters of the Book of Acts (13–28) focus on his missionary labors. Thus Paul is the author or subject of nearly one-third of the NT and the most important interpreter of the teachings of Christ and of the significance of His life, death, and resurrection.

▲ The Cleopatra Gate at Tarsus commemorating Mark Antony's meeting of Cleopatra at this ancient city, also home of Paul the apostle.

Early Life and Training, AD 1–35
Birth and Family Background

Paul was born in a Jewish family in Tarsus of Cilicia (Acts 22:3), probably sometime during the first decade of the first century. According to Jerome, Paul's family moved to Tarsus from Gischala in Galilee. Paul's family was of the tribe of Benjamin (Phil. 3:5), and he was named for the most prominent member of the tribe—King Saul. Paul probably came from a family of tent makers or leatherworkers and, according to Jewish custom, was taught this trade by his father. Apparently the business thrived, and Paul's family became moderately wealthy. Paul was a citizen of the city of Tarsus, "an important city" (Acts 21:39). According to one ancient writer, the property qualification for Tarsian citizenship was five hundred drachmae, a year and a half's wages.

Roman Citizenship

More importantly, Paul was born a Roman citizen. Many speculate that Paul's father or grandfather was honored with citizenship because of some special service rendered to a military proconsul. However, early Christian tradition preserved by Jerome and Photius stated that Paul's parents had been carried as prisoners of war from Gischala to Tarsus, enslaved to a Roman citizen, then freed and granted citizenship. Regardless of how Paul's parents received their citizenship, the Book of Acts states three times that he possessed it, and his citizenship was accompanied by important rights that would benefit him in his missionary labors. The Roman citizen had the right of appeal after a trial, exemption from imperial service, right to choose between a local or Roman trial, and protection from degrading forms of punishment like scourging. Paul might have carried a wax tablet that functioned as a birth certificate or certificate of citizenship in order to prove his Roman citizenship. However, most people who claimed citizenship were trusted since the penalty for impersonating a Roman citizen was death.

Rabbinic Training

Acts 22:3 shows that Paul grew up in Jerusalem. Paul used this fact to prove that he was no Diaspora Jew who was more influenced by Gentile culture than Jewish ways. He was educated in Jerusalem in the Jewish religion according to the traditions of his ancestors (Acts 22:3). The Mishnah taught: "At five years old [one is fit] for the Scripture, at ten years for the Mishnah, at thirteen [for the fulfilling of] the commandments, at fifteen for the Talmud, at eighteen for the bride-chamber, at twenty for pursuing a calling, at thirty for authority." This is probably a fairly accurate description of the regimen of training that Paul experienced. Acts 22 says that Paul was trained by Rabbi Gamaliel I, the member of the Sanhedrin mentioned in Acts 5:33-39. Gamaliel was a leading Jewish teacher in Paul's day. The Mishnah mentions Gamaliel I frequently and expresses many of his opinions. Gamaliel was listed among 13 great rabbis whose deaths marked the decline of Judaism: "When Rabbi Gamaliel the Elder died, the glory of the Law ceased and purity and abstinence died." The passage implies that Gamaliel was as renowned for his high moral standards as for his interpretation of the Scriptures. Paul quickly excelled as a Jewish rabbinical student. As Paul says in Galatians 1:14, "I advanced in Judaism beyond many contemporaries among my people, because I was extremely zealous for the traditions of my ancestors." In Philippians 3 Paul describes himself as "circumcised the eighth day; of the people of Israel, of the tribe of Benjamin, a Hebrew born of Hebrews; as to the law, a Pharisee; as to zeal, persecuting the church; as to the righteousness that is in the law, blameless." In Acts 26:5 Paul again identifies himself with the sect of the Pharisees. His father had also been a Pharisee (Acts 23:6).

Persecution of Christians

As an ideal Pharisee Paul was probably active as a Jewish missionary winning Gentiles as proselytes. He may have been like the Pharisees Jesus described who traveled "over land and sea to make one convert" (Matt. 23:15). Paul's words "If I still preach circumcision" may allude to his past as a Jewish missionary (Gal. 5:11). Paul, more than his mentor Gamaliel (Acts 5:34-39), recognized the serious threat that the followers of Jesus posed to the traditional Jewish religion. The Mishnah taught that a Jewish male was ready for a position of authority at age 30. Thus Paul was probably in his thirties when he, with authorization from the chief priest, began to imprison believers first in the synagogues of Jerusalem and then later in Damascus. Perhaps Paul's clearest description of persecution is found in Acts 26:9-11, "I myself supposed it was necessary to do many things in opposition to the name of Jesus the Nazarene. This I actually did in Jerusalem, and I locked up many of the saints in prison, since I had received authority for that from the chief priests. When they were put to death, I cast my vote against them. In all the synagogues I often tried to make them blaspheme by punishing them. Being greatly enraged at them, I even pursued them to foreign cities." Some believe this reference to casting a vote (literally "casting a pebble"—black for no or white for yes) implies that Paul was a member of the Sanhedrin. However, it is difficult to imagine that Paul would not have explicitly stated this especially on those occasions in which he highlights his devout Jewish pedigree. Most commentators thus take the statement as a metaphor implying that Paul consented to the execution of believers or suggest that he was a member of a committee appointed by the Sanhedrin and vested with this authority. Paul's initial and adamant rejection of Jesus as the Messiah may largely have been motivated by Jesus' ignoble death. Death by crucifixion was indicative of divine curse (Deut. 21:23). Certainly the Messiah could not have died under the curse of God. But when Paul wrote his first epistle, this death curse was recognized as the grounds for substitutionary atonement (Gal. 3:10-14). In 1 Corinthians 1 Paul explained that the idea of a crucified Messiah was a stumbling block to the Jews. Probably Paul was speaking from his own past experience.

▲ Wall of the New Testament period in Damascus from which Paul escaped to begin his ministry.

Paul's Conversion (p. 358)

While Saul was on his way to Damascus to arrest and imprison believers there, the resurrected and glorified Christ appeared to him with blinding radiance. Christ's words "It is hard for you to kick against the goads" indicate that God had already begun His convicting work earlier. Like an ox kicking against a goad in the hand of the ox driver, Paul had been resisting divine guidance and leadership resulting in his own harm and pain. At the appearance of Christ, Saul immediately surrendered to His authority and went into the city to await further orders. There his blindness was healed, received the Holy Spirit, and accepted believer's baptism. No doubt Ananias shared with Paul the message that the Lord had given him in a vision: "This man is My chosen instrument to carry My name before Gentiles, kings, and the sons of Israel. I will certainly show him how much he must suffer for My name!" Paul spent a few days with the disciples in Damascus.

Ruins of Antioch of Syria on hill above the modern town of Antakya, Turkey. It was from Antioch that Paul's mission to the Gentiles was launched.

Paul's Missionary Travels (AD 35–61)

Early Travels

Soon after his conversion, Paul traveled to Arabia where he began evangelization of the Nabatean Arabs (Gal. 1:17; 2 Cor. 11:32-33) and probably experienced his first opposition to the gospel from political authorities. He then returned to Damascus where he began to go into the synagogues to preach the message that had been revealed to him on the Damascus road: Jesus is the Son of God and the promised Messiah. The Jews in Damascus watched the city gates in order to kill Paul and he had to escape through a window in the wall by being lowered in a basket (Acts 9:22-25).

Paul then traveled to Jerusalem. Church leaders were initially suspicious of Paul but Barnabas intervened in his behalf (Acts 9:26-30; Gal. 1:18). After 15 days in Jerusalem, visiting with Peter and James, the Lord's brother, Paul returned to Tarsus evangelizing Syria and Cilicia for several years. Doubtless he heard them describe Jesus' life and teachings, though Paul's gospel was already clearly defined even before this visit. While in Syria, Barnabas contacted Paul and invited him to become involved in the Antioch church, where large numbers of Gentiles were responding to the gospel. The church at Antioch collected money to carry to the believers who suffered in Judea during a period of famine. Barnabas and Paul were chosen by the church to carry the gift to Jerusalem (Acts 11:27-30). This probably was the occasion of the conference described by Paul in Galatians 2:1-10. Many equate this with the Jerusalem Council (Acts 15), but if Galatians were written after an official ruling by the apostles, Paul would only have to display the letter from the apostles to discredit the Judaizers. Furthermore, this conference (Gal. 2:1-10) appears to have been a private meeting rather than a public affair. The pillars of the Jerusalem church, Peter, John, and James the brother of Jesus, approved the no-Law gospel preached by Paul and his focus on Gentile evangelism.

The tell of Lystra near the Turkish village Khatyn Serai.

First Missionary Journey (p. 359)

Paul and Barnabas soon began their first missionary journey, traveling through Cyprus and Anatolia probably during the years AD 47–48. The missionary team carried the gospel to the cities of Pisidian Antioch, Iconium, Lystra, and Derbe. These cities were located in the Roman province of Galatia, and it is probably these churches in south Galatia to which the epistle to the Galatians is addressed. Galatians was probably written during this journey.

Jerusalem Council

When Paul returned to Antioch from the first missionary journey, he found himself embroiled in controversy over requirements for

Gentile salvation. Peter and even Barnabas were vacillating on the issue of Jew-Gentile relationships. Even worse, some false teachers from the Jerusalem church had infiltrated congregations in Antioch and were teaching "unless you are circumcised according to the custom taught by Moses, you cannot be saved." The church appointed Paul and Barnabas to go to Jerusalem and settle the matter. A council was convened in AD 49 that included the missionary team, those who insisted upon circumcision as a requirement for salvation, and the apostles. The Apostle Peter and James the brother of Jesus spoke in defense of Paul's Law-free gospel, and a letter was sent to the Gentile churches confirming the official view. Paul returned to Antioch and remained there from 49 to 51.

Second Missionary Journey (p. 360)

The second missionary journey carried Paul through Macedonia and Achaia in AD 50–52. Paul and Barnabas parted company early in this journey in a disagreement about the participation of Barnabas's nephew John Mark. Mark had abandoned the team on the first journey (Acts 15:38). Paul took Silas and established churches in Philippi, Thessalonica, and Berea. Barnabas went with John Mark. Paul also spent 18 months in Corinth strengthening a fledgling church there. Four of Paul's letters are addressed to churches known from this second journey. Most scholars believe that 1 and 2 Thessalonians were written during this journey.

Overlooking Berea in Macedonia. This is the city to which Paul escaped after the Jews of Thessalonica sought to harm him.

The theater at Ephesus was built in the third century BC.

Third Missionary Journey (p. 364)

Paul's third missionary journey (AD 53–57) focused on the city of Ephesus where Paul spent the better part of three years. Toward the end of this journey Paul worked hard to collect another relief offering for Jerusalem believers. Paul wrote 1 and 2 Corinthians and Romans during this journey.

Panorama from atop ancient Corinth. Roman walls are joined with walls from the period of the Crusades.

Final Years

Paul carried the relief offering to Jerusalem. While in the temple performing a ritual to demonstrate his Jewish faithfulness to some of the Jerusalem believers, Jewish opponents incited a riot, and Paul was arrested (AD 57). Paul was sent to Caesarea to stand trial before the procurator Felix. After two years of procrastination on the part of his detainers, Paul finally appealed to the Roman emperor for trial. After arriving in Rome Paul spent two years under house arrest awaiting his trial. Paul wrote Philemon, Colossians, Ephesians, and Philippians during this first Roman imprisonment.

The record of Acts ends at this point so information as to the outcome of the trial is sketchy. Early church tradition suggests that Paul was acquitted (ca. AD 63) or exiled and fulfilled the dream expressed in Romans 15:23-29 of carrying the gospel to Spain (AD 63–67). Paul probably wrote 1 and 2 Timothy and Titus during the period between his acquittal and a second Roman imprisonment. According to church tradition Paul was arrested again and subjected to a harsher imprisonment. He was condemned by the emperor Nero and beheaded with the sword at the third milestone on the Ostian Way, at a place called Aquae Salviae, and lies buried on the site covered by the basilica of St. Paul outside the Walls. His execution probably occurred in AD 67.

Head of Nero, Roman emperor from AD 54 to 68. Both Paul and Peter died in the wake of the severe persecution launched by Nero.

Paul's Appearance

No biblical record of the appearance of Paul or his physical condition exists. We know that he must have been a hearty individual to endure the abuses and trials that he suffered as an apostle (2 Cor. 11:23-29). He was evidently the victim of some serious eye disease (Gal. 4:12-16). This may account for his characteristically large signature appended to letters which were penned by a secretary (Gal 6:11). The earliest description of Paul's appearance appears in a book from the NT Apocrypha which says that Paul was "a man small of stature, with a bald head and crooked legs, in a good state of body, with eyebrows meeting and nose somewhat hooked, full of friendliness; for now he appeared like a man, and now he had the face of an angel." The writer attributes the description of Paul to Titus, and it may have some historical basis. Although it sounds unflattering to moderns, several of the physical features mentioned were considered to be traits of the ideal Roman.

Paul's Gospel

Paul's gospel indicted all humanity for the crime of rejecting God and His rightful authority. Under the influence of Adam's sin, mankind plunged into the depths of depravity so that they were utterly unable to fulfill the righteous demands of God (Rom. 1:18-32; 3:9-20; 9:12-19) and deserved only the wrath of God (Rom. 1:18; 2:5-16). The sinner was alienated from God and at enmity with Him (Col. 1:21). Consequently, the sinner's only hope was the gospel which embodied God's power to save those who had faith in Christ (Rom. 1:16). The focus of Paul's gospel was Jesus Christ (Rom. 1:3-4).

Paul affirmed Jesus' humanity and His deity. Christ was a physical descendent from the line of David (Rom. 1:2), came in the likeness of sinful man (Rom. 8:3), and had assumed the form of a humble obedient servant (Phil. 2:7-8). Yet He was the visible form of the invisible God (Col. 1:15), all the fullness of deity living in bodily form (Col. 2:9), the very nature of God (Phil. 1:6), and possessed the title "Lord" (Greek title for the God of the OT), the name above all names (Phil. 2:9-11). Paul believed that by virtue of His sinlessness, Jesus was qualified to be the sacrifice which would make sinners right with God (2 Cor. 5:21). In His death on the cross, Jesus became the curse for sin (Gal. 3:10-14), and the righteous died for the unrighteous (Rom. 5:6-8). Salvation is a free gift granted to believers and grounded solely in God's grace. Salvation is not dependent upon human merit, activity, or effort, but only upon God's undeserved love (Eph. 2:8-10; Rom. 6:23). Those who trust Jesus for their salvation, confess Him as Lord, and believe that God raised Him from the dead (Rom. 10:9) will be saved from God's wrath, become righteous in God's sight (Rom. 5:9), adopted as God's children (Rom. 8:15-17), and transformed by the Spirit's power (Gal. 5:22-24). At the coming of Christ, believers will be resurrected (1 Cor. 15:12-57), will partake fully of the Son's righteous character (Phil. 3:20-21), and will live forever with their Lord (1 Thess. 4:17). By his union with Christ through faith, the believer participated spiritually in Christ's death, resurrection, and ascension (Rom. 6:1-7:6; Eph. 2:4-5). Consequently, the believer has been liberated from the power of sin, death, and the Law. He is a new, though imperfect, creation that is continually being made more Christlike (Col. 3:9-10; 2 Cor. 5:17). Although the believer is no longer under the authority of the written Law, the Holy Spirit functions as a new internal law which leads him to naturally and spontaneously fulfill the Law's righteous demands (Rom. 8:1-4). As a result, the Law-free gospel does not encourage unrighteous behavior in believers. Such behavior is contrary to their new identity in Christ.

The union of believers with Christ brings them into union with other believers in the body of Christ, the church. Believers exercise their spiritual gifts in order to help one another mature, to serve Christ, and glorify Him, which is the church's highest purpose (Eph. 3:21; 4:11-13). Christ now rules over the church as its Head, its highest authority (Eph. 1:22). When Christ comes again, His reign over the world will be consummated and all that exists will be placed under His absolute authority (Phil. 2:10-11; 4:20; Eph. 1:10). He will raise the dead: unbelievers for judgment and punishment; believers for glorification and reward (2 Thess. 1:5-10).

St. Paul outside the Walls where Paul was buried.

176 PAUL'S CONVERSION AND EARLY MINISTRY

LEGEND

- City
- ▲ Mountain peak
- ✕ Pass
- ← Paul sent to Damascus
- ← Paul spends time in Arabia
- ← Paul returns to Jerusalem
- ← Paul flees from Hellenists
- ← Paul and Barnabas travel to Antioch
- ← Paul and Barnabas sent to Jerusalem
- ← Paul and Barnabas return to Antioch
- Kingdom of Agrippa I

6. Paul and Barnabas establish a strong church where believers were first called Christians.

7. Paul and Barnabas travel to Jerusalem with aid for famine.

8. Paul and Barnabas return to Antioch.

3. Paul baptized and preaches about his newfound faith.

5. Paul returns to his hometown of Tarsus.

2. Paul has a vision of Jesus and converts.

4. Paul flees to Arabia then returns to Jerusalem.

1. Paul sanctioned to arrest followers in Damascus.

Galatians 1:18-21

Then after three years I did go up to Jerusalem to get to know Cephas, and I stayed with him 15 days.

But I didn't see any of the other apostles except James, the Lord's brother. Now in what I write to you, I'm not lying. God is my witness.

Afterwards, I went to the regions of Syria and Cilicia.

177 THE FIRST MISSIONARY JOURNEY OF PAUL

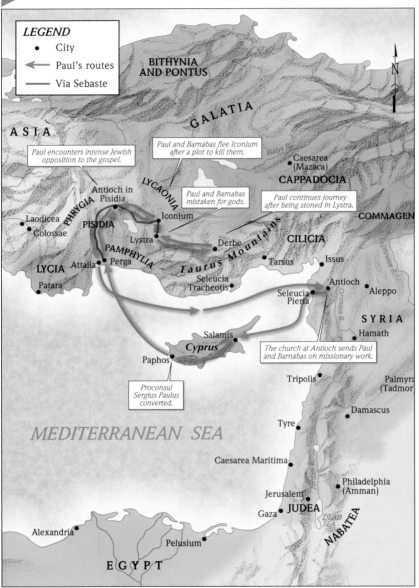

LEGEND
- City
- Paul's routes
- Via Sebaste

BITHYNIA AND PONTUS

GALATIA

ASIA

Paul encounters intense Jewish opposition to the gospel.

Paul and Barnabas flee Iconium after a plot to kill them.

Halys R.

Caesarea (Mazaca)

CAPPADOCIA

Antioch in Pisidia

LYCAONIA

Paul and Barnabas mistaken for gods.

Paul continues journey after being stoned in Lystra.

COMMAGEN

PHRYGIA

Laodicea
Colossae

PISIDIA

Iconium

Lystra

Derbe

CILICIA

Tarsus

Issus

PAMPHYLIA

Taurus Mountains

LYCIA

Attalia

Perga

Seleucia Tracheotis

Antioch

Aleppo

Patara

Seleucia Pieria

Orontes R.

Euphrates R.

SYRIA

Hamath

Salamis

Cyprus

Paphos

The church at Antioch sends Paul and Barnabas on missionary work.

Tripoli

Palmyra (Tadmor)

Proconsul Sergius Paulus converted.

Damascus

MEDITERRANEAN SEA

Tyre

Caesarea Maritima

Jordan R.

Philadelphia (Amman)

Jerusalem

Gaza

JUDEA

DEAD SEA

Alexandria

Pelusium

NABATEA

EGYPT

Acts 13:4-5

Being sent out by the Holy Spirit, they came down to Seleucia, and from there they sailed to Cyprus.

Arriving in Salamis, they proclaimed God's message in the Jewish synagogues. They also had John as their assistant.

178▶ THE SECOND MISSIONARY JOURNEY OF PAUL

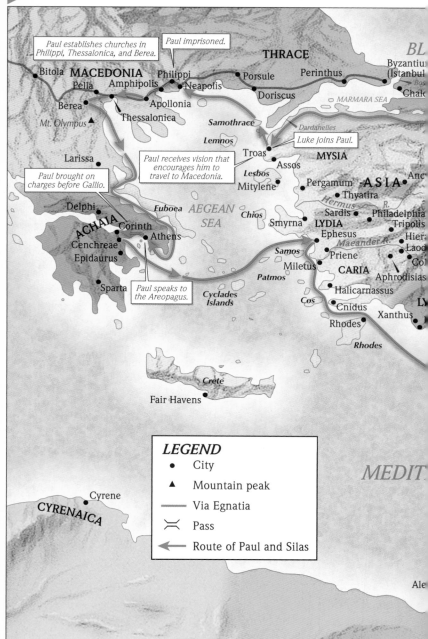

Paul establishes churches in Philippi, Thessalonica, and Berea.

Paul imprisoned.

THRACE

BL

Byzantiu
(Istanbul

Bitola **MACEDONIA** Philippi Porsule Perinthus

Pella Amphipolis Neapolis Doriscus Chal

Berea Apollonia *MARMARA SEA*

Mt. Olympus ▲ Thessalonica

Larissa *Samothrace* Dardanelles

Lemnos *Luke joins Paul.*

Paul receives vision that encourages him to travel to Macedonia. Troas **MYSIA**

Assos

Lesbos Ance

Mitylene Pergamum **ASIA**

Delphi *Euboea* *Chios* Thyatira

AEGEAN SEA Sardis Philadelphia

ACHAIA Corinth Smyrna **LYDIA** Tripolis

Cenchreae Athens Ephesus Hier

Epidaurus *Maeander R.* Lao

Samos Priene Co

Miletus **CARIA** Aphrodisias

Patmos

Sparta *Paul speaks to the Areopagus.* *Cyclades Islands* Halicarnassus Ly

Cos

Cnidus

Xanthus

Rhodes

Rhodes

Paul brought on charges before Gallio.

Crete

Fair Havens

LEGEND
- • City
- ▲ Mountain peak
- — Via Egnatia
- ⋈ Pass
- ← Route of Paul and Silas

MEDIT

Cyrene

CYRENAICA

Ale

Acts 16:6-9

They went through the region of Phrygia and Galatia and were prevented by the Holy Spirit from speaking the message in the province of Asia. When they came to Mysia, they tried to go into Bithynia, but the Spirit of Jesus did not allow them. So, bypassing

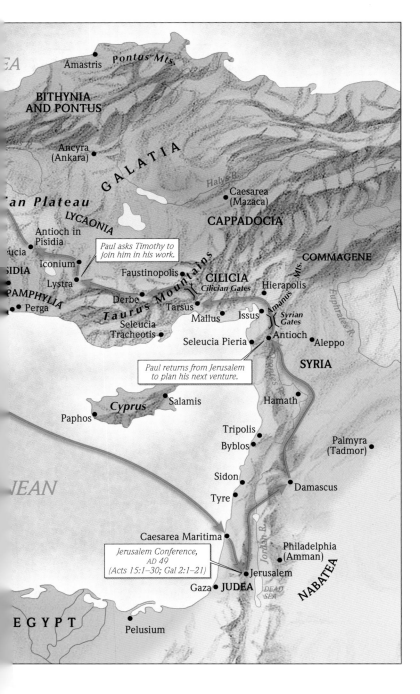

Mysia, they came down to Troas. During the night a vision appeared to Paul: a Macedonian man was standing and pleading with him, "Cross over to Macedonia and help us!"

179 ▶ FIRST-CENTURY ATHENS, GREECE

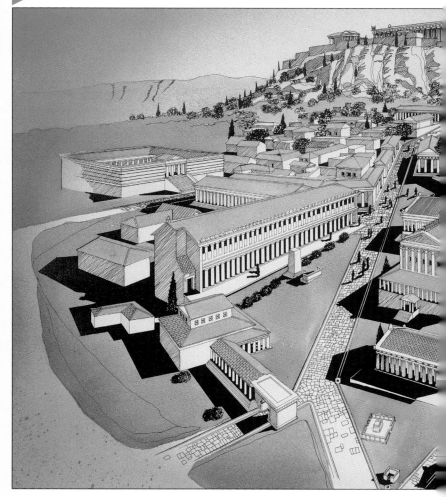

Acts 17:16-28

While Paul was waiting for them [Silas and Timothy] in Athens, his spirit was troubled within him when he saw that the city was full of idols. So he reasoned in the synagogue with the Jews and with those who worshiped God, and in the marketplace every day with those who happened to be there. Then also, some of the Epicurean and Stoic philosophers argued with him. Some said, "What is this pseudo-intellectual trying to say?"

Others replied, "He seems to be a preacher of foreign deities"— because he was telling the good news about Jesus and the resurrection.

They took him and brought him to the Areopagus, and said, "May we learn about this new teaching you're speaking of? For what you say sounds strange to us, and we want to know what these ideas mean." Now all the Athenians and the foreigners residing there spent their time on nothing else but telling or hearing something new.

Then Paul stood in the middle of the Areopagus and said: "Men of Athens! I see that you are extremely religious in every respect. For as I was passing through and observing the objects of your worship, I even found an altar on which was inscribed: TO AN UNKNOWN GOD. Therefore, what you worship in ignorance, this I proclaim to you. The God who made the world and everything in it—He is Lord of heaven and earth and does not live in shrines made by hands. Neither is He served by human hands, as though He needed anything, since He Himself gives everyone life and breath and all things. From one man He has made every nation of men to live all over the earth and has determined their appointed times and the boundaries of where they live, so that they might seek God, and perhaps they might reach out and find Him, though He is not far from each one of us. For in Him we live and move and exist, as even some of your own poets have said, 'For we are also His offspring.'"

180▶ THE THIRD MISSIONARY JOURNEY OF PAUL

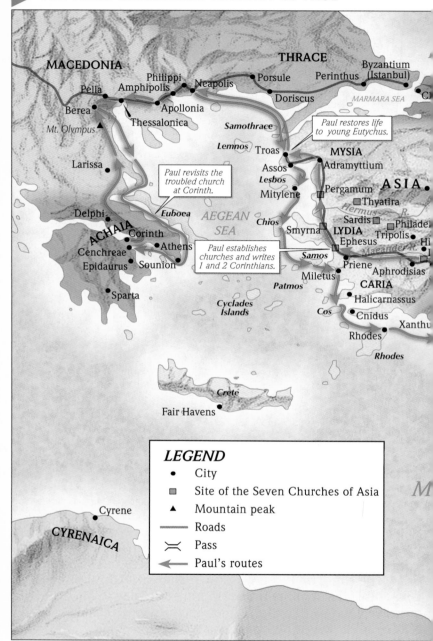

LEGEND

•	City
▪	Site of the Seven Churches of Asia
▲	Mountain peak
—	Roads
⋈	Pass
⟵	Paul's routes

Acts 20:13-17

Then we went on ahead to the ship and sailed for Assos, from there intending to take Paul on board. For these were his instructions, since he himself was going by land. When he met us at Assos, we took him on board and came to Mitylene. Sailing from there, the next day we arrived off Chios. The following day we crossed over to

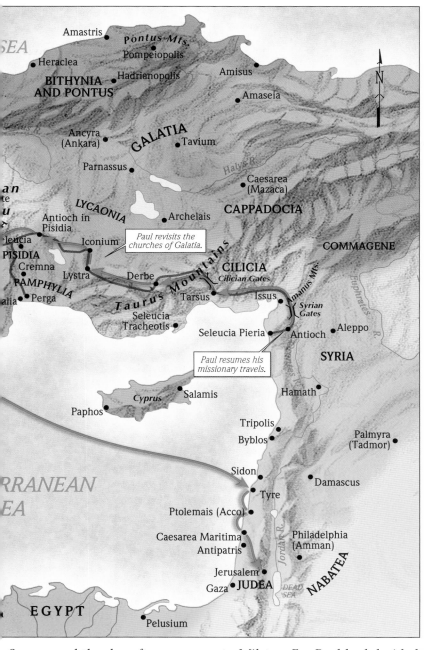

Samos, and the day after, we came to Miletus. For Paul had decided to sail past Ephesus so he would not have to spend time in the province of Asia, because he was hurrying to be in Jerusalem, if possible, for the day of Pentecost.

Now from Miletus, he sent to Ephesus and called for the elders of the church.

181 ▶ PAUL'S ARREST AND IMPRISONMENT

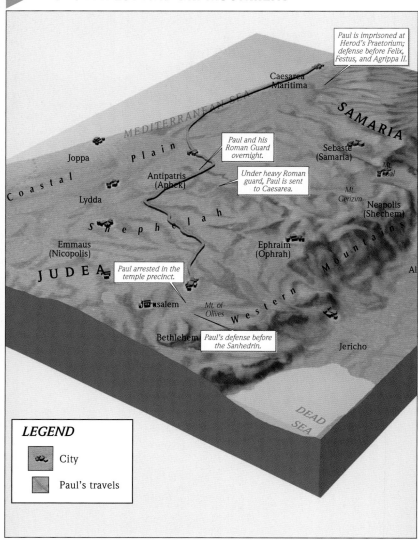

Paul is imprisoned at Herod's Praetorium; defense before Felix, Festus, and Agrippa II.

Paul and his Roman Guard overnight.

Under heavy Roman guard, Paul is sent to Caesarea.

Paul arrested in the temple precinct.

Paul's defense before the Sanhedrin.

Caesarea Maritima

SAMARIA

MEDITERRANEAN SEA

Joppa

Coastal Plain

Antipatris (Aphek)

Lydda

Sebaste (Samaria)

Mt. Ebal

Mt. Gerizim

Neapolis (Shechem)

Shephelah

Emmaus (Nicopolis)

JUDEA

Ephraim (Ophrah)

Western Mountains

Al

Jerusalem

Mt. of Olives

Bethlehem

Jericho

DEAD SEA

LEGEND

City

Paul's travels

Acts 23:31-33

Therefore, during the night, the soldiers took Paul and brought him to Antipatris as they were ordered. The next day, they returned to the barracks, allowing the cavalry to go on with him. When these men entered Caesarea and delivered the letter to the governor, they also presented Paul to him.

182 CAESAREA MARITIMA

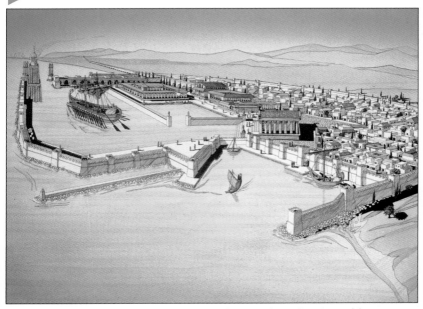

Reconstruction of Caesarea Maritima where Paul was imprisoned for two years before his journey to Rome (Acts 23:31–26:32).

The turbulent waters of the Mediterranean Sea as seen from Caesarea Maritima.

183> PAUL'S VOYAGE TO ROME

Rome — Paul spends two years preaching the gospel as he awaits his appeal to Nero.

ADRIATIC SEA

MACEDONIA

Three Taverns • Puteoli
Forum of Appius • Pompeii
Brundisium
Amphipolis
Berea • Thessa

Tarentum

TYRRHENIAN SEA

Larissa •

Messana • Rhegium

Delphi •

Sicily

Olympia •

ACHAIA

Syracuse

Sparta •

Sytris Minor

Malta

Ship lost in storm.

Ship smashes into reef and all aboard swim to shore.

MEDITERRANE

Phoenix
Caud

Cyrene •

Syrtis Major

CYRENAICA

LEGEND
- • City
- ⬊ Etesian winds
- ← Paul's routes
- — Appian Way

| 0 | 100 | 200 | 300 Miles |
| 0 | 100 | 200 | 300 Kilometers |

Acts 27:13-26

When a gentle south wind sprang up, they thought they had achieved their purpose; they weighed anchor and sailed along the shore of Crete. But not long afterwards, a fierce wind called the "northeaster" rushed down from the island.

Since the ship was caught and was unable to head into the wind, we gave way to it and were driven along. After running under the shelter of a little island called Cauda, we were barely able to get control of the skiff. After hoisting it up, they used ropes and tackle and girded the ship. Then, fearing they would run aground on the Syrtis, they lowered the drift-anchor, and in this way they were driven along. Because we were being severely battered by the storm, they began to jettison the cargo the next day. On the third day, they

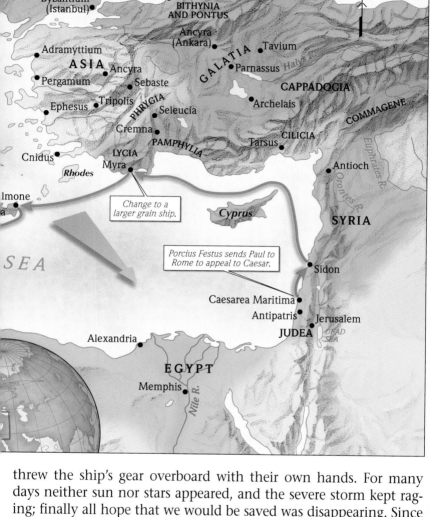

BLACK SEA

Sinope

RACE

Heraclea

Byzantium
(Istanbul)

BITHYNIA
AND PONTUS

Ancyra
(Ankara)

Tavium

Adramyttium

ASIA Ancyra

GALATIA Parnassus Halys

Pergamum

Sebaste

CAPPADOGIA

COMMAGENE

Ephesus Tripolis PHRYGIA

Archelais

Seleucia

Cremna

PAMPHYLIA

CILICIA

Tarsus

Cnidus

LYCIA

Euphrates R.

Rhodes

Myra

Antioch

Imone

Change to a
larger grain ship.

Cyprus

Oronte R.

SYRIA

SEA

Porcius Festus sends Paul to
Rome to appeal to Caesar.

Sidon

Caesarea Maritima

Antipatris Jerusalem

Alexandria

JUDEA DEAD
SEA

EGYPT

Memphis

Nile R.

threw the ship's gear overboard with their own hands. For many
days neither sun nor stars appeared, and the severe storm kept rag-
ing; finally all hope that we would be saved was disappearing. Since
many were going without food, Paul stood up among them and said,
"You men should have followed my advice not to sail from Crete
and sustain this damage and loss. Now I urge you to take courage,
because there will be no loss of any of your lives, but only of the
ship. For this night an angel of the God I belong to and serve stood
by me, saying, 'Don't be afraid, Paul. You must stand before Caesar.
And, look! God has graciously given you all those who are sailing
with you.' Therefore, take courage, men, because I believe God that
it will be just the way it was told to me. However, we must run
aground on a certain island."

184 RECONSTRUCTION OF ROME

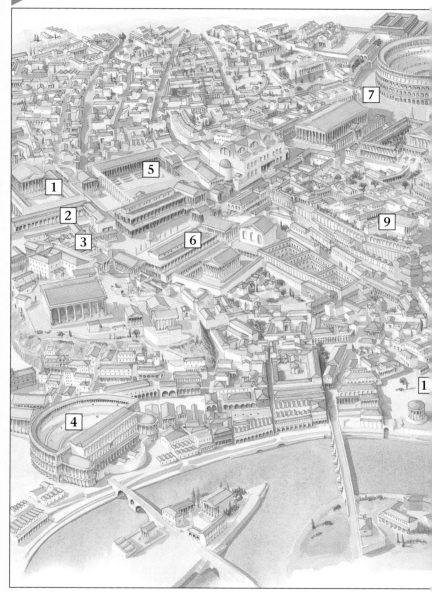

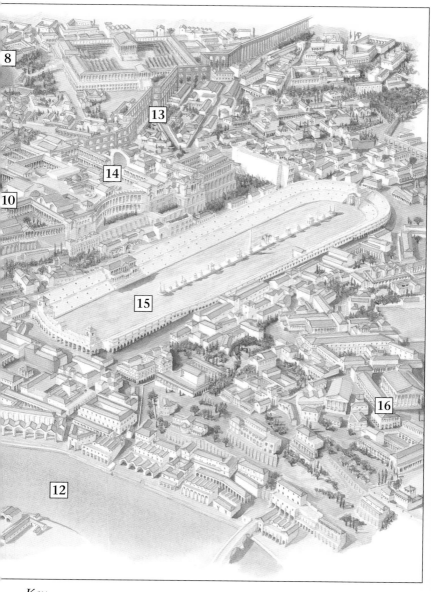

Key

1. Forum of Augustus
2. Forum of Julius
3. Temple of Vespasian
4. Theatre of Marcellus
5. Forum of Peace
6. Basilica Julia
7. Colossus of Nero
8. Flavian Amphitheatre
9. Temple of Cybel
10. Temple of Apollos
11. Temple of Hercules
12. Tiber River
13. Claudian Aquaduct
14. Domitian Hippodrome
15. Circus Maximus
16. Temple of Diana

185 THE FIRST JEWISH REVOLT

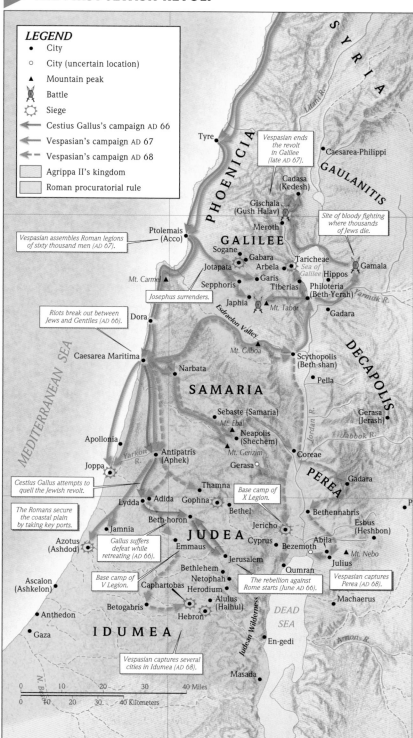

LEGEND
- City
- ○ City (uncertain location)
- ▲ Mountain peak
- ⚙ Battle
- ✿ Siege
- ← Cestius Gallus's campaign AD 66
- ← Vespasian's campaign AD 67
- ←- Vespasian's campaign AD 68
- Agrippa II's kingdom
- Roman procuratorial rule

Vespasian ends the revolt in Galilee (late AD 67).

Vespasian assembles Roman legions of sixty thousand men (AD 67).

Site of bloody fighting where thousands of Jews die.

Josephus surrenders.

Riots break out between Jews and Gentiles (AD 66).

Cestius Gallus attempts to quell the Jewish revolt.

The Romans secure the coastal plain by taking key ports.

Gallus suffers defeat while retreating (AD 66).

Base camp of X Legion.

Base camp of V Legion.

The rebellion against Rome starts (June AD 66).

Vespasian captures Perea (AD 68).

Vespasian captures several cities in Idumea (AD 68).

SYRIA

PHOENICIA

GAULANITIS

GALILEE

DECAPOLIS

SAMARIA

PEREA

JUDEA

IDUMEA

MEDITERRANEAN SEA

DEAD SEA

Tyre

Caesarea-Philippi

Cadasa (Kedesh)

Gischala (Gush Halav)

Meroth

Ptolemais (Acco)

Sogane

Gabara

Taricheae

Hippos

Gamala

Jotapata

Arbela

Sea of Galilee

Mt. Carmel ▲

Sepphoris

Garis

Tiberias

Philoteria (Beth-Yerah)

Yarmuk R.

Dora

Japhia

Mt. Tabor ▲

Gadara

Esdraelon Valley

Mt. Gilboa

Scythopolis (Beth-shan)

Caesarea Maritima

Narbata

Pella

Sebaste (Samaria)

Mt. Ebal ▲

Neapolis (Shechem)

Gerasa (Jerash)

Apollonia

Mt. Gerizim ▲

Jabbok R.

Antipatris (Aphek)

Gerasa ○

Coreae

Joppa

Yarkon R.

Jordan R.

Gadara

Thamna

Lydda

Adida

Gophna

Bethel

Bethennabris

Esbus (Heshbon)

Beth-horon

Jericho

Jamnia

Cyprus

Abila

Azotus (Ashdod)

Emmaus

Bezemoth

Mt. Nebo ▲

Jerusalem

Julius

Ascalon (Ashkelon)

Bethlehem

Netophah

Qumran

Caphartobas

Herodium

Machaerus

Betogabris

Alulus (Halhul)

Anthedon

Hebron

Judean Wilderness

En-gedi

Gaza

Arnon R.

Masada

0 10 20 30 40 Miles
0 10 20 30 40 Kilometers

186 TITUS'S CAMPAIGNS

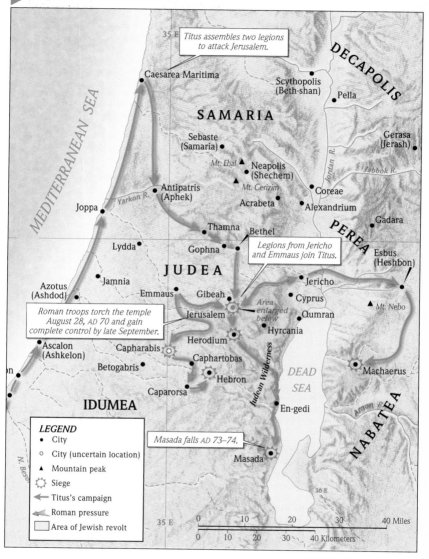

Titus assembles two legions to attack Jerusalem.

MEDITERRANEAN SEA

DECAPOLIS

Caesarea Maritima

Scythopolis (Beth-shan)

Pella

SAMARIA

Sebaste (Samaria)

Mt. Ebal

Neapolis (Shechem)

Mt. Gerizim

Gerasa (Jerash)

Jordan R.

Jabbok R.

Antipatris (Aphek)

Yarkon R.

Coreae

Acrabeta

Joppa

Alexandrium

Thamna

Bethel

Gophna

PEREA

Gadara

Legions from Jericho and Emmaus join Titus.

Lydda

JUDEA

Esbus (Heshbon)

Azotus (Ashdod)

Jamnia

Emmaus

Gibeah

Jericho

Cyprus

Mt. Nebo

Roman troops torch the temple August 28, AD 70 and gain complete control by late September.

Jerusalem

Area enlarged below

Qumran

Hyrcania

Herodium

Capharabis

Caphartobas

Ascalon (Ashkelon)

Betogabris

Hebron

Judean Wilderness

DEAD SEA

Machaerus

Caparorsa

IDUMEA

En-gedi

Amon R.

NABATEA

N. Bes

Masada falls AD 73–74.

Masada

LEGEND
- City
○ City (uncertain location)
▲ Mountain peak
⚙ Siege
← Titus's campaign
← Roman pressure
☐ Area of Jewish revolt

35 E

0   10   20   30   40 Miles

0   10   20   30   40 Kilometers

36 E

187 THE SIEGE OF JERUSALEM

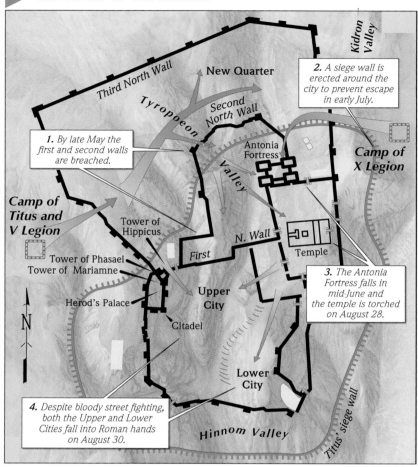

1. By late May the first and second walls are breached.

2. A siege wall is erected around the city to prevent escape in early July.

3. The Antonia Fortress falls in mid-June and the temple is torched on August 28.

4. Despite bloody street fighting, both the Upper and Lower Cities fall into Roman hands on August 30.

Third North Wall

New Quarter

Tyropoeon

Second North Wall

Antonia Fortress

Camp of X Legion

Camp of Titus and V Legion

Tower of Hippicus

Valley

N. Wall

Tower of Phasael
Tower of Mariamne

First

Temple

Herod's Palace

Upper City

Citadel

Lower City

Hinnom Valley

Titus' siege wall

Kidron Valley

N

Luke 19:41-44

As He approached and saw the city, He wept over it, saying, "If you knew this day what [would bring] peace—but now it is hidden from your eyes. For the days will come on you when your enemies will build an embankment against you, surround you, and hem you in on every side. They will crush you and your children within you to the ground, and they will not leave one stone on another in you, because you did not recognize the time of your visitation."

"Now who is there that revolves these things in his mind, and yet is able to bear the sight of the sun, though he might live out of danger? Who is there so much his country's enemy, or so unmanly, and so desirous of living, as not to repent that he is still alive? And I cannot but wish that we had all died before we had seen that holy city demolished by the hands of our enemies, or the foundations of our holy temple dug up after so profane a manner."—*Flavius Josephus, The Wars of the Jews VII.8.7*

188▶ ROMAN SIEGE TOWER

Matthew 24: 1-2
 As Jesus left and was going out of the temple complex, His disciples came up and called His attention to the temple buildings. Then He replied to them, "Don't you see all these things? I assure you: Not one stone will be left here on another that will not be thrown down!"

189 ROMAN BATTERING RAM

190 ROMAN ARCHER'S MACHINE

191 ► CHURCHES OF THE REVELATION

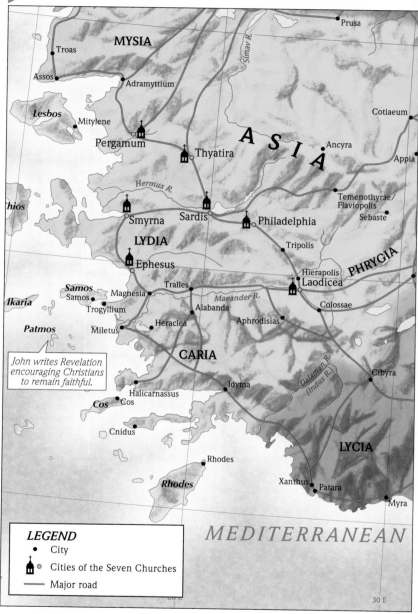

Revelation 1:19-20

Therefore write what you have seen, what is, and what will take place after this. The secret of the seven stars you saw in My right hand, and of the seven gold lampstands, is this: the seven stars are the angels of the seven churches, and the seven lampstands are the seven churches.

192 ▸ MILLENNIAL PERSPECTIVE ON REVELATION

POINT OF INTERPRETATION	AMILLENNIAL	HISTORICAL PREMILLENNIAL	DISPENSATIONAL PREMILLENNIAL
Description of View	Viewpoint that the present age of Christ's rule in the church is the millennium; holds to one resurrection and judgment marking the end of history as we know it and the beginning of life eternal	Viewpoint that Christ will reign on earth for a thousand years following His second coming; saints will be resurrected at the beginning of judgment	Viewpoint that after the battle of Armageddon, Christ will rule through the Jews for a literal thousand years accompanied by two resurrections and at least three judgments
Book of Revelation	Current history written in code to confound enemies and encourage Asian Christians; message applies to all Christians	Immediate application to Asian Christians; applies to all Christians throughout the ages, but the visions also apply to a great future event	"Unveiling" of theme of Christ among churches in present dispensation, also as Judge and King in dispensations to come
Seven candlesticks (1:13)	Churches		Churches, plus end-time application
Seven stars (1:16,20)	Pastors	Symbolizes heavenly or supernatural character of the church (some believe refers to pastors)	Pastors or saints
Churches addressed (chaps. 2–3)	Specific historical situations, truths apply to churches throughout the ages; do not represent periods of church history		Specific historical situations and to all churches throughout the ages; shows progress of churches' spiritual state until end of church age
Twenty-four elders (4:4,10; 5:8,14)	Twelve patriarchs and twelve apostles; together symbolize all the redeemed	Company of angels who help execute God's rule (or elders represent twenty-four priestly and Levitical orders)	The rewarded church; also represents twelve patriarchs and twelve apostles
Sealed book (5:1-9)	Scroll of history; shows God carrying out His redemptive purpose in history	Contains prophecy of end events of chapters 7–22	Title deed to the world
144,000 (7:4-8)	Redeemed on earth who will be protected against God's wrath	Church on threshold of great tribulation	Jewish converts of tribulation period who witness to Gentiles (same as 14:1)
Great multitude (7:9-10)	Uncountable multitude in heaven praising God for their salvation	Church, having gone through great tribulation, seen in heaven	Gentiles redeemed during tribulation period through witness of 144,000
Great tribulation (first reference in 7:14)	Persecution faced by Asian Christians of John's time; symbolic of tribulation that occurs throughout history	Period at end time of unexplained trouble, before Christ's return; church will go through it; begins with seventh seal (18:1) which includes trumpets 1–6 (8:2–14:20)	Period at end time of unexplained trouble referred to in 7:14 and described in chapters 11–18; lasts three and a half years, the latter half of seven-year period between rapture and millennium

POINT OF INTERPRETATION	AMILLENNIAL	HISTORICAL PREMILLENNIAL	DISPENSATIONAL PREMILLENNIAL
"Star" (9:4)	Personified evil	Represents an angelic figure divinely commissioned to carry out God's purpose	The leader of apostasy during the great tribulation
Forty-two months (11:2);1,260 days (11:3)	Indefinite duration of pagan desolation	A symbolic number representing period of evil with reference to last days of age	Half of seven-year tribulation period
Two witnesses (11:3-10)	Spread of gospel in first century	Two actual historical persons at end of time who witness to Israel	A witnessing remnant of Jews in Jerusalem testifying to the coming kingdom and calling Israel to repent
Sodom and Egypt (11:8)	Rome as seat of Empire	Earthly Jerusalem	
Woman (12:1-6)	True people of God under Old and New Covenants (true Israel)		Indicates Israel, not church; key is comparison with Gen. 37:9
Great red dragon (12:3)	All views identify as Satan		
Manchild (12:4-5)	Christ at His birth, life events, and crucifixion, whom Satan sought to kill	Christ, whose work Satan seeks to destroy	Christ but also the church (head and body); caught up on throne indicates rapture of church
1,260 days (12:6)	Indefinite time	Symbolic number representing period of evil with special reference to last days of age	First half of great tribulation after church is raptured
Sea beast (13:1)	Emperor Domitian, personification of Roman Empire (same as in chap. 17)	Antichrist, here shown as embodiment of the four beasts in Daniel 7	A new Rome, satanic federation of nations that come out of old Roman Empire
Seven heads (13:1)	Roman emperors	Great power, shows kinship with dragon	Seven stages of Roman Empire; sixth was imperial Rome (John's day); last will be federation of nations
Ten horns (13:1)	Symbolize power	Kings, represent limited crowns (ten) against Christ's many	Ten powers that will combine to make the federation of nations of new Rome
Earth beast (13:11)	*Concilia*, Roman body in cities responsible for emperor worship	Organized religion as servant of first beast during great tribulation period; headed by a false prophet	Antichrist, who will head apostate religion, a Jewish leader described in Daniel 11:36-45 (some identify as assistant to the Antichrist)

Note: Postmillennialism is the viewpoint that Christ's reign on earth is spiritual not physical. Christ returns after the millennium that is established by gospel preaching.

MILLENNIAL PERSPECTIVE ON REVELATION, cont.

POINT OF INTERPRETATION	AMILLENNIAL	HISTORICAL PREMILLENNIAL	DISPENSATIONAL PREMILLENNIAL
666 (13:18)	Imperfection, evil; personified as Domitian	Symbolic of evil, short of 777; if a personage meant, he is unknown but will be known at the proper time	Not known but will be known when time comes
144,00 on Mount Zion (14:1)	Total body of redeemed in heaven		Redeemed Jews gathered in earthly Jerusalem during millennial kingdom
River of blood (14:20)	Symbol of infinite punishment for the wicked	Means God's radical judgment crushes evil thoroughly	Scene of wrath and carnage that will occur in Palestine
Babylon (woman—17:5)	Historical Rome	Capital city of future Antichrist	Apostate church of the future
Beast	Domitian	Antichrist	Head of satanic federation of nations of revived Roman Empire; linked with apostate church (seventh head)
Seven mountains (17:9)	Pagan Rome, which was built on seven hills	Indicate power, so here means a succession of empires, last of which is end-time Babylon	Rome, revived at end time
Seven heads (17:7) and seven kings (17:10)	Roman emperors from Augustus to Titus, excluding three brief rules	Five past godless kingdoms; sixth was Rome; seventh would arise in end time	Five distinct forms of Roman government prior to John; sixth was imperial Rome; seventh will be revived Roman Empire
Ten horns (17:7) and ten kings (17:12)	Vassal kings who ruled with Rome's permission	Symbolic of earthly powers that will be subservient to Antichrist	Ten kingdoms arising in future out of revived Roman Empire
Waters (17:15)	People ruled by Roman Empire	Indicates complex civilization	People dominated by apostate church
Bride, wife (19:7)	Total of all the redeemed		The church; does not include Old Testament saints or tribulation saints
Marriage supper (19:9)	Climax of the age; symbolizes complete union of Christ with His people	Union of Christ with His people at His coming	Union of Christ with His church accompanied by Old Testament saints and tribulation saints
One on white horse (19:11-16)	Vision of Christ's victory over pagan Rome; return of Christ occurs in connection with events of 20:7-10	Second coming of Christ	

POINT OF INTERPRETATION	AMILLENNIAL	HISTORICAL PREMILLENNIAL	DISPENSATIONAL PREMILLENNIAL
Battle of Armageddon (19:19-21; see 16:16)	Not literally at end of time but symbolizes power of God's Word overcoming evil; principle applies to all ages	Literal event of some kind at end time but not literal battle with military weapons; occurs at Christ's return at beginning of millennium	Literal bloody battle at Armageddon (valley of Megiddo) at end of great tribulation between kings of the East and federation of nations of new Rome; they are all defeated by blast from Christ's mouth and then millennium begins
Great supper (19:17)	Stands in contrast to marriage supper		Concludes series of judgments and opens way for kingdom to be established
Binding of Satan (20:2)	Symbolic of Christ's resurrection victory over Satan	Curbing of Satan's power during the millennium	
Millennium (20:2-6)	Symbolic reference to period from Christ's first coming to His second	A historical event, though length of one thousand years may be symbolic, after Armageddon during which Christ rules with His people	A literal thousand-year period after the church age during which Christ rules with His people but especially through the Jews
Those on thrones (20:4)	Martyrs in heaven; their presence with God is a judgment on those who killed them	Saints and martyrs who rule with Christ in the the millennium	The redeemed ruling with Christ, appearing and disappearing on earth at will to oversee life on earth
First resurrection (20:5-6)	The spiritual presence with Christ of the redeemed that occurs after physical death	Resurrection of saints at beginning of millennium when Christ returns	Includes three groups: (1) those raptured with church (4:1); (2) Jewish tribulation saints during tribulation (11:11); (3) other Jewish believers at beginning of millennium (20:5-6)
Second death (20:6)	Spiritual death, eternal separation from God		
Second resurrection (implied)	All persons, lost and redeemed, rise when Christ returns in only resurrection that takes place	Nonbelievers, resurrected at end of millennium	
New heavens and earth (21:1)	A new order; redeemed earth		
New Jerusalem (21:2-5)	God dwelling with His saints in the new age after all other end-time events		
New Jerusalem (21:10– 22:5)	Same as 21:2-5		Millennial Jerusalem from which the world will be ruled; the bride as well as the home of the saints

REVELATION

Revelation was written during a time of intense persecution of Christians. The date of writing is likely the last decade of the first century during the reign of either Domitian or Trajan. Rome's arena of death, the Colosseum, was a place where Christians were pitted against lions. Construction on the Colosseum took ten years and was completed in AD 80. It seated about 55,000 spectators. The word Colosseum derives from a colossal statue that stood near the arena whose official name was the Flavian Ampitheater. Beneath the floor of the Colosseum were numerous cells which held wild animals, gladiators, convicted criminals, and Christians.

 The interior of the Colosseum at Rome showing the area beneath the arena.

▲ The famous Colosseum at Rome was built in the latter years of the first century AD.

Revelation 7:13-17

Then one of the elders asked me, "Who are these people robed in white, and where did they come from?" I said to him, "Sir, you know." Then he told me: These are the ones coming out of the great tribulation. They washed their robes and made them white in the blood of the Lamb. For this reason they are before the throne of God, and they serve Him day and night in His sanctuary. The One seated on the throne will shelter them: no longer will they hunger; no longer will they thirst; no longer will the sun strike them, or any heat. Because the Lamb who is at the center of the throne will shepherd them; He will guide them to springs of living waters, and God will wipe away every tear from their eyes.

193 PROPHECIES OF JESUS' SECOND COMING

SUBJECT	BIBLE REF.	DESCRIPTION
Certainty of Coming	Heb. 9:28	He will bring salvation.
	Matt. 16:27	He will reward according to what each has done.
	John 14:3	We will be with Him in place He prepared.
	1 Thess. 4:16	He will descend from heaven with shout and trumpet.
	2 Thess. 1:7-8	He will take vengeance on those who do not know and obey Him.
	Acts 1:11	He will return just as He ascended.
	Rev. 3:11	He is coming quickly; hold fast to faith; do not let anyone take it away.
	Rev. 22:12	He is coming with reward for every person according to what each has done.
Time Is Unknown	Matt. 24:44	Be ready; Son of Man is coming when you do not expect Him.
	Matt. 25:13	Be alert; you do not know day or hour.
	Mark 13:32	No person nor angel, not even Jesus, only the Father knows the hour of His return.
Resurrection of All Dead	Matt. 25:32	All nations will stand before Him.
	John 5:28-29	All in graves come forth; good to resurrection of life; evil to resurrection of judgment.
Judgment	Matt. 25:31-33	Son of Man will sit on throne and put sheep on His right and goats on His left.
	Rev. 14:14	Son of Man will come on cloud with sharp sickle harvesting the earth.
	2 Thess. 1:7-10	He is coming to be glorified by His saints and admired by those who have believed, but with destruction for disobedient.
	1 Cor. 4:5	Judge nothing now; the Lord will come and reveal the intentions of the hearts.
	Jude 14-15	He is coming with holy ones to convict ungodly of their ungodly deeds.
	Rev. 22:12	He is coming quickly with reward for each person.
Glorification of Those Who Believe	Mark 13:26-27	He is coming in power and glory to gather His elect to the end of the earth.
	Phil. 3:20-21	He will change our bodies to be like His glorious body by His power to subject everything to Himself.
	Col. 3:4	We will be revealed with Messiah in glory.

SUBJECT	BIBLE REF.	DESCRIPTION
Glorification of Those Who Believe (cont.)	2 Thess. 1:10	He will come to be glorified by His saints and admired by those who have believed.
	1 John 3:2	We are God's children and will be like Him when He appears.
	1 Pet. 5:2	Those who shepherd God's flock willingly will receive unfading crown of glory when the Chief Shepherd appears.
	2 Tim. 4:7	I have kept the faith so a crown of righteousness is reserved for me and for all who have loved His appearing.
	1 Thess. 4:16-18	We will always be with the Lord.
Destruction of the World	2 Pet. 3:10-13	Day of the Lord comes as thief; heavens and earth will be destroyed, but we wait for new heavens and new earth.
Delivers Kingdom to the Father	1 Cor. 15:23-28	He will put all enemies under His feet, even death, and then will subject Himself to God, all in all.
Hope of Second Coming Is Call to Obedience and Faithfulness	2 Pet. 3:14, 17-18	Make every effort to be found without spot or blemish before Him; grow in grace and knowledge of Jesus.
	Rev. 3:3,11	Remember what you have received and heard and repent; Jesus will come at hour you do not know; let no one take your crown.
	1 Thess. 3:12	Lord cause you to increase in love that He may make your hearts holy at the coming of Jesus with His saints.
Signs of Coming	Luke 21:29-36	See the signs and know the kingdom is near.
Assurance of Second Coming	John 14:27-31	Jesus gives His peace to us so that we need not be afraid; He will come again to us.
	Phil. 1:6	God will complete the good work He started in you until the day of Christ.
	James 5:7	Be patient like farmer waiting for the rains; for the coming of the Lord is getting near.
	Heb. 10:36	Be enduring to receive what was promised.
	Acts 1:10-11	No reason to gaze into heaven in wonder; Jesus will come again.
	Rev. 22:20	I am coming quickly.
Coming Revealed in Lord's Supper	1 Cor. 11:26	When you eat and drink the Supper, you proclaim the Lord's death until He comes.

194 ▶ PALESTINE FROM AD 73 TO 135

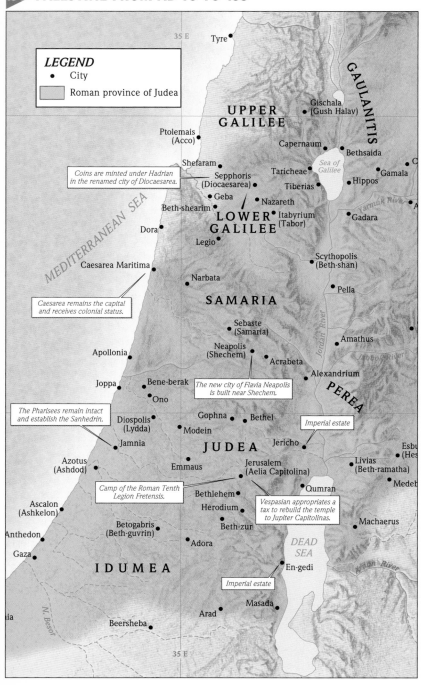

LEGEND
- City
- Roman province of Judea

Tyre

35 E

GAULANITIS

UPPER GALILEE

Gischala (Gush Halav)

Ptolemais (Acco)

Capernaum

Bethsaida

Shefaram

Taricheae

Sea of Galilee

Gamala

Coins are minted under Hadrian in the renamed city of Diocaesarea.

Sepphoris (Diocaesarea)

Hippos

Geba

Nazareth

Tiberias

Beth-shearim

LOWER GALILEE

Itabyrium (Tabor)

Gadara

Yarmuk River

Dora

Legio

Scythopolis (Beth-shan)

Caesarea Maritima

Narbata

Pella

Caesarea remains the capital and receives colonial status.

SAMARIA

Sebaste (Samaria)

Amathus

Neapolis (Shechem)

Apollonia

Acrabeta

Alexandrium

PEREA

Jordan River

Joppa

Bene-berak

The new city of Flavia Neapolis is built near Shechem.

Ono

The Pharisees remain intact and establish the Sanhedrin.

Gophna

Bethel

Diospolis (Lydda)

Modein

Imperial estate

Jamnia

JUDEA

Jericho

Esbu (Hes

Azotus (Ashdod)

Emmaus

Jerusalem (Aelia Capitolina)

Livias (Beth-ramatha)

Medeb

Camp of the Roman Tenth Legion Fretensis.

Qumran

Ascalon (Ashkelon)

Bethlehem

Herodium

Vespasian appropriates a tax to rebuild the temple to Jupiter Capitolinas.

Anthedon

Betogabris (Beth-guvrin)

Beth-zur

Machaerus

Gaza

Adora

DEAD SEA

IDUMEA

En-gedi

Arnon River

Imperial estate

N. Besor

Masada

ia

Arad

Beersheba

35 E

MEDITERRANEAN SEA

195► THE BAR KOKHBA REVOLT

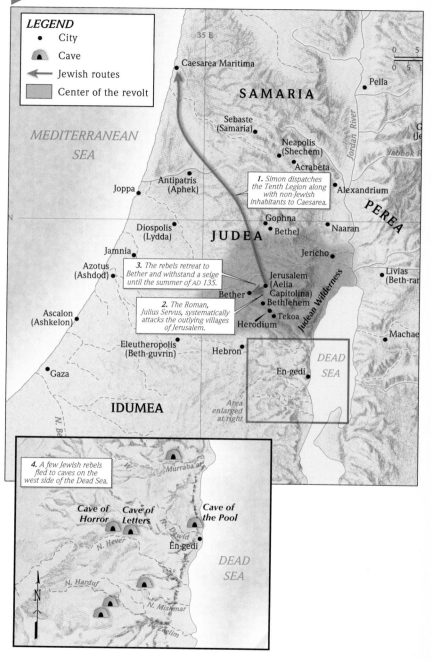

LEGEND
- • City
- ⌂ Cave
- ← Jewish routes
- ▦ Center of the revolt

1. Simon dispatches the Tenth Legion along with non-Jewish inhabitants to Caesarea.

3. The rebels retreat to Bether and withstand a seige until the summer of AD 135.

2. The Roman, Julius Servus, systematically attacks the outlying villages of Jerusalem.

4. A few Jewish rebels fled to caves on the west side of the Dead Sea.

MEDITERRANEAN SEA

SAMARIA

Caesarea Maritima

Pella

Sebaste (Samaria)

Neapolis (Shechem)

Acrabeta

Antipatris (Aphek)

Joppa

Alexandrium

PEREA

Gophna

Diospolis (Lydda)

Bethel

Naaran

JUDEA

Jamnia

Jericho

Azotus (Ashdod)

Jerusalem (Aelia Capitolina)

Bether

Bethlehem

Livias (Beth-rar

Ascalon (Ashkelon)

Tekoa

Herodium

Judean Wilderness

Machae

Eleutheropolis (Beth-guvrin)

Hebron

DEAD SEA

Gaza

En-gedi

IDUMEA

Area enlarged at right

N. Be

Murraba'at

Cave of Horror

Cave of Letters

Cave of the Pool

N. Hever

En-gedi

N. David

DEAD SEA

N. Harduf

N. Mishmar

N. Zeelim

Jordan River

Jabbok R

196 THE EXPANSION OF CHRISTIANITY IN THE SECOND AND THIRD CENTURIES AD

NORTH SEA

Eburacum

BRITANNIA
Londinium

Rhine R.

Cologna
BELGICA   GERMANIA
Trier   Mainz

Seine R.

LUGDUNENSIS

Loire R.

NORICUM

PANNONIA

Lugdunum
(Lyons)   Rhone R.
AQUITANIA   Vienna   Parentium   ILLYRICUM
(DALMATIA)

NARBONENSIS   RAETIA

Salona

Tiber R.   ITALIA   ADRIATIC
SEA

Corsica   Rome   Dyrrhach
Leon   Ostia
TARRACONENSIS   Saragossa   Antium   Apol
Ebro R.   Puteoli

Balearic Islands   Sardinia   TYRRHENIAN
SEA

rida

Corduba   Sicily
BAETICA   Carthago Nova   Syracuse

Hippo Regius   Carthage
Sitifis   Cirta   Sicca   AFRICA   Malta
Lambesis   Madaurus   Uthina
MAURETANIA   NUMIDIA   Hadrumetum   M

TRIPOLITANIA

Sahara Des

LEGEND
- City
- Site of key churches
- Territory under Roman control
- Extent of Christian influence, second century AD
- Core areas of Christianity, third century AD

0   250
0   250   500

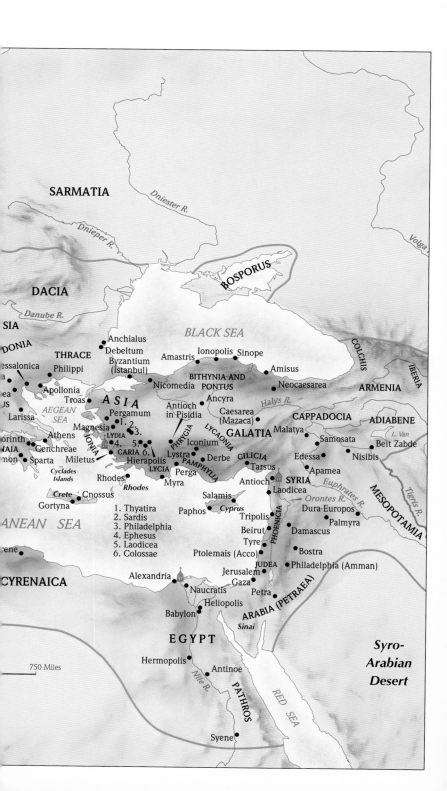

SARMATIA

Dniester R.

Dnieper R.

Volga

DACIA

BOSPORUS

Danube R.

SIA

BLACK SEA

THRACE

Anchialus
Debeltum
Byzantium
(Istanbul)

Amastris Ionopolis Sinope

COLCHIS

IBERIA

DONIA

essalonica
a

Philippi

Nicomedia

BITHYNIA AND
PONTUS

Amisus

Neocaesarea

ARMENIA

Apollonia
Troas

Antioch
in Pisidia

Ancyra

ea
US

ASIA

Caesarea
(Mazaca)

Halys R.

CAPPADOCIA

ADIABENE

*AEGEAN
SEA*

Pergamum

PHRYGIA

LYCAONIA

GALATIA

Malatya

Samosata

L. Van

Beit Zabde

Larissa

Magnesia

1. 2.
3.

orinth

Athens

LYDIA

Iconium

Edessa

Nisibis

IAIA

Cenchreae

4. 5.

Lystra Derbe

CILICIA

Apamea

non

Sparta

CARIA 6.

Hierapolis

PAMPHYLIA

Tarsus

MESOPOTAMIA

Tigris R.

Miletus

LYCIA

Perga

Euphrates R.

*Cyclades
Islands*

Rhodes

Myra

Antioch

SYRIA

Rhodes

Laodicea

Orontes R.

Dura-Europos

Crete Cnossus

Salamis

Palmyra

ANEAN SEA

Gortyna

1. Thyatira
2. Sardis
3. Philadelphia
4. Ephesus
5. Laodicea
6. Colossae

Paphos

Cyprus

Tripolis

PHOENICIA

Damascus

Beirut

Tyre

Bostra

rene

CYRENAICA

Alexandria

Ptolemais (Acco)

JUDEA

Jerusalem

Philadelphia (Amman)

Naucratis

Gaza

Petra

Heliopolis

Babylon

ARABIA (PETRAEA)

Sinai

*Syro-
Arabian
Desert*

EGYPT

750 Miles

Hermopolis

Antinoe

Nile R.

PATHROS

*RED
SEA*

Syene

197▶ ANCIENT VERSIONS OF BIBLICAL TEXT

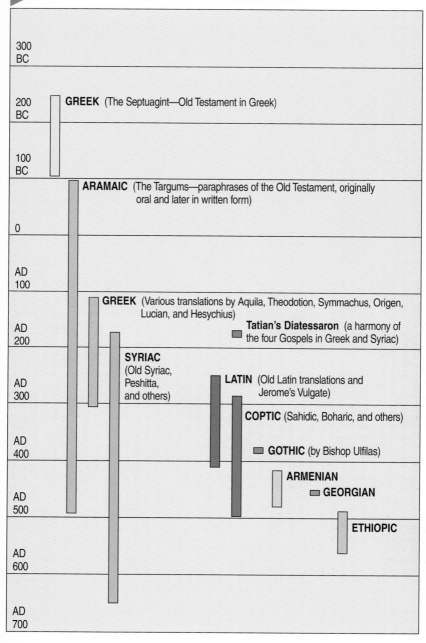

198▸ THE HEBREW CANON OF THE OLD TESTAMENT

CLASSIFICATION OF THE BOOKS	HEBREW NAMES FOR THE BOOKS	ENGLISH NAMES FOR THE BOOKS
THE LAW (Torah)	In the beginning These are the names And He called In the wilderness These are the words	Genesis Exodus Leviticus Numbers Deuteronomy
FORMER PROPHETS	Joshua Judges 1 Samuel 2 Samuel 1 Kings 2 Kings	Joshua Judges 1 Samuel 2 Samuel 1 Kings 2 Kings
LATTER PROPHETS	Isaiah Jeremiah Ezekiel The Book of the Twelve (which includes) Hosea Joel Amos Obadiah Jonah Micah Nahum Habakkuk Zephaniah Haggai Zechariah Malachi	Isaiah Jeremiah Ezekiel Hosea Joel Amos Obadiah Jonah Micah Nahum Habakkuk Zephaniah Haggai Zechariah Malachi
THE WRITINGS (HAGIOGRAPHA)	Praises Job Proverbs Ruth Song of Songs The Preacher How! Esther Daniel Ezra Nehemiah 1 The words of the days 2 The words of the days	Psalms Job Proverbs Ruth Song of Solomon Ecclesiastes Lamentations Esther Daniel Ezra Nehemiah 1 Chronicles 2 Chronicles

COMPARISON LISTS OF OLD TESTAMENT BOOKS

RABBINIC CANON 24 BOOKS	SEPTUAGINT 53 BOOKS	ROMAN CATHOLIC OLD TESTAMENT 46 BOOKS
The Law	*Law*	*Law*
Genesis	Genesis	Genesis
Exodus	Exodus	Exodus
Leviticus	Leviticus	Leviticus
Numbers	Numbers	Numbers
Deuteronomy	Deuteronomy	Deuteronomy
The Prophets	*History*	*History*
The Former Prophets		
Joshua	Joshua	Joshua
Judges	Judges	Judges
1-2 Samuel	Ruth Ruth	
1-2 Kings	1 Kingdoms (1 Samuel)	1 Samuel (1 Kingdoms)
The Latter Prophets	2 Kingdoms (2 Samuel)	2 Samuel (2 Kingdoms)
Isaiah	3 Kingdoms (1 Kings)	1 Kings (3 Kingdoms)
Jeremiah	4 Kingdoms (2 Kings)	2 Kings (4 Kingdoms)
Ezekiel	1 Paralipomena (1 Chronicles)	1 Chronicles (1 Paralipomena)
The Twelve	2 Paralipomena (2 Chronicles)	2 Chronicles (2 Paralipomena)
Hosea	1 Esdras (Apocryphal Ezra)	Ezra (1 Esdras)
Joel	2 Esdras (Ezra-Nehemiah)	Nehemiah (2 Esdras)
Amos	Esther (with Apocryphal additions)	Tobit
Obadiah	Judith	Judith
Jonah	Tobit	Esther
Micah	1 Maccabees	1 Maccabees
Nahum	2 Maccabees	2 Maccabees
Habakkuk	3 Maccabees	
Zephaniah	4 Maccabees	*Poetry*
Haggai		Job
Zechariah	*Poetry*	Psalms
Malachi	Psalms	Proverbs
	Odes (includes prayer of Manasseh)	Ecclesiastes
The Writings	Proverbs	Song of Songs
Poetry	Ecclesiastes	Wisdom of Solomon
Psalms	Song of Songs	Ecclesiasticus (The Wisdom of
Proverbs	Job	Jesus the son of Sirach)
Job	Wisdom (of Solomon)	

RABBINIC CANON 24 BOOKS	SEPTUAGINT 53 BOOKS	ROMAN CATHOLIC OLD TESTAMENT 46 BOOKS
Rolls—"the Festival Scrolls"	Sirach (Ecclesiasticus or The Wisdom of Jesus the son of Sirach)	*Prophecy*
Song of Songs		Isaiah
Ruth	Psalms of Solomon	Jeremiah
Lamentations		Lamentations
Ecclesiastes	*Prophecy*	Baruch (including Letter of Jeremiah)
Esther	The Twelve Prophets	Ezekiel
Others (History)	Hosea	Daniel
Daniel	Amos	Hosea
Ezra-Nehemiah	Micah	Joel
1–2 Chronicles	Joel	Amos
	Obadiah	Obadiah
	Jonah	Jonah
	Nahum	Micah
	Habakkuk	Nahum
	Zephaniah	Habakkuk
	Haggai	Zephaniah
	Zechariah	Haggai
	Malachi	Zechariah
	Isaiah	Malachi
	Jeremiah	
	Baruch	
	Lamentations	*Appendix*
	Letter of Jeremiah	The Prayer of Manasseh
	Ezekiel	The two apocryphal books of Esdras
	Daniel (with apocryphal additions, including the Prayer of Azariah and the Song of the Three Children, Susanna, and Bel and the Dragon)	

The Canonical Books of the Old Testament *

	Books of Law
	Books of History
	Books of Poetry and Wisdom
	Books of the Major Prophets
	Books of the Minor Prophets

* Grouped according to the Christian canon

200▶ THE APOCRYPHA

TITLES (listed alphabetically)	APPROX-IMATE DATES	LITERARY TYPES	THEMES	IN SEPTUAGINT?	IN ROMAN CATHOLIC CANON?
Baruch 60 BC	150– (composite)	Wisdom & narrative promise of hope, opposition to idolatry	Praise of wisdom, law	Yes	Yes
Bel and the Dragon	100 BC	Detective narrative at end of Daniel	Opposition to idolatry	Yes	Yes
Ecclesiasticus (Wisdom of Jesus Sirach)	180 BC in Hebrew; 132 BC Greek Translation	Wisdom, patriotism; temple worship; retribution; free will	Obedience to law; praise of patriarchs; value of wisdom	Yes	Yes
I Esdras	150	History (621–458 BC)	Proper worship; power of truth	Yes	No
2 Esdras	AD 100	Apocalypse with Christian preface & epilogue	Preexistent, dying Messiah: punishment for sin; salvation in future; inspiration; divine justice; evil	No	No
Additions to Esther (103 verses)	114 BC	Religious amplification	Prayer; worship; revelation; God's activity; providence	Yes	Yes
Letter of Jeremiah	317 BC	Homily added to Baruch based on Jer. 29	Condemn idolatry	Yes	Yes
Judith	200– 100 BC	Historical novel	Obedience to law; prayer; fasting; true worship; patriotism	Yes	Yes
1 Maccabees	90 BC	History (180–134 BC)	God works in normal human events; legitimate Hasmonean kings	Yes	Yes
2 Maccabees	90 BC	History (180–161 BC)	Resurrection; creation from nothing; miracles; punishment for sin; martyrdom; temple angels	Yes	Yes
3 Maccabees	75 BC	Festival legend	Deliverance of faithful; angels	Some mss.	No
4 Maccabees	10 BC; AD 20–54	Philosophical treatise based on 2 Macc. 6–7	Power of reason over emotions; faithfulness to law; martyrdom; immortality	Some mss.	No
Prayer of Azariah and Song of Three Young Men	100 BC	Liturgy; hymn & additions to Dan. 3:23	Praise; God's response to prayer	Yes	Yes
Prayer of Manasseh	200– 201 BC	Prayer of penitence based on 2 Kings 21:10-17 2 Chron. 33:11-19	Prayer of repentance	Yes	No
Psalm 151	?	Victory hymn	Praise to God who uses young & inexperienced	Yes	No
Susanna	100 BC	Detective story at end of Daniel	Daniel's wisdom; God's vindication of faithfulness	Yes	Yes
Tobit	200– 100 BC	Folktale	Temple attendance; tithing; charity; prayer; obedience to Jewish law; guardian angel; divine justice and retribution; personal devotion	Yes	Yes
Wisdom of Solomon	10 BC in Egypt	Wisdom personified; Jewish apologetic	Value of wisdom and faithfulness, immortality	Yes	Yes

201 ▶ STAGES IN THE DEVELOPMENT OF THE NEW TESTAMENT CANON

BOOKS OF THE CANON	Quoted by Irenaeus (ca. AD 130–200), Bishop of Lyons, in his work *Against Heresies*	Listed in the *Muratorian Canon* (ca. AD 170–210)—a Latin manuscript	Listed by Eusebius (ca. AD 260–340), in his work *Ecclesiastical History*, 3.25	Listed by Athanasius Bishop of Alexandria, Egypt, in his thirty-ninth Paschal Letter (AD 367)	List is "closed" by Council of Carthage (AD 397)
REVELATION			*		
JUDE			* *		
3 JOHN			* *		
2 JOHN					
1 JOHN			*		
2 PETER					
1 PETER			*		
JAMES					
HEBREWS					
PHILEMON					
TITUS					
2 TIMOTHY					
1 TIMOTHY					
2 THESSALONIANS					
1 THESSALONIANS					
COLOSSIANS					
PHILIPPIANS					
EPHESIANS					
GALATIANS					
2 CORINTHIANS					
1 CORINTHIANS					
ROMANS					
ACTS					
JOHN					
LUKE					
MARK					
MATTHEW					

* "Disputed Books" (not yet universally accepted)—according to Eusebius

Legend:
- LETTER BY UNKNOWN AUTHOR
- GENERAL, OR "CATHOLIC," LETTERS
- BOOK OF PROPHECY
- GOSPELS
- BOOK OF HISTORY OF THE EARLY CHURCH
- LETTERS OF PAUL (probably collected before the end of the first century)

TABLE OF WEIGHTS AND MEASURE

	BIBLICAL UNIT	LANGUAGE	BIBLICAL MEASURE	U.S. EQUIVALENT
WEIGHT	Gerah	Hebrew	1/20 shekel	1/50 ounce
	Bekah	Hebrew	1/2 shekel or 10 gerahs	1/5 ounce
	Pim	Hebrew	2/3 shekel	1/3 ounce
	Shekel	Hebrew	2 bekahs	2/5 ounce
	Litra (Pound)	Greco-Roman	30 shekels	12 ounces
	Mina	Hebrew/Greek	50 shekels	1 1/4 pounds
	Talent	Hebrew/Greek	3000 shekels, 60 minas	75 lbs/88 lbs
LENGTH	Handbreadth	Hebrew	1/6 cubit or 1/3 span	3 inches
	Span	Hebrew	1/2 cubit or 3 handbreadths	9 inches
	Cubit/Pechys	Hebrew/Greek	2 spans	18 inches
	Fathom	Greco-Roman	4 cubits	2 yards
	Kalamos	Greco-Roman	6 cubits	3 yards
	Stadion	Greco-Roman	1/8 milion or 400 cubits	1/8 mile
	Milion	Greco-Roman	8 stadia	1,620 yards
DRY MEASURE	Xestēs	Greco-Roman	1/2 cab	1 1/6 pints
	Cab	Hebrew	1/18 ephah	1 quart
	Choinix	Greco-Roman	1/18 ephah	1 quart
	Omer	Hebrew	1/10 ephah	2 quarts
	Seah/Saton	Hebrew/Greek	1/3 ephah	7 quarts
	Modios	Greco-Roman	4 omers	1 peck or 1/4 bush
	Ephah [Bath]	Hebrew	10 omers	3/5 bushel
	Lethek	Hebrew	5 ephahs	3 bushels
	Cor [Homer] /Koros	Hebrew/Greek	10 ephahs	6 bushels or 200 quarts/ 14.9 bushels or 500 quarts
LIQUID MEASURE	Log	Hebrew	1/72 bath	1/3 quart
	Xestēs	Greco-Roman	1/8 hin	1 1/6 pints
	Hin	Hebrew	1/6 bath	1 gallon or 4 quarts
	Bath/Batos [Ephah]	Hebrew/Greek	6 hins	6 gallons
	Metretes	Greco-Roman	10 hins	10 gallons
	Cor [Homer] /Koros	Hebrew/Greek	10 baths	60 gallons

METRIC EQUIVALENT	VARIOUS TRANSLATIONS
.6 gram	gerah; oboli
5.7 grams	bekah; half a shekel; quarter ounce; fifty cents
7.6 grams	2/3 of a shekel; quarter
11.5 grams	shekel; piece; dollar; fifty dollars
.4 kilogram	pound; pounds
.6 kilogram	mina; pound
34 kilograms/40 kilograms	talents/talent; 100 pounds
8 centimeters	handbreadth; three inches; four inches
23 centimeters	span
.5 meter	cubit(s); yard; half a yard; foot
2 meters	fathom; six feet
3 meters	rod; reed; measuring rod
185 meters	miles; furlongs; race
1.5 kilometer	mile
.5 liter	pots; pitchers; kettles; copper pots; copper bowls; vessels of bronze
1 liter	cab; kab
1 liter	measure; quart
2 liters	omer; tenth of a deal; tenth of an ephah; six pints
7.3 liters	measures; pecks; large amounts
9 liters	bushel; bowl; peck-measure; corn-measure; meal-tub
22 liters	bushel; peck; deal; part; measure; six pints; seven pints
110 liters	half homer; half sack
220 liters/525 liters	cor; homer; sack; measures; bushels/sacks; measures; bushels; containers
.3 liter	log; pint; cotulus
.5 liter vessels of bronze	pots; pitchers; kettles; copper pots; copper bowls;
4 liters	hin; pints
22 liters	gallon(s); barrels; liquid measure/gallons; barrels; measures
39 liters	firkins; gallons
220 liters	cor; homer; sack; measures; bushels/sacks; measures; bushels; containers

PHOTO AND ART CREDITS
(All Rights Reserved)

Arnold, Nancy. Freelance photographer. Nashville, Tennessee: 36, 49 lower, 248, 367 lower, 382.

Artist, Linden. *Biblical Illustrator*. London, England: 224, 259, 370-371.

Biblical Illustrator: 228, 230.

Brisco, Thomas V. Dean, Logsdon School of Theology, Hardin-Simmons University. Abilene, Texas: 29, 54, 60, 61, 64, 68, 119 lower.

Corel: 288.

Couch, Ernie. Photographer. *Biblical Illustrator*. Nashville, Tennessee: 40 middle.

Langston, Scott. Associate Dean and Professor of Biblical Studies, Southwest Baptist University. Bolivar, Missouri: 43 upper, 46, 49 upper, 63, 74, 75, 118.

Latta, Bill. Latta Art Services. Mt. Juliet, Tennessee: 126 upper, 126 lower, 166-167, 170, 173, 193, 207, 279, 280-281, 315 upper, 315 lower, 330, 336-337, 339, 340-341, 342, 362-363, 367 upper, 375, 376 upper, 376 lower.

McLemore, James. Photographer. Nashville, Tennessee: 114, 177, 292, 351.

Rogers, David. Photographer. *Biblical Illustrator*. Nashville, Tennessee: 23 lower, 43 lower, 59, 78, 103, 178 right, 190, 191 left, 191 right, 229, 348.

Schatz, Bob. Photographer. *Biblical Illustrator*. Nashville, Tennessee: 40 lower, 51, 69, 101, 102, 116, 164, 165, 176, 178 lower left, 178 middle, 179, 192, 194, 195, 220, 223 upper, 240, 241 upper, 241 lower, 284, 286, 287, 295, 332, 352, 353, 354 upper, 354 lower, 355, 357.

Scofield Collection, Dargan Research Library. Nashville, Tennessee: 23 upper, 40 upper, 45, 58 upper, 83, 89, 247, 350.

Smith, Stephen. Freelance photographer. Nashville, Tennessee: 383 lower.

Stephens, William H. Retired Senior Curriculum Coordinator, LifeWay Christian Resources. Nashville, Tennessee: 66, 117, 136, 231, 244.

Tolar, William B. Distinguished Professor of Biblical Backgrounds, Southwestern Baptist Theological Seminary. Fort Worth, Texas: 44, 58 lower, 72, 115 upper, 115 lower, 119 upper, 221, 223 lower, 290.

Touchton, Ken. Photographer. *Biblical Illustrator*. Nashville, Tennessee: 41, 47, 48, 50, 87, 90, 137, 157, 242, 289, 383 upper.